Six Years

Six Years: The dematerialization of the art object from 1966 to 1972: a cross-reference book of information on some esthetic boundaries: consisting of a bibliography into which are inserted a fragmented text, art works, documents, interviews, and symposia, arranged chronologically and focused on so-called conceptual or information or idea art with mentions of such vaguely designated areas as minimal, anti-form, systems, earth, or process art, occurring now in the Americas, Europe, England, Australia, and Asia (with occasional political overtones), edited and annotated by Lucy R. Lippard.

UNIVERSITY OF CALIFORNIA PRESS
Berkeley · Los Angeles · London

University of California Press
Berkeley and Los Angeles, California

University of California Press, Ltd.
London, England

First California Paperback Printing 1997

Library of Congress Cataloging-in-Publication Data

Lippard, Lucy R.
    Six years : the dematerialization of the art object from 1966 to
1972 . . . / edited and annotated by Lucy R. Lippard.
        p.   cm
    Previously published: New York : Praeger, 1973.
    Includes bibliographical references and index.
    ISBN 0-520-21013-1 (paperback : alk. paper)
    1. Conceptual art.   2. Art, Modern—20th century.   I. Title.
N6494.C63L56   1997
709′.04′075—dc21   96-47552
                                                         CIP

Printed in the United States of America

    2 3 4 5 6 7 8 9

The paper used in this publication meets the minimum requirements of American National Standard for Information Sciences—Permanence of Paper for Printed Library Materials, ANSI Z39.48-1984. ⊚

CONTENTS

ESCAPE ATTEMPTS

Conceptual artists are mystics rather than rationalists. They leap to con-clusions that logic cannot reach . . . Illogical judgements lead to new ex-perience. —Sol LeWitt, 1969[1]

I. A Biased History

The era of Conceptual art—which was also the era of the Civil Rights Movement, Vietnam, the Women's Liberation Movement, and the counter-culture—was a real free-for-all, and the democratic implications of that phrase are fully appropriate, if never realized. "Imagine," John Lennon exhorted us. And the power of imagination was at the core of even the stodgiest attempts to escape from "cultural confine-ment," as Robert Smithson put it, from the sacrosanct ivory walls and heroic, patriar-chal mythologies with which the 1960s opened. Unfettered by object status, Con-ceptual artists were free to let their imaginations run rampant. With hindsight, it is clear that they could have run further, but in the late sixties art world, Conceptual art seemed to me to be the only race in town.

On a practical level, Conceptual artists offered a clear-eyed look at what and where art itself was supposed to be; at the utopian extreme, some tried to visualize a new world and the art that would reflect or inspire it. Conceptual art (or "ultra-conceptual art," as I first called it, in order to distinguish it from Minimal painting and sculpture, earthworks, and other grand-scale endeavors which appeared in the early sixties as abnormally cerebral) was all over the place in style and content, but materially quite specific.

Conceptual art, for me, means work in which the idea is paramount and the mater-ial form is secondary, lightweight, ephemeral, cheap, unpretentious and/or "demate-rialized." Sol LeWitt distinguished between conceptual art "with a small c" (e.g. his own work, in which the material forms were often conventional, although generated by a paramount idea) and Conceptual art "with a capital C" (more or less what I have described above, but also, I suppose, anything by anyone who wanted to belong to a movement). This has not kept commentators over the years from calling virtually anything in unconventional mediums "Conceptual art." And this book muddies the waters as well, since it documents the whole heady scene that provided my narrower definition of Conceptual art with its context.

There has been a lot of bickering about what Conceptual art is/was; who began it; who did what when with it; what its goals, philosophy, and politics were and might have been. I was there, but I don't trust my memory. I don't trust anyone else's either. And I trust even less the authoritative overviews by those who were not there. So I'm going to quote myself a lot here, because I knew more about it then than I do now, despite the advantages of hindsight.

The times were chaotic and so were our lives. We have each invented our own his-tory, and they don't always mesh; but such messy compost is the source of all ver-sions of the past. Conceptual artists, perhaps more concerned with intellectual dis-tinctions in representation and relationships than those who rely on the object as vehicle/receptacle, have offered posterity a particularly tangled account. My own version is inevitably tempered by my feminist and left politics. Almost thirty years later my memories have merged with my own subsequent life and learnings and leanings. As I reconstitute the threads that drew me into the center of what came to be Conceptual art, I'll try to arm you with the necessary grain of salt, to provide a context, within the ferment of the times, for the personal prejudices and viewpoints that follow. I'm not a theoretician. This is an occasionally critical memoir of a small group of young artists' attempts to escape from the frame-and-pedestal syndrome in which art found itself by the mid-1960s.

When the decade began I was a free-lance researcher, translator, indexer, bibliographer, and would-be writer in New York. I began to publish regularly in 1964. The mid-to-late sixties were one of the most exciting times of my life on every level: I began to make a living from free-lance writing (at almost the exact moment my son was born). I curated my first exhibition, gave my first lectures, published my first two books, began to travel, wrote some fiction, got unmarried, got politicized. Conceptual art was an integral part of the whole process. I came to it, as did most of my artist colleagues, through what came to be called Minimalism. But we converged from very different directions and eventually went off again in others.

The word Minimal suggests a tabula rasa—or rather the failed attempt at a clean slate, a utopian wish of the times that never came true but was important for the goals and desires it provoked. It was and still is an idea that appeals to me, though not for its reality quotient. In graduate school I had written a long paper about a tabula rasa swept clean by the Zen monk's broom and Dada's vitriolic humor. I saw materialist echoes of these impossible longings in the paintings of Robert Ryman and Ad Reinhardt. From 1960 to 1967, I lived with Ryman, who was never called a Minimalist in those days because the roots of his white paintings from the late fifties were in Abstract Expressionism; he was "discovered" around 1967 through the advent of the messier "process art" and was included in a surprising number of "Conceptual art" shows, although the term is really inappropriate for his obsession with paint and surface, light and space. We lived on Avenue A and Avenue D and then on the Bowery. Sol LeWitt was a close friend of ours, and my major intellectual influence at the time. (We had all worked at The Museum of Modern Art in the late fifties. Ryman was a guard; LeWitt was at the night desk; I was a page in the library.)

On and around the Bowery, an art community formed that included LeWitt, Ray Donarski, Robert Mangold, Sylvia Plimack Mangold, Frank Lincoln Viner, Tom Doyle, and Eva Hesse. My own history of Conceptual art is particularly entwined with that studio community, and with LeWitt's work and writings; through him, around 1965–66, I met or saw the work of Dan Graham, Robert Smithson, Hanne Darboven, Art & Language, Hilla and Bernd Becher, Joseph Kosuth, and Mel Bochner.

Around 1964–65, Kynaston McShine and I had begun work at The Museum of Modern Art on what became the "Primary Structures" exhibition he curated for The Jewish Museum in 1966. That year I also wrote the catalogue for The Jewish Museum's retrospective of Ad Reinhardt, the reluctant hero of one branch of what was to become Conceptual art. Joseph Kosuth's storefront Museum of Normal Art was "dedicated" to him. Around the same time, I met Carl Andre, whose poetic detours around art-as-art made him a cantankerous part of the Conceptual community in spite of himself; he never liked or sympathized with the products, although he hung out with the artists. Donald Judd was also a powerful figure, an obdurately blunt artist and writer who was a model for many younger artists. And Robert Morris, elusive and virtually styleless, was the progenitor of many soon-to-be "seminal" concepts.

In 1967, John Chandler and I wrote the article on "The Dematerialization of Art" that was published in the February 1968 *Art International*, in which we saw "ultra-conceptual art" emerging from two directions: art as idea and art as action. In late 1967, I went to Vancouver and found that Iain and Ingrid (then Elaine) Baxter (the N. E. Thing Co.) and others there were on a wavelength totally unconnected yet totally similar to that of many New York friends. This and later encounters in Europe confirmed my belief in "ideas in the air"—"the spontaneous appearance of similar work totally unknown to the artists that can be explained only as energy generated by [well-known, common] sources and by the wholly unrelated art against which all the potentially 'conceptual' artists were commonly reacting," as I once described the phenomenon.

The question of sources has since become a sore point. Marcel Duchamp was the obvious art-historical source, but in fact most of the artists did not find his work all that interesting. The most obvious exceptions, perhaps, were the European-connected Fluxus artists; around 1960 Henry Flynt coined the term "concept art," but few of the artists with whom I was involved knew about it, and in any case it was a different kind of "concept"—less formal, less rooted in the subversion of art-world assumptions and art-as-commodity. As responsible critics we had to mention Duchamp as a precedent, but the new art in New York came from closer to home: Reinhardt's writings, Jasper Johns's and Robert Morris's work, and Ed Ruscha's deadpan photo-books, among others. Duchampian "claiming," however, was an occasional strategy: the N. E. Thing Co. categorized its work as ACT (Aesthetically Claimed Things) or ART (Aesthetically Rejected Things); Robert Huot, Marjorie Strider, and Stephen Kaltenbach all did pieces that "selected" art-like objects from real life in the city.

In my own experience, the second branch of access to what became Conceptual art was a jurying trip to Argentina in 1968. I returned belatedly radicalized by contact with artists there, especially the Rosario Group, whose mixture of conceptual and political ideas was a revelation. In Latin America I was trying to organize a "suitcase exhibition" of dematerialized art that would be taken from country to country by "idea artists" using free airline tickets. When I got back to New York, I met Seth Siegelaub, who had begun to reinvent the role of the "art dealer" as distributor extraordinaire through his work with Lawrence Weiner, Douglas Huebler, Robert Barry, and Joseph Kosuth. Siegelaub's strategy of bypassing the art world with exhibitions that took place outside of galleries and/or New York and/or were united in publications that were art rather than merely *about* art dovetailed with my own notions of a dematerialized art that would be free of art-world commodity status. A practical man, unencumbered at the time by addiction to ideology or esthetics, Siegelaub went right ahead and did what had to be done to create international models for an alternative art network.

On my return from Latin America I was also asked to co-curate (with painter Robert Huot and political organizer Ron Wolin) an exhibition of important Minimal artworks against the Vietnam war, as a benefit for Student Mobilization and the opening show at Paula Cooper's new Prince Street space. (It included LeWitt's first public wall drawing.) In January 1969 the Art Workers Coalition (AWC) was formed on a platform of artists' rights which was soon expanded into opposition to the Vietnam war. (Anti-racism and then anti-sexism were soon added to the anti-war agenda.) The AWC provided a framework and an organizational relationship for artists who were mixing art and politics that attracted a number of "Conceptual artists." Kosuth designed a fake membership card for entrance to The Museum of Modern Art—one of our major targets—with AWC rubberstamped in red across it. Andre was the resident Marxist. Smithson, Judd, and Richard Serra were skeptical, non-participating presences. The Guerrilla Art Action Group (GAAG), consisting at that time of Jean Toche, Jon Hendricks, Poppy Johnson, and Silvianna, was a major force in the AWC's Action Committee, though maintaining its own identity. While GAAG's almost Dada letters to President Nixon ("Eat What You Kill") and other world leaders were in the spirit of the general "Conceptual movement," their blood-and-guts performance style and their connections to Europe, via Fluxus and Destruction Art, separated them from the cooler, Minimal art-oriented Conceptual mainstream.

> *Concept art is not so much an art movement or vein as it is a position or worldview, a focus on activity.* —Ken Friedman, formerly head of Fluxus West, San Diego, 1971

So "Conceptual art"—or at least the branch of it in which I was involved—was very much a product of, or fellow traveler with, the political ferment of the times, even if that spirit had arrived belatedly in the art world. (A small group of artists, including Rudolph Baranik, Leon Golub, Nancy Spero, and Judd had been organizing against the war for several years by then. Even earlier, Reinhardt had also spoken out and demonstrated against intervention in Vietnam, but the Reinhardtian attitude remained that art was art and politics were politics and that when artists were activists they were acting as artist citizens rather than as esthetic arbiters.) The strategies with which we futilely schemed to overthrow the cultural establishment reflected those of the larger political Movement, but the most effective visual antiwar imagery of the period came from outside the art world, from popular/political culture.

For me, Conceptual art offered a bridge between the verbal and the visual. (I was writing abstract, conceptual "fiction" then; at one point I tried alternating pictorial and verbal "paragraphs" in a narrative; nobody got it) By 1967, although I had only been publishing art criticism for a few years, I was very aware of the limitations of the genre. I never liked the term critic. Having learned all I knew about art in the studios, I identified with artists and never saw myself as their adversary. Conceptual art, with its transformation of the studio into a study, brought art itself closer to my own activities. There was a period when I saw myself as a writer-collaborator with the artists, and now and then I was invited by artists to play that part. If art could be anything at all that the artist chose to do, I reasoned, then so could criticism be whatever the writer chose to do. When I was accused of becoming an artist, I replied that I was just doing criticism, even if it took unexpected forms. I organized my first exhibition ("Eccentric Abstraction") at the Fischbach Gallery in 1966, when critics rarely curated, and considered it, too, just another kind of "criticism." (At the height of my conceptually hybrid phase, Kynaston McShine asked me to write a text for The Museum of Modern Art's Duchamp catalogue. I constructed it of "readymades" chosen by a "random system" from the dictionary, and to my amazement, they used it.)

I also applied the conceptual freedom principle to the organization of a series of four exhibitions which began in 1969 at the Seattle Art Museum's World's Fair annex. They included wall works, earthworks, and sculptural pieces as well as more idea-oriented pieces. Three aspects (or influences) of Conceptual art were incorporated in these shows: the titles ("557,087" in Seattle) were the current populations of the cities; the catalogues were randomly arranged packs of index cards; and with a team of helpers, I executed (or tried to) most of the outdoor works myself, according to the artists' instructions. This was determined as much by economic limitations as by theory; we couldn't afford plane fare for the artists.

When the show went to Vancouver, it acquired a new title ("955,000"), additional cards, a bibliography, and many new works, which were shown in two indoor locations (the Vancouver Art Gallery and the Student Union at the University of British Columbia) and all over the city. My texts in the card catalogues included aphorisms, lists, and quotes and were mixed in, unsequentially, with the artists' cards. The idea was that the reader could discard whatever s/he found uninteresting. Among my cards:

> *Deliberately low-keyed art often resembles ruins, like neolithic rather than classical monuments, amalgams of past and future, remains of something "more," vestiges of some unknown venture. The ghost of content continues to hover over the most obdurately abstract art. The more open, or ambiguous, the experience offered, the more the viewer is forced to depend upon his [sic] own perceptions.*

The third version, in 1970, was a more strictly conceptual and portable exhibition that originated at the Centro de Arte y Comunicación in Buenos Aires as "2,972,453"; it included only artists not in the first two versions: among others, Siah Armajani, Stanley Brouwn, Gilbert & George, and Victor Burgin. The fourth version, in 1973, was "c. 7,500"—an international women's Conceptual show that began at the California Institute of the Arts in Valencia, California, and traveled to seven venues, ending in London. It included Renate Altenrath, Laurie Anderson, Eleanor Antin, Jacki Apple, Alice Aycock, Jennifer Bartlett, Hanne Darboven, Agnes Denes, Doree Dunlap, Nancy Holt, Poppy Johnson, Nancy Kitchel, Christine Kozlov, Suzanne Kuffler, Pat Lasch, Bernadette Mayer, Christiane Möbus, Rita Myers, Renee Nahum, N. E. Thing Co., Ulrike Nolden, Adrian Piper, Judith Stein, Athena Tacha, Mierle Laderman Ukeles, and Martha Wilson. I list all these names here, as I said on a catalogue card at the time, "by way of an exasperated reply on my own part to those who say 'there are no women making conceptual art.' For the record, there are a great many more than could be exhibited here."

The inexpensive, ephemeral, unintimidating character of the Conceptual mediums themselves (video, performance, photography, narrative, text, actions) encouraged women to participate, to move through this crack in the art world's walls. With the public introduction of younger women artists into Conceptual art, a number of new subjects and approaches appeared: narrative, role-playing, guise and disguise, body and beauty issues; a focus on fragmentation, interrelationships, autobiography, performance, daily life, and, of course, on feminist politics. The role of women artists and critics in the Conceptual art flurry of the mid-sixties was (unbeknownst to us at the time) similar to that of women on the Left. We were slowly emerging from the kitchens and bedrooms, off the easels, out of the woodwork, whether the men were ready or not—and for the most part they weren't. But even lip service was a welcome change. By 1970, thanks to the liberal-to-left politics assumed by many male artists, a certain (unprecedented) amount of support for the feminist program was forthcoming. Several men helped us (but knew enough to stay out of the decision-making) when the Ad Hoc Women Artists Committee (an offshoot of the AWC) launched its offensive on the Whitney Annual exhibition. The "anonymous" core group of women faked a Whitney press release stating that there would be fifty percent women (and fifty percent of them "non-white") in the show, then forged invitations to the opening and set up a generator and projector to show women's slides on the outside walls of the museum while a sit-in was staged inside. The FBI came in search of the culprits.

One of the reasons we were successful in forcing the Whitney to include four times as many women as before in that year's sculpture show was the establishment of the Women's Art Registry, initiated in angry response to the "There-are-no-women-who . . ." (make large sculpture, Conceptual art, kinetic art, etc., etc.) syndrome. As a freelance writer I was unaware of personal gender discrimination (it's hard to know what jobs you don't get), but it was easy enough to perceive when it came to women artists, who were virtually invisible in the mid-sixties, with a very few exceptions: Lee Bontecou, Carolee Schneemann, and Jo Baer being practically the only ones around my age; the others were older, second-generation Abstract Expressionists. A brilliant horde was waiting in the wings.

In terms of actual Conceptual art, the major female figure in New York in the 1960s was Lee Lozano, who had shown her huge industrial/organic paintings at Dick Bellamy's cutting-edge Green Gallery. She was making extraordinary and eccentric art-as-life Conceptual works in the late sixties: a "general strike piece," an "I Ching piece," a "dialogue piece," a "grass piece," and "infofictions." "Seek the extremes," she said, "That's where all the action is." (When the Women's Movement began, Lozano made the equally eccentric decision never to associate with women.)

Yoko Ono, who had participated in Fluxus since the early 1960s, continued her independent proto-Conceptual work. In 1969 Agnes Denes began her *Dialectic Triangulation: A Visual Philosophy*, involving rice, trees, and haiku as well as mathematical diagrams. Martha Wilson, still a student at the Nova Scotia College of Art and Design, began her examinations of gender and role playing that evolved into performance and continue today in her "impersonations" of Nancy Reagan, Tipper Gore, and other friends of the arts. Christine Kozlov, who was also very young, was Joseph Kosuth's collaborator in the Museum of Normal Art and other enterprises and did her own rigorously "rejective" work. Yvonne Rainer's drastic alterations of modern dance were also very influential. On the West Coast, Eleanor Antin pursued the whimsical, narrative vein that was to lead her to neo-theatrical performance and filmmaking, especially with her cinematic *100 Boots* postcards (1971), in which pairs of rubber boots wandered out of the gallery to explore the real world, traveling through the U.S. mails.

By the end of the decade Adrian Piper (also very young then) had made a series of mapping pieces and intellectual actions that explored philosophical/spatial concepts, somewhat reminiscent of LeWitt and Huebler. By 1970 she had launched into her own totally original identity works—the Catalysis series, in which she recreated or destroyed her own image/identity in bizarre public activities. Conceptual art has continued to be the basis of much important postmodern feminist work, from Piper, Antin, Martha Rosler (who was making photo-text pieces in Los Angeles in 1970), Suzanne Lacy, Susan Hiller, and Mary Kelly to Barbara Kruger, Jenny Holzer, and Lorna Simpson, among others.

II. Outside the Frame

For years people have been concerned with what goes on inside *the frame. Maybe there's something going on* outside *the frame that could be considered an artistic idea.* —Robert Barry, 1968

Ideas alone can be works of art; they are a chain of development that may eventually find some form. All ideas need not be made physical. . . . The words of one artist to another may induce an idea chain, if they share the same concept. —Sol LeWitt, 1969

I was beginning to suspect that information could be interesting in its own right and need not be visual as in Cubist, etc. art. —John Baldessari, 1969

Although Conceptual art emerged from Minimalism, its basic principles were very different, stressing the acceptively open-ended in contrast to Minimalism's rejectively self-contained. If Minimalism formally expressed "less is more," Conceptual art was about saying more with less. It represented an opening up after Minimalism closed down on expressionist and Pop excesses. As Robert Huot said in a 1977 billboard piece: "Less Is More, But It's Not Enough."

I'm often asked by younger students of the period why I talk about Conceptual art in political terms when, looking back, most of it seems supremely apolitical. Part of the answer is relative. With a few exceptions, the art was apolitical, but in an art world that still idolized Clement Greenberg (who in turn publicly abhorred Pop and Minimal art), that denied even the presence of political concerns, and offered little or no political education or analysis, Conceptual artists—most of whom were then in their twenties and thirties—looked and sounded like radicals. Now, with a few exceptions, their art looks timid and disconnected in comparison to the political activism of the sixties and the activist art of the late seventies and eighties, much of which is Conceptually aligned. The prime exceptions were GAAG and the work of the Uruguayan expatriate Luis Camnitzer.

Writing from a consciousness almost non-existent in the American art world, Camnitzer wrote in 1970 that despite the fact that so many people in the world were starving to death, "artists continue to produce full-belly art." He mused about why the phrase "Colonial Art" was art-historically positive, and applied only to the past, because "In reality it happens in the present, and with benevolence it is called 'international style.'" In perhaps the most inspired political Conceptual artwork, Orders & Co. (Camnitzer) sent a letter to Pacheco Areco, president of Uruguay in 1971, ordering him to do things he could not help doing, so as to expose the dictator to dictatorship: "The 5th of November you will simulate normal walking but you will be conscious that for this day Orders & Co. have taken possession of every third step you take. It is not necessary for you to obsess yourself with this."

Around the same time, Hans Haacke wrote:

Information presented at the right time and in the right place can potentially be very powerful. It can affect the general social fabric. . . . The working premise is to think in terms of systems: the production of systems, the interference with and the exposure of existing systems. . . . Systems can be physical, biological, or social.[2]

One could argue that art is rarely in the right place, but Haacke's statement was sharpened when his 1971 exhibition of systems was canceled by the Guggenheim Museum (his champion, curator Edward Fry, was also fired). The offending piece was "social," a thoroughly-researched work on actual absentee landlords, with whom the Guggenheim apparently shared an intense class-identification. Censorship sent

Haacke's art in a more political direction, his "museum-quality" resistance eventually providing a bridge between Conceptualism, activism, and postmodernism.

However, it was usually the form rather than the content of Conceptual art that carried a political message. The frame was there to be broken out of. Anti-establishment fervor in the 1960s focused on the de-mythologization and de-commodification of art, on the need for an independent (or "alternative") art that could not be bought and sold by the greedy sector that owned everything that was exploiting the world and promoting the Vietnam war. "The artists who are trying to do non-object art are introducing a drastic solution to the problems of artists being bought and sold so easily, along with their art. . . . The people who buy a work of art they can't hang up or have in their garden are less interested in possession. They are patrons rather than collectors," I said in 1969. (Now *that's* utopian . . .)

It was also becoming clear how authorship and ownership were intertwined. In Paris, in 1967, Daniel Buren (whose first striped works had been made in 1966), Olivier Mosset, and Niele Toroni invited reviewers to make or claim their paintings: "In order to discuss a forgery," wrote the critic Michel Claura, "one must refer to an original. In the case of Buren, Mosset, Toroni, where is the original work?" In Holland, in 1968, Jan Dibbets, who had stopped painting in 1967, said: "Sell my work? To sell isn't part of the art. Maybe there will be people idiotic enough to buy what they could make themselves. So much the worse for them." Carl Andre said of his outdoor line of hay bales at Windham College in Vermont in 1968 (another Siegelaub enterprise) that it "is going to break down and gradually disappear. But since I'm not making a piece of sculpture for sale . . . it never enters the property state." This attack on the notion of originality, "the artist's touch," and the competitive aspects of individual style constituted an attack on the genius theory, the hitherto most cherished aspect of patriarchal, ruling-class art.

Some Conceptualists took a page from Pop (imagery and techniques) and Minimalism (fabrication out of the artist's hands) by assuming an "industrial" approach. Ruscha had said, early on, that his photographic artist's books were not "to house a collection of art photographs—they are technical data like industrial photography." He eliminated text so the photos would become "neutral." There was a cult of "neutrality" in Minimalism, applied not only to the execution of objects but to the ferocious erasure of emotion and conventional notions of beauty. (Morris's 1963 *Card File* and *Statement of Esthetic Withdrawal* were precedents.) In 1967, LeWitt said "The idea becomes a machine that makes the art." Bochner curated an exhibition of "working drawings" at the School of Visual Arts, which included "non-art" as well as businesslike art diagrams. Andre explained his work, based on "particles" of material, in Marxist terms. Dennis Oppenheim did two large-scale earthworks that were about (and resulted in) wheat production. In Germany, Hilla and Bernd Becher were offering a new framework for documentary photography with their frontal, unmodulated images of industrial sites. And in England John Latham initiated the Artists Placement Group (APG), which placed artists in "real world" workplaces. Frequently perceptible beneath the surface of such statements was the need to identify art with respectable work, and on a more superficial level, with the working class.

A related notion, also designed to avoid the isolation of art from the "ordinary" world, was a new angle on style and authorship, which led to post-Dada appropriation. Reviewing "557,087" in *Artforum*, Peter Plagens suggested that "There is a total style to the show, a style so pervasive as to suggest that Lucy Lippard is in fact the artist and that her medium is other artists." Of course a critic's medium is always artists; critics are the original appropriators. Conceptual artists followed the Dadas into this territory. Starting from their Duchampian notion of "claiming," appropriation in the 1960s became more political as art-world artists borrowed John Heartfield's classic poster-makers' technique or co-opting media and other familiar images for new and often satirical ends (the "corrected billboard" of the later 1970s expanded this idea). Information and systems were seen as fair game, in the public domain. The appropriation of other artists' works or words, sometimes mutually agreed-upon as a kind of collaboration, was another Conceptual strategy. A combative attitude toward art as individual product was also implied, in line with the general sixties appeal of the collective act. Barthelme took on the alter ego James Robert Steelrails; a pseudonymous Arthur R. Rose (a multiple pun, perhaps, on Rrose Sélavy, Barbara Rose, Art, Author/ity, tumescence, etc.) interviewed artists; I quoted the mythical Latvan (later Latvana) Greene. In 1969, the Italian artist Salvo appropriated the letters of Leonardo da Vinci to Lodovico il Moro. In 1970, Eduardo Costa mocked the art world's first-come-first-served bias in *A Piece That Is Essentially The Same As A Piece Made By Any Of The First Conceptual Artists, Dated Two Years Earlier Than The Original And Signed By Somebody Else*.

In *Robert Barry Presents A Work By Ian Wilson* (July 1970), the work was *Ian Wilson*, a fragment of the elusive "Oral Communication," which Wilson once described as taking "the object or the idea of oral communication out of its natural context" and putting it in an art context, by speaking it, at which point "it became a concept." In another work from this series of "presentations" of others' work, Barry kidnapped three of my card catalogues and a review as the total contents of his 1971 Paris exhibition. In one particularly convoluted interchange, I wrote something about all this mutual appropriation, much enjoying the twists and turns on art, plagiarism, and criticism encountered, and my text became simultaneously part of two different artworks—by Douglas Huebler and David Lamelas. "It's all just a matter of what to call it?" I asked rhetorically. "Does that matter?" (I still wonder and I still try to blur the boundaries between art and everything else as much as possible.) This is as close as Conceptual art came to the meaningful play of Dada, and these were, actually, political questions that affected the whole conception of what art was and what art could do.

> The root word "image" need not be used only to mean representation (in the sense of one thing referring to something other than itself). To re-present can be defined as the shift in referential frames of the viewer from the space of events to the space of statements or vice versa. Imagining (as opposed to imaging) is not a pictorial preoccupation. Imagination is a projection, the exteriorizing of ideas about the nature of things seen. It re-produces that which is initially without product. —Mel Bochner, 1970

For artists looking to restructure perception and the process/product relationship of art, information and systems replaced traditional formal concerns of composition, color, technique, and physical presence. Systems were laid over life the way a rectangular format is laid over the seen in paintings, for focus. Lists, diagrams, measurements, neutral descriptions, and much counting were the most common vehicles for the preoccupation with repetition, the introduction of daily life and work routines, philosophical positivism, and pragmatism. There was a fascination with huge numbers (Mario Merz's pseudo-mathematical Fibonacci series, Barry's *One Billion Dots* (1969), Kawara's *One Million Years* (1969), and with dictionaries, thesauruses, libraries, the mechanical aspects of language, permutations (LeWitt and Darboven), the regular, and the minute (for example, Ian Murray's 1971 *Twenty Waves In A Row*). Lists of words were equally popular, e.g. Barry's 1969 piece that included its own "refinement" as it progressed at least into 1971, which began: "It is whole, determined, sufficient, individual, known, complete, revealed, accessible, manifest, effected, effectual, directed, dependent."

Austerity took precedence over hedonism, even to the point of deliberate "boredom" (sanctified by Minimalism as an alternative to frenetic expressionist individualism and crowd-pleasing Pop). There was a decidedly puritanical cast to much Conceptual art, as well as a fascination with pseudo-scientific data and neo-philosophical gobbledygook. One elegant precedent was Graham's *March 31, 1966*, which listed distances from "1,000,000,000,000,000,000,000,000.00000000 miles to edge of known universe" through celestial, geographic, then local sectors to the artist's typewriter and glasses to ".00000098 miles to cornea from retinal wall." Donald Burgy's 1968 *Rock* series combined this impetus with the notion of context and took it to an almost absurd extreme, documenting "selected physical aspects of a rock; its location in, and its conditions of, time and space," including weather maps, electron microscopy, X-ray photographs, spectrographic and petrographic analysis. "The scale of this information extends, in time," said Burgy, "from the geologic to the present moment; and, in size of matter, from the continental to the atomic." Sometimes a certain wit was involved, as in Dibbet's manipulations of perspective so that non-rectangles appeared rectangular; he did this on walls, on the ground, and, in 1968, on television, showing a tractor furrowing ground with perspective corrections matching the rectangular frame of the TV screen.

The emphasis on process also led to art-as-life, life-as-art pieces, like Lozano's, Piper's, and Gilbert & George's living sculptures, and especially Mierle Laderman Ukeles's "Maintenance Art" series, which began in 1969. In 1971, as Haacke's real-estate piece was being censored, Allan Kaprow published his influential text on "the education of the un-artist," and Christopher Cook executed a grand-scale "art-as-life" work by assuming the directorship of the Institute of Contemporary Art in Boston as a year-long piece. In performance, conceptualized improvisation played a similar role, as in Vito Acconci's "following" piece, or his *Zone* (1971), in which he tried to keep a cat confined in a taped square for half an hour, blocking its moves by walking, no hands. The later work of Linda Montano, Lynn Hershman, and Tehching Hsieh inherited and extended this legacy.

Communication (but not community) and distribution (but not accessibility) were inherent in Conceptual art. Although the forms pointed toward democratic outreach, the content did not. However rebellious the escape attempts, most of the work remained art-referential, and neither economic nor esthetic ties to the art world were fully severed (though at times we liked to think they were hanging by a thread). Contact with a broader audience was vague and undeveloped.

Surprisingly little thought was given in the United States (as far as I know) to education, especially within or as alternatives to the existing institutions. In 1967, Amsterdam artists Dibbets, Ger van Elk, and Lucassen began the short-lived "International Institute for the Reeducation of Artists." The most powerful model was Joseph Beuys, who said in 1969:

*To be a teacher is my greatest work of art. The rest is the waste product,
a demonstration. . . . Objects aren't very important for me any more. . . . I
am trying to reaffirm the concept of art and creativity in the face of Marxist doctrine. . . . For me the formation of the thought is already sculpture.*

Verbal strategies enabled Conceptual art to be political, but not populist. Commu-
nication between people was subordinate to communication about communication.
"Whereas it took years to get a work to Europe or California [from New York]," said
Siegelaub, "now it takes a telephone call. These are significant differences. The idea
of swift communication implies that no one has anything." In the era of faxes and the
Internet, this seems quaint, but at the time the adoption of telex technology by N. E.
Thing Co. and Haacke seemed daringly "beyond art."

Occasionally the content seemed relatively accessible, as in James Collins's Introduction Pieces of 1970–71, in which he introduced two total strangers in a public
place, photographed them shaking hands, then asked them to sign an "affidavit" on
the transaction. However, there was also a "semiotic" component to these works
that effectively academicized them: "That the message functioned *disjunctively* culturally was employed as a device to re-align the recipients' relationship to the message, as a theoretical construct."

For the most part communication was perceived as distribution, and it was in this
area that populist desires were raised but unfulfilled. Distribution was often built into
the piece. Weiner offered the most classic and concise examination of this issue in
the stipulations for "ownership" (or for avoiding ownership) that accompanied all of
his works:

1. The artist may construct the piece.
2. The piece may be fabricated.
3. The piece need not be built.
*Each being equal and consistent with the intent of the artist, the decision
as to condition rests with the receiver upon the occasion of receivership.*

Since novelty was the fuel for the conventional art market, and novelty depended
upon speed and change, Conceptual artists gloried in speeding past the cumber-
some established process of museum-sponsored exhibitions and catalogues by
means of mail art, rapidly edited and published books of art, and other small-is-bet-
ter strategies. "Some artists now think it's absurd to fill up their studios with objects
that won't be sold, and are trying to get their art communicated as rapidly as it is
made. They're thinking out ways to make art what they'd like it to be in spite of the
devouring speed syndrome it's made in. That speed has not only to be taken into
consideration, but to be utilized," I told Ursula Meyer in 1969; "the new dematerialized art . . . provides a way of getting the power structure out of New York and
spreading it around to wherever an artist feels like being at the time. Much art now is
transported by the artist, or *in* the artist himself [sic], rather than by watered-down,
belated circulating exhibitions or by existing information networks."

*Communication relates to art three ways: (1) Artists knowing what other
artists are doing. (2) The art community knowing what artists are doing. (3)
The world knowing what artists are doing. . . . It's my concern to make it
known to multitudes. [The most suitable means are] books and catalogues. —Seth Siegelaub, 1969*

One of the things we often speculated about in the late sixties was the role of the art magazine. In an era of proposed projects, photo-text works, and artists' books, the periodical could be the ideal vehicle for art itself rather than merely for reproduction, commentary, and promotion. At one point I recall brainstorming with friends about a parasite magazine, each "issue" of which would appear noted as such in a different "host" magazine each month. The idea was to give readers first-hand rather than second-hand information about art. (Kosuth, Piper, and Ian Wilson published works as "ads" in newspapers at the time; in the 1980s this strategy was revived by Haacke and Group Material.)

In 1970, Siegelaub, with the enthusiastic support of editor Peter Townsend, took over an issue of the then lively British journal *Studio International* and made it a kind of magazine exhibition with six "curators" (critics David Antin, Germano Celant, Michel Claura, Charles Harrison, Hans Strelow, and myself). We were each given eight pages and could fill them however we liked, with whatever artists we liked, doing whatever they liked. Claura chose only Buren, who striped his pages in yellow and white; Strelow chose Dibbets and Darboven; the rest of us chose eight artists with a page each. My "show" was a round robin. I asked each artist to provide a "situation" within which the next artist was to work, so the works created one cumulative, circular piece. (For example: Weiner to Kawara: "Dear On Kawara, I must apologize but the only situation I can bring myself to impose upon you would be my hopes for your having a good day. Fond Regards, Lawrence Weiner." Kawara replied with a telegram: I AM STILL ALIVE, sent to LeWitt, who responded by making a list of seventy-four permutations of that phrase.)

Decentralization and internationalism were major aspects of the prevailing distribution theories. This sounds odd now, when the "art world" extends to most of the western world (though "global" is still out of reach, "Magiciens de la terre" and the Bienal de La Habana notwithstanding). In the sixties, however, New York was resting in a self-imposed, and self-satisfied, isolation, having taken the title of world art capital from Paris in the late fifties. At the same time, the political struggles of the sixties were forging new bonds among the youth of the world. (The Parisian Situationists, though rarely mentioned in the Conceptual art literature, paralleled its goals in many ways, although the French focus on media and spectacle was far more politically sophisticated.)

The easily portable, easily communicated forms of Conceptual art made it possible for artists working out of the major art centers to participate in the early stages of new ideas. Huebler, for instance, one of the most imaginative and broad-ranging early Conceptualists, lived in Bradford, Massachusetts. They could also carry their work with them as they moved around the country or world. When artists travel more, I argued at the time—not to sightsee, but to get their work out—they take with them the ambience, stimulus, and energy of the milieu in which the work was made (New York was still implied as the prime source of that energy): "People are exposed directly to the art and to the ideas behind it in a more realistic informal situation." (This was before the "visiting artist" lecture series became an American academic institution; with the artists' slide registry, which came out of the Women's Movement, such series transformed the American art student's education and voided the curatorial excuse, "there are no good artists out there.") Spirits were high. In a de-commodified "idea-art," some of us (or was it just me?) thought we had in our hands the weapon that would transform the art world into a democratic institution.

By the end of the decade, connections had been made between "idea artists" and their supporters around the United States and in England, Italy, France, Germany, Holland, Argentina, and Canada (Vancouver and Halifax in particular). By 1970 Australia (the Inhibodress group in Sydney) and Yugoslavia (the OHO group) had also kicked in. We began to see that Europe was more fertile ground than the United States for these new networks and means of dissemination. As younger American artists were invited to Europe, younger European artists began to show up in New York independently, making contact with their peers, cooking up inexpensive but expansive international "projects" unaffiliated with the commercial gallery system; French was the lingua franca, as few then spoke good English. The generous government funding in Europe (and more curatorial sympathy on the intellectual/political level) and, in Germany, the Kunsthalle system made more and quicker experimentation possible. The New York art world was so full of itself that it didn't need to pay much attention to the Conceptual gnats nipping at its fat flanks. The British critic Charles Harrison pointed out that in the late 1960s, Paris and the various European cities were in the position that New York was around 1939: a gallery and museum structure existed, but it was so dull and irrelevant to new art that there was a feeling that it could be bypassed. "Whereas in New York," I said, "the present gallery-money-power structure is so strong that it's going to be very difficult to find a viable alternative to it."

Kynaston McShine's fully international "Information" show at The Museum of Modern Art in the summer of 1970 was an unexpected exception. Born of an art-oriented interest in systems and information theory, and then transformed by the national rage attending Kent State and Cambodia, it became a state-of-the-art exhibition unlike anything else that cautious and usually unadventurous institution had attempted to date. The handsome catalogue looked like a Conceptual artist's book, with its informal "typewritten" text and wild range of non-art imagery from anthropology to computer science, and an eclectic, interdisciplinary reading list. I am listed in the table of contents with the artists because of the weird critical text I contributed (from Spain, where I was writing a novel deeply influenced by Conceptual art), and elsewhere as a "critic" (in quotation marks). Many of the artists might have preferred the quotation-marks treatment too, as a way of distancing themselves from predictable roles. Another departure for the time: films, videos, books, and John Giorno's Dial-A-Poem were among the exhibits. Adrian Piper's contribution was a series of notebooks filled with blank pages in which the viewers were

> requested to write, draw, or otherwise indicate any response suggested by this situation (this statement, the blank notebook and pen, the museum context, your immediate state of mind, etc.)

III. The Charm of Life Itself

At its most inventive, it has the mystery and charm of life itself. It is the toughness of art that is lacking. —Amy Goldin on Conceptual art, 1969.

Inevitably, the issues of Conceptual art as "not art," "non-art," and "anti-art" was raised in the face of all these typed and xeroxed pages, blurry photographs, and radical (sometimes preposterous or pretentious) gestures. Frederick Barthelme (who later gave up his cantankerous forays into "visual" art to become a well-known novelist) rejected the notion of [art] by refusing to say the word:

I do not agree that by putting something into an   context one admits to making   . . . . I do not like the word   . I do not like the body of work defined by the word   . What I do like is the notion production. *I produce in order to pass the time.*

It was sometimes a question of who was an artist and to what extent art is style. The late Australian artist Ian Burn, who was an early member of Art & Language, stated the anti-style position of many Conceptualists when he said in 1968: "Presentation is a problem because it can easily become a form in itself, and this can be misleading. I would always opt for the most neutral format, one that doesn't interfere with or distort the information."

There is something about void and emptiness which I am personally very concerned with. I guess I can't get it out of my system. Just emptiness. Nothing seems to me the most potent thing in the world. —Robert Barry, 1968

One of the suggested solutions was a tabula rasa. In 1970, John Baldessari cremated all his art dated May 1953 to March 1966, thereby giving himself a fresh start. Kozlov showed an empty film reel, and made rejection itself her art form, conceptualizing pieces and then rejecting them, freeing herself from execution while remaining an artist. In England, Keith Arnatt titled a work *Is It Possible For Me To Do Nothing As My Contribution To This Exhibition?* and mused on "Art as an Act of Omission." In Australia, Peter Kennedy made a ten-minute piece that transferred bandages from a microphone onto a camera, forming a doubly muted transition between silence and invisibility.

In 1969 I organized an exhibition at the Paula Cooper Gallery, a benefit for the Art Workers Coalition, in which the symptoms of dematerialization were well advanced: an (apparently) "empty" room contained Haacke's *Air Currents* (a small fan), Barry's invisible *Magnetic Field*, Weiner's *Minute Pit In The Wall From One Air-Rifle Shot*, Wilson's "Oral Communication," a "secret" by Kaltenbach, a small black blip painted on the wall by Richard Artschwager, Huot's "existing shadows," and a tiny cable wire piece by Andre on the floor. The smallest room was, by contrast, crammed with printed matter—photo, text, xerox, and otherwise shrunken art.

This was a relatively conservative statement. Barry rejected the closed claustrophobic spaces of the gallery system by closing the gallery for one of his shows. Buren sealed off the entrance to a gallery space in Milan with his trademark white-and-one-color striped fabric, "opening" and "closing" the show in one move. In Argentina, Graciela Carnevale welcomed opening visitors to a totally empty room; the door was hermetically sealed without their knowing it: "The piece involved closing access and exits, and the unknown reactions of the visitors. After more than an hour, the 'prisoners' broke the glass window and 'escaped.'"

Such escape attempts were in fact being made by the artists rather than by the audiences. In this case the audience was forced to act out the artists' desires—to break out of the system. Much of this discussion had to do with boundaries—those imposed by conventional art definitions and contexts, and those chosen by the artists to make points about the new, autonomous lines they were drawing. "All legitimate art deals with limits," said Smithson. "Fraudulent art feels that it has no limits." Some, like Huebler and Oppenheim, focused on the redistribution of site or place, although the more abstract notions of space and context usually prevailed over local specificity.

> The more successful work from the minimal syndrome rejected itself, allowing the viewer a one-to-one confrontation with pure limit or bounds. This displacement or sensory pressures from object to place will prove to be the major contribution of minimalist art. —Dennis Oppenheim, 1969

Huebler "dematerialized" place (or space) in his many map pieces, which in a quintessentially "Conceptual" manner disregarded time and space limitations, and in works like one from 1970, which consisted of a vertical line drawn on a sheet of paper with the line below it reading: "the line above is rotating on its axis at a speed of one revolution each day." Bochner, who made a series of works delineating interior architectural measurements, wrote the same year: "A fundamental assumption in much recent past art was that things have stable properties, i.e. boundaries. . . . Boundaries, however, are only the fabrication of our desire to detect them." Applying the idea to a social context, Baldessari executed a "ghetto boundary" piece with George Nicolaidis for "557,087" in Seattle in 1969 which, although intended as a consciousness-raising device, would probably be perceived as racist today: they affixed small silver and black labels to telephone poles or street signs along the boundary of an African-American neighborhood.

> I'm beginning to believe that one of the last frontiers left for radical gestures is the imagination. —David Wojnarowicz, 1989 [3]

Even in 1969, as we were imagining our heads off and, to some extent, out into the world, I suspected that "the art world is probably going to be able to absorb conceptual art as another 'movement' and not pay too much attention to it. The art establishment depends so greatly on objects which can be bought and sold that I don't expect it to do much about an art that is opposed to the prevailing systems." (This remains true today—art that is too specific, that names names, about politics, or place, or anything else, is not marketable until it is abstracted, generalized, defused.) By 1973, I was writing with some disillusion in the "Postface" of *Six Years*: "Hopes that 'conceptual art' would be able to avoid the general commercialization, the destructively "progressive" approach of modernism were for the most part unfounded. It seemed in 1969 . . . that no one, not even a public greedy for novelty, would actually pay money, or much of it, for a xerox sheet referring to an event past or never directly perceived, a group of photographs documenting an ephemeral situation or condition, a project for work never to be completed, words spoken but not recorded; it seemed that these artists would therefore be forcibly freed from the tyranny of a commodity status and market-orientation. Three years later, the major conceptualists are selling work for substantial sums here and in Europe; they are represented by (and still more unexpected—showing in) the world's most prestigious galleries. Clearly, whatever minor revolutions in communication have been achieved by the process of dematerializing the object . . . , art and artists in a capitalist society remain luxuries."

Yet, with a longer view, it is also clear that the Conceptual artists set up a model that remains flexible enough to be useful today, totally aside from the pompous and flippant manner in which it has sometimes been used in the art context. Out of that decade from 1966 to 1975 came a flock of cooperative galleries (55 Mercer and A. I. R. being the notable survivors), a tide of artists' books (which led to the formation in 1976 of Printed Matter and the Franklin Furnace Archive), another activist artists' organization led by former Conceptualists (Artists Meeting for Cultural Change) after the AWC faded with the Vietnam war, and an international performance art and video network. Activist and ecological/site-specific work that had its beginnings in the 1960s in Conceptual-related projects has seen a revival in the 1980s and 1990s; the much-maligned Whitney Biennial of 1993 featured more-and-less "political" art that recalled its Conceptual sources; and feminist activists like the Guerrilla Girls and the Women's Action Coalition (WAC) also renewed 1960s and early 1970s concerns with women's representation in the media, daily life, and role playing/gender-bending.

Perhaps most important, Conceptualists indicated that the most exciting "art" might still be buried in social energies not yet recognized as art. The process of extending the boundaries didn't stop with Conceptual art: These energies are still out there, waiting for artists to plug into them, potential fuel for the expansion of what "art" can mean. The escape was temporary. Art was recaptured and sent back to its white cell, but parole is always a possibility.

Notes
1. Sol LeWitt, "Sentences on Conceptual Art," in Lucy R. Lippard, *Six Years: The Dematerialization of the Art Object from 1966 to 1972* (New York: Praeger, 1973), 75.
2. Jeanne Siegel, "An Interview with Hans Haacke," *Arts Magazine* 45, no. 7 (May 1971): 21.
3. David Wojnarowicz, "Post Cards from America: X-Rays from Hell," In *Witnesses: Against Our Vanishing*, exh. cat. (New York: Artists Space, 1989), 10.

For Sol

"To discuss what one is *doing* rather than the artwork which results, to attempt to unravel the loops of creative activity, is, in many ways, a behavioural problem. The fusion of art, science and personality is involved. It leads to a consideration of our total relationship to a work of art, in which physical moves may lead to conceptual moves, in which Behaviour relates to Idea. . . . 'An organism is most efficient when it knows its own internal order.'"
—Roy Ascott, "The Construction of Change," *Cambridge Opinion* 37 (January, 1964).

AUTHOR'S NOTE

(1973) *Six years* . . . is basically a bibliography and list of events, arranged chronologically. Each year begins with a list of the *books* published then and a few general events that could not be listed under specific months. The book list is followed by a monthly breakdown of periodicals, exhibitions, catalogues, and works included in these; symposia; articles, interviews, and works by individual artists (alphabetically); and general articles and events—usually in that order.

All factual information (bibliographical, chronological, and general) is in bold type; all anthological material (excerpts, statements, art works, symposia) is in roman type; and all commentary by the editor is in italics.

The following abbreviations have been used throughout: CAYC—Centro de Arte Y Communicacion; *APB—Art and Project Bulletin; Arts—Arts Magazine;* NETCo.—N.E. Thing Co.; NSCAD—Nova Scotia College of Art and Design; MOMA—Museum of Modern Art; (Rep.)—reproduction.

· · ·

(1996) When I compiled *Six Years: The Dematerialization of the Art Object* . . . in 1972–73, I described it in the nearly 100-word title as ". . . focused on so-called conceptual or information or idea art with mentions of such vaguely designated areas as minimal, antiform, systems, earth or process art . . ." The initial manuscript was about twice the size of that which was finally published (The Archives of American Art has the rest of the stuff), and even at its published length, I was convinced that no one would ever read the thing through. When it appeared, I was amazed to hear that some eccentric souls were unable to put it down and a lot of people seemed to be plowing through it, plugging into the hidden narrative that I thought would be an involuntary secret. Then the book went out of print for over a decade and became, ironically, a very expensive collector's item, paralleling the fate of the art it espoused.

I'm delighted that University of California Press editor Charlene Woodcock kept at me to help her reprint *Six Years.* My recalcitrance was due to laziness, exhaustion with digging up the past (which has become inexplicably fascinating to too many graduate students, gratifying though it may be), and the pressure of current work, which always interests me much more. However, I am constantly struck by how often my current work—involving feminism or photography or public art or art by contemporary Native Americans—recalls past events in Conceptual art. It was a far richer vein than any of us could have realized at the time. Looking back through this book, I am always amazed by the density and diversity of the genre(s).

PREFACE

Because this is a book about widely differing phenomena within a time span, not about a "movement," there is no precise reason for certain inclusions and exclusions except personal prejudice and an idiosyncratic method of categorization that would make little sense on anyone else's grounds. I planned this book to expose the chaotic network of ideas in the air, in America and abroad, between 1966 and 1971. While these ideas are more or less concerned with what I once called a "dematerialization" of the art object, the form of the book intentionally reflects chaos rather than imposing order. And since I first wrote on the subject in 1967, it has often been pointed out to me that dematerialization is an inaccurate term, that a piece of paper or a photograph is as much an object, or as "material," as a ton of lead. Granted. But for lack of a better term I have continued to refer to a process of dematerialization, or a deemphasis on material aspects (uniqueness, permanence, decorative attractiveness).

"Eccentric Abstraction," "Anti-Form," "Process Art," "Anti-Illusionism," or whatever, did come about partly as a reaction against the industrialized geometry and sheer bulk of much minimal art. Yet minimal art was itself anti-formalist in its nonrelational approach, its insistence on a neutralization of "composition" and other hierarchical distinctions. Sol LeWitt's premise that the concept or idea was more important than the visual results of the system that generated the object undermined formalism by insisting on a return to content. His exhaustive permutations reintroduced chance into a systematic art, an idea that he has successfully investigated in his serial drawings, which are executed directly on the wall according to very specific instructions that allow for infinite generalization, or variety. Other artists were more concerned with allowing materials rather than systems to determine the form of their work, reflected in the ubiquity of temporary "piles" of materials around 1968 (done by, among others, Andre, Baxter, Beuys, Bollinger, Ferrer, Kaltenbach, Long, Louw, Morris, Nauman, Oppenheim, Saret, Serra, Smithson). This premise was soon applied to such ephemeral materials as time itself, space, nonvisual systems, situations, unrecorded experience, unspoken ideas, and so on.

Such an approach to physical materials led directly to a similar treatment of perception, behavior, and thought processes *per se.* The most effective method in this case has often been the accent or overlay of an art context, an art framework, or simply an art awareness, that is, the imposition of a foreign pattern or substance on existing situations or information (e.g., Barry, Dibbets, Huebler, Oppenheim, Smithson, Weiner, and others). The addition of accents rather than the delineation of an independent form led away from marking the object into remarking direct experience. ("Ephemeralization" is the term Buckminster Fuller uses for "the design science

5

strategy of doing even more with even less per unit of energy, space, and time.") Fragmentation is more like direct communication than the traditionally unified approach in which superfluous literary transitions are introduced. Criticism itself tends to clog up these direct reactive processes with irrelevant information, while the terseness and the isolation of much of the art reproduced here forces mental jumps; these in turn facilitate a heightened alertness to sensorial or visual phenomena.

I would like this book to reflect that gradual deemphasis of sculptural concerns, and as the book evolves, I have deliberately concentrated increasingly on textual and photographic work. This is not to say, of course, that many artists whose work greatly interests me have not continued to work in sculpture or painting, but simply that the phenomena examined in this book tend to avoid those solutions. The anti-individualistic bias of its form (no single artist's sequential development or contribution can be traced without the help of the index) will hopefully emphasize timing, variety, fragmentation, and interrelationships above all. In fact, I have included some of the work here because it illustrates connections to or even exploitation of other, stronger work, or repetition of ideas considered from very different viewpoints, or how far certain ideas can be taken before they become exhausted or totally absurd. In any case, I enjoy the prospect of forcing the reader to make up his or her own mind when confronted with such a curious mass of information.

Proto-conceptual art in the guise of the Fluxus group's "concept art," the performance and body works of the Japanese Gutai group, Happenings, concrete poetry, most performances and street works, and even such impressively eccentric manifestations as Ray Johnson's use of the postal system or Arakawa's exotically referential canvases have been omitted partly through spatial necessity and partly because, confused as the issues are, they would be unmanageable if *some* similarity of esthetic intention were not maintained. This is not a book about *all* dematerialized art and the point I want to make is phenomenological rather than historical. I am probably safe in saying, as I have of some exhibitions I have organized, that no one but me (and my editors) will read the whole book through.

Because *Six Years* is about ideas changing over a period of time, it seems only fair to subject myself to the same lack of hindsight about which the artists themselves had reservations when I asked permission to use old work or old statements. Therefore, the following excerpts from a December, 1969, interview by Ursula Meyer with me, have not been revised according to what I think now, but stand as things looked then. The Postface offers some contradictions.

*

LL: A lot of this business about object art and non-object art gets very confused. People use it like a value judgment. "It's still an object" or "he's finally got past the object." It isn't really a matter of how much materiality a work has, but what the artist is doing with it.

UM: But I think it is very obvious that concern with the object is the fundamental issue of what has been going on the last few years.

LL: Probably it's typical of the first half of the twentieth century. Ad Reinhardt's making black-square identical paintings in 1960 was by implication a very important ending point. Now I think things have opened up to where the business of going "beyond" anything is less important. The fragmentation is so obvious. There's more chance of people doing what they want and not having it measured against the Greenbergian standard of "advance", or anybody else's standards. . . . It's strange how Reinhardt relates to much of the new art, because these artists often make art out of unadulterated life situations and Reinhardt was so very determined that art should relate to nothing but art. Doug Huebler sees the connection between his work and Reinhardt's in the way he imposes an art framework on life. In a broad sense, anyone taking a photograph is geometricizing life. Most of the artists who are now called "conceptual" were doing "minimal" work in 1967–68. Weiner and Kosuth, maybe Barry and Huebler less so, are very much concerned with Art, with retaining a consistency, or coherency. They work in a straight, definite line and exclude far more than they include, which is fundamentally a formal or structural point of view. Morris and Baxter and Nauman come closer to a Dada-Surrealist viewpoint, an acceptive instead of a rejective approach. There's always been that kind of split. It used to be the old classical-romantic thing, but in the last couple of years those terms have become pretty irrelevant, or confused. Barry, for instance, is a very classical and a very romantic artist at the same time. The break, and it's often a very subtle one too, comes through acceptance or rejection of the multiplicity of non-art subject matter, or in the case of Barry or Huebler or Weiner, who use non-art, immaterial situations, it's the imposition of a closed instead of an open system. Barry doesn't "claim" all psychic phenomena, as Iain Baxter might; he selects his pieces very strictly even when he can't know or name the phenomena, but can only impose conditions on them. Fundamentally it's a matter of *degree* of acceptance.

UM: Do you think visual art may eventually function in a different context altogether?

LL: Yes, but there's going to have to be an immense educational process to get people to even begin to look at things, to say nothing of look at things the way artists look at things. . . . Some artists now think it's absurd to fill up their studios with objects that won't be sold, and are trying to get their art communicated as rapidly as it is made. They're thinking out ways to make art what they'd like it to be in spite of the devouring speed syndrome it's made in. That speed has not only to be taken into consideration, but to be utilized.

UM: What do you think about the way the art journals have been pertaining to the new art?

LL: For the most part they haven't pertained, or even entertained the idea that ideas can be art. They're just beginning to realize they're going to have to treat this new art seriously. Generally, though, the artists are so much more intelligent than the writers on the subject that the absence of critical comment hasn't been mourned. . . . If *Time* and *Newsweek* were more accurate, they'd probably be better art magazines than most of the art magazines. The trouble is they hand out incorrect and oversimplified information. . . . If you respect the art, it becomes more important to transmit the information about it accurately than to judge it. Probably the best way of doing that is through the artists. Let the readers make their own distinctions about the extent to which the artist is slinging it. That way they have to look at his or her work too, and they're getting first-hand rather than second-hand information.

UM: Do you believe the impact of what is happening now—with conceptual art and what I call the other culture—that impact is going to hit the so-called art world, the galleries, the museums? What changes do you envisage?

LL: Unfortunately I don't think there are going to be many changes taking place immediately. I think the art world is probably going to be able to absorb conceptual art as another "movement" and not pay too much attention to it. The art establishment depends so greatly on objects which can be bought and sold that I don't expect it to do much about an art that is opposed to the prevailing systems. Whenever I lecture and start talking about the possibility of no art or non-art in the future, I have to admit I think *I'm* going to be able to tell who the artists are anyway. Maybe another culture, a new network will arise. It's already clear that there are very different ways of seeing things and thinking about things within the art world even as it stands now, not as clear as the traditional New York "uptown" and "downtown" dichotomy, but it has something to do with that.

One of the important things about the new dematerialized art is that it provides a way of getting the power structure out of New York and spreading it around to wherever an artist feels like being at the time. Much art now is transported by the artist, or *in* the artist himself, rather than by watered-down, belated circulating exhibitions or by existing information networks such as mail, books, telex, video, radio, etc. The artist is traveling a lot more, not to sightsee, but to get his work out. New York is the center because of the stimulus here, the bar and studio dialogue. Even if we get the art *works* out of New York, even if the objects do travel, they alone don't often provide the stimulus that they do combined with the milieu. But when the artists travel, whether they're liked or disliked, people are exposed directly to the art and to the ideas behind it in a more realistic, informal situation. . . . Another idea that has come up often recently that interests me very much is that of the artist working as an interruptive device, a jolt, in present societal systems. Art has always been that, in a way, but John Latham and his APG group in London, among others, are trying to deal with it more directly.

UM: There's a strange reawakening in Europe now.

LL: It may be more fertile for new ideas and new ways of disseminating art than the United States. Certainly Canada is. Charles Harrison has pointed out that Paris and the various European cities are in the position that New York was in around 1939. There is a gallery and museum structure, but it is so dull and irrelevant to new art that there's a feeling that it can be bypassed, that new things can be done, voids filled. Whereas in New York, the present gallery-money-power structure is so strong that it's going to be very difficult to find a viable alternative to it. The artists who are trying to do non-object art are introducing a drastic solution to the problem of artists being bought and sold so easily, along with their art. Not, God knows, that the artists making conventional objects want that any more than anyone else, but their work unfortunately lends itself more easily to capitalist marketing devices. The people who buy a work of art they can't hang up or have in their garden are less interested in possession. They are patrons rather than collectors. That's why all this seems so inapplicable to museums, because museums are basically acquisitive.

UM: That one word "idea" contradicts any sort of central establishment. You might have many idea centers that are made by living artists rather than one chauvinistic art enterprise.

LL: Yes. I was politicized by a trip to Argentina in the fall of 1968, when I talked to artists who felt that it was immoral to make their art in the society that existed there. It becomes clear that today everything, even art, exists in a political situation. I don't mean that art itself has to be seen in political terms or *look* political, but the way artists handle their art, where they make it, the chances they get to make it, how they are going to let it out, and to whom—it's all part of a life style and a political situation. It becomes a matter of artists' power, of artists achieving enough solidarity so they aren't at the mercy of a society that doesn't understand what they are doing. I guess that's where the other culture, or alternative information network, comes in—so we can have a choice of ways to live without dropping out.

ACKNOWLEDGMENTS

My particular thanks go to Roberta Berg Handler for her impressive (and unpaid) work on the bibliography; as well as to Renata Karlin and Vieri Tucci for translations, Poppy Johnson for photographic research, Nancy Landau and Gerald Barrett for typing and transcriptions, Brenda Gilchrist for her sympathetic editorial help, Gilda Kuhlman for designing the book, Nora Conover for a painstaking job of copy-editing, Carl Andre for the index, and the following for support and information: Ursula Meyer, Germano Celant, Seth Siegelaub, Art & Project (Amsterdam), Konrad and Erika Fischer, Ken Friedman, Lisa Béar, Willoughby Sharp, and Charlotte Townsend. And especially to all the artists represented here, who provided not only their work, but the impetus to do the book in the first place.

My thanks to Russell Ferguson and LAMOCA for allowing us to reprint the introductory text from their *Reconsidering the Object Of Art* catalogue (1995) and to John Alan Farmer for his editorial work.

Left: Bruce Nauman. Untitled. Latex with cloth backing, 72″ x 15″ x 2″ (approx.). 1965–66. Nicholas Wilder Gallery, Los Angeles. *Right:* Bruce Nauman. *Thighing.* Still from 16-mm., 8–10-minute color film, with sound. 1967. Courtesy Leo Castelli Gallery, New York.

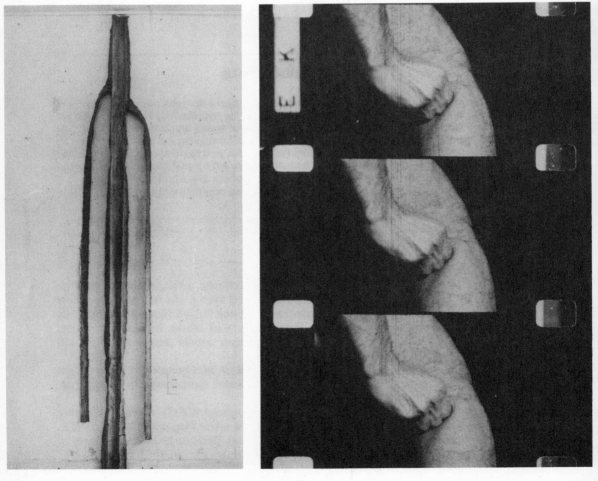

1966

BOOKS

Brecht, George. *Chance-Imagery.* **New York, 1966. Independently and in association with the Fluxus group, Brecht has been making "events" that anticipate a stricter "conceptual art" since around 1960. For example:**

Three Aqueous Events, summer, 1961: ice · water · steam.

Time-Table Event, spring, 1961: To occur in a railway station. A time-table is obtained. A tabled time indication is interpreted in minutes and seconds (7:16 equaling, for example, 7 minutes and 16 seconds). This determines the duration of the event.

Two Exercises, fall, 1961: Consider an object. Call what is not the object "other." Add to the object, from the "other," another object, to form a new object and a new "other." Repeat until there is no more "other." Take a part from the object and add it to the "other," to form a new object and a new "other." Repeat until there is no more object.

Kaprow, Allan. *Assemblage, Environments and Happenings.* **New York, Harry N. Abrams, 1966.**

Nauman, Bruce. *Pictures of Sculpture in a Room.* **Los Angeles, winter, 1965–66. (Rep.)**

Nauman's first show is held at Nicolas Wilder, Los Angeles, May 10–June 2, 1966. During this year he makes a series of punning color photographs and continues to make body works (begun with a calisthenics piece in 1965) and films: Bouncing Ball, Playing Violin, Pacing in the Studio *(1965).*

Films are about seeing. I wanted to find out what I would look at in a strange situation, and I decided that with a film and a camera I could do that. In one film I did, the title was straight and everything else tipped on its side, partly because you could get more in the picture that way and partly as a concession to art—so it looked like I did something to it, changed it. The films I did with Bill Allan are the closest to just making a film, without considering art. We made a film called *Fishing for Asian Carp.* Bill Allan got into his boots and we went to the creek. We ran the film until Allan caught the fish. . . . When you want to make a film, you don't know how long it will take, and so you pick something to make it about that will determine how long it will be. When he caught the fish, it ended. (*Art News,* summer, 1967.)

Ruscha, Edward. *Every Building on the Sunset Strip.* **Los Angeles, 1966. Two-sided, fold-out, boxed. Ruscha's extremely influential "antiphotography" books first appeared in 1962. They were:** *Twenty-six Gasoline Stations* **(1962),** *Various Small Fires* **(1964) (Rep.),** *Some Los Angeles Apartments* **(1965), and others that are listed below chronologically.**

11

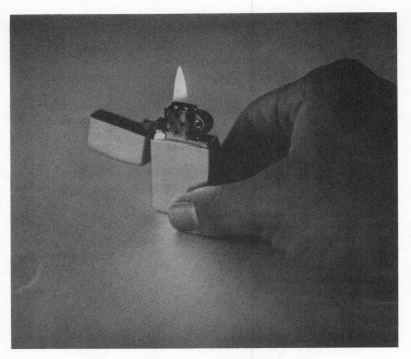

Ed Ruscha. Plate from *Various Small Fires.* 1964.

Nor am I really interested in books as such, but I am interested in unusual kinds of publications. . . . Above all, the photographs I use are not "arty" in any sense of the word. I think photography is dead as a fine art; its only place is in the commercial world, for technical or information purposes. Thus [*Small Fires*] is not a book to house a collection of art photographs—they are technical data like industrial photography. . . . One of the purposes of my book has to do with making a mass-produced object. The final product has a very commercial, professional feel to it. . . . I have eliminated all text from my books—I want absolutely neutral material. My pictures are not that interesting, nor the subject matter. They are simply a collection of "facts"; my book is more like a collection of "readymades." (Excerpt from an interview with Ruscha by John Coplans, *Artforum,* February, 1965.)

Williams, Mason. *The Night I Lost My Baby: A Las Vegas Vignette.* Los Angeles, 1966. Designed by Ed Ruscha.

Vancouver, B.C.: Founding of "IT," an anonymous art group.
An artist with the need to create original and radical works must first get sick and tired of all the work he sees. Only then is he left with a clear field to look into. . . . You don't have to use accepted methods. You can use anything that comes—people, things, it's easy. (From the manifesto; one of the participants became the N. E. Thing Co.)

Among the early earthworks executed during this year (see below for others) were Richard Long's in England, (Rep.) *Robert Morris's model for* Project in Earth and Sod, *and Robert Smithson's* Tar Pool and Gravel Pit, *a model shown at the Dwan Gallery in the fall, which he later described as a proposal that "makes one conscious of the primal ooze. A molten substance is poured into a square sink that is surrounded by another square sink of coarse gravel. The tar cools and flattens into a sticky level deposit. This carbonaceous sediment brings to mind a tertiary world of petroleum, asphalts, ozokerite, and bituminous agglomerations." (Artforum, September, 1968.) In 1960, Lawrence Weiner did an "exhibition" in Mill Valley, California, which consisted of a crater executed by explosives. See also de Maria, below.*

New York: Bernar Venet begins his "presentation and utilization of linguistic and logical diagrams in order to present abstract content devoid of any formalistic/aesthetic content" with works "based on school mathematics, physics, chemistry and industrial drawing, and a manifesto against sensibility, against the expression of the individual's personality."

January, 1966: Yoko Ono gives a lecture at Wesleyan University:
All my work in fields other than music have an *Event bent* . . . event, to me, is not an assimilation of all the other arts as Happening seems to be, but an extrication from the various sensory perceptions. It is not a *get togetherness* as most happenings are, but a dealing with oneself. Also, it has no script as Happenings do, though it has something that starts it moving—the closest word for it may be a *wish* or *hope*. . . . After unblocking one's mind, by dispensing with visual, auditory and kinetic perceptions, what will come out of us? Would there be anything? And my events are mostly spent in wonderment. . . . We never experience things separately . . . but if that is so, it is all the more reason and challenge to create a sensory experience isolated from other sensory experiences, which is something rare in daily life. Art is not merely a duplication of life. . . . Among my instructions paintings, my interest is mainly in "painting to construct in your head" . . . the movement of the molecule can be continuum and discontinuum at the same time. . . . There is no visual object that does not exist in comparison to or simultaneously with other objects, but these characteristics can be eliminated if you wish. . . . The painting method derives as far back as the time of the Second World War, when we had no food to eat, and my brother and I exchanged menus in the air.

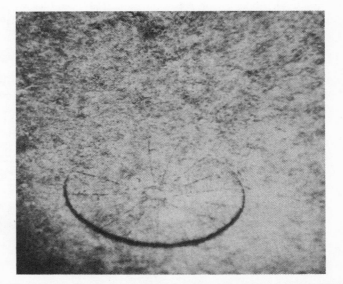

Richard Long.
England. 1966.

Some earlier works by Ono, who was associated then with the Fluxus group:
"Listen to the sound of the earth turning" (spring, 1963); "Take the sound of the stone aging" (*Tape Piece I*, autumn, 1963); "Take the sound of the room breathing: at dawn, in the morning, in the evening, before dawn. . . . Bottle the smell of the room of that particular hour as well" (*Tape Piece II*, autumn, 1963); "Use your blood to paint. Keep painting until you faint (*a*). Keep painting until you die (*b*)" (spring, 1960).

See also Emily Wasserman, "Yoko Ono at Syracuse: 'This Is Not Here,'" *Artforum*, January, 1972.

N. E. Thing Co. (Iain & Ingrid Baxter). *Bagged Place*. University of British Columbia Fine Arts Gallery, Vancouver, February 2–16, 1966. A four-room apartment with every item in it encased in plastic bags. Reviewed by Alvin Balkind, *Artforum*, May, 1968; see also F. Danieli in *Artscanada*, February, 1967.

Daniel Buren. Galerie Fournier, Paris, March, 1966. First public exhibition of vertically striped paintings which, in one form or another, Buren has continued to make until the present. The stripe paintings were first shown to a few friends in a garage in Paris in December, 1965.

Dan Graham. *March 31, 1966* (shown November, 1967, Finch College, New York):

1,000,000,000,000,000,000,000,000,000.00000000	miles to edge of known universe
100,000,000,000,000,000,000,000.00000000	miles to edge of galaxy (Milky Way)
3,573,000,000.00000000	miles to edge of solar system (Pluto)
205.00034600	miles to Washington, D.C.
2.85100000	miles to Times Square, New York, N.Y.
.38600000	miles to Union Square subway stop
.11820000	miles to corner 14th St. and First Ave.
.00367000	miles to front door, Apt. 1D, 153 First Ave.
.00021600	miles to typewriter paper page
.00000700	miles to lens of glasses
.00000098	miles to cornea from retinal wall

March, San Diego: John Baldessari stops making works by his own hand and signature. He has been working with words since c. 1959; by 1966, "I was beginning to suspect that information could be interesting in its own right and need not be visual as in Cubist, etc. art." (See below for word paintings done in this period and shown at Molly Barnes Gallery, 1968.)

Wilson, William. "New York Correspondance School." *Art and Artists*, April, 1966.

Kosuth, Joseph, and Kozlov, Christine. *Ad Reinhardt: Evolution into Darkness—The Art of an Informal Formalist; Negativity, Purity, and the Clearness of Ambiguity*. Unpublished typescript for the School of Visual Arts, New York, May, 1966.

Collins, James; Haw, Kenneth; Sullivan, John. *Teaching Notes*. London, June, 1966. 31 pp. mimeographed sheets on semiotics and art.

Bochner, Mel. "Primary Structures: A Declaration of a New Attitude as Revealed by an Important Current Exhibition." *Arts*, June, 1966.

August, London: John Latham, "Art and Culture" (Rep.):
A book called Art & Culture—a collection of essays written by Clement Green-

THE ART SHOW 1963

This tableau is just what the title says. It is an art show set in a commercial gallery in either Los Angeles (slacks on the women) or New York (coats and galoshes). On the walls (or standing on the floor, hanging from the ceiling) is displayed the newest annual fad. These will be invented works in an invented style for an invented artist by the name of Christian Carry.

Mingling among each other and the art works are the art lovers. This should be an interesting bunch, wearing all styles of personalities and faces. I will probably place this tableau in 1966 to be able to use mini-skirts on some of the lovelies.

Also, I plan sound recordings of actual gallery openings, and a desiccated punch bowl.

PRICE: Part One $ 15,000.00
           Part Two $ 1,000.00
           Part Three   Costs plus artist's wages

Above: Edward Kienholz. *The Art Show.* Concept tableau. 1963. Right: *The Art Show.* Concept tableau. 1963 (formalized in 1966).

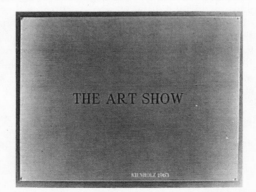

THE ART SHOW

KIENHOLZ 1963

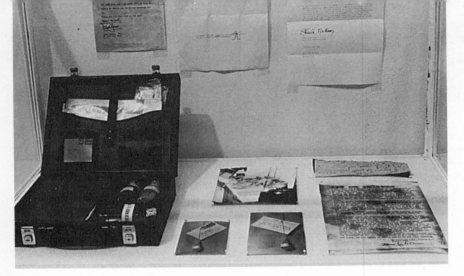

John Latham. *Art and Culture.* Case, papers, miscellany. August, 1966.

berg—having been published in America early in the 1960's, had found its way into the library of St. Martins School of Art. In August, 1966, having regard for both the persuasive power of the book among students and for the provocative title, the book was withdrawn in the name of John Latham, and an event organized at his home together with the sculptor Barry Flanagan, who then was in the role of "student." The event was called "STILL & CHEW," and many artists, students, and critics were invited.

When the guests arrived they were each asked to take a page from Art & Culture and to chew it—after which they could if necessary spit out the product into a flask provided. About a third of the book was so chewed, and there was some selective choosing as to the pages. The chewed pages were later immersed in acid—30% sulphuric—until the solution was converted to a form of sugar, and this was then neutralized by addition of quantities of sodium bicarbonate.

The next step was the introduction of an Alien Culture, a yeast. After which several months went by with the solution bubbling gently.

Nearly a year after the Chewing, at the end of May, 1967, a postcard arrived addressed to Mr. Latham with a red label on it saying VERY URGENT. On the back was a plea for the return of the book "wanted urgently by a student, Art & Culture."

A distilling apparatus was assembled, and a suitable glass container procured for the book to be returned to the librarian. When this had been done a label was fixed to the glass saying what it was and together with the postcard it was presented to her back in the school, where for some years John Latham had been engaged as a part-time instructor. After the few minutes required to persuade the librarian that this was indeed the book which was asked for on the postcard, he left the room.

In the morning postal delivery a day later a letter arrived from the principal of St. Martins addressed to Mr. Latham. It said he was sorry, he was unable to invite him to do any more teaching.

Wolfram, Eddie. "In the Beginning Was the Word." *Art and Artists,* August, 1966.

Eccentric Abstraction. Fischbach Gallery, New York, September 20–October 8, 1966. Organized by Lucy R. Lippard. Brief text with vinyl announcement. Adams, Bourgeois, Hesse, Kuehn, Nauman, Potts, Sonnier, Viner. Reviewed by Hilton Kramer, *New York Times,* September 25; David Antin, *Artforum,* November; Mel Bochner, *Arts,* November; Dore Ashton, *Studio International,* November. Long article by Lippard based on the show and other similar work, internationally, in *Art International,* November, 1966.

October–November: Terry Atkinson and Michael Baldwin meet at Lanchester Polytechnic, Coventry. Baldwin has made contact with LeWitt in New York, in March.

Robert Huot. Stephen Radich Gallery, New York, fall, 1966.
  Exhibition of reductive paintings with conceptual bases. One "minimal" artist's reaction was "this is not painting, it's just ideas." In 1967, Huot worked primarily with Areas in which canvases of different sizes contained the same area of color in different manners; they were often hung at an extended distance from each other to emphasize the visual-memory factor at the conception. One painting of this year consisted simply of a nubbly semitransparent nylon surface over a stretcher with one curved edge. Huot's interest in integrating the wall with his painting continued in monochrome paintings. The play between the two-dimensional surface and the objectness of painting led him to work in 1968 with lines of tape, attached directly to the wall, which stressed or counterpointed architectural detail, and then with similar effects with moldings, quarter-rounds, white paints of different gloss levels on the same wall, the shadows of architectural elements, luminescent tape points indoors and out marking the spaces. (See March, 1969 show at Paula Cooper, below.) By the end of 1969, Huot was working anonymously and giving works away while refusing to sell them. By 1970, he was devoting an increasing amount of time to film.

Hutchinson, Peter. "Is There Life on Earth?" *Art in America,* October–November, 1966.

Gruppe Handwagen 13, Joseph Beuys. Kopenhagen Galleri 101, October 14–15, 1966. See also *Hvedekorn* (Copenhagen), no. 5, 1966. Includes statements and reproductions by Joseph Beuys and articles on him by Per Kirkeby, Henning Christiansen, and Hans-Jorgen Nielsen; mimeographed text by Troels Andersen from *Blockade* (see below 1969), first printed in *Billedkunst* (Copenhagen), no. 4, 1966, on the action "Eurasia":
  At first glance he belongs to the fantastic characters somewhere between clown

Joseph Beuys. *Eurasia.* Action. Vienna, 1967.   Joseph Beuys. *Eurasia.* Action. Berlin. 1968.

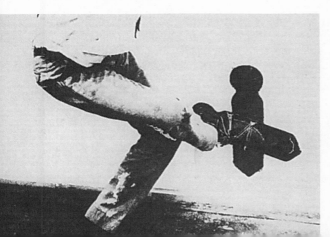

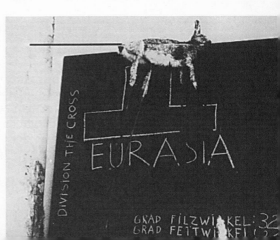

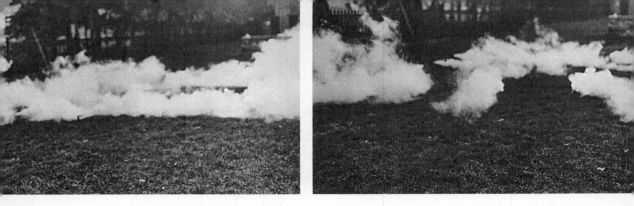

Robert Morris. *Steam Cloud.* 1966. As executed at the Corcoran Gallery of Art, Washington, D.C., 1969.

and gangster. In action he is changed, absorbed into his performance, intense and suggestive. He uses very simple symbols. His performance was the 32nd section from the *Siberian Symphony,* and lasted an hour and a half. The introductory motif was "the division of the cross." Kneeling, Beuys slowly pushed two small crosses which were lying on the floor towards a blackboard; on each cross was a watch with an adjusted alarm. On the board he drew a cross which he then half erased; underneath he wrote "Eurasia."

The remainder of the piece consisted of Beuys maneuvering, along a marked line, a dead rabbit whose legs and ears were extended by long, thin black wooden poles. When the rabbit was on his shoulders, the poles touched the floor. Beuys moved from the wall to the board where he deposited the rabbit. On the way back, three things happened; he sprinkled white powder between the rabbit's legs, put a thermometer in its mouth, and blew into a tube. Afterwards he turned to the board with the erased cross and allowed the rabbit to twitch his ears while he himself allowed one foot, which was tied to an iron plate, to float over a similar plate, on the floor.

This is the main content of the action. The symbols are completely clear and they are all translatable. The division of the cross is the split between East and West, Rome and Byzantium. The half cross is the United Europe and Asia, to which the rabbit is on its way. The iron plate on the floor is a metaphor—it is hard to walk and the ground is frozen. The three interruptions on the way back signify the elements snow, ice, wind. All this is understandable only when the word Siberia is caught. But the symbols' significance are of secondary importance. Beuys is performing no cultural philosophical sketch. That is made clear by his extreme concentration. A man who spends himself to such an extent before an audience does this not only for the sake of certain rules set up for this particular situation. His actions require perspective and are penetrating because they are part of a larger context. . . . He uses the expression "counterspace" and "countertime" to indicate the psychic factors which make it possible to realize such a relationship to and experience of the materially given space. When the legs of the rabbit quiver, the poles sway out of their position—as they do incessantly during this exciting trip—and when he has great difficulty bringing them back to their proper position—for a moment then, our relationship to space breaks down. Something within us is set into motion. It is logical that sweat flows in streams from Beuys, that he looks like a person in great pain. He must continually restate the

18

balance, even if he stands on only one leg. . . . Man and animal compose a weak unity against space, which surrounds them.

Joseph Beuys in conversation with Ursula Meyer: "A rabbit running from one 'Fat Corner' to the next can do more for mankind than the SDS, which deals with Marxist thoughts without understanding them. . . .

"People assume immediately, if a work is not visible, it is particularly conceptual. That is a very materialistic way of thinking if one takes any thought and reverses it in itself. That is incredibly primitive because it is evidently the same thought only in reverse. Nothing has changed at all."

November 21, 1966: Dan Graham publishes his piece "Detumescence" as a classified advertisement in the *National Tatler* (also printed in *Screw* and *New York Review of Sex* in 1969).

LeWitt, Sol. "Ziggurats." *Arts,* November, 1966.

Smithson, Robert, and Bochner, Mel. "The Domain of the Great Bear." *Art Voices,* November, 1966.

Smithson, Robert. "Quasi-Infinities and the Waning of Space." *Arts,* November, 1966. "Actuality is . . . the interchronic pause when nothing is happening. It is the void between events"—George Kubler.

***Working Drawings and Other Visible Things on Paper Not Necessarily Meant to Be Viewed as Art.* Visual Arts Gallery, New York, December, 1966. Organized by Mel Bochner. The exhibition**

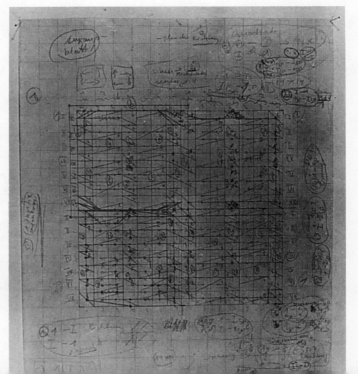

Hanne Darboven. *Permutational Drawing.* Pencil on graph paper. 1966.

consisted of several large looseleaf notebooks containing xerox copies of the drawings and placed on "pedestals" in an otherwise empty room. (Rep. Darboven.)

December, Paris: Buren, Toroni, Parmentier, and Mosset form a group on the principle of each artist's making one painting over and over again for whatever situation comes up. (See January, 1967.)

Graham, Dan. "Homes for America." *Arts,* December–January, 1966–67. (Rep.)

Dan Graham. *Homes for America.* 1966. Collection of Herman J. Daled, Brussels.

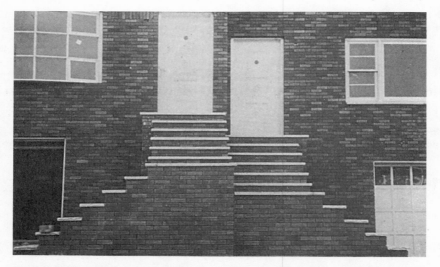

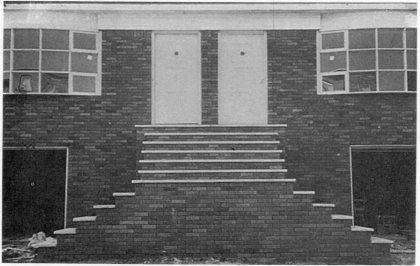

1967

Books

Atkinson, Terry, and Baldwin, Michael. *Air Show/Air-Conditioning Show.* **Coventry, England, Art-Language Press. Excerpt from** *Air Show* **thesis (1966–67):**
The macroscopic aggregate can be subjected to a micro-reductive examination. The horizontal dimensions of a "column" of air, atmosphere, "void," etc., can be indicated and established (for all "external" and practical purposes) by a visible demarcation in terms of horizontal dimensions, axis, etc. This could be done in a number of ways: e.g., through the indication of some points of contiguity with other "things," or through the computation of a particular physical magnitude: e.g., temperature or pressure differences, etc. (this is not necessarily to advocate an instrumental situation). None of this is to say that a complete, if only "factual" or constructual, specification is to be expected.

Obviously, when one talks of a column, there is some reference to a visual situation (from whence the vocabulary may or may not find support). There is a comparison to be made here between the "air-conditioning situation" and the fog bank, in which the obvious physical differences between the "matter" which constitutes the indicators of this or that "boundary" can be made out. This is not to describe the difference between boundaries per se, nor is it to exclude the possibility of regarding "boundaries" as "entifications" of geometrical gaps.

Mostly, anyway, the questions of "demarcation" are external ones of a practical nature. Still, they remain securely rooted in the perusal tradition, so long as one considers them in the context of particularizing characteristics at an observational level.

A lot of emphasis was placed on the microscopic mechanical aspects of procedure and process in the air-conditioning situation; it's easy to raise and answer the same sort of question here. The objection to doing this is based in a rejection of the problems of "visualization" (and "identification" in that context) on theoretical grounds. The microscopic picture has a counterweight origin in the macroscopic aspect of a situation. Whilst articulation on and identification of air as a "thing" conforms to this tradition, the molecular mechanical concept of "particle," "flux" (of energy), and the "thing," "particle" identity systems appear to be incompatible. What is interesting about thermodynamics is that it is restricted to the formulation of necessary conditions for an occurrence.

———. *Hot Warm Cool Cold.* Coventry, Art-Language Press.

———. *Frameworks.* Coventry, Art-Language Press.

Ramsden, Mel. *The Black Book.* **New York, 1967.**

Ruscha, Edward (with Mason Williams and Patrick Blackwell). *Royal Road Test.* **Los Angeles:**
   Date: Sunday, August 21, 1966. Time: 5:07 P.M. Place: U.S. Highway 91 (Interstate Highway 15) traveling South-Southwest, approximately 122 miles Southwest of Las Vegas, Nevada. Weather: perfect. Speed: 90 m.p.h. [Documentation of the destruction of a vintage Royal typewriter thrown from the window of a 1963 Buick Le Sabre.] "It was too directly bound to its own anguish to be anything other than a cry of negation; carrying within itself the seeds of its own destruction." (Rep.)

———. *Thirty-four Parking Lots in Los Angeles.* **Los Angeles.**

Young, Lamonte, and MacLow, Jackson, eds. *An Anthology.* **Munich, Heiner Friedrich, 1967 (first printed in 1963). Includes "Concept Art" by Henry Flynt. (Rep.)**

New York: Robert Barry makes paintings in which 2″ × 2″ squares of stretched canvas demark and enclose a rectangular space on the wall; makes hanging wire and nylon sculptures that are virtually invisible; makes film *Scenes***, in which long periods of white screen are broken by flashes of scenery.**

New York: Rick Barthelme makes tape paintings (or sculptures) consisting simply of geometric areas demarked on floors, walls, and ceilings. (Rep.)

Amsterdam: Jan Dibbets, Ger van Elk, and Lucassen found the International Institute for the Reeducation of Artists. Dibbets makes his first earth sculptures (grass squares, rolls of turf).

Michael Heizer makes his first earthworks.

Christine Kozlov sends out xeroxed calender strips systematically canceled.

London: NOIT chair of nonentity founded by John Latham.

Ed Ruscha. Plate from *Royal Road Test*. 1967.

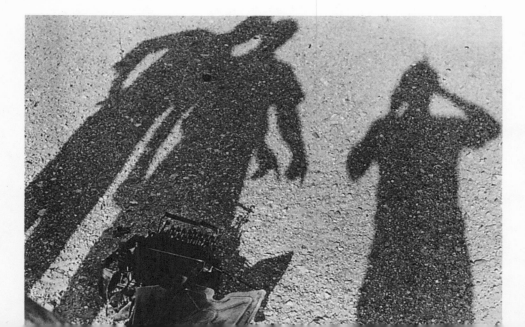

Frederick Barthelme. Untitled.
Tape. 1967.

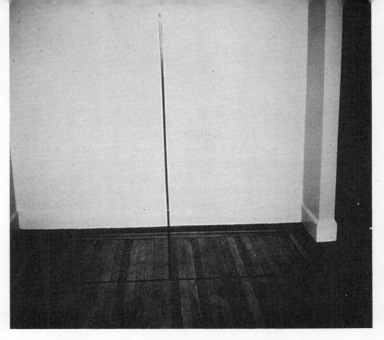

NOIT states gratuitously an axiomatic base (no it) for the conception of all things making up the "real" world. . . . A terminology that is so firmly embedded in the premise that "matter" is somewhere a solid is in great difficulty, and the resultant problems and compensatory devices for reassuring everybody that all is well show up in every department of life. NOIT proposes a different logic that places extension in time the key dimension of "real" phenomena, and proceeds from there to suggest that a least event could lead to the apparent but very misleading "particle." NOIT is a stratagem.

Richard Long executes a cycling sculpture in Middlesex, Oxfordshire, Buckinghamshire, Northamptonshire, Leicestershire, Cambridgeshire, Suffolk, and Essex.

Dennis Oppenheim makes his first earthwork (a five-foot wedge from a mountain in Oakland, California, lined with plexiglass; it follows his aluminum "site markers").

Bernar Venet decides to present during the next four years: Astrophysics, Nuclear Physics, Space Sciences, Mathematics by Computation, Meteorology, Stock Market, Meta-Mathematics, Psychophysics and Psychochronometry, Sociology and Politics, Mathematical Logic, etc.

For each discipline an authority advised me upon the subjects to be presented: these subjects were chosen according to their *importance.* . . . The question was not to make a new object, a new readymade out of mathematics. I attributed a *didactic* goal to their presentation. *Scientific diagrams were painted, at first by hand, on large canvases; later some were accompanied by taped lectures and the "paintings" became photographic blow-ups of texts or diagrams directly from books (see p. 105).*

William Wiley and Terry Fox (among others working with Wiley) make *Dust Exchange,* dust having been used as a medium by Marcel Duchamp in 1920, by Barry Le Va in 1968, and Bruce Nauman (flour dust) 1968.

January 2, 1967, Paris: Buren, Mosset, Parmentier, and Toroni work in public for the duration of the opening of the Salon de la Jeune Peinture, each making "his own" painting: Buren, vertical stripes; Mosset, a small black circle centered on a white canvas; Parmentier, sprayed horizontal bands; Toroni, "imprints of a No. 50 brush at 30-cm. distances." During this period a loudspeaker blares in three languages: "Buren, Mosset, Parmentier, and Toroni advise you to become intelligent."

A tract is distributed which reads, in part: "Inasmuch as painting is a game. . . . Inasmuch as to paint is to represent the external (or interpret it or appropriate it or dispute it or present it). . . . Inasmuch as to paint is a function of estheticism, flowers, woman, eroticism, the daily environment, art, dada, psychoanalysis, the war in Vietnam, WE ARE NOT PAINTERS."

January 3: The four withdraw from the Salon because, among other reasons, "Painting is by nature objectively reactionary."

Adrian, Dennis. "Walter de Maria: Word and Thing." *Artforum,* January, 1967.

Nonanthropomorphic Art by Four Young Artists: Joseph Kosuth, Christine Kozlov, Michael Rinaldi, Ernest Rossi, at the Lannis Gallery on 315 East 12th Street, near Second Avenue, opening February 19, 12 to 12: Four Statements.

Christine Kozlov, *Compositions for Audio Structures:*

The numbers on the left indicate the different sounds. The horizontals corresponding to each number indicate both placement (in relation to the other sounds) and duration in counts of sound (the numbers on top of the horizontals). In structure number 1, for instance, number 1's first duration is 12 counts of sound, stopping for 1 count, continuing for 11, stopping for 2, continuing for 10, and so on.

The sounds sounding together are realized by reading downward until the sound-indicating numbers repeat; so that again in structure number 1, the first 6 counts of sound, sound 1, 3 and 5 (the constant) are sounding; at the end of count 6 sound 4 enters lasting for 12½ counts, or until the middle of sound 1 and 3's second duration; after sound 1 and 3's first stop and until sound 1 and 3 start again sound 2 is sounding.

The structures are concerned with symmetry, asymmetry, progression, or with their own intrinsic logic.

The structure's development in sound would incorporate either constant sounds, or sounds with equal beat durations or both.

$$* \quad * \quad *$$

Joseph Kosuth:

My art objects are total, complete, and disinterested. They are made of non-organic, non-polar, completely synthetic, completely unnatural, yet of conceptual rather than found materials. (June, 1966)

If a growth seems to exist to those familiar with my comparatively short history as a maker of art objects, it is an illusion. Each art object exists as an isolated event, without reference to time. When each art object was made I had a particular interest. If there is a continuum it exists in the similarity of my interests.

When I say that "Each art object exists as an isolated event, without reference to time," I could add as well, "or meaning." Yet, I do not intend to deny or reject its philosophical implications. Its uselessness, on another level, leaves little but that as a quality. An art object concerned totally with art (inasmuch as it is concerned with nothing else) must take the properties of an order, a logic of one kind or another to keep from taking the shape of other things which cannot be controlled, as well as to eliminate an association with elements embodying their own particular qualities. (September, 1966)

Several artists in process today are over-using mathematics, in one way or another, in their work. This is unfortunate. There is no sense in glorifying mathematics. Math is merely a tool. Artists use tools. Math is either math or it is not math, but it is not art. Mathematics does make it possible for a structure or object to have an order not associated with natural or useful objects. But orders can have their limitations. Particular artists not very interested in art get "hung-up" in the order. Art *is* boring. . . .

Order, when used by particular artists, becomes a "hidden motive" and a secret inside. (November, 1966)

It is not by mere chance that all of the work done by me included in this exhibit is labeled "model." All I make are models. The actual works of art are ideas. Rather than "ideals" the models are a visual approximation of a particular art object I have in mind. It does not matter who actually makes the model, nor where the model ends up. The models are real and actual and are beautiful in more or less proportion to other models and who they are being viewed by. Insofar as they are, as models, objects concerned with art—they are art objects. (February, 1967)

Graham, Dan. "Muybridge Moments." *Arts,* February, 1967.

Monuments, Tombstones, and Trophies. Museum of Contemporary Crafts, New York, March 17–May 14. No catalogue. Carl Andre contributes *Grave,* a conical sculpture executed by dropping sand from a stairway above, which was decomposed in time, constituting (according to Dan Graham) a pun on gravity and corporeal disintegration. Mel Bochner contributes "Four Statements Concerning Monuments," quotations from Duchamp, Sartre, Webster's Dictionary, and John Daniels. Reviewed by Dan Graham, "Models and Monuments." *Arts,* March, 1967.

0–9. Editors: Vito Hannibal Acconci and Bernadette Mayer. New York. No. 1, April, 1967; No. 2, August, 1967; No. 3, January, 1968. See June, 1968, January, 1969, and July, 1969, below, for last three numbers.

William Anastasi. Dwan Gallery, April–May, 1967. Exhibition consists of paintings of the walls on which the paintings hang (reduced by 10 per cent).

Sol LeWitt. One Set of Nine Pieces. Dwan Gallery, Los Angeles, April, 1967. Notes: "The individual pieces are composed of a form set equally within another and centered. Using this premise as a guide, no further design is necessary." See Lucy R. Lippard, "Sol LeWitt: Non-Visual Structures," *Artforum,* April, 1967.

April 11–May 3, 1967: Robert Ryman's *Standard* series (his first one-man show) at the Bianchini Gallery, New York.

These thirteen all-white brushstrokes on steel sheets were hung flat against the wall plane, denying object-quality to concentrate on surface, paint, and process, which, in 1968, became a "trend" called "antiform" and later "anti-illusionism," etc. Ryman had made a group of paintings without stretchers in 1964, and in 1967 began to tape or staple or paint (using paint as the adhesive) his white sheets of painted paper directly to the wall. Since then, he has continued to work with surfaces flat to the

Robert Ryman. *Adelphi*. Oil on linen with wax paper, frame, and tape, 110″ x 110″. 1967.

walls, as in: the grid-paneled Classico *series; a painting stapled to the wall with a blue line drawn* on *the wall from the upper right corner leftward till it meets the ceiling; a painting with a broad yellow "frame" painted directly on the wall wherever it is hung, or* Adelphi, *which has a replaceable "frame" of waxed paper. (Rep.) Ryman is primarily a painter, but these strategies enabled him to concentrate more fully on painting* per se *and freed him from a bulky, difficult-to-transport object; as such, this work is notable within the "dematerialization" process.*

*   *   *

When you made the Standard *paintings, were you trying to get away from the notion of objecthood?*

The traditional surface for painting has been canvas. . . . I use it and so do most painters, simply because it's the best; it's the lightest, it can be constructed large or small, in all kinds of shapes. . . . But there are other things: paper, plastics, masonite, on and on. . . . Rothko was the first, I guess, to make the point that painting was an esthetic object. That point was made over and over again through the 60's (I'm talking

26

about abstract painters) and I had done it myself [by painting around the edges of my stretcher in 1958]. The point had really gotten across strongly that the painting was an object. So, I wanted to make a painting getting the paint across. That's really what a painting is basically about, whether you talk about figurative painting or abstract painting. . . . I wanted to point out the paint and paint surface and not so much the objectness. Of course, they are always objects. . . . You can't get away from that. (From an interview by Phyllis Tuchman with Robert Ryman, *Artforum,* May, 1971.)

Rose, Barbara. "The Value of Didactic Art." *Artforum,* April, 1967.

Chandler, John, and Lippard, Lucy. "Visible Art and the Invisible World." *Art International,* May, 1967.

15 People Present Their Favorite Book. Lannis Gallery–Museum of Normal Art, New York, spring, 1967.

Serielle Formationen. Goethe Universität, Frankfurt am Main, May 22–June 30, 1967. Essays by Paul Maenz and Peter Roehr. Includes LeWitt, Dibbets, Andre, etc.

Burnham, Jack. "Hans Haacke: Wind and Water Sculpture." *Tri-Quarterly Supplement,* no. 1, spring, 1967 (Evanston, Northwestern University Press).

Language to Be Looked at and/or Things to Be Read. Dwan Gallery, New York, June 3–28, 1967. Xeroxed checklist and typed illiterate statement by "Eton Corrasable."

June 2, Paris: Buren, Mosset, Parmentier, and Toroni each hang their canvases (always identical to those made in January) in the auditorium of the Museé des Arts Décoratifs; a paying audience waits for an hour; at 10:15 a tract is distributed saying, "obviously this is only a matter of looking at the paintings of Buren, Mosset, Parmentier and Toroni," and describing each painting in detail.

Graham, Dan. "The Book as Object." *Arts,* June, 1967.

Morris, Robert. "Notes on Sculpture, Part 3: Notes and Nonsequiturs." *Artforum,* June, 1967.
  In 1963, Robert Morris made two extremely influential pieces that anticipated so-called conceptual art to a great degree. One was Card-File *(Rep.), a hanging series of plastic-encased cards with notes, references, and cross-references to the process of compiling the file. The second was a notarized "Statement of Esthetic Withdrawal," dated November 15, 1963, in which he withdrew from his construction* Litanies *"all esthetic quality and content" and declared that "from the date hereof said construction has no such quality and content." Other pieces from the period that bear mentioning in this context are two process works—*Metered Bulb, *and an electroencephalogram. Morris's* Twelve Bottles of Fresh Air, *also 1963, refers directly to Duchamp's* 50cc of Paris Air *(1919), as his telegram reading "use this," contributed to the* March, 1969, *exhibition (see below), referred directly to Rauschenberg's earlier telegram, "This is a portrait of Iris Clert if I say it is."*

Smithson, Robert. "Towards the Development of an Air Terminal Site." *Artforum,* June, 1967. (Rep.) At this point, the esthetics of the earthwork begins to be formalized. Smithson was "artist consultant" for the development of an air terminal between Dallas and Fort Worth,

Texas. Plans at one point included earth-aerial sculptures by Smithson, Morris, LeWitt; seminal ideas by Tony Smith and Carl Andre are cited:

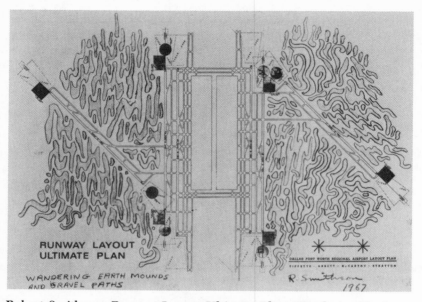

Robert Smithson. *Runway Layout Ultimate Plan; Wandering Earth Mounds and Gravel Paths.* Drawing. 1967. Courtesy John Weber Gallery, New York.

Our whole notion of airflight is casting off the old meaning of speed through space, and developing a new meaning based on instantaneous time. . . . The farther out an object goes in space, the less it represents the old rational idea of visible speed. The stream-lines of *space* are replaced by crystalline structure of *time*. . . . Language problems are often at the bottom of most rationalistic "objectivity." One must be conscious of the changes in language before one attempts to discover the form of an object or fact.

Robho no. 1 appears in Paris, edited by Jean Clay and Julien Blaine; newspaper format, each issue printed in a different color. July, 1967, issue contains Clay's "La Peinture est finie" (translated in *Studio International,* July–August, 1967, as "Painting—A Thing of the Past").

LeWitt, Sol. "Paragraphs on Conceptual Art." *Artforum,* summer, 1967:
I will refer to the kind of art in which I am involved as conceptual art. In conceptual art the idea or concept is the most important aspect of the work. (In other forms of art the concept may be changed in the process of execution.) When an artist uses a conceptual form of art, it means that all of the planning and decisions are made beforehand and the execution is a perfunctory affair. The idea becomes a machine that makes the art. . . .
Conceptual art is not necessarily logical. The logic of a piece or series of pieces is a device that is used at times only to be ruined. . . . The ideas need not be complex.

Most ideas that are successful are ludicrously simple. . . . Ideas are discovered by intuition.

What the work of art looks like isn't too important. It has to look like something if it has physical form. No matter what form it may finally have it must begin with an idea. It is the process of conception and realization with which the artist is concerned. . . .

Conceptual art doesn't really have much to do with mathematics, philosophy or any other mental discipline. The mathematics used by most artists is simple arithmetic or simple number systems. The philosophy of the work is implicit in the work and is not an illustration of any system of philosophy. . . .

Conceptual art is only good when the idea is good.

Robert Morris. *Card File.* **47″ x 10 1/2″ x 2″.
1962. Courtesy Dwan Gallery, New York.**

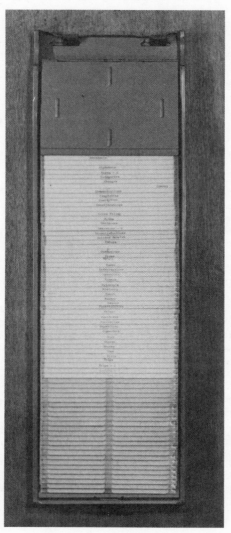

July–September: Terry Atkinson travels to New York, meets LeWitt, Graham, Andre, Smithson, after having corresponded with the first two for some time.

Bochner, Mel. "Serial Art Systems: Solipsism." *Arts,* summer, 1967.

Fall, New York: Claes Oldenburg is asked to participate in a city outdoor sculpture show; he (1) suggests calling Manhattan a work of art, (2) proposes a scream monument wherein a piercing scream is broadcast through the streets at 2 a.m., and (3) finally has a 6′ × 6′ × 3′ trench dug behind the Metropolitan Museum by union gravediggers, under his supervision, and then filled up again.

19:45–21:55. Organized by Paul Maenz on the property of Dorothy Loehr, Frankfurt am Main, September–November, 1967: Dibbets, Flanagan, Höke, Johnson, Long, Lueg, Posenenske, Roehr. Dibbets's sawdust oval to be perceived as a circle (his first perspective correction) was photographed every five minutes in the process of destruction by visitors. Long marked out with loosely touching pieces of wood the shape of the room in Frankfurt, and repeated it outdoors in Bristol, England.

September, Buenos Aires: Oscar Bony exhibits a bare room with a tape-recorded loop describing the room's measurements and features in minute detail.

September, Paris: At the Paris Biennale, canvases by Buren, Mosset, Parmentier, and Toroni are presented with miscellaneous slides and a synchronized tape giving a series of definitions:
    Art is the illusion of disorientation, the illusion of liberty, the illusion of presence, the illusion of the sacred, the illusion of Nature. . . . Not the painting of Buren, Mosset, Paramentier or Toroni. . . . Art is a distraction, art is false. Painting begins with Buren, Mosset, Parmentier, Toroni.

Arte Povera/Im Spazio. Galleria La Bertesca, Genoa, October, 1967. Two separate exhibitions organized and prefaced by Germano Celant. *Arte Povera* also shown at the Instituto di storia dell'arte at Genoa University (Boetti, Fabro, Kounellis, Paolini, Pascali, Prini); symposium with these artists plus Pistoletto (who cut his wife's hair), Anselmo, Merz, Zorio. Some of the artists appeared simultaneously in *Contemplazione* at the Galleria Sperone, Turin, and Galeria Flaviana, Lugano (organized by Daniela Palozzoli). The shows were reviewed in *Lavoro Nuovo,* October 10; *Corriere Mercantile,* October 27; *Casabella,* October; *Bit,* November, December; *Arte Oggi,* December (see Celant, *Art Povera,* for full bibliography).

October, 1967: Opening of Konrad Fischer Gallery in Düsseldorf with Carl Andre's first one-man show in Europe. Fischer continues to exhibit minimal and "conceptual" artists in Europe, giving first European shows to Artschwager, Huebler, LeWitt, Nauman, Ryman, Smithson, Weiner, Wilson; first one-artist shows anywhere to Darboven, Long, Panamarenko, Rinke, Rückriem, Ruthenbeck; first German shows to Boetti, Buren, Dibbets, Fulton, McLean, and Merz.

Dies alles Herzchen wird einmal dir Gehören. Galerie Loehr, Frankfurt, October, 1967. Dibbets, Long, etc.

"New York Correspondance [*sic*] School." *Artforum,* October, 1967.

Opening Exhibition: Normal Art, directed by Joseph Kosuth. (Rep.) The Lannis Museum of Normal Art, New York, November, 1967. Andre, Barthelme, Bochner, Darboven, de Maria, Kawara, Kozlov (Rep.), LeWitt, Lozano, Morris, Rockburne, Ryman, Smithson, etc.

Left: Joseph Kosuth. *"Titled" (Art as Idea as Idea).* Negative photostat, mounted. 1967. *Right:* Christine Kozlov. No title. Transparent film #2, white—16 mm. 1967.

Art in Series. Finch College, New York, November, 1967. Text by Elayne Varian, statements by the artists, among whom were Bochner, Darboven, Graham, Hesse, Lee, LeWitt. Discussed by Mel Bochner in "The Serial Attitude," *Artforum,* December, 1967, and David Lee in "Serial Art," *Art News,* December, 1967.

Robert Morris gives a lecture November, 1967, at the Guggenheim Museum, New York, consisting of several tape-recorded talks by himself on aspects of his art, life, esthetic, art-making process, criticism, each played for five minutes, consecutively, for an hour.

Artschwager, Richard. "The Hydraulic Doorcheck." *Arts,* November, 1967 (Rep.):
The most striking property of doors (although not unique to doors) is RESONANCE between two states, which can be conveniently labeled as "open" and "closed." Resonance is never a simple, unqualified fluctutation between two states; even so in this case. A door—at any given moment—is in a state of being closed with the possibility of its being opened, or in a state of being open with the possibility of its being closed. This is not a speculative model for a door but a description of the state of affairs which immediately existed when the first door was brought into being. . . .
The properties of "open" and "closed" cannot be divorced from the "geography" of the door, i.e., without reference to that which the door opens or closes. It becomes obvious that to speak of a door as being "open" or "closed" is in fact a contradiction in terms. Can this be remedied by saying that the door when closed is "in the act" of closing itself? God forbid! Or in the act of closing that to which it is appended? Not quite. The act is not the transformation. The act takes place in stages. Otherwise it is not an act. At any rate there is no such thing (in our terms of reference) as somewhat open, or somewhat closed. In other words the tiniest crack is open, and closed is closed. . . . This can be carried on indefinitely, so one has to say that one cannot define a minimal open position which is DIFFERENT from a closed position.
Having effectively closed the door we may now direct our attention to the partition to which the door is appended.

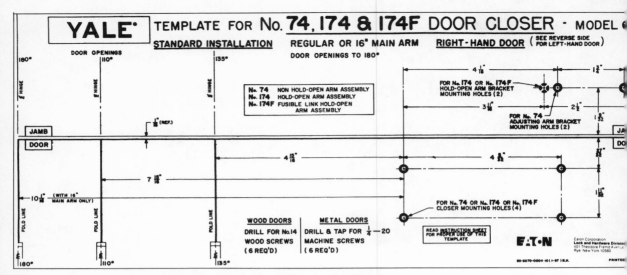

Richard Artschwager. *Hydraulic Doorcheck.* 1968.

The main obstacle to the elimination of history from art is art itself. Conventionality in art resides in the convention of art. This sounds like proclaiming democracy in art by applying to each of its practitioners, without fear or favor, the same coat of tar and feathers. Once this stricture has been tentatively accepted it can be eased somewhat by issuing a like set of stigmata to practitioners of some of the other conventions: inventors of social and economic systems, revealers of metaphysical truths, etc.

I am arguing the subjectivity and consequent self-conscious posture of all world views and their practitioners. The conception-practice of horizon making is, moreover, not just a fact of human life but is altogether appropriate human posture and behavior.

Mel Ramsden, New York, makes a painting that is canvas stretched, front to the wall, labeled on the back: Title "UNTITLED (NONVISUAL ART)," dated November, 1967.

Müller, Grégoire. "Quatre non peintres." *Robho,* no. 2, November–December, 1967. On Buren, Mosset, Parmentier, and Toroni. In the same issue: Hans Haacke, a special section including statements by the artist and an interview with Jack Burnham.

December 5–25, Paris 8, rue Montfaucon: Buren, Mosset, and Toroni each paint their own "usual" works and those of the other two as well. Buren and Toroni do a similar work in Lugano in December, under the title "Buren, Toroni or anybody," inviting reviewers to make or to claim their paintings. Two-page brochure by Michel Claura: "In order to discuss a forgery, one must refer to an original. In the case of Buren, Mosset, Toroni, where is the original work?"

Aspen, no. 5–6, fall–winter, 1967. Edited by Brian O'Doherty. Boxed; in separate booklets or envelopes: a "structural play" by O'Doherty, "Serial Project #1,1966," Sol LeWitt; excerpt from *Site,* a film by Morris and Vanderbeek; "Seven Translucent Tiers," Mel Bochner; texts by R. Barthes, S. Sontag ("The Aesthetics of Silence"), G. Kubler, M. Butor, and others; scores, works, records, etc.; reviewed by Dore Ashton, *Studio International,* May, 1968. Also included, Dan Graham:

Schema for a Set of Pages whose component variants are to be published in various places. In each published instance, or example, it is set in its final form (so it defines itself) by the editor of the particular publication where it is to appear, the exact data used to correspond in each specific instance to the specific fact(s) of the published final appearance. The work defines itself in place only as information with simply the external support of the facts of its external appearance as information (or art); as the sign of its own appearance or presence in print in place of the object. (1966):

(number of)	adjectives
(number of)	adverbs
(percentage of)	area not occupied by type
(percentage of)	columns
(number of)	conjunctions
(depth of)	depression of type into page surface
(number of)	gerunds
(number of)	infinitives
(number of)	letters of alphabet
(number of)	lines
(number of)	mathematical symbols
(number of)	nouns
(number of)	numbers
(number of)	participles
(perimeter of)	page
(weight of)	paper sheet
(type of)	paper stock
(number of)	prepositions
(number of)	pronouns
(number of point)	size type
(name of)	typeface
(number of)	words
(number of)	words capitalized
(number of)	words italicized

December, Turin: Pistoletto's show at Galleria Sperone states:
With this show, I have liberated my studio, which is open to welcome young people who want to present their work, make things, discover themselves.

In his book *Le ultime parole famose,* published at the same time, Pistoletto wrote:
There is no goal before us with laurels for the winner and ashes for the loser. The world race for this abstract point structures itself into a system of battles between both individuals and masses. When we move ahead by stepping to one side, the race between individuals becomes a series of parallels, since every individual proceeds individually, without projecting himself out of himself onto abstract points or other individuals. When we move in this way there are no such things as better and worse, since everybody is what he is and does what he does. Nobody needs to pretend to prove that he is better, and communication grows very easy without the structures of language, since it's easy to understand who everybody is and what he's like. For communication and understanding, we will finally be able to develop all of the possibilities of the mechanism of perception.

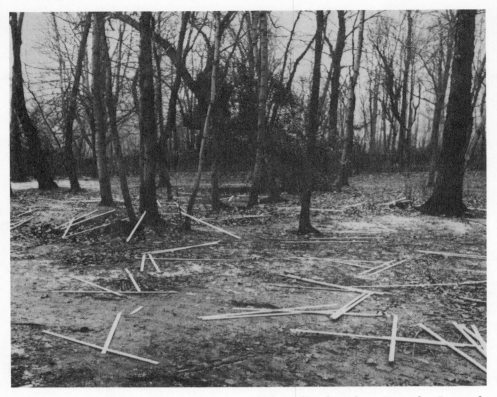

Roelof Louw. *300 Wooden Slats Scattered in Holland Park at Irregular Intervals.* London. October, 1967.

December: Michael Snow's film *Wavelength* (December, 1966–May, 1967) wins first prize at the Fourth International Experimental Film Festival, Knokke-le-Zoute, Belgium.
I was thinking of, planning for, a time monument in which the beauty and sadness of equivalence would be celebrated, thinking of trying to make a definitive statement on pure film space and time, a balancing of "illusion" and "fact," all about seeing. The space starts at the camera's (spectator's) eye, is in the air, then is on the screen, then is within the screen (the mind). (From the catalogue.)

If *Wavelength* is metaphysics, *New York Eye and Ear Control* [1964 film] is philosophy and will be physics. . . . My films are (to me) attempts to suggest to the mind a certain state or certain states of consciousness. They are drug relatives in that respect. (From "Letter from Michael Snow" to P. Adams Sitney and Jonas Mekas, August 21, 1968; first published in *Film Culture,* no. 46, autumn, 1968.)

Hutchinson, Peter. "The Fictionalization of the Past." *Arts,* December, 1967.

Smithson, Robert. "The Monuments of Passaic." *Artforum,* December, 1967.

Danieli, Fidel A. "The Art of Bruce Nauman." *Artforum,* December, 1967.

Morris, Robert. "A Method for Sorting Cows." *Art and Literature,* no. 11, winter, 1967.

1968

BOOKS

Acconci, Vito Hannibal. *Four Book.* 0 to 9 Books, New York, 1968.

Atkinson, Terry, and Baldwin, Michael. *22 Sentences: The French Army* (October, 1967). Coventry, Precinct Publications, 1968:

KEY:
FA   —French Army
CMM   —Collection of Men and Machines
GR   —Group of Regiments

Assertions. Explicata.

The context of identity statements in which collection of men and machines appears as a covering concept is a relativistic one. Identity is not simply built into that concept. The "sense" of identity is contrasted with the constitutive one.

The FA is regarded as the same CMM as the GR and the GR is the same CMM as (e.g.) "a new order" FA (e.g., morphologically a member of another class of objects): by transitivity the FA is the same CMM as the "new Shape/Order one."

It's all in support of the constitutive sense that the FA is the same CMM as the GR. The inference is that the FA and the CMM have the same life history (both the FA and the CMM are decimated) and in which case CMM fails as a covering concept. If the CMM isn't decimated (no identity) the predicate fails. The "constitutive" concept stays. And its durability doesn't come from a distorted construction of "Collection."

The concept of collection or manifold is one for which there can be no empty or null collection. The manifold FA; a domain, a regiment; it's all one whether the elements are specified as the battalions, the companies or single soldiers.

(This doesn't work for classes).

The elements are intended to define and exhaust the "whole." If the CMM is to be regarded as no more and no less tolerant of damage and replacement of parts as FA, then the right persistence-conditions and configuration of CMM can be ensured only by grafting on the concept FA, and this is to "decognize" thing-matter equations.

The rest is not equivocation. "Concrete" and "steel" are not, in this framework, the sortals with classificatory purport (and in the terminological context, the sense does not emanate from them). And the same for all the constituents which may be specified at different dates for the FA.

Barry, Robert. *360° Book.* New York. Unique copy. The 360 degrees of a circle drawn off degree by degree on graph paper. Collection Panza di Biumo, Milan.

Bochner, Mel. *The Singer Notes.* Four xerox books published by the artist, New York, 1968; also, *Eight Times Eight Times Eight.*

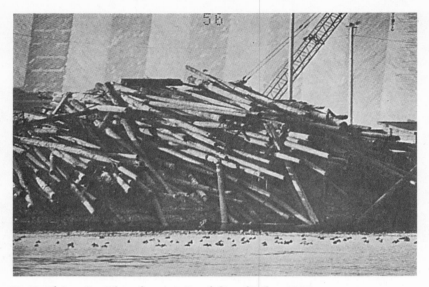

N. E. Thing Co. Plate from *A Portfolio of Piles.* 1968.

Burnham, Jack. *Beyond Modern Sculpture.* New York, George Braziller, 1968.

Calvesi, Maurizio, ed. *Teatro delle Mostre.* Rome, Lerici, 1968. Book after exhibition in Rome (May 6–31) in which one artist per day performed a piece.

Marchetti, Walter. *Arpocrate seduto sul loto.* Madrid, Zaj, 1968.

N. E. Thing Co. *A Portfolio of Piles.* (Rep.) Fine Arts Gallery, University of British Columbia, Vancouver, February, 1968. Fifty-nine photographs of found "piles" ranging from dirt to chains to breasts to doughnuts to barrels, etc., plus a list of locations and a map of Vancouver. Introduction by Kurt von Meier, note from the president of NETCo. Reviewed by Alvin Balkind, *Artforum,* May 1968 and in *Artscanada,* August, 1968.
    It is the visual Unknown that challenges the N. E. Thing researchers. Like researchers anywhere, they seek to add to the world's store of knowledge—by exploratory research on the frontiers of basic theory, by product research for results in specific tangible forms, by production research for processes that yield precise end products. These probings of the why and how of visual things and their combinations are efforts to discover distinct properties or effects and the means of putting them into operation. (1968 Company statement.)

Ramsden, Mel. *Abstract Relations.* New York, 1968.

Ruscha, Edward. *Nine Swimming Pools and a Broken Glass.* Los Angeles, 1968 (in color).

Ruscha, Edward, and Bengston, Billy Al. *Business Cards.* Los Angeles, 1968.

Walther, Franz Erhard. *Objekte, benutzen.* Cologne, Gebr. König; New York, 1968: "These objects are instruments, they have little perceptual significance. The objects are important only through the possibilities originating from their use." Walther has made instrument-objects since 1963. (Rep.)

Weiner, Lawrence. *Statements.* **Seth Siegelaub, Louis Kellner Foundation, New York, 1968. Divided into "General Statements":**
A field cratered by structured simultaneous TNT explosions
A removal to the lathing or support wall of plaster or wall board from a wall
One standard dye marker thrown into the sea
Common steel nails driven into the floor at points designated at time of installation

And "Specific Statements":
One hole in the ground approximately one foot by one foot/One gallon water-base white paint poured into this hole
One aerosol can of enamel sprayed to conclusion directly upon the floor
One quart exterior green enamel thrown on a brick wall
A 2″ wide 1″ deep trench cut across a standard one-car driveway

Mel Ramsden, New York. *Secret Piece,* **1968 ("Envelope #1 encloses specific documentation of content of Envelope #2"; "Envelope #2 encloses specific documentation of content of Envelope #1"). And** *Secret Painting* **(1967–68). Acrylic on canvas, photostat: "the content of this painting is invisible, the character and dimensions of the content are to be kept permanently secret, known only to the artist."**

Ian Burn has been working with Ramsden since the mid-1960's (at one point, with Roger Cutforth, they formed The Society for Theoretical Art and Analysis). In an interview with Joel Fischer, Burn said:
Presentation is a problem because it can easily become a form in itself, and this can be misleading. I would always opt for the most neutral format, one that doesn't interfere with or distort the information. For example, this interview published in the context of an art-magazine would be natural as a format; one's intake capacity for the information is therefore at its highest. But if I photo-enlarge the pages and mounted them on a gallery wall, then one's conceptual intake is considerably lowered.

Hans Haacke. **Howard Wise Gallery, New York, January 13–February 3, 1968:**
A "sculpture" that physically reacts to its environment is no longer to be regarded as an object. The range of outside factors affecting it, as well as its own radius of action, reaches beyond the space it materially occupies. It thus merges with the environment in a relationship that is better understood as a "system" of interdependent processes. These processes evolve without the viewer's empathy. He becomes a witness. A system is not imagined, it is real. (H. H.)

Franz Erhard Walther. *#29 (1967) from 1. Werksatz (Demonstration).* **Courtesy Videogalerie Gerry Schum, Dusseldorf.**

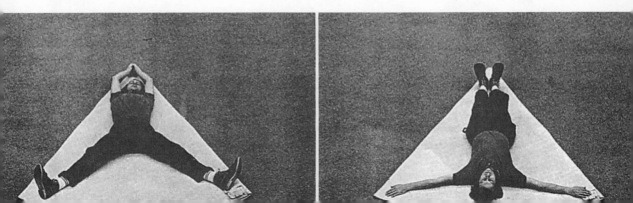

Haacke built his first water box, exploring natural systems of condensation and contained waves, in Germany in 1963. These led to ice pieces, work with actual biological growth (grass, hatching chickens) and more open and unlimited weather pieces (see Wind in Water, December, 1968, below). In January, 1965, he wrote the following notes:

. . . make something which experiences, reacts to its environment, changes, is nonstable . . .

. . . make something indeterminate, which always looks different, the shape of which cannot be predicted precisely . . .

. . . make something which cannot "perform" without the assistance of its environment . . .

. . . make something which reacts to light and temperature changes, is subject to air currents and depends, in its functioning, on the forces of gravity . . .

. . . make something which the "spectator" handles, with which he plays, and thus animates it . . .

. . . make something which lives in time and makes the "spectator" experience time . . .

. . . articulate something Natural . . .

Michael Snow Sculpture. Poindexter Gallery, New York, January 27–February 16, 1968. Metal sculpture on themes of perception:

First to Last (1967) is a kind of absolute that frames things that are fortuitous. It is totally symmetrical, a perfect square in middle-grey, turned in on itself. . . . When you look through the slots, first you see the shiny aluminum that is the inner basis of the work, and then you realize you are seeing a prism of some kind. . . . The sculpture is internal (but) it feeds on what is external. . . . Art is often a limitation, a focusing-in on things. . . .

For the last 3 or 4 years I have been influenced by films and by the camera. When you narrow down your range and are looking through just that small aperture of the lens, the intensity of what you see is so much greater. (From an interview by Dorothy Cameron with Michael Snow, May 23, 1967.)

Hanne Darboven. One page of Jan. 23, 1968. From one of six volumes of the year 1968.

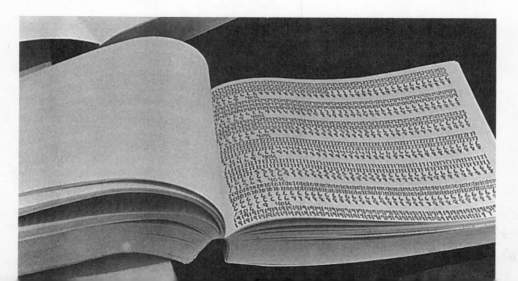

Bruce Nauman. Leo Castelli, New York, January 27–February 17, 1968. Booklet reproducing forty-four works from 1965 to 1968; "notes" by David Whitney.

Hutchinson, Peter. "Dance Without Movement." *Art in America,* January–February, 1968.

Diacono, Mario. "Arakawa: A Quadridimensional Geometry of Imagination." *Art International,* January, 1968.

Random Sample, N-42. "An exhibition organized by Arnold Rockman, of randomly selected and randomly displayed contemporary artifacts." Fine Arts Gallery, University of British Columbia, Vancouver, February, 1968. Reviewed by Alvin Balkind, *Artforum,* May, 1968.

From a letter dated October, 1967, from Arnold Rockman to Alvin Balkind, director of the UBC Fine Arts Gallery:

The Random Sample show is growing in my mind all the time. As I conceive of it now, I shall make it an assignment for my students in the communications course I teach at York University. I shall ask them to supply photos of rooms in their own homes, plus photos I shall take in my own home and in the street downtown. Then we shall enlarge the photos, place a plastic grid over them, and select squares from a table of random numbers. The objects in the squares then become the objects in the show. You will get a list of the objects divided into "inside objects" and "outside objects." I should like a line drawn or taped on the floor of the gallery to divide the two selections or samples. When you get the list, either you yourself, or people selected by you then collect the Vancouver examples of the objects described. Suppose one of the objects is "bedroom chair with clothes which have been taken off for the night thrown over it." Then you get any chair from anybody's bedroom with their clothes on it, just as it is. In every case, no attempt must be made to arrive at an "aesthetic" arrangement. We're interested in naturalism and natural history. . . . As for the arrangement of the objects in the gallery, again that ought to be arrived at through the use of chance procedures. . . . You can decide on the mode of presentation that way too. Some would be wall-pieces—"paintings"—while others would be "sculptures"—either on the floor or on plinths.

From Rockman's catalogue introduction:

The cultural historian Johann Huizinga and the sociologist Emile Durkheim both felt that the distinction between the sacred and the profane is crucial for our understanding of such phenomena as the arts and religious ritual. As soon as a particular space is set aside for an activity that is regarded as different from the ordinary profane activities of ordinary life, then that special space, and the activities performed in it, acquire a sacred character. . . .

If we think about the simplest set of combinations of sacred and profane spaces, we can clearly discern four main types of aesthetic performance or exhibition: (a) sacred things displayed in sacred spaces (the traditional aesthetic of performance and display); (b) profane things displayed in profane spaces (exhibitions and performances such as *Random Sample* and *Piles*); (c) profane things displayed in profane spaces (ordinary events and activities that take place in the city streets without any conscious aesthetic intention); (d) sacred things displayed in profane spaces (sculpture in the street; a Mardi Gras parade; early Soviet agit-prop theatre; medieval mystery plays in the marketplace). . . .

The performance called *Random Sample, N-42* is intended to illustrate two sentences which are significant in the history of equalitarianism and democracy in the arts. The first sentence is by John Constable, the English landscape painter and precursor of the French impressionists: "My limited and abstracted art is to be found under every hedge and in every lane, and therefore nobody thinks it worth picking up." The second sentence is by Georg Simmel, the German aesthetician and sociologist: "To treat not only every person but every *thing* as if it were its own end: this would be a cosmic ethic."

Arte Povera. Galleria de Foscherari, Bologna, February, 1968; Centro Arte Viva Feltrinelli, Trieste, March, 1968. Texts by Germano Celant.

Carl Andre, Robert Barry, Lawrence Weiner. Bradford Junior College, Bradford, Mass., February 4–March 2, 1968. Organized by Seth Siegelaub. Symposium with the artists and the organizer on February 8. Some excerpts from the unpublished tape-recording:
SS: What are the revolutionary aspects of the philosophy behind this work?

RB: Well, revolutionary is a strong term. I hesitate to use it, but I guess it has to do with my purpose in art and the things that I deal with. I try to paint what I don't know. It seems to me to be a very boring thing to make paintings which predict what I know. In other words, I want to take a chance. I may be dealing with things I don't completely understand myself. I try to deal with things that maybe other people haven't thought about, emptiness, making a painting that isn't a painting. For years people have been concerned with what goes on *inside* the frame. Maybe there's something going on *outside* the frame that could be considered an artistic idea. That isn't to say they are experiments. I think of them as complete artistic ideas in themselves. . . .

CA: I don't feel terribly revolutionary. I don't really think that word applies to the making of art. At least for myself, I make art because it is the only thing I know how to do. . . .

LW: I suspect revolution never has anything to do with something new. I don't think very much is ever added. It is like fashion. There are ages of faith and ages of skepticism alternating in the course of human history—struggle and counterstruggle. I don't think anything is particularly added . . . so I would say the true revolutionary act just changes the balance of things already existing.

RB: Why the void and not the created space? There is something about void and emptiness which I am personally very concerned with. I guess I can't get it out of my system. Just emptiness. *Nothing* seems to me the most potent thing in the world.

CA: I would say a thing is a hole in a thing it is not. Our whole education is conducted by linguistic means. Language is mostly devoted to symbols, and art has very little to do with that. Any artist can symbolize but very few artists can execute. I would say that all ideas are the same except in execution. They lie in the head. In terms of the artist, the only difference between one idea and another is how it is executed. . . . Art doesn't come from the mouth, you know. It is not a telling experience. We want experience to *tell* us something, but I don't think that understanding has to do with telling anything. . . . Science is creating and comparing, and art is creating conditions that do not quite exist. That is why art is different from science. The ideal of science is to create at least theoretical models of things we hope have some correspondence with what exists; whereas with art, you try as a human being to create something that wouldn't exist unless you made it.

February, Paris: Buren, Mosset, and Toroni each show one painting in a friend's apartment.

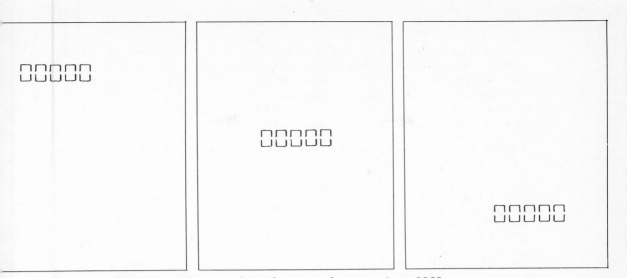

Peter Downsbrough. Segment of Staple on graph paper piece. 1968.

Parinaud, André. "Interview with Daniel Buren." *Galerie des Arts,* **no. 50, February, 1968. The following excerpt from this December, 1967, interview was translated by L. R. L.:**

AP: If I understand correctly, you wish to provide information at the zero degree of painting?

DB: I'll push it further. I believe we are the only ones to be able to claim the right of being "looked at," in the sense that we are the only ones to present a thing which has no didactic intention, which does not provide "dreams," which is not a "stimulant." Each individual can dream himself, and without doubt much better than by the trickery of an artist, however great he may be. The artist appeals to laziness, his function is emollient. He is "beautiful" for others, "talented" for others, "ingenious" for others, which is a scornful or superior way of considering "others." The artist brings beauty, dreams, suffering, to their domiciles, while "the others," whom I myself consider *a priori* as talented as artists, must find their own beauty, their own dream. In a word, become adults. Perhaps the only thing that one can do after having seen a canvas like ours is total revolution.

AP: You have been making the same painting for two years?

DB: The color is decided by what they offer me when I buy the cloth. I do not choose. I have fifty meters of red. This is to avoid always making the same canvas—*which is not decided in advance either*—finding myself after ten years with a magnificent arch-classic oeuvre of a Buren who will have made the same canvas for ten years, and finally, my canvas will have become "Buren." . . . I can fall into other traps which I haven't yet discovered, but that one I have perceived, so I try to avoid it. Now, the only way of avoiding it is not to give any significance to color, and to do so seems to suffice to demonstrate that I personally don't give a damn about this color, that I fixed on one color, even taken at random. And the same goes for form, that is, if I always make the same form; even if at the beginning that form seems bizarre or neutral, that bizarre form will end by being beautiful and that neutral form will end by not being neutral any more.

I am not saying pink is neutral, or gray is neutral, but a gray striped canvas then a blue striped one then another in green, and so on, infinitely, hinders by successive and equal repetition any significance for any of them. It is the destruction of the notion of "the work of art." So, to say that a painting can be neutral is to say something differing radically from everything that painting has until now affirmed. I mean to say, things could open up (but that no longer concerns us, in the sense that I am not a prophet and I completely forbid myself to be one) into a kind of painting which, if it exists, if it can be made, will be radically different, because there will no longer be any possibility of evolution, nor of perfectability. . . . My painting, at the limit, can only signify itself. *It is.* So much so, and so well, that anyone can make it and claim it. It is outside of me—by me but also by Toroni and anybody else.

It is a painting which must completely escape from its creator and, moreover, when I say that I have no illusions, I am transcribing a certain sensibility of my epoch of which I am the product and the actor like anyone else, but it is very difficult for me to affirm it.

AP: You refuse to be a person in this society?

DB: In the sense that artists play it, yes.

Sol LeWitt. *46 3-Part Variations on 3 Different Kinds of Cubes.* Dwan Gallery, New York, February, 1968; later published as a book, *49 3-part Variations Using 3 Different Kinds of Cubes/1967–68,* Zurich, Bruno Bischofberger, 1969. (Rep.)

Lippard, Lucy R., and Chandler, John. "The Dematerialization of Art," *Art International,* February, 1968:

During the 1960's the anti-intellectual, emotional intuitive processes of art-making characteristic of the last two decades have begun to give way to an ultra-conceptual art that emphasizes the thinking process almost exclusively. As more and more work is designed in the studio, but executed elsewhere by professional craftsmen, as the object becomes merely the end product, a number of artists are losing interest in the physical evolution of the work of art. The studio is again becoming a study. Such a trend appears to be provoking a profound dematerialization of art, especially of art as

Sol LeWitt. *46 3-Part Variations on 3 Different Kinds of Cubes.* Baked enamel/ aluminum, 45″ x 15″ x 15″ each. 1967. Courtesy Dwan Gallery.

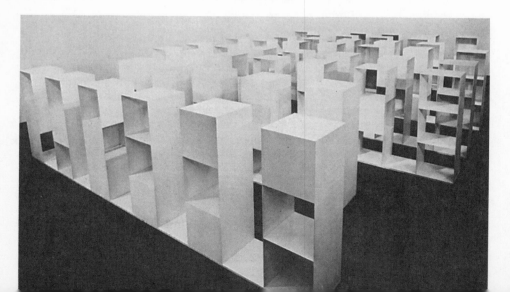

object, and if it continues to prevail, it may result in the object's becoming wholly obsolete.

The visual arts at the moment seem to hover at a crossroad that may well turn out to be two roads to one place, though they appear to have come from two sources: art as idea and art as action. In the first case, matter is denied, as sensation has been converted into concept; in the second case, matter has been transformed into energy and time-motion.

February–March, Rosario, Argentina: The Rosario group, hitherto concerned with a version of Minimal art, organizes the Ciclo de Arte Experimental to show works questioning permanence, commercialism, materialism, and chauvinism. For instance, Renzi sent cards to people all over the world saying "write me a card saying 'I am sending you water from New York' (or wherever)." The cards received were exhibited and the piece called *Water from All over the World* (though no water per se was involved). Graciela Carnevale accumulated each day all the daily Buenos Aires newspapers in separate piles, to remark upon the variations of information received by the public.

Minimal Art. **Gemeentemuseum, The Hague, March 23–May 26, 1968. Includes Andre, Smithson, Morris, and others; texts by Enno Develing and Lucy R. Lippard; slightly different catalogue published for showing January 17–February 23, 1969, at the Städtische Kunsthalle und Kunstverein, Düsseldorf.**

Air Art. **Organized and text by Willoughby Sharp. First shown at the Arts Council YM/YWHA, Philadelphia, March 13–31. Statements by the artists (among them, Haacke, Morris, van Saun, Medalla); brief biographies and bibliographies. Discussed by Sharp in "Air Art,"** *Studio International,* **May, 1968; by Jorge Glusberg in** *Art and Artists,* **January, 1969 (see also Eventstructure Research Group, "Air Art Two," same issue).**

Unpublished letter-essay from the Art-Language group, Coventry, to Lucy Lippard and John Chandler "Concerning the article 'The Dematerialization of Art,'" March 23, 1968. An excerpt:
All the examples of art-works (ideas) you refer to in your article are, with few exceptions, art-objects. They may not be an art-object as we know it in its traditional matter-state, but they are nevertheless matter in one of its forms, either solid-state, gas-state, liquid-state. And it is on this question of matter-state that my caution with regard to the metaphorical usage of dematerialization is centred upon. Whether for example, one calls Carl Andre's "substance of forms" empty space or not does not point to any evidence of dematerialization because the term "empty space" can never, in reference to terrestrial situations, be anything more than a convention describing how space is filled rather than offering a description of a portion of space which is, in physical terms, empty. Andre's empty space is in no sense a void. . . . Consequently, when you point, among many others, to an object made by Atkinson, "Map to not indicate etc.," that it has "almost entirely eliminated the visual-physical element," I am a little apprehensive of such a description. The map is just as much a solid-state object (i.e., paper with ink lines upon it) as is any Rubens (stretcher-canvas with paint upon it) and as such comes up for the count of being just as physically-visually perusable as the Rubens. . . .

Matter is a specialized form of energy; radiant energy is the only form in which energy can exist in the absence of matter. Thus when dematerialization takes place, it means, in terms of physical phenomena, the conversion (I use this word guardedly) of a state of matter into that of radiant energy; this follows that energy can never be

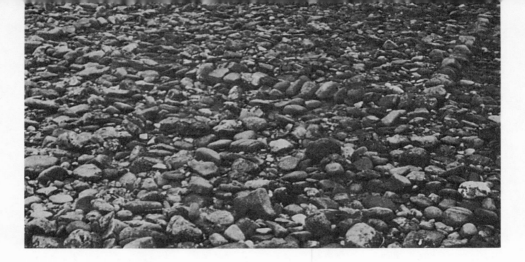

Richard Long. England. 1968.

created or destroyed. But further, if one were to speak of an art-form that used radiant energy, then one would be committed to the contradiction of speaking of a formless form, and one can imagine the verbal acrobatics that might take place when the romantic metaphor was put to work on questions concerning formless-forms (non-material) and material forms. The philosophy of what is called aesthetics relying finally, as it does, on what it has called the content of the art work is, at the most, only fitted with the philosophical tools to deal with problems of an art that absolutely counts upon the production of matter-state entities. The shortcomings of such philosophical tools are plain enough to see inside this limit of material objects; once this limit is broken these shortcomings hardly seem worth considering as the sophistry of the whole framework is dismissed as being not applicable to an art procedure that records its information in words, and the consequent material qualities of the entity produced (i.e., typewritten sheet, etc.) do not necessarily have anything to do with the idea. That is, the idea is "read about" rather than "looked at." That some art should be directly material and that other art should produce a material entity only as a necessary by-product of the need to record the idea is not at all to say that the latter is connected by any process of dematerialization to the former.

Beuys. Municipal van Abbe-Museum, Eindhoven, March 22–May 5, 1968. Text by Otto Mauer.

Boudaille, Georges. "Entretien avec Daniel Buren: L'Art n'est plus justifiable ou les points sur les 'i'" ("Art is no longer justifiable"). *Les Lettres Françaises,* March 13, 1968.

Smithson, Robert. "A Museum of Language in the Vicinity of Art." *Art International,* March, 1968:
   In the illusory babels of language, an artist might advance specifically to get lost, and to intoxicate himself in dizzying syntaxes, seeking odd intersections of meaning, strange corridors of history, unexpected echoes, unknown humors, or voids of knowledge . . . but this quest is risky, full of bottomless fictions and endless architectures and counter-architectures . . . at the end, if there is an end, are perhaps only meaningless reverberations. The following is a mirror structure built of macro

and micro orders, reflections, critical laputas, and dangerous stairways of words, a shaky edifice of fictions that hangs over inverse syntactical arrangements ... coherences that vanish into quasi-exactitudes and sublunary and translunary principles. Here language covers rather than "discovers" its sites and situations. Here language "closes" rather than "discloses" doors to utilitarian interpretations and explanations. The language of the artists and critics referred to in this article becomes paradigmatic reflections in a looking-glass babel that is fabricated according to Pascal's remark, "Nature is an infinite sphere whose center is everywhere and whose circumference is nowhere."

De France, James. "Some New Los Angeles Artists: Barry Le Va." *Artforum,* March, 1968.

Straight, no. 1. New York, School of Visual Arts, April, 1968. Edited by Joseph Kosuth ("Editorial in 27 Parts"), with text on rock music by Dan Graham.

Bochner, Mel. "A compilation for Robert Mangold." *Art International,* April, 1968. A series of quotations from other artists and writers that apply to Mangold's works.

April 27, Paris: Daniel Buren's "Proposition Didactique" presented inside the Salon de Mai (green and white striped floor to ceiling, two walls) and outside (two men with striped sandwich boards for one full day; striped billboards in over 200 locations around the city). See *Robho,* no. 4, 1968, for an account. (Rep.)

"Eye liners and some leaves from Barry Flanagan's Notebook." *Art and Artists,* April, 1968.

Hutchinson, Peter. "Perception of Illusion: Object and Environment." *Arts,* April, 1968.

Morris, Robert. "Anti-Form." *Artforum,* April, 1968:
  The process of "making itself" has hardly been examined. ... Of the Abstract

Left: Daniel Buren. Outside the Salon de Mai, Paris, 1967. *Right:* Barry Le Va. *Strips and Particles.* Gray felt, 35' x 45' (approx.). 1968.

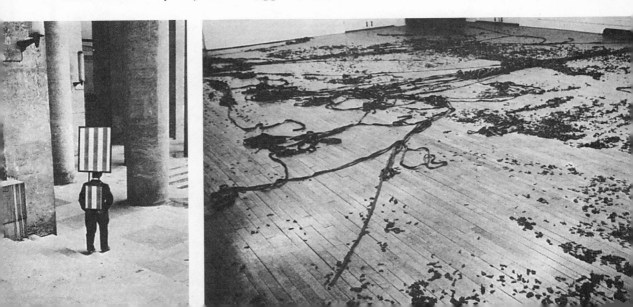

Expressionists only Pollock was able to recover process and hold on to it as part of the end form of the work. . . . In object-type art process is not visible. Materials often are. . . . Recently, materials other than rigid industrial ones have begun to show up. Oldenburg was one of the first to use such materials. A direct investigation of the properties of these materials is in progress. This involves a reconsideration of the use of tools in relation to material. In some cases these investigations move from the making of things to the making of the material itself. Sometimes a direct manipulation of a given material without the use of any tool is made. In these cases considerations of gravity become as important as those of space. The focus on matter and gravity as means results in forms which were not projected in advance. Considerations of ordering are necessarily casual and imprecise and unemphasized. Random piling, loose stacking, hanging, give passing form to the material. Chance is accepted and indeterminacy is implied since replacing will result in another configuration. Disengagement with preconceived enduring forms and orders for things is a positive assertion. It is part of the work's refusal to continue estheticizing form by dealing with it as a prescribed end. (Reproductions of work by Bollinger, Morris, Oldenburg, Paul, Pollock, Saret, Serra accompany this article.)

Junker, Howard. "Idea Art." Unpublished manuscript, spring, 1968; in part a commentary on Lippard and Chandler, "Dematerialization of Art."

Carl Andre, Robert Barry, Lawrence Weiner. **Windham College, Putney, Vt., April 30–May 31. Outdoor exhibition conceived by Chuck Ginnever as a follow-up to Bradford exhibition of same artists (see above); organized by Seth Siegelaub. Andre:** *Joint,* **183 units of uncovered common bailed hay end-to-end from woods into a field (Rep.); Barry: 1,206′ of half-inch woven nylon cord, 25′ off the ground stretched between two buildings; Weiner: a grid of "staples, stakes, twine, turf," 70′ × 100′ with a 10′ × 20′ notch removed, 6″ off the ground, topologically variable. "As far as I know, this was the first time artists were asked to build a show around**

Carl Andre. *Joint.* Uncovered common baled hay, 183 units, 14″ x 18″ x 36″ each. 1968. Courtesy Seth Siegelaub.

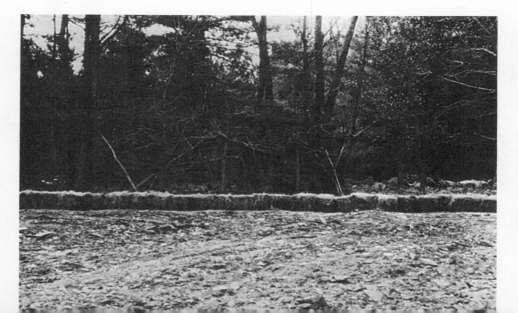

whatever situation they found operating at a preordained location and time, with the additional handicap of a nearly nonexistent budget." (Ginnever.)

April 30: Symposium at the college moderated by Dan Graham. Some excerpts:

DG: One of the concepts I want to introduce is the idea of place. Carl Andre?

CA: Yes, that's an idea I've had for quite a long time. Part of it came from working for four years for the Pennsylvania Railroad, as a freight brakeman and freight conductor in Northern New Jersey, to the New Jersey meadows, where all the highways from the West come into New York. It's an enormous plain, with long lines of freight cars lined up in the freight yards, and vast swampy meadows. It became a strong influence on my work. The kind of place I mean is not to be confused with an environment. It is futile for an artist to try to create an environment because you have an environment around you all the time. Any living organism has an environment. A place is an area within an environment which has been altered in such a way as to make the general environment more conspicuous. Everything is an environment, but a place is related particularly to both the general qualities of the environment and the particular qualities of the work that has been done.

LW: The idea of building a piece of sculpture outdoors has always intrigued me. . . . I'd liken it to walking in the woods, when you come upon a gravestone that is half buried. Now, if a piece of sculpture can exist within a landscape in that sense, whatever is around the landscape is heightened and brought out. It's a matter of what you can displace with what you are doing to the place.

RB: I guess for the last few years I've thought about a place when I make paintings where I would try to utilize the wall as part of the painting. When I made movies I tried to use the auditorium and the darkness and the sound of the projector in my movie. I am primarily an indoor person, having been born and raised in New York, so I use rooms, walls, floors in my sculpture. When I came up here a few months ago to look over the scene, I wanted to use the land, drive something into the land, circle it some way, emphasize it, create something in proportion to the buildings around it, to the piece of land itself. In the piece I did, I tried to use those same ideas, the fact that there were workmen working underneath this, it's all part of it, the sky above and the mud below and the buildings are all sort of tied together by the nylon cord.

CA: This chance to work here in Windham is a learning experience for me. I've learned a hell of a lot because heretofore I have worked only in inside spaces. I didn't know whether I could make a piece of sculpture outside, but when Chuck Ginnever and I talked about coming up here, I said I certainly wanted to do it because I did not have the chance to work outside in New York. I said I may get up there and find out I don't have any ideas for outdoor sculpture, but I'd be willing to explain to people why I couldn't do it at a symposium or something. . . . I selected hay because I had to work with materials that were available. It is rather materialistic in the Marxian sense that you can't do something that does not exist for you. If you don't have control of the means of production, you can't produce anything, so you have to find the means of production that you can control. Hay was this means at Windham College. I always use particles, so a bale of hay was a particle of sufficient size to remain in a coherent array. The hay, of course, is going to break down and gradually disappear. But since I'm not making a piece of sculpture for sale, neither the college nor anyone else is, it never enters the property state. . . . My particles are all more or less standards of the economy because I believe in using the materials or the society in the form the society does not use them; whereas works like Pop art use the forms of society but make them from different materials.

47

LW: One thing I would like to bring up about my piece was that it could have been placed anywhere; all it required was a reasonably flat area. The piece would have existed wherever it was put; it was in relationship to an outdoor space, as opposed to a *specific* outdoor space. The piece is low enough that it has to be walked over, or through; it can always be viewed by standing inside or sitting inside of it. . . . I was trying to figure out what material could be easily handled by more or less unskilled workers. I originally wanted to use barbed wire, because of the riots . . . a misplaced sense of humanity, so to speak, kept me from using barbed wire. The material was chosen about a half hour before we bought it; it was just available, and was within the price range, and it was attractive enough and not preordained at all. . . .

When we came up in the middle of the winter, and I had been speaking of using a grid, we were discussing the way you bought one square inch in the Yukon and they split it up with strings and you could own each of these squares by sending in a box top and a quarter, or whatever.

May, New York: The New York Graphic Workshop (founded in the winter of 1964–65 to make FANDSO—Free Assembleable Nonfunctional Disposable Serial Objects) sends out its *First-Class Mail Art Exhibition* # 1, in two parts:

(1) Luis Camnitzer's nine gummed labels each inscribed with one art work, such as: "A perfect circular horizon"; "A straight thick line that runs from here through you to the end of the room"; "This is a mirror. You are a written sentence." (2) Liliana Porter's wrinkle print to be crumpled and wrinkled again on receipt. Exhibition # 2 is José Castillo's sheet of paper marked with horizontal dotted lines and the directions "fold here."

May 25–June 22: Group show at Bykert Gallery, New York, includes Ian Wilson's *Chalk Circle*, drawn directly on the floor. (Rep.)

Language II. Dwan Gallery, New York, May 25–June 22. The use of language in and as art in regard to this show is discussed at length by John Chandler, "The Last Word in Graphic Art," _Art International,_ November, 1968: "Now it seems that art is once more accepted as a

Ian Wilson. *Chalk Circle.* 6′ in diameter (approx.). 1968.

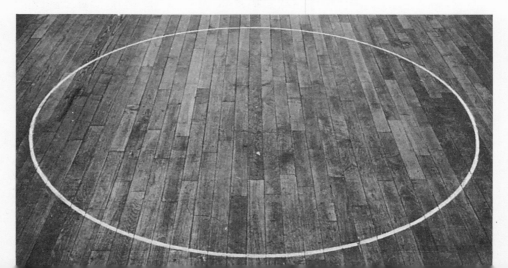

language and the questions now are whether this language is to be esoteric or exoteric, and whether this language is to be lingual or literal." (See also Robert White and Gary M. Dault, "Word Art & Art Word," *Artscanada,* June, 1968.)

"'Where Does the Collision Happen?' John Latham in Conversation with Charles Harrison." *Studio International,* May, 1968.

May 27–28, New York: *Relativity's Track* by Bernar Venet is performed at the Judson Memorial Church with the help of physicists Jack Ullman, Edward Macagno, and Martin Krieger, who lecture simultaneously on the subject of relativity; and of Stanley Taub, M.D., who lectures with a film on the larynx.

Harrison, Charles. "Barry Flanagan's Sculpture." *Studio International,* May, 1968.

June 16: The following item appears as an advertisement in the Sunday *New York Times* art section: IAN WILSON.

0 to 9, no. 4, June. Among contributors: Graham, LeWitt, Perreault, H. Weiner.

Metro, nos. 14 and 15, June, July, 1968: Alfieri, Bruno, "Come andare avanti," "La Cultura sconcertata"; and Lea Vergine, "Torino '68: Nevrosi e sublimazioni."

June–October, Rosario, Argentina: The Rosario group begins its "Experimental Art Cycle." Each artist has a period of time in which he or she works in- or out-doors. Among the pieces described in the catalogue are: Lia Maisonnave, June 17–29: an empty room with a square drawn on the floor; each spectator is given a page reproducing the square with detailed directions on the possibility of constructing a similar work indoors or outdoors at their own homes. "The work is not the square that has been executed nor the ones that could be executed by the spectators according to the directions I give them. What is important in this action, this plan, is all that which it provokes in the spectator."
Noemi Escandell, July 15–27: a speech given on the 20th of June.
Eduardo Favario, September 9–21: the exhibition space is closed and the visitor finds a sign that tells him how he can follow the development of the work in another part of the city.
Graciela Carnevale, October 7–19: a totally empty room, the window wall covered to provide a neutral ambiance, in which are gathered the people who came to the opening; the door is hermetically sealed without the visitors' being aware of it. The piece involved closing access and exits, and the unknown reactions of the visitors. After more than an hour, the "prisoners" broke the glass window and "escaped."
Other participants: Boglione, Bortolotti, Elizade, Gatti, Ghilioni, Greiner, Navanjo, Puzzolo, Renzi and Rippa.

July: On Kawara, in Brazil, begins the "I met" and "I went" notebook pieces (July 1, 1968–June 30, 1969)—typed lists of every person encountered each day and a mapped record of his movements. During this period he lived in South America, Europe, Japan, and New York.
Kawara is one of the most important, and one of the most elusive and isolated, artists working in this general direction. In 1966, he began an immense and continuing series of "date paintings," small canvases with the stenciled date, executed almost daily and accompanied by a clipping from the day's newspaper, kept in notebooks. He also made a series of paintings marking location by longitude and latitude, a continuing series of "I got up" postcards (see p. 125) and of telegrams (see p. 180), a numerical cipher piece, and the One Million Years *book (see p. 211). The fascination exerted by Kawara's obsessive and precise notations of his place in the world (time and location)*

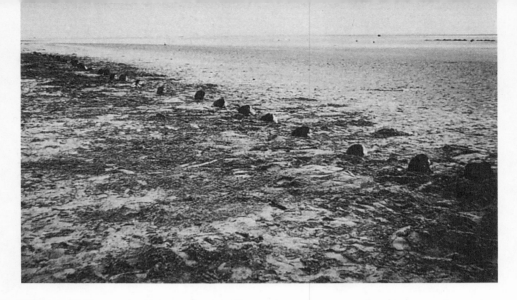

Keith Arnatt. *Liverpool Beach-Burial.* 1968.

imply a kind of self-reassurance that the artist does, in fact, exist. At the same time, they are totally without pathos, their objectivity establishing the self-imposed isolation which marks his way of life as well as his art.

Junker, Howard. "The New Art: It's Way, Way Out." *Newsweek,* July 29, 1968.

Kaprow, Allan. "The Shape of the Art Environment." *Artforum,* summer, 1968. (Concerning Morris's Anti-Form article.)

Prospekt 68. Kunsthalle, Düsseldorf, September 20–29. Organized by Konrad Fischer and Hans Strelow. Catalogue published after the exhibition consists primarily of articles and reviews of the exhibition, which included Anselmo, Beuys, Buren, Merz, Morris, Nauman, Panamarenko, Ruthenbeck, Serra, Zorio.

August 26, 1968: Founding of Art and Project, Amsterdam, by Adriaan van Ravesteijn and Geert van Beijeren. First bulletin-exhibition mailed September 16 (Charlotte Posenenske).

September, 1968, Keith Arnatt, *Liverpool Beach-Burial* (Rep.):
    In 1967 I was teaching a sculpture course at Manchester College of Art and I discussed with my students the possibility of sculpture's being what I called "situational." By this I meant that the focus of attention could be upon what one did with an "object" rather than the object *itself.* Context itself became the determining factor in what we did. In other words, revealing an aspect of a particular (physical) context became the point of our activity. . . . The focus of attention was on behavior patterns themselves. Both the beach-burial and my "self-burial" piece were the outcome of these kinds of considerations—they were both essentially "behavioristic."
    The burial involved the following pattern of behavior: (1) Choosing a site and marking out a *straight* line. (2) Marking off four-foot intervals. Each mark representing a digging position for each of the hundred plus participants. (3) Each participant

chose a site on the line and dug his/her own hole. (4) When the holes were deep enough the participants were "buried" by nonparticipants.

September 26, Amsterdam: Boezem sends out map and documentation of the day's weather report and meteorological analysis entitled "Medium for the Furtherance of Renewed Experiences."

September 4, 1968, Bradford, Mass., Donald Burgy, *Rock # 5 (Rep.):*
   "Documentation of selected physical aspects of a rock; its location in, and its conditions of, time and space," including, among others: daily weather map and charts (on several resolution levels, continental, U.S.A., local surface observations); electron beam x-ray photographs; electron microscopy; location photographs and maps (on several resolution levels—satellites, airplanes, walking); mass spectographic analysis; petrographic analysis and photographs; weight and density data, etc.
   "The scale of this information extends, in time, from the geologic to the present moment; and, in size of matter, from the continental to the atomic." In later works, Burgy documented: himself—all physical data collected through a variety of tests undergone during a voluntary stay in the hospital (January, 1969); a pregnancy and birth (March, 1969); and executed a lie-detector test with another artist (Douglas Huebler) in which the information was partly relevant to "life," partly to "art" (March, 1969).

Buren, Daniel. "Is Teaching Art Necessary?" (June, 1968). *Galerie des Arts,* September, 1968. Partial text follows:
   The dispute with tradition, etc., is already found in the 19th century (so as not to go back too far). However, since then, so many traditions, so many academisms, so many new tabus and new schools have been created and replaced!
   Why? Because these phenomena against which the artist struggles are only epiphenomena or, more precisely, these are only the superstructures compared to the foundation which conditions art and is art. And art has changed 100 times, if not more, its tradition, academism, tabus, school, etc., because anything superficial has by nature to be changed constantly; and since the foundation remains untouched, obviously nothing is fundamentally changed.

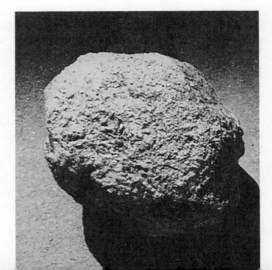

Donald Burgy. From *Rock Series #1.* 1968.

And thus art evolves and thus there is a history of art. The artist disputes the easel by painting surfaces too large to be supported by an easel; then he dispenses with the easel and the overlarge surface by making a canvas more of an object, then an object, then the object to make for the object made, then a mobile or untransportable object, etc. This is only an example, but one which demonstrates that if a dispute is possible, it cannot be formal, it can only be fundamental, on the level of art, and not on the level of the forms given to art.

The artist, in regard to the art, wants it to evolve. *In regard to the art, the artist is reformist, he is not revolutionary.*

The difference between art and the world, between art and being, is that the world and being are perceived by real facts (physical, emotional, intellectual) and art visualizes this reality.

If the artist's vision of the world were concerned this could be a veritable consciousness of reality. But it concerns a product, art—that is, the thing seen by the consumer; thus a fixed and arbitrary reality is proposed, a reality deformed by the individual who, wanting to express his own vision of the world, no longer expresses the real but makes an illusion of reality.

Then the artist undertakes his dictatorial task. He imposes purely and simply on the consumer his vision of the world (which is, in the consumer's product, the illusion of the world and of being). And still he finds that he alone knows how to express it, he is accepted as the guide; it is thus that one chooses one's master. What is more, by acknowledging that art is enlightened—as one would say of a despot—what dialogue can be established, since the basis of discussion is false. This is a dialogue of illusionists. And thus what reality can be discovered through art, inasmuch as the art is false, and from the outset fixes the viewer's thought in a false direction—one prehension of the world by art. It will always be the same as long as art merely approaches the real and not reality proper.

Concretely, the way things are today, the role of the artist is not of great consequence. He produces for a culturally formed bourgeois minority. Consciously or not, he plays the game of the bourgeoisie which is his public, and, reciprocally, the bourgeoisie accepts at first glance the product proposed by his artist-producer. It is even especially partial to any art called subversive (mental or political), not only to save its conscience, but because it relishes the "revolution" when it is hung "on the line" in galleries or nicely disposed of in its apartments.

Let us take, then, as a working hypothesis, that it is necessary to change radically the circuit "imposed" up until now on the artistic product, in order to find a new public, other consumers, even those who haven't the right to "culture." For example, show art in the factories.

At this point, the truly evil role of the artist will be sharply revealed. The system is not afraid of seeing art in the factories. On the contrary. The enterprise of alienation will be completed when "anyone" can participate in culture. For culture, and art, such as they are currently conceived, are most certainly the alienating element among others. Because here we discuss the political and even intellectual virtue of art: *distraction.* Some art is only illusion, illusion of the real; it is necessarily distraction from the real, a false world, a false semblance of itself. "Art is the blindfold over the spectator's eyes which allows him not to return to his reality or the world's reality" (Michel Claura).

Under these conditions, art in the factory will have as a positive result improvement of the working environment, no more, no less. Pushed to extremes, this will create esthetic quarrels where otherwise the urge to revolution might have been born.

Art is the safety valve of our repressive system. As long as it exists, and, better yet, the more prevalent it becomes, art will be the system's distracting mask. And a system has nothing to fear as long as its reality is masked, as long as its contradictions are hidden.

Art is inevitably allied to power. This was not yet known at the beginning of the century, when Impressionist or Fauve exhibitions were closed down. But today it is so obvious that 5,000 policemen are sent to defend an avant-garde biennale.

The artist, if he wants to work for another society, must begin by fundamentally contesting art and assuming his total rupture with it. If not, the next revolution will take over his responsibility.

Daniel Buren. Photo-souvenir of the work made in Milan, Galerie Apollinaire, October, 1968. Vertical stripes, white and green, glued over and thereby sealing the door of the gallery and "closing" the "show."

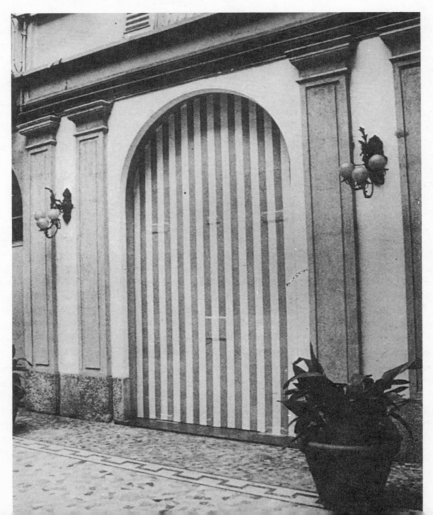

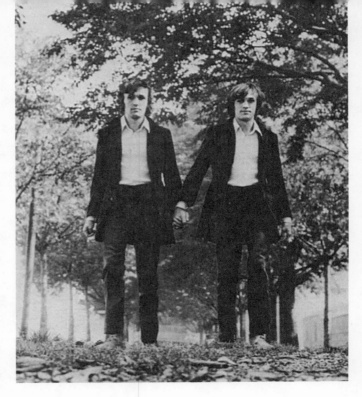

Alighiero Boetti. *Twins.* 1968.

Art is the most beautiful ornament of society as it is now, and not the warning signal for society as it should be—never that.

How can the artist contest society when his art, all art, "belongs" objectively to that society?

He believes, alas, in the myth of revolutionary art.

But art is objectively reactionary.

Walter de Maria: *50 M³ (1,600 Cubic Feet) Level Dirt/ The Land Show: Pure Dirt/ Pure Earth/ Pure Land.* **Galerie Heiner Friedrich, Munich, September 28–October 12, 1968. In May, 1960, de Maria wrote "Art Yard" (published in the Young-MacLow** *Anthology,* **1963). Excerpts follow:**

I have been thinking about an art yard I would like to build. It would be sort of a big hole in the ground. Actually it wouldn't be a hole to begin with. That would have to be dug. The digging of the hole would be part of the art. Luxurious stands would be made for the art lovers and spectators to sit in.

They would come to the making of the yard dressed in tuxedoes and clothes which would make them aware of the significance of the event they would see. Then in front of the stand of people a wonderful parade of steamshovels and bulldozers will pass. Pretty soon the steamshovels would start to dig. And small explosions would go off. What wonderful art will be produced. Inexperienced people like La Monte Young will run the steamshovels. From here on out what goes on can't easily be said. (It is hard to explain art.) As the yard gets deeper and its significance grows, people will run into the yard, grab shovels, do their part, dodge explosions. This might be considered the first meaningful dance. People will yell "Get that bulldozer away from my child."

Bulldozers will be making wonderful pushes of dirt all around the yard. Sounds, words, music, poetry. (Am I too specific? optimistic?) . . .

I have just been thinking about this wonderful art, already it is being killed in my mind. Is nothing safe? Perhaps you haven't thought me serious? Actually I am. And if this paper should fall into the hands of someone who owns a construction company and who is interested in promoting art and my ideas, please get in touch with me immediately. Also if someone owns an acre or so of land (preferably in some large city . . . for art . . . thrives there) do not hesitate.

In 1962, de Maria projected a series of "works in the desert," some of which were executed in 1968: (1) Nevada, U.S.A.: Two Parallel Lines—*12' apart—in chalk, running for a full mile across the desert (Rep.); (2) Three-Continent Project: Square in U.S. desert, Horizontal Line in the Sahara, Vertical Line in India. "When all of the lines are photographed from the air, the photos are placed one on top of the other, the image will reveal a cross in a square. Three continents are needed for this image, which can be photographed in one day by a satellite." A related project was executed for* Landart *(April, 1969, see below): a film entitled* Two Lines Three Circles on the Desert, *executed in the Mojave Desert, March, 1969. The lines were drawn on the desert and the circles were provided by the movement of the camera.*

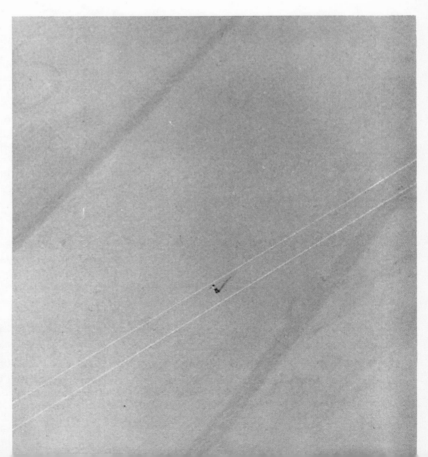

Walter de Maria. *Mile-Long Drawing.* 2 parallel chalk lines, 12' apart. Mohave Desert, California. 1968. Courtesy Dwan Gallery, New York.

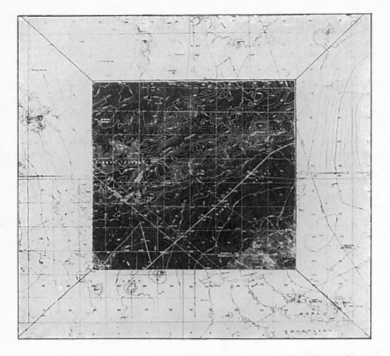

Robert Smithson. *Map for a Double Nonsite.* 1968.

Smithson, Robert. "A Sedimentation of the Mind: Earth Projects." *Artforum,* **September, 1968:**
The earth's surface and the figments of the mind have a way of disintegrating into discrete regions of art. . . . One's mind and the earth are in a constant state of erosion: mental rivers wear away abstract banks, brain waves undermine cliffs of thought, ideas decompose into stones of unknowing, and conceptual crystallizations break apart into deposits of gritty reason. Vast moving faculties occur in this geological miasma, and they move in the most physical way. This movement seems motionless, yet it crushes the landscape of logic under glacial reveries. This slow flowage makes one conscious of the turbidity of thinking. Slump, debris slides, avalanches all take place within the cracking limits of the brain. The entire body is pulled into the cerebral sediment, where particles and fragments make themselves known as solid consciousness. A bleached and fractured world surrounds the artist. To organize this mess of corrosion into patterns, grids, and subdivisions is an esthetic process that has scarcely been touched. . . .

Look at any *word* long enough and you will see it open up into a series of faults, into a terrain of particles each containing its own void. This discomforting language of fragmentation offers no easy gestalt solution; the certainties of didactic discourse are hurled into the erosion of the poetic principle.

Alloway, Lawrence. "Christo and the New Scale." *Art International,* **September, 1968.**

Burnham, Jack. "Systems Aesthetics." *Artforum,* **September, 1968.**

September 22, Frankfurt: Total eclipse of the sun claimed as an art work by Timm Ulrichs, who also removes a section of the exterior layer of a stucco house as a wall removal to the bricks.

Brown, Gordon. "The De-materialization of the Object." *Arts,* September–October, 1968.

Calvesi, Maurizio. "Lo Spazio, La Vita e L'Azione." *L'Espresso,* Rome, September 15, 1968.

Earthworks. Dwan Gallery, New York, October 5–30. Includes Andre, de Maria, Heizer, Morris, Oldenburg, Oppenheim, LeWitt, Smithson, Kaltenbach, and Herbert Bayer's 1955 *Earth Mound,* "a sculptured garden project." Reviewed by John Perreault, *Village Voice,* October 17.

Anti-form. John Gibson Gallery, New York, October–November 7, 1968. Hesse (Rep.) Panamarenko, Ryman, Serra, Saret, Sonnier, Tuttle.

October 4–6, Amalfi: *Arte Povera piu azione povere.* Organized by Germano Celant on the occasion of the "RA3" of the Centro Studi Colautti di Salerno. Three days of events and collective works by artists and writers including, among others, Boetti, Dibbets, Gilardi, Long, Mario and Marisa Merz, Prini, Trini, Celant, van Elk, Zorio. Published as *Rassegna di Amalfi #3,* Salerno, Rumma editore, 1969. See also Tommaso Trini, "Rapporto da Amalfi," *Domus,* no. 468, November, 1968.

Andre. Städtisches Museum, Mönchengladbach, October 18–December 15, 1968. Boxed catalogue contains self-interview and elongated "tablecloth" multiple.

October, New York: Sol LeWitt does his first serial drawing in pencil directly on the wall (temporary) at the Paula Cooper Gallery for the *Art for Peace* exhibition.

Douglas Huebler, *The Windham Piece.* A one-day, one-piece show at Windham College, Putney, Vt., October 23, 1968, a "site sculpture project" in which a hexagon was drawn on a map of the area and the five points were photographed. The "exhibition" at the college consisted of the photographs and samples of the dirt from each of the points.

Hutchinson, Peter. "Science-Fiction: An Aesthetic for Science." *Art International,* October, 1968.

Eva Hesse. *Sequel.* Latex, sheet: 30″ x 32″; balls: 2 1/2″ in diameter. 1967–68. Courtesy Fourcade-Droll, Inc., New York.

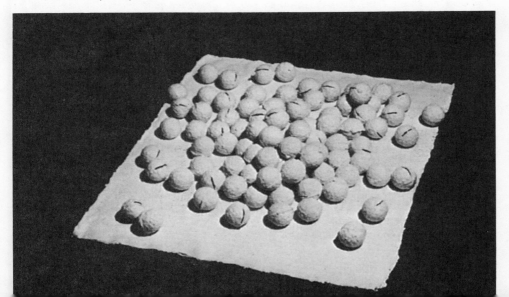

John Baldessari. *Everything Is Purged . . . 60″x45″.* 1966–67.

EVERYTHING IS PURGED FROM THIS PAINTING
BUT ART, NO IDEAS HAVE ENTERED THIS WORK.

John Baldessari. Molly Barnes Gallery, Los Angeles, October, 1968. Paintings executed by a sign painter containing words alone (Rep.), such as: *A painting that is its own documentation;* and *Painting for Kubler: This painting owes its existence to prior paintings. By liking this solution you should not be blocked in your continued acceptance of prior inventions. To attain this position, ideas of former painting had to be rethought in order to transcend former work. To like this painting, you will have to understand prior work. Ultimately this work will amalgamate with the existing body of knowledge.*

Also included in the show are paintings that are photographs of National City locations with address as text, texts quoted from art books with matched photos, and "narrative paintings" with text only, such as: *Semi-close-up of girl by geranium (soft view) finishes watering it—examines plant to see if it has any signs of growth—finds slight evidence—smiles—one part is sagging—she runs fingers along it—raises hand over plant to encourage it to grow.*

Museumjournaal (Amsterdam), ser. 13, no. 4, 1968. Includes Piero Gilardi's "Microemotive Art" and Robert H. F. Hartzema on Dibbets. Gilardi text translated as "Primary Energy and the Microemotive Artists," in *Arts,* September–October, 1968.

Bonfiglio, Pietro, ed. *La Povertà dell'arte.* Bologna, Edizione Galleria de Foscherari, October, 1968. A collection of writings in reaction to Germano Celant's original texts on Arte Povera, most of which were published in catalogues and magazines elsewhere first. Contributions by Apollonio, Arcangeli, Barilli, Bonfiglio, Bonito Oliva, Calvesi, Celant, Del Guercio, de Marchis, Fagiolo, Gottuso, Pignotti. For additional writings on the subject, see the bibliography of Celant's book and catalogue (1969, 1970).

Burgin, Victor. "Art-Society System." *Control,* no. 4, 1968.

Robho, no. 4, fall, 1968. Jean Clay, "Art Sauvage: La fin de galeries"; "Lygia Clark: Fusion Généralisée." Statement by Jan Dibbets (in toto):

I stopped painting in 1967. Before that I made assemblages of monochrome canvases. In April 1967 I realized my last assemblage, a superimposition of blank canvases entitled "My Last Painting." In September, in Frankfurt, I presented in a gallery a show of water. The floor of the gallery was regularly furrowed a meter in length. Simultaneously I began my "corrected perspective"; an ellipse, which, seen from the entrance to a garden, looked like a circle out of balance in relation to the ground. I worked with all sorts of perspectives. They must be seen from a precise point. Some were made along a railroad track. The spectator would see them from his seat in passing.

I make most of these works with ephemeral materials: sand, growing grass, etc. These are demonstrations. I do not make them to keep, but to photograph. The work of art is the photo. Anyone ought to be able to reproduce my work.

At the recent congress of Amalfi (October, 1968), I placed eight sticks in the water twenty centimeters below the surface of the sea. From where we were—fifty meters above—one saw the sticks oscillate in the water; that was the work.

Right now I am preparing a transmission for television to Berlin. People will have a Dibbets in their house for five minutes. The work: a tractor furrowing in the ground a trapezoid which, with perspective correction, will exactly match the rectangular frame of the TV screen.

My works are not exactly made to be seen. They are more there so that you are given the fleeting feeling that something isn't right in the landscape.

Sell my work? To sell isn't part of the art. Maybe there will be people idiotic enough to buy what they could make themselves. So much the worse for them.

November. Tucuman, Argentina: The Rosario group of artists undertakes a political "exhibition" in conjunction with the labor unions (CGT) to protest workers' conditions in Tucuman, in northwest Argentina. (Rep.)

November 17, New York: Tiny Events, organized by Hannah Weiner at the Longview Country Club (annex to Max's Kansas City). Artists and poets performed short events or actions. Among them, Acconci, Costa, Giorno, Perreault, Schjeldahl, Weiner.

Rosario group, Argentina. *Tucuman.* First stage of the publicity campaign. 1968.

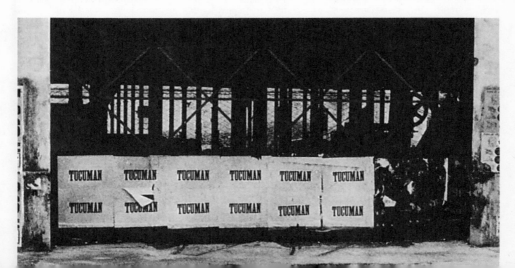

Barthelme, Frederick. *The Complex Figure-Ground Issue as Dealt with by the Young Artist David Frame.* Signed and dated on rear. November, 1958 (35-page booklet of the same photo and title).

November, New York: L.R.L. receives a group of temporary photographic works from "James Robert Steelrails" dated November, 1958, and November, 1968; after more texts and art and mysterious phone calls, the artist is identified as Frederick Barthelme. Some excerpts:

I do not agree that by putting something into an   context one admits to making   . It is natural to invite to view the work those persons who are most likely to find interest in it.

The   that I have made recently has as its base the desire to literally *carry* (and in that sense potentially transmit or communicate) certain information. The   and the information are mutually interdependent.

The information is by choice not very important, both in the formal   sense as is pointed out on another page, and in fact. At the same time the information is not trivia. It has about it a quality of *regularity* which is, it seems to me, appropriate. The work as a whole cannot be called   because of the failure of the information to "stamp itself out" and it cannot be called bad   because the formal stance is so strong.

I do not like the word   . I do not like the body of work defined by the word   . What I do like is the notion *production.* I produce in order to pass the time.

Whenever I develop a system such as this one (in which I say that *all* future work, and present work for that matter, will be issued in such and such a format), I feel it important to destroy the system almost at once. The destruction does not render the system useless, it only changes its aspect. It makes plain the fact that in the bottom half of the twentieth century it is only possible to be half-serious. Accordingly I have signed and redated one of the works included here.

*   *   *

Insofar as the visual and literary information on each sheet can be removed from the sheet presentation proper, that information could be called "subject matter."

There is the danger of viewing the information in such terms with the resultant criticism that "the presentation is ahead of the   ." Since the information is not intended to function as   but as a *unit distinguishing figure,* equivalent say of any mark, I suggest that such conventional   historical terms are not relevant. At the same time, the presentation itself, inclusive of whatever mark and format, is, in conception, the substance of the   in those same conventional terms. Simply, the conception and presentation of the work in the form that it is presented comprises the   .

Douglas Huebler: November, 1968. Seth Siegelaub, New York. Catalogue of first exhibition to exist solely as a catalogue in which the work and its documentation appear. (Rep.)

I was still trying to define my own reasons for doing some of the early things, the site sculptures, the hexagons or circles imposed on a map. Bob Barry said, why don't you just put a dot on the map; why do you join them together for lines? I said, so that you can read it as different from everything else on a map. It's only a convention. It could have been a circle or a number of things. All it was doing was creating a similar relationship to a conceptually transferred location. There's no inside, no outside. These are little points described on a map, described by language as to what they stand for, but in actual physical fact of course there was nothing there. There's nothing to be perceived through normal experience. And for me, this was an irony,

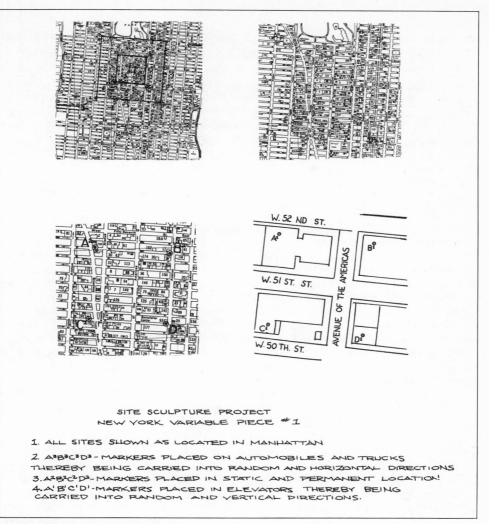

SITE SCULPTURE PROJECT
NEW YORK VARIABLE PIECE #1

1. ALL SITES SHOWN AS LOCATED IN MANHATTAN

2. A³B³C³D³ - MARKERS PLACED ON AUTOMOBILES AND TRUCKS THEREBY BEING CARRIED INTO RANDOM AND HORIZONTAL DIRECTIONS
3. A²B²C²D² - MARKERS PLACED IN STATIC AND PERMANENT LOCATION!
4. A'B'C'D' - MARKERS PLACED IN ELEVATORS THEREBY BEING CARRIED INTO RANDOM AND VERTICAL DIRECTIONS.

Douglas Huebler. New York. 1968.

that the experience of nature is bound by conventions. We take a chunk of it and put a frame around it and the frame can be like the frame on these paintings or the frame can be language, the frame can be documents. (Huebler, March 31, 1970, NSCAD lecture, Halifax.)

* * *

42nd Parallel. 11 certified postal receipts (sender); 10 certified postal receipts (receiver); 3,040 miles (approximate). 14 locations, A'–N', are towns existing either exactly or approximately on the 42° parallel in the United States. Locations have been marked by the exchange of certified postal receipts sent from and returned to "A"—Truro, Massachusetts. Documentation: ink on map; receipts.

* * *

61

A system existing in the world disinterested in the purpose of art may by "plugged into" in such a way as to produce a work that possesses a separate existence and that neither changes nor comments on the system to be used. *42nd Parallel* used an aspect of the United States Postal Service for a period of time to describe 3,000 miles of space and was brought into its completed existence through forms of documentation that in fact "contain" sequential time and linear space in present time and place.

An inevitable destiny is set in motion by the specific process selected to form such a work, freeing it from further decisions on my part.

I like the idea that even as I eat, sleep or play, the work is moving towards its completion. (D.H., 1969 statement, slightly revised.)

November 30, Coney Island: Hans Haacke executes *Live Random Airborne Systems*, sea gulls retrieving bread thrown on the water.

Hutchinson, Peter. "Earth in Upheaval." *Arts*, November, 1968.
Adrian Piper. Untitled, fall, 1968:
This square should be read as a whole; or, these two vertical rectangles should be read from left to right or right to left; or, these two horizontal rectangles should be read from top to bottom or bottom to top; or, these four squares should be read from upper left to upper right to lower right to lower left or upper left to upper right to lower left to lower right or upper left to lower left to lower right to upper right or upper left to lower left to lower right to upper right or upper left to lower right to lower left to upper right or upper left to lower right to upper right to lower left or upper right to lower right to lower left to upper left or upper right to lower right to upper left to lower left or upper right to upper left to lower left to lower right or upper right to upper left to lower right to lower left or upper right to lower left to upper left to lower right or upper right to lower left to lower right to upper left or lower right to lower left to upper left to upper right or lower right to lower left to upper right to upper left or lower right to upper right to upper left to lower left or lower right to upper right to lower left to upper left or lower right to upper left to upper right to lower left or lower right to upper left to lower left to upper right or lower left to upper right or lower left to upper left to upper right to lower right or lower left to upper left to lower right to upper right or lower left to lower right to upper left to upper right or lower left to lower right to upper left or lower left to lower right to upper left to upper right or lower left to upper right to upper left to lower right or lower left to upper right to lower left to upper right or lower left to upper right to lower right to upper left or lower left to upper right to upper left to lower right; or, these eight horizontal rectangles should be read from top left to top right to upper middle right to lower middle right to bottom right to bottom left to lower middle left to upper middle left or top left to top right to upper middle left to upper middle right to lower middle left to lower middle right to bottom left to bottom right or top left to upper middle left to lower middle left to bottom left to bottom right to lower middle

Strelow, Hans. "Zahlen blätter als Bilder für das geistige Auge." *Rheinische Post*, November 15, 1968 (on Hanne Darboven).

Livingston, Jan. "Barry Le Va: Distribution Sculpture." *Artforum*, November, 1968.

Junker, Howard. "The New Sculpture: Getting Down to the Nitty Gritty." *Saturday Evening Post*, November 2, 1968.

***Nine at Leo Castelli*. Organized by Robert Morris at Leo Castelli's warehouse, December, 1968. Anselmo, Bollinger, Hesse, Kaltenbach, Nauman, Saret, Serra (Rep.), Sonnier, (Rep.) Zorio.**

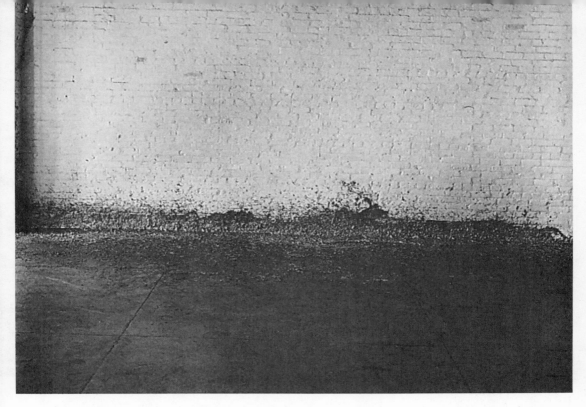

Above: Richard Serra. *Splashing.* Molten lead. New York. 1968. Courtesy Leo Castelli Gallery, New York. *Below:* Keith Sonnier. *Mustee.* Latex, flock, and string, 12′ long. 1969. Courtesy Leo Castelli Gallery, New York.

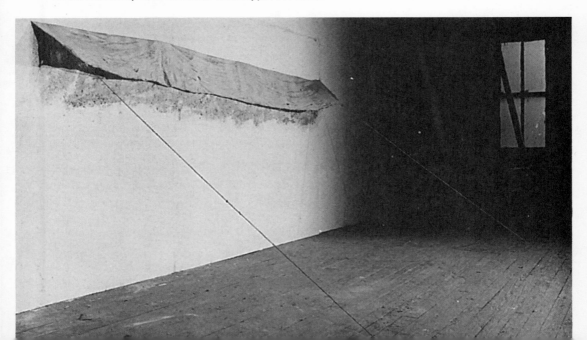

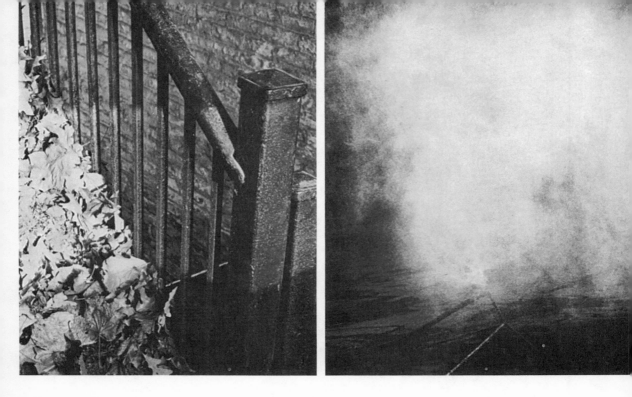

Left: Rafael Ferrer. *Staircase—3 Landings—Leaves.* In the Stairwell of Leo Castelli's warehouse, Dec. 4, 1968. *Right:* Hans Haacke. *Wind in Water (Mist).* New York. 1968.

Reviewed by Max Kozloff, "9 in a Warehouse: An Attack on the Status of the Object," *Artforum,* **February, 1969; Grégoire Müller, "Robert Morris Presents Anti-Form,"** *Arts,* **February, 1969; Philip Leider, "The Properties of Materials: In the Shadow of Robert Morris,"** *New York Times,* **December 22, 1968.**

December 4, New York: Rafael Ferrer's *Three Leaf Pieces* **appear unexpectedly on the staircase at the opening of the Castelli warehouse show (Rep.), in the elevator of 29 West 57th St., where the Dwan Gallery is located, and in the Leo Castelli Gallery proper, on East 77th St.**
　　In my work, starting with the *Three Leaf Pieces* of '68 and the ice and grease pieces at the Whitney [Anti-Illusion show], I find that time restrictions became an energizing factor in the decision making. . . . I would rather eliminate my performing as much as I can. In that sense, the grease and the ice and the leaves and most of these materials that tend to have a life of their own, continue to react after you have done something to them. This takes away the interest in performance. (Ferrer catalogue, Institute of Contemporary Art, Philadelphia, 1971.)

Carl Andre, Robert Barry, Douglas Huebler, Joseph Kosuth, Sol LeWitt, Robert Morris, Lawrence Weiner **(The Xerox Book). Seth Siegelaub, John Wendler, New York, December, 1968. Each artist was given twenty-five pages with which he made a piece more or less utilizing the xerox medium.**

Series Photographs. School of Visual Arts Gallery, New York, December 3–January, 1969. Graham, LeWitt, Muybridge, Nauman, Ruscha, Smithson, et al.

December, Palermo: Buren and Toroni participate in the Palermo Festival, show their work indoors and outdoors, on the floor or ground, and on the walls. Afterward they distribute a tract saying all the art in the world is "reactionary" and their room is closed by the authorities.

December 14–15: Hans Haacke, *Wind in Water* show on his studio roof. One day it consists simply of untouched snow; another, of artificial mist. (Rep.)

Bourdon, David. "Walter de Maria: The Singular Experience." *Art International,* December, 1968.

N. E. Thing Co. Project Dept., Ecological Projects. *Right 90° Parallel Turn.* 100′ turn in 6″ powdered snow. Mt. Seymour, B.C., Canada. 1968.

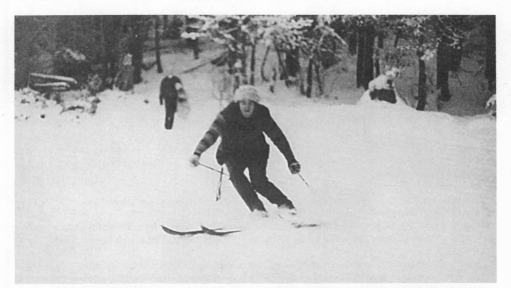

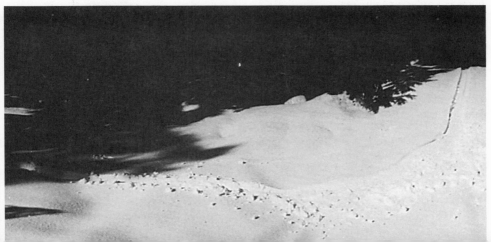

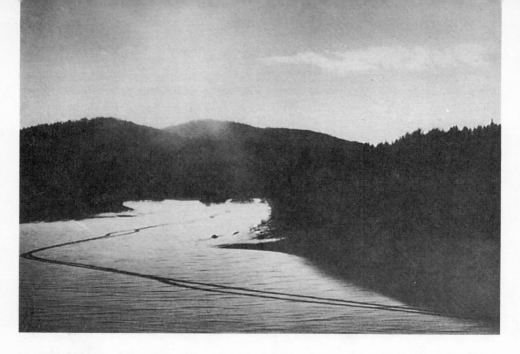

Dennis Oppenheim. *Time Line* (detail). 3 miles long. U.S.A./Canadian boundary, along frozen St. John River near Fort Kent, Maine. 1968.

Alloway, Lawrence. "The Expanding and Disappearing Work of Art." Lecture given December 7, 1968, at Parke-Bernet Galleries, New York, and repeated on Channel 13 TV; published in *Auction,* October, 1969.

Tillim, Sidney. "Earthworks and the New Picturesque." *Artforum,* December, 1968.

During 1968, Stephen Kaltenbach makes three Time Capsules (see pp. 84–85) and four bronze sidewalk plaques (Bone, Blood, Flesh, Skin).

During 1968, Dennis Oppenheim makes numerous outdoor pieces, including several snow projects in northern Maine (Rep. and see p. 184), and Iain Baxter (the N.E. Thing Company) makes snow pieces on the west coast of Canada (side steps, skiing, snow over frame) (Rep.).

November, 1968, Vancouver: N. E. Thing Co., ACT and ART. Photographs accompanied by stamped certificates of approval (claim) or rejection assert:
All men are to recognize and note for posterity that: ACT #000 (example: a great thing, the Acme Glacier, Coldtown, N.W.T. Canada) on the ——day of ——, 19——, has met the stringent requirements of sensitivity information as set forth by the N. E. Thing Co. It is hereby and henceforth elevated for eternity to the realm of Aesthetically Claimed Things. It is to be known from this day on by all men as an ACT. The N. E. Thing Co. reserves the right to redo or duplicate any ACT as a future project.

*   *   *

All men are to recognize and note for posterity that: ART #0000 (example: An Inferior Thing, John Doe's painting, "Summertime," 1955) on this ——day of ——, 19——, has not met the stringent requirements of sensitivity information as set forth

66

by the N. E. Thing Co. It is hereby and henceforth banished for eternity to the rank and file of Aesthetically Rejected Things. It is to be known from this day on by all men as ART.

It has occurred to us that Duchamp all his life tried to find an unaesthetic object but really could not do this because any object becomes good with time, social and cultural conditions, etc. Thus all his readymades are N. E. Thing Co. ACTS. . . . While on the other hand our Research Department in cooperation with the Art Department has come up with the following important discovery—that an aesthetic object, one which does not meet the stringent visual sensitivity information requirements of the N. E. Thing Co., is called ART because it is within what gets called ART that the 5th rate unaesthetic object fails. (NETCo. letter to L.R.L., November, 1968.)

When I visited Vancouver in February, 1968, and met Iain and Elaine Baxter (now Ingrid) for the first time, I was struck again by the phenomenon of "ideas in the air." NETCo's ideas for nonart object exhibitions, nonobject art exhibitions, imaginary visual experiences, and photographic projects (capitalizing upon the artist's isolation from New York and "provincial" dependence on reproduction rather than on first-hand experience) often coincided point by point with those unpublished projects in the planning stages in New York and Europe at the time, with which the Baxters could not have been familiar. The points of departure were, of course, the same (Morris, Nauman, Ruscha, etc.) but the spontaneous appearance of similar work totally unknown to the artists can be explained only as energy generated by these sources and by the wholly unrelated art against which all the potentially "conceptual artists" were commonly reacting. (Adapted from Lucy R. Lippard, "Letter from Vancouver," *Art News,* September, 1968.)

Soft and Apparently Soft Sculpture. Circulating exhibition for the American Federation of Arts, 1968–69; organized by Lucy R. Lippard, spring, 1968. Baxter, Bourgeois, Hesse, Kaltenbach, Kusama, Linder, Nauman, Oldenburg, Paul, Serra, Simon, Sonnier, Viner, Winsor.

Extensions, edited by Suzanne Zavrian and Joachim Neugroschel, New York. No. 1, 1968, includes work by Acconci, Graham, Perreault, H. Weiner; no. 2, 1969, work by Acconci, Graham.

Ian Burn and Mel Ramsden. "Excerpts from 'Six-Negatives' Book." New York, winter, 1968–69:
"Six Negatives" was conceived in the following way. The tabular synopsis of categories was appropriated per se from Roget's Thesaurus. There are six classifications stated for dealing with ideas (I. ABSTRACT RELATIONS. II. SPACE. III. MATTER. IV. INTELLECT. V. VOLITION. VI. AFFECTIONS), of which two (class IV and V) each have two divisions. Each class or division of class formed a separate page in the work. Within each class is listed a number of sections and within each of these is listed a number of categories or heads, being arranged in two columns, the left listing the positive words denoting categories and the right listing the negative or contrasting. Having accepted the synopsis of categories as a basis for working, a process of negation was imposed: this was formed by four distinct attitudes: (i) the imposing of the process negating the possible role which the synopsis of categories could assume in the work; (ii) the physical striking-out or negating of each word in the column of positive words; (iii) as a result, a vocabulary of negative or contrasting words remains; (iv) finally, the entire work made into a photographic negative of its completed state.

1969

BOOKS

Acconci, Vito Hannibal. *Transference: Roget's Thesaurus.* 0–9 Books, New York, 1969.

Andre, Carl. *Seven Facsimile Notebooks of Poetry,* etc. Seth Siegelaub and the Dwan Gallery, New York, 1969. Limited edition of 36. Notebooks date from 1960–69; "Passport," "A Theory of Poetry," "American Drill," "Shape and Structure," "Three Operas," "One Hundred Sonnets," "Lyrics and Odes." Poems, collages, letters, photographs, and drawings.

Borofsky, Jon. *Thought Process.* New York, 1969–70. Unique copy (xerox). Contents: (1) Thoughts nos. 1–36; (2) Time thoughts nos. 5–9; Thought procedures A.B.C. (June–July, 1969); (3) Brain exercises nos. 16–22, 25, 27, 28, 29 (August, 1969); (4) Thought Process M, pages 1–118: illustrations regarding the meaning of time (August–December, 1969); (5) Brain exercises no. 31, with procedural diagrams (December, 1969); (6) Thought process M continued, pages 119–178: illustrations regarding the meaning of time (December–January, 1970); (7) Brain exercise no. 32, with procedural diagram (January, 1970). (Rep.)

Brouwn, Stanley. *Potentiële beginpunten van this way brouwn's in Hamburg.* Hamburg, Hansen Verlag, 1969. Stanley Brouwn began his walking and direction pieces in 1960 in Amsterdam. One of his early projects was an exhibition of all the shoe stores in Amsterdam. An early book was titled *Brouwnhair* and each page contained a sample of the artist's hair. The following three pieces date from 1962:
1. a walk through a grass field
2. a walk during one week
3. a walk from a to b

Castillejo, José Luis. *The Book of i's.* Bonn, 1969.

Celant, Germano, ed. *Arte Povera.* Milan, Mazzotta, 1969. (London, Studio Vista, and New York, Praeger, as *Art Povera: Earthworks, Impossible Art, Actual Art, Conceptual Art.*) Celant text, pp. 225–30, plus bibliography. The rest of the book consists of work and statements by the artists: Andre, Anselmo, Barry, Beuys, Boetti, Boezem, Calzolari, de Maria, Dibbets, Fabro, Flanagan, Haacke, Heizer, Hesse, Huebler, Kaltenbach, Kosuth, Kounellis, Long, Merz, Morris, Nauman, Oppenheim, Paolini, Penone, Pistoletto, Prini, Ruthenbeck, Serra, Sonnier, van Elk, Walther, Weiner, Zorio.

Cutforth, Roger. *The ESB.* New York, Art Press, 1969.

———. *The Empire State Building: A Reference Work,* New York, 1969.

Finch, Christopher, ed. *Form Follows Function.* Special issue of *Design Quarterly,* no. 73, 1969. Includes pieces by Tony Shafrazi.

Jonathan Borofsky. *Time Thought # 8,* page 7. 1969.

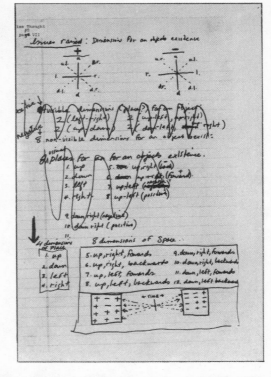

————, ed. *Process and Imagination.* Special issue of *Design Quarterly,* no. 74–75, 1969. Includes pieces by or on Ferriss, Wright, Goff, Soleri, Fuller, Frei Otto, Archigram, Oldenburg, e. t. and d. w. bowen, Le Va, Armajani.

Gins, Madeleine. *Word Rain.* New York, Grossman, 1969. A novel.

Graham, Dan. *End Moments.* New York, 1969. Unpublished or partially published writings from 1966. Includes an article on Sol LeWitt.

Higgins, Ed, and Vostell, Wolf, eds. *Pop Architecture/Concept Art.* Düsseldorf, Droste, 1969.

Jacks, Robert. [tiny untitled book of increasing lines]. New York, 1969.

Kinmont, Robert. *Eight Natural Handstands* and *My Favorite Dirt Roads.* San Francisco, 1969. (Rep.)

LeWitt, Sol. *Four basic kinds of straight lines . . . and their combinations.* London, Studio International, 1969.

Mayer, Rosemary. *Book: 41 Fabric Swatches,* 0–9 Books, New York, 1969. Typed descriptions of fabrics from a standard catalogue.

Nauman, Bruce. *Clea Rsky.* Los Angeles, 1969.

————. *Burning Small Fires.* Los Angeles, 1969. On burning a copy of Ed Ruscha's Small Fires book.

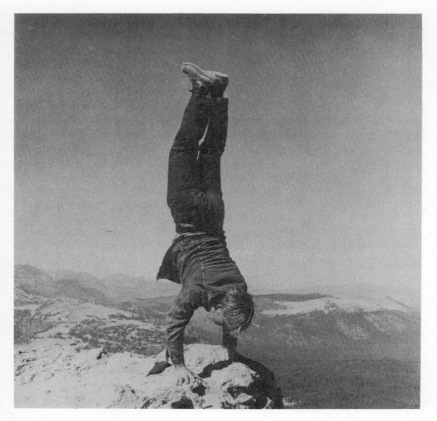

Bob Kinmont. Plate # 1 from *Eight Natural Handstands.* 1969. Courtesy Reese Palley, San Francisco.

Piper, Adrian. Untitled piece in booklet form based on proportional enlargement of one mapped block of New York City. 0 to 9 Books, New York, 1969.

————. Untitled piece in booklet form based on decreasing sizes of squares on graph paper. 0 to 9 Books, New York, 1969.

————. Untitled piece in booklet form based on Hagstrom maps of the five New York boroughs. 0 to 9 Books, New York, 1969.

Ruscha, Edward. *Crackers.* Heavy Industry Publications, Hollywood, 1969. With Leon Bing, Larry Bell, Rudi Gernreich, Tommy Smothers; photos by Ken Price, Joe Goode, Ed Ruscha (film made in 1971).

Salvo. Letters of Leonardo da Vinci to Ludovico il Muro, 1969:
  Dear Gianenzo:
  Now that I have examined and adequately considered the experiments of all those who consider themselves masters and creators of military machines, and having seen that the inventions and operations of these implements are in no way out of the ordinary, I shall attempt to explain myself to you, revealing my secrets and then offering them for your pleasure at any time at your convenience.
  (Enclosed please find lists)
  In peacetime, I think that I can perform as well as anyone else in architecture

designing public and private buildings and transporting water from place to place, etc. What is more, I will create works of sculpture and painting which will bear comparison to any others. What is more, I shall be able to paint your portrait, which will reflect immortal glory and eternally honor your memory.

And if any of the things mentioned above should seem impossible to anyone, I believe I am perfectly ready to demonstrate my claims in any situation of your choice concerning that position for which I most humbly recommend myself.

Salvo

Seery, John. *12 Thought Forms.* New York, July, 1969.

Weidman, Phil. *Slant Step Book.* The Art Co., Sacramento, Calif., 1969. Concerning the history of an unidentified object (Slant Step) found in 1965 in a Mill Valley junk shop by William Wiley, bought by Bruce Nauman, source of various works of art by San Francisco artists and a show at the Berkeley Gallery, fall, 1966, from which it was stolen and taken to New York by Richard Serra, later copied in plastic as a design object by Steve Kaltenbach, et passim.

Weiner, Lawrence. *Terminal Boundaries,* 1969. Dummy lost and book never published. Among the 42 pieces to be included:
An intrusion into an eastward flowing stream
An intrusion into a westward flowing stream
On or near the Continental Divide U.S.A.

50 pounds of lead placed upon the ocean north of the Coaxial Cable
50 pounds of lead placed upon the ocean south of the Coaxial Cable

A concise explosion at the boundary common to three countries

An object tossed from one country to another

A rubber ball thrown into the American Falls Niagara Falls
A rubber ball thrown into the Canadian Falls Niagara Falls

A rubber ball thrown at the sea
A rubber ball thrown on the sea

January 5–31, 1969. Seth Siegelaub, New York. Barry, Huebler, Kosuth, Weiner. Exhibition held at 44 East 52nd St., the McLendon Building. "The exhibition consists of (the ideas communicated in) the catalog; the physical presence (of the work) is supplementary to the catalog" (S.S.). Discussed by Gregory Battcock, "Painting Is Obsolete," *New York Free Press,* January 23, 1969; John Perreault, "Art: Disturbances," *Village Voice,* January 23, 1969; and "Four Interviews with Arthur Rose," *Arts,* February, 1969 (with Barry, Huebler, Kosuth, Weiner), from which excerpts follow:
Robert Barry:
"Arthur Rose": How did you arrive at the kind of work you are now doing?
RB: It's a logical continuation of my earlier work. A few years ago when I was painting, it seemed that paintings would look one way in one place and, because of lighting and other things, would look different in another place. Although it was the same object, it was another work of art. Then I made paintings which incorporated as part of their design the wall on which they hung. I finally gave up painting for the wire installations (two of which are in the show). Each wire installation was made to suit the place in which it was installed. They cannot be moved without being destroyed.
Color became arbitrary. I started using thin transparent nylon monofilament.

Eventually the wire became so thin that it was virtually invisible. This led to my use of a material which is invisible, or at least not perceivable in a traditional way. Although this poses problems, it also presents endless possibilities. It was at this point that I discarded the idea that art is necessarily something to look at.

Q: If your work is not perceivable, how does anyone deal with it or even know of its existence?

RB: I'm not only questioning the limits of our perception, but the actual nature of perception. These forms certainly do exist, they are controlled and have their own characteristics. They are made of various kinds of energy which exist outside the narrow arbitrary limits of our own senses. I use various devices to produce the energy, detect it, measure it, and define its form.

By just being in this show I'm making known the existence of the work. I'm presenting these things in an artistic situation using the space and the catalogue. I think this will be less of a problem as people become more acclimated to this art. As with any art, an interested person reacts in a personal way based on his own experience and imagination. Obviously, I can't control that.

Q: Exactly what kind of energy do you use?

RB: One kind of energy is electromagnetic waves. There is a piece in the show which uses the carrier wave of a radio station for a prescribed length of time, not as a means of transmitting information, but rather as an object. Another piece uses the carrier wave of a citizens band transmitter to bridge two distant points in New York and Luxembourg several times during the run of the show. Because of the position of the sun and favorable atmospheric conditions during January—the month of the show—*this* piece could be made. At another time, under different conditions, other locations would have to be used. There are two smaller carrier-wave pieces which have just enough power to fill the exhibition space. They are very different in character, one being AM, the other being FM, but both will occupy the same space at the same time—such is the nature of the material.

Also in the show will be a room filled with ultrasonic sound. I've also used microwaves and radiation. There are many other possibilities which I intend to explore—and I'm sure there are a lot of things we don't yet know about, which exist in the space around us, and, though we don't see or feel them, we somehow know they are out there.

* * *

Joseph Kosuth—some works listed in the catalogue:
- Four titles, 1966, glass, 4 glass sheets at 3′ × 3′.
- Art idea made with white words on nine gray painted square canvases, 1966, liquitex on canvas, 9 panels each 2½′ × 2½′.
- Titled (Art as idea as idea), 1967, photographic process, 4′ × 4′.
- Insurance (Art as idea as idea), 1968, insurance form and canceled airplane tickets.
- VI. Time (Art as idea as idea), 1968 (published in:) *The London Times: The Daily Telegraph* (London): *The Financial Times* (London): *The Observer* (London) all in the December 27, 1968 issue.
  "Note: The art is formless and sizeless; however the presentation has specific characteristics."

Statement by Kosuth:
My current work, which consists of categories from the Thesaurus, deals with the multiple aspects of an idea of something. I changed the form of presentation from the

mounted photostat, to the purchasing of spaces in newspapers and periodicals (with one "work" sometimes taking up as many as five or six spaces in that many publications—depending on how many divisions exist in the category). This way the immateriality of the work is stressed and any possible connections to painting are severed. The new work is not connected with a previous object—it's accessible to as many people as are interested, it's non-decorative—having nothing to do with architecture; it can be brought into the home or museum, but wasn't made with either in mind; it can be dealt with by being torn out of its publication and inserted into a notebook or stapled to the wall—or not torn out at all—but any such decision is unrelated to the art. My role as an artist ends with the work's publication.

*   *   *

Lawrence Weiner:

"Arthur Rose": When you did your early pieces which consisted of paint being applied directly on the floor or wall (I am thinking of "the spray on the floor for so many minutes" pieces . . . the paint thrown on the wall piece, and the paint poured on the floor piece) what did you have in mind?

LW: Making art.

Q: It has been said that some of the "Anti-form" artists have been influenced by the look of some of your work. Is this true, and what is the primary difference between their work and yours?

LW: I can't imagine how, as they are primarily concerned with making objects for display—which has nothing to do with the intent of my work.

Q: An integral aspect of your work is the existence of a receiver. The receiver—as I understand it—decides whether you will build the piece, have the piece fabricated, or not build it at all. Why?

LW: Because it doesn't matter.

Q: What doesn't matter?

LW: The condition of the piece. If I were to choose the condition, that would be an art decision which would lend unnecessary and unjustified weight to what amounts to presentation—and that has very little to do with the art.

Q: What is your interest in removing as an art process?

LW: I'm not interested in the process. Whereas the idea of removal is just as interesting as (if not more so) the intrusion of a fabricated object into a space, as sculpture is.

Q: What role does time play in your work?

LW: As a designation of quantity.

Q: What is the subject matter of your work, would you say?

LW: Materials.

Q: You state that the subject matter of your work is material, yet you claim that you are not a materialist—how does this follow?

LW: Materialist implies a primary involvement in materials, but I am primarily concerned with art. One could say the subject matter is materials, but its reason to be goes way beyond materials to something else, that something else being art.

1968 statement by Lawrence Weiner in the January, 1969, show catalogue (and consistently repeated thereafter in relation to all of his work):

1. The artist may construct the piece.
2. The piece may be fabricated.
3. The piece need not be built.

Each being equal and consistent with the intent of the artist, the decision as to condition rests with the received upon the occasion of receivership.

In 1970 (*Art in the Mind*), Weiner amplified this statement somewhat:
As to construction, please remember that as stated above there is no correct way to construct the piece as there is no incorrect way to construct it. If the piece is built it constitutes not how the piece looks but only how it could look.

Douglas Huebler, statement in catalogue:
The world is full of objects, more or less interesting; I do not wish to add any more. I prefer, simply, to state the existence of things in terms of time and/or place.

More specifically, the work concerns itself with things whose interrelationship is beyond direct perceptual experience.

Because the work is beyond direct perceptual experience, awareness of the work depends on a system of documentation.

This documentation takes the form of photographs, maps, drawings and descriptive language.

January, 1969: Judy (Gerowitz) Chicago makes firework piece, *Orange Atmosphere,* Brookside Park, Pasadena, the first of 13 powdered color pieces made over a 16-month period.

January 10, Dartmoor, England: Richard Long makes a sculpture for Martin and Mia Visser, Bergeijk, which is photographically recorded and published as "seven views of a sculpture" by Fernsehgalerie Gerry Schum, Düsseldorf, 1969: "According to Richard Long's idea the photographs in hand [the book] do not have the function of documentation: It *is* the 'Sculpture made for Martin and Mia Visser.'"

January 20, St. Martins School, London: Gilbert and George perform first version of their "singing sculpture."
January 26, London: First Showing of Gilbert Proesch's *Readings from a Stick* at the Geffrye Museum. 100 color slides of a resin walking stick. After the one-hour showing Gilbert shook hands with everyone at the door as they left. Some people refused to shake his hand.
During the same month, Gilbert and George (Passmore) presented their Interview Sculpture at St. Martins and two other art schools.

Christine Kozlov, in London, conceives of a "following" piece to be executed in the street, then rejects it.

***The New York Graphic Workshop,* Museo de Bellas Artes, Caracas, January, 1969. Texts by Luis Camnitzer and Donald Karshan.**
0–9, no. 5, January, 1969. Includes Yvonne Rainer's "Lecture for a Group of Expectant People" and Robert Smithson's "Non-Site Map of Mono Lake, California"; poems by Acconci, H. Weiner, Perreault; two untitled pieces by Piper; "The Disposable Transient Environment" by Les Levine:
Painting breaks the real time, real place experience. It separates the environment and introduces a focal point for abstract time. All paintings are landscapes. . . . They allow the viewer to leave the time of his environment intellectually and enter into the time of the painting. *Looking at paintings may be like going to sleep.* . . . Environmental art can have no beginnings or endings. . . . It can have no time. Time is the essential difference between theatre and environmental art. . . . Previous ideas in art have been covered with the notion that you have to stop seeing what you see, in order to see art. With environmental art . . . you see as you move and you move as you see. Art becomes *transient, not kinetic.* . . . History is the consciousness of development of all that has come before us. If we can extract from history the awareness of the process-development in our lives, we can go forward and extend our own consciousness. . . . It is conceivable that as it becomes unnecessary to hold onto

things and with the advantage of not using our minds as *storage bins,* that mankind could achieve a level of consciousness never before attained.

And "Sentences on Conceptual Art," by Sol LeWitt:

1. Conceptual Artists are mystics rather than rationalists. They leap to conclusions that logic cannot reach.
2. Rational judgements repeat rational judgements.
3. Illogical judgements lead to new experience.
4. Formal Art is essentially rational.
5. Irrational thoughts should be followed absolutely and logically.
6. If the artist changes his mind midway through the execution of the piece he compromises the result and repeats past results.
7. The artist's will is secondary to the process he initiates from idea to completion. His wilfulness may only be ego.
8. When words such as painting and sculpture are used, they connote a whole tradition and imply a consequent acceptance of this tradition, thus placing limitations on the artist who would be reluctant to make art that goes beyond the limitations.
9. The concept and idea are different. The former implies a general direction while the latter are the components. Ideas implement the concept.
10. Ideas alone can be works of art; they are in a chain of development that may eventually find some form. All ideas need not be made physical.
11. Ideas do not necessarily proceed in logical order. They may set one off in unexpected directions but an idea must necessarily be completed in the mind before the next one is formed.
12. For each work of art that becomes physical there are many variations that do not.
13. A work of art may be understood as a conductor from the artist's mind to the viewer's. But it may never reach the viewer, or it may never leave the artist's mind.
14. The words of one artist to another may induce an idea chain, if they share the same concept.
15. Since no form is intrinsically superior to another, the artist may use any form, from an expression of words (written or spoken) to physical reality, equally.
16. If words are used, and they proceed from ideas about art, then they are art and not literature; numbers are not mathematics.
17. All ideas are art if they are concerned with art and fall within the conventions of art.
18. One usually understands the art of the past by applying the conventions of the present thus misunderstanding the art of the past.
19. The conventions of art are altered by works of art.
20. Successful art changes our understanding of the conventions by altering our perceptions.
21. Perception of ideas leads to new ideas.
22. The artist cannot imagine his art, and cannot perceive it until it is complete.
23. One artist may mis-perceive (understand it differently than the artist) a work of art but still be set off in his own chain of thought by that misconstrual.
24. Perception is subjective.
25. The artist may not necessarily understand his own art. His perception is neither better nor worse than that of others.

26. An artist may perceive the art of others better than his own.
27. The concept of a work of art may involve the matter of the piece or the process in which it is made.
28. Once the idea of the piece is established in the artist's mind and the final form is decided, the process is carried out blindly. There are many side-effects that the artist cannot imagine. These may be used as ideas for new works.
29. The process is mechanical and should not be tampered with. It should run its course.
30. There are many elements involved in a work of art. The most important are the most obvious.
31. If an artist uses the same form in a group of works, and changes the material, one would assume the artist's concept involved the material.
32. Banal ideas cannot be rescued by beautiful execution.
33. It is difficult to bungle a good idea.
34. When an artist learns his craft too well he makes slick art.
35. These sentences comment on art, but are not art.

Sol LeWitt. *Drawing.* Ink on paper, 18″ x 24″. October, 1969. Courtesy Art & Project, Amsterdam.

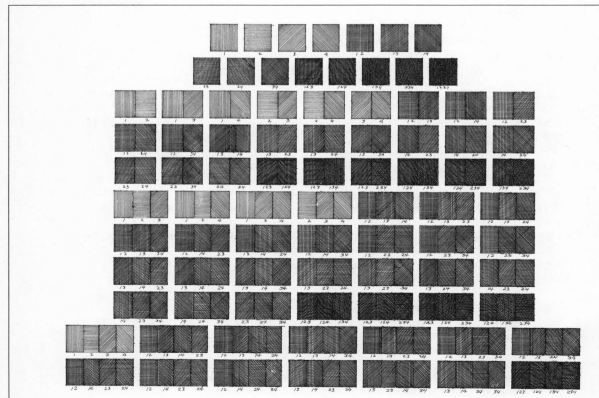

Trini, Tommaso. "Nuovo alfabeto per corpo e materia." *Domus,* no. 470, January, 1969.

Rose, Barbara. "The Politics of Art: Part II." *Artforum,* January, 1969.

Kramer, Hilton. "The Emperor's New Bikini." *Art in America,* January–February, 1969.

February, Düsseldorf: Joseph Beuys accepts full responsibility for any snowfall from February 15 to 20.

February 2, New York; Dennis Oppenheim, *Removal Transplant New York Stock Exchange.*

"This is to verify that on Wednesday, Feb. 19, 1969, there was an aborted symbolic assassination of: Richard Serra, Robert Smithson, Robert Morris, Michael Heizer, Carl Andre and Lucy Lippard." (Saul Ostrow, a propos of a panel on "order" with these participants at the School of Visual Arts.)

February 28, Frankfurt, Galerie Patio: Timm Ulrichs makes a text-environment measuring a room and marking its measurements on the surfaces.

Hanne Darboven. Städtisches Museum, Mönchengladbach, February 25–April 1, 1969. Six film projections after six books from 1968. Boxed catalogue with brief text by Johannes Cladders (see below), indexes to books, and a booklet of blank graph paper. Reviewed by Hans Strelow, "Zeit als Zahl," *Frankfurter Allgemeine Zeitung,* March 22, 1969.

The drawings (constructions) by Hanne Darboven, contained in 6 books, deal with the year 1969 and derive from the individual dates beginning with 1.1.1969 and ending with 31.12.1969. As a result each book has the same number of pages, namely 365, and the theme remains constant. The books differ from each other, however, through a processive reduction. Nevertheless, this reduction affects neither the numbers of pages nor the theme. It does though affect the "spacial" expansion of the drawings formed by numbers of squares.

Hanne Darboven's own index to each book provides the code to each respective reduction, that is to say, to the respective units from which basis springs the development of the drawing which remains constant in quantity and content. (The denotation "K" represents "Construction.")

Index I

The constructions derive from the dates forming cross-sums. The numbers 6 and 9 of the year's denotation are always dealt with separately. All other numbers with double-figures are treated as units. The cross-sums resulting from the dates become progressively larger from 17 to 68, increase in the frequency of occurrence from 1 to 12, and decrease again back to 1. The index expounds the respective cross-sum and the frequency of its occurrence. In all, 42 different cross-sums derive from the dates. Example:

$$1.\ 1.69 = 1 + 1 + 6 + 9 = 17 \qquad 1x$$
$$2.\ 1.69 = 2 + 1 + 6 + 9 = 18 \left.\begin{array}{l} \\ \text{but also} \\ 1.\ 2.69 = 1 + 2 + 6 + 9 = 18 \end{array}\right\} 2x-11$$

The frequency of the occurrence of a cross-sum corresponds to the frequency of the repetition of the resulting construction. Constructions, from which bases a cross-sum occurs only 1x, appear only once in the book; those which occur 12x appear 12x in succession on respective pages, thus accounting for 365 pages.

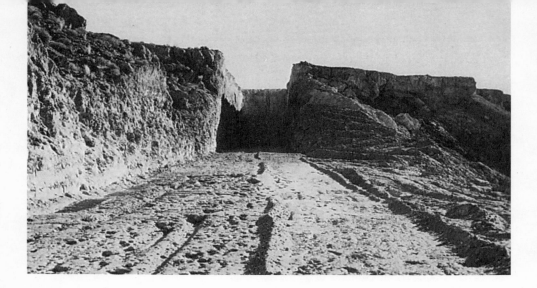

Michael Heizer. *Double Negative.* 1100′ x 42′ x 30′, 40,000 tons displaced. Virgin River Mesa, Nevada. 1969. Collection Virginia Dwan.

All constructions in the book dealt with in Index 1 are written out in numbers. Moreover every number is repeated as often as the number denotes.

Lee Lozano, *General Strike Piece* (started February 8, 1969):
Gradually but determinedly avoid being present at official or public "uptown" functions or gatherings related to the "art world" in order to pursue investigation of *total personal and public revolution.* Exhibit in public only pieces which further the sharing of ideas and information related to total personal and public revolution. In process at least through summer, 1969.

Blockade '69. **Galerie Rene Block, Berlin, February 28–November 22, 1969. Rooms by Beuys, Giese, Hodicke, Lohaus, Knoebel, Palermo, Panamarenko, Polke, Ruthenbeck. Text on Beuys's "action"—Eurasia (first done in 1965) by Troels Andersen. (see above, pp. 17–19).**

Earth Art. **Andrew Dickson White Museum, Cornell University, Ithaca, N.Y., February 19–March 16, 1969. Foreword by Thomas Leavitt, texts by William C. Lipke and by the organizer, Willoughby Sharp; statements by the artists, bibliography, and excerpts from a symposium held February 16. Artists: Dibbets, Haacke, Jenney, Long, Medalla, Morris, Oppenheim, Smithson, Uecker.**
I believe we are still carrying this heavy burden of "visual" art. When this term "aesthetics" was brought up in this discussion, it was immediately coupled with the *looks* of something. I believe art is not so much concerned with the looks. It is more concerned with concepts. What you see is just a vehicle for the concept. Sometimes you have a hard time seeing this vehicle, or it might even not exist, and there is only verbal communication or a photographic record or a map or anything that could convey the concept. (Haacke, from symposium.)

Earth Art **reviewed by David Bourdon, "What on Earth," *Life,* April 29, 1969; John Perreault, "Art-Down to Earth," and "Earth Show," *Village Voice,* February 13 and 27, 1969; Max Kozloff,**

The Nation, March 17, 1969; Dore Ashton, *Arts,* April, 1969. Les Levine made an exhibition, or environment, at the Phyllis Kind Gallery, Chicago, April, 1969; from 1,000 copies of each of 31 photographs taken on a press flight from New York to Ithaca; it was called *Systems Burn-Off X Residual Software.*

Robbin, Anthony. "Smithson's Non-Site Sights." *Art News,* February, 1969. Smithson is quoted as saying: "I think the major issue now in art is what are the boundaries. For too long artists have taken the canvas and stretchers as given, the limits."

Meadmore, Clement. "Thoughts on Earthworks, Random Distribution, Softness, Horizontality and Gravity." *Arts,* February, 1969.

Perreault, John. "Nonsites in the News" (Smithson). *New York,* February 24, 1969.

Trini, Tommaso. "L'Imaginazione Conquista il Terrestre." *Domus,* no. 471, February, 1969.

March 1–31, 1969. Seth Siegelaub, New York. First exhibition to exist in catalogue form alone; distributed free worldwide. Reviewed by John Perreault, "Off the Wall," *Village Voice,* March 13, 1969; Lawrence Alloway, *The Nation,* April 7, 1969; Grace Glueck, *New York Times,* March 16, 1969. Works from the exhibition:

SETH SIEGELAUB

Dear Mr. _____,

I am organizing an International Exhibition of the "work" of 31 artists during each of the 31 days in March 1969. The exhibition is titled "One Month."

The invited artists and their dates are:

March				
1	Carl Andre	17	On Kawara	
2	Mike Asher	18	Joseph Kosuth	
3	Terry Atkinson	19	Christine Kozlov	
4	Michael Baldwin	20	Sol LeWitt	
5	Robert Barry	21	Richard Long	
6	Rick Barthelme	22	Robert Morris	
7	Iain Baxter	23	Bruce Nauman	
8	James Byars	24	Claes Oldenburg	
9	John Chamberlain	25	Dennis Oppenheim	
10	Ron Cooper	26	Alan Ruppersberg	
11	Barry Flanagan	27	Ed Ruscha	
12	Dan Flavin	28	Robert Smithson	
13	Alex Hay	29	De Wain Valentine	
14	Douglas Huebler	30	Lawrence Weiner	
15	Robert Huot	31	Ian Wilson	
16	Stephen Kaltenbach			

You have been assigned March __, 1969.

Kindly return to me, as soon as possible, any relevant information regarding the nature of the "work" you intend to contribute to the exhibition on your day.

Your reply should specify one of the following:
1) You want your name listed, with a description of your "work" and/or relevant information.
2) You want your name listed, with no other information.
3) You do not want your name listed at all.

A list of the artists and their "work" will be published, and internationally distributed. (All replies become the property of the publisher.)

Kindly confine your replies to just verbal information.

All replies must be received by February 15th. If you do not reply by that time, your name will not be listed at all.

Thank you for your cooperation.

Sincerely,

SETH SIEGELAUB

21 January 1969   1100 Madison Avenue, New York 10028. (212) 288-5031

Oldenburg:
My Work: "Things Colored Red."

Alex Hay:
I will place a piece of chemical filter paper 60″ × 60″ on the roof of the building at 27 Howard Street, Manhattan, for the 24 hours of Thursday, March 13, for whatever it accumulates.

Rick Barthelme:
I have set down below the relevant information appropriate use of which will avail anyone anywhere of the work.

Four individual works—

Being, in the physical condition—facing north
Being, in the physical condition—facing south
Being, in the physical condition—facing east
Being, in the physical condition—facing west

About the works it can be said:

1. The works include and accept but do not determine everything (perceptual and conceptual) that occurs while in the condition.
2. The works can only be accomplished personally, and as such exist as fields of potential delimited by the physical condition.

Christine Kozlov. *Information: No Theory,* spring, 1969 (revised version of piece in March catalogue):
1. The recorder is equipped with a continuous loop tape.
2. The recorder will be set at *record.* All the sounds audible in the room will be recorded.
3. The nature of the loop tape necessitates that new information erases old information. The "life" of the information, that is, the time it takes for the information to go from "new" to "old" is the time it takes the tape to make one complete cycle.
4. Proof of the existence of the information does in fact not exist in actuality, but is based on probability.

Op Losse Schroeven: Situaties en Cryptostructuren (Square Pegs in Round Holes). Stedelijk Museum, Amsterdam, March 15–April 27, 1969. Texts by Wim Beeren, Piero Gilardi, Harald Szeeman; catalogue in two parts; Part II is a booklet of squared graph paper, a "page project" by artists. Participants: Andre, Anselmo, Beuys, Bollinger, Calzolari, de Maria, Dibbets, van Elk, Ferrer, Flanagan, Heizer, Huebler, Icaro, Jenney, Kaks, Kounellis, Long, Merz (Mario), Merz (Marisa), Morris, Nauman, Oppenheim, Panamarenko, Prini, Ruthenbeck, Ryman, Saret, Serra, Smithson, Sonnier, Viner, Weiner, Zorio.
Dennis Oppenheim (from catalogue):
In ecological terms what has transpired in recent art is a shift from "primary" homesite to the alternate of "secondary" homesite. With the fall of galleries, artists have sensed a similar sensation as do organisms when curtailed by disturbances of environmental conditions. This results in extension or abandonment of homesite. The loft organism stifled by the rigidity of his habitat works on not recognizing his out-put waning to the contemplation of new ways to work within old bounds.

The more successful work from the minimal syndrome rejected itself, allowing the viewer a one-to-one confrontation with pure limit or bounds. This displacement of sensory pressures from object to place will prove to be the major contribution of minimalist art. However, when one's energy can be absorbed so wantonly, by the "place you put your thing" . . . it's time to consider a more deserving location. . . .

This summer I will work within the mid-western United States, using the wheat production and processing industry as a framework. Each stage of this media gridwork will be inspected and rearranged in accordance with a strict aesthetic masterplan. Last July, I directed the linear harvest of a 300' × 900' oat field in Hamburg, Pennsylvania. This time, isolated episodes will be directed towards a core network involving every permutation (from planting to distributing the product). The aesthetic effect of the interaction will permeate the range in which it deals—communication outside the system will come in the form of photographic documentation, excursions, and an annual report.

When Attitudes Become Form. Kunsthalle, Bern, March 22–April 27, 1969. Organized by Harald Szeeman. Catalogue texts by Szeeman, Scott Burton, Grégoire Müller, Tommaso Trini; bibliographies, biographies. Artists: Andre, Anselmo, Artschwager, Bang, Bark, Barry, Beuys, Boetti, Bochner, Boezem, Bollinger, Buthe, Calzolari, Cotton, Darboven, de Maria, Dibbets, van Elk, Ferrer, Flanagan, Glass (Ted), Haacke, Heizer, Hesse, Huebler, Icaro, Jacquet, Jenney, Kaltenbach, Kaplan, Kienholz, Klein, Kosuth, Kounellis, Kuehn, LeWitt, Lohaus, Long, Louw, Medalla, Merz, Morris, Nauman, Oldenburg, Oppenheim, Panamarenko, Pascali, Pechter, Pistoletto, Prini, Raets, Ruppersberg, Ruthenbeck, Ryman, Sandback, Saret, Sarkis, Schnyder, Serra, Smithson, Sonnier, Tuttle, Viner, Walther, Wegman, Weiner, Wiley, Zorio. The exhibition, somewhat revised, went to the ICA in London in August—September. Charles Harrison directed it and wrote a new catalogue essay also published as "Against Precedents" in *Studio International,* September, 1969.

Op Losse Schroeven and *When Attitudes Become Form* reviewed by Jean-Christophe Amman, "Schweizerbrief," *Art International,* May, 1969; Tommaso Trini, "Trilogia del creator prodigo," *Domus* 478, September, 1969; C. Blok, "Letter from Holland," *Art International,* May, 1969; Scott Burton, *Art and Artists,* August, 1969.

March 17, New York: "Time: A Panel Discussion." The New York Shakespeare Theater, for the Benefit of the Student Mobilization Committee to End the War in Vietnam. Seth Siegelaub, moderator; Carl Andre, Michael Cain representing Pulsa; Douglas Huebler, Ian Wilson. Transcript edited by Lucy R. Lippard and published in *Art International,* November, 1969. Excerpts follow:

MC: I am here as a representative of a group of artists who work together collaboratively. And since I guess no one here is familiar with the work of the Pulsa group, I'll describe it for just a moment. We're involved in considering the use of time and actually manipulating time as a material in works of art. Our group, consisting of ten members, is involved in research with programming environments through electronic technology. The environments we work with are varied: interior spaces, public places outdoors, country landscapes. In each case, a particular system capable of emanating (and whenever possible, totally controlling, or at least giving forth) perceptible energies, wave energies—light and sound—is set up and controlled through an electronic system that we've designed. All of our work is, therefore, time-extended. Generally our environments run from a period of from ten hours, uninterruptedly, each evening, for a period of a couple of weeks to several months. They're usually programmed so that they're different each night. The large membership of the group is involved in implementing these works, which are very large in scale and, technologically, extremely complex.

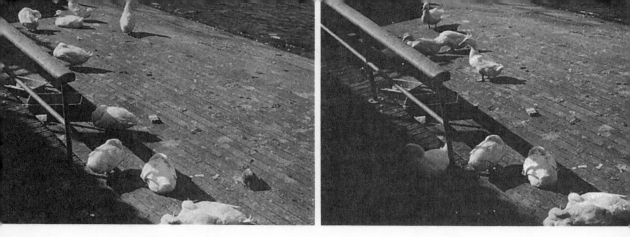

Douglas Huebler. *Duration Piece # 7.* New York City. April, 1969.

On March 17, 1969, fifteen photographs were made, at one-minute intervals, of an area in Central Park occupied by eleven ducks and an occasional pigeon.

Fifteen photographs (presented with no sequential order) join with this statement to constitute the form of this piece.

Our interest in time is, of course, manifold. In any situation, in any cultural situation, in any society, time (which I think is itself a phenomenon lacking any kind of absolute definition, especially in terms of Einsteinian relativity), time itself has no absolute rate of flow, nor do events have any absolute succession. Instead, the rate of flow and the succession of events is determined by the position of the observer, the speed at which he's moving, gravitational fields, temperature conditions, etc. All this is quite familiar, but it implies that a given culture has to set up some kind of a framework in which people can relate to time. An individual has the same problem. His experience of time consists of nothing more than a succession of events and consciousnesses which he has to order in some way from which he projects principles or discerns certain rates of flow. The fact that an individual isolated in a sensory deprivation chamber experiences a complete disorientation of time is indicative of the fact that we depend on a flow of events to keep us tuned in to our society's peculiar involvement with temporal structure. Our environment is totally dominated by electronic phenomena. Our total environment, at least at night, is electric. The rate at which actions occur within it, the nature of our experiences in life occur in particular rates and successions determined by electronic technology.

In such an environment, it seems critical to the Pulsa group that a public art form be developed, to deal with these phenomena to create an abstract, meaningful art force which deals specifically with the experiences people have today, in terms of time and also of space in the world. . . . Our intention through all of this is to find a way of rendering people's experience of the environment in which they live more integrated, or at least more richly intelligible. . . .

SS: Do you people think time could ever be a concrete value as now we feel space is a concrete value? Can you envisage our knowing as much about time in relation to art or to life, as we know about space?

DH: I don't think we know any more about space than we do about time. At least I don't think I do. We measure space through objects existing in the world, and I think we measure time the same way. They're both rather boundless; they're only conventions that we use. Let me answer the first part of what Seth said too. I think it's perfectly fair to say that time is what each of us says it is at any given moment. But as a convention, it suits our purposes within the terms of the particular structure that we want to give to it. I work in an extremely neutral way. I'm altogether incompetent to work with the kinds of elements and materials that Pulsa does. But I am interested in being able to take some very small piece of life, of the world, and doing something with it in terms of time, that is, by demonstrating how objects or the position of things change. I've done that by having elements, events, or materials actually change as they would normally in sequential time, documenting the changes photographically, and then scrambling the photographs so that there's no priority of the linear. It's just a way of pulling something out of a series of possibilities and calling it a work. . . .

IW: As far as I'm concerned, time is just a vast illusion, it's just a never-ending illusion without any possible understanding of it. I don't really use it in this sense, though. I use it just as a word that has suitable characteristics, but one of the facts is that it is a word, and that it is so nebulous, such an enigma, that you can't pin anything on it; it's so vague, it's not even there. The word, when said, is like a sound: it vanishes in its moment of execution, the sound vanishes, just like time. But this is really what I'm trying to do. The same principles carry over to oral communication, and I'm not involved with time now, I'm involved with oral communication. . . .

I can go right back to the primitive philosophies of Greece. Pythagoras and Socrates (not so much Plato) were aware, obviously, of the animation of ideas presented through oral communication. They never went near the printed word, and so oral communication comes out of that tradition. But it also comes out of today, and today's art. I came up through the art of Primary Structures, etc., and I'm very much a part of it. I try all the time to keep things at a primary state and present subjects as directly as possible. If you have the subject of, say, oral communication, it can't be written because you can't write an orally communicated thing. Obviously you apply the medium that presents the idea as directly as possible, and you end up with

Pulsa. *Continuing Research Project.* Computer and strobe lights on Yale Golf Course, New Haven. Winter, 1969.

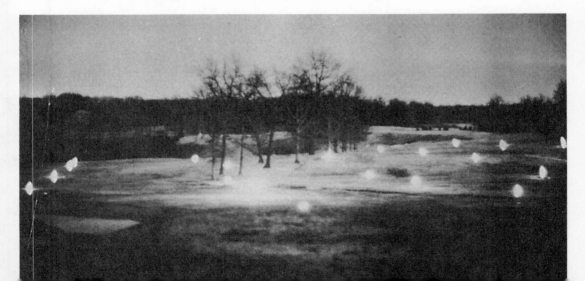

yourself saying it—oral communication—just directly. The animation of the situation is not destroyed.

CA: There's one thing that troubles me personally. I said that I did sculpture and I did poetry, and I'm willing to accept Ian's oral communication as an art form related to poetry, but not related to sculpture or painting, because I feel that if you can write or say something adequately, there's no need to make a painting or sculpture of it. In other words, painting and sculpture explicitly concern themselves with aspects of human sensibility which cannot adequately be dealt with in language. So that's why I wonder, is Ian here as a poet, in a sense?

IW: I certainly am not a poet, I'm a very bad writer; probably that's why I'm talking about oral communication. I'm not a poet and I'm considering oral communication as a sculpture. Because, as I said, if you take a cube, someone has said you imagine the other side because it's so simple. And you can take the idea further by saying you can imagine the whole thing without its physical presence. So now immediately you've transcended the idea of an object that was a cube into a word without a physical presence. And you still have the essential features of the object at your disposal. So now, if you just advance a little, you end up where you can take up a word like time and you have the specific features of the word "time." You're just moving this idea of taking a primary structure and focusing attention on it.

Norvell, Patricia Ann. *Eleven Interviews,* **March–July, 1969. Tape recordings, unpublished; each tape indexed in typescript plus bibliographies and biographies; Hunter College Library, New York. Andre, Barry, Huebler, Kaltenbach, Kosuth, LeWitt, Morris, Oppenheim, Siegelaub, Smithson, Weiner.**

Stephen Kaltenbach (edited by L. R. L. and the artist):
SK: Over the past two years, previous to January, 1967, I had been removing the number of elements in my work one by one; they were becoming simpler and simpler. I realized that you could only remove so many elements from a volumetric form and still have a volumetric form. Finally it has to go, so if I wanted to continue working that way I would have had to begin reducing the number of elements in the environment which intrude and complicate the visual experience. I decided I would take over the space and control everything from the door in; I made a series of drawings which I guess you have seen—the room constructions, which are completely normal rooms in every aspect from color to ceiling features to door with one single manipulation. For instance, a floor that was shaped like a pyramid, but was covered with carpet. There was no flat floor in the room; it went to the edge of the walls. That's the first thing that was really very consciously cerebral about my work. . . . Also at that time I began to smoke grass. That was very important. . . . I felt that in a sense I could remove myself from my ego a little bit, and see myself and my work more clearly. I was stoned when I had an experience that started me on the drapery things I did. . . . I would simply come up with a shape of cloth, for instance a square, and I would decide on five or ten different ways to fold it that looked nice. If a person wanted one they would choose the color and size and kind of cloth and follow my directions. That suggested the possibility that as an artist I didn't have to control everything. In fact, some of the things I'm interested in now are things that I control hardly at all. Another thing I was thinking about from January to March 1967 was legality and laws and the fact that a great many things that are illegal aren't immoral. . . . I thought of the possibility of breaking some of these laws that really aren't unethical and sealing the evidence of it

into a time capsule so I could document my feelings about the laws but not pay the piper for what I'd done. I made three capsules between November 1967 and June 1968. . . . I never say anything about the contents and I won't even admit that there are contents, although I don't swear that there aren't. The secret quality itself, and the enclosure of whatever was inside, if anything, was really important. . . . One was for Bruce Nauman, who was a primary influence on me over all other people; and one was for Barbara Rose, which says: "Barbara Rose: Please open this capsule when in your opinion I have achieved national prominence as an artist." The one at the Museum of Modern Art is to be opened when I die. . . . The contents of the capsules are limited by what I can imagine, what I can accept as appropriate, what I can accept as art. Although I guess lately there is nothing that I can't accept as art. . . .

PN: Do you feel we are taking any bigger step in opening up the art field than in the past? That this whole year has been exciting?

SK: Culturally we are permitted to move faster now. I like being in a looser, faster moving, developing kind of thing. The developing has really become primary. I'm

---

Dan Graham. One still from *Two Correlated Rotations.* 2 Super-8 film projections. 1969.

Two performers with camera's viewfinder to their eyes are each other's subjects (observed) as they are simultaneously each other's objects (observers) are subjects to each other's objects in the filming of each other; the process is a relation of dependent, reciprocal feedback.

In the gallery, the spectator "sees" the feedback loop in a very close time between the cameras' recorded images: 2 object/subject *I*'s in relation to his *I* on 2 screens at right angles to each other.

The 2 cameramen spiral counterdirectionally, the outside performer walking outward while his opposite walks inside toward the center. The filming ends when the inside performer approaches the inward limits of the center of his spiral. As they walk, their "objective" is to as nearly as is possible be continuously centering their camera's view on the position of the other. This is more complex at times for the inside performer who, in order to maintain a continuous view of the outer walker would have to swivel on his neck a complete 360°. So it is necessary for him to shift at times his vantage from over one shoulder to over the other side of his neck (the movement of this is seen in the film as a rapid, approximately 100° pan along the horizon line).

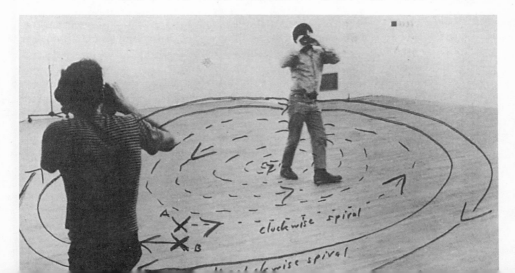

having a hard time making objects now, and the objects that I do make seem to sort of drop out, as evidence of my discoveries. Anything I can understand seems to become potentially a way of working, so that as I get and understand information, and if I do anything to that information myself, then I'm really anxious to pass it on. The traditional method of passing it on was doing a work and having people see it and understand what is new in it and do it themselves. Now, instead, you can simply pass on the information. I like to do it very underhandedly, so I come up with devices for doing it that way. . . .

I used to be an incredible daydreamer. I could dream up color and three-dimensional imagery. I though that with all the evidence of ESP and that kind of thing, it may be a muscle that can be developed as much as any other muscle. Someday an artist may simply expose his head directly to other people, and that may be the way he expresses himself. Being unable to do that, I felt there might be other ways to go directly from head to head, and this was obviously through language, so I got into writing things. . . .

I've been thinking of presenting something in a theater situation, kind of a mind play, where instead of having the acting going on on the stage, the cues would come from the stage and would go on in the person's head. . . .

PN: You haven't talked about the *Artforum* pieces [one-line statements or commands ("Art works," "Become a legend") published as advertisements in *Artforum,* 1968–69].

SK: And I haven't talked about the influence pieces. They come first. When I first got to New York I showed a friend of mine a specific group of my own work; we were working with the same materials and generally the same approach. I came to his studio about three months later and I saw a lot of my pieces around, all done his way, much bigger and much better. Of course at first I felt the whole thing artists feel when they think someone else is taking their work. Then I realized it was sort of a compliment. He liked my work well enough to extend it. It seemed ludicrous to be uptight about it. That suggested the possibility of trying to do my work through other people. When I was talking to an artist who had interests like mine I would nonchalantly give him whatever I had that might help him, and wait and see what would happen. I would write down what I'd given. It didn't always bear fruit. But that kind of thing is very hard to measure. Often I suspect ideas I gave were ideas they already had, so quantitatively there was no way for me to decide if what happened was my work. Nevertheless, I felt I was really doing work, and it occurred to me that this was another way to escape my own taste, by taking a principle I was working with and channeling it through someone else.

PN: Are you publicizing any of this?

SK: It is potentially loaded ego-wise, and I'm not into causing anybody any uptightness or feelings that I'm trying to get credit for what they did; besides, the same thing is happening to me. I'd be blind if I didn't admit it. I have good examples, like the sidewalk plaques, which are almost duplicates of Bruce Nauman's work, which keeps me from getting any god-like feelings.

Since then I've gone on to other things. I'm into what I call teach-art now, with my students. It's the more traditional way of doing the same thing, and in a sense it is more logical and less specific because I'm trying not to give them my ideas but to push them to get their own ideas. But again I can accept that as my work. Because anything can be your work, anything you feel, anything you can imagine. Teaching art is one way of expressing myself. It is a two-way thing. I get a lot of ideas from my students and the exchange clarifies my own ideas.

PN: On what grounds does an observer judge, evaluate your work?

SK: The idea can be evaluated. Nothing else can. People are accepting the possibility that you can't criticize this kind of work, and as a result the really imaginative art critics are into passing out information rather than making their own value judgments. In a sense, they are really becoming artists. In fact, just living could really be a valid means for an artist to express himself.

PN: That's what you're getting into. A style of life.

SK: So were guys like Yves Klein and Duchamp, although I didn't realize it until I understood it myself. At first I thought that was my idea. I want to become a legend, which is the next ad coming out in *Artforum*. There are 14,000 copies of *Artforum*, so instead of sitting down and talking to you, I'm talking to 14,000 people. Except a lot of things I put in *Artforum* are not understandable to a lot of people who read the magazine. In fact they aren't even identified as information. They are passing on possibilities. A lot of them are very straightforward, like the command things: "Build a Reputation," "Tell a Lie," "Perpetuate a Hoax." Some of the others were much less so. They are time pieces, in a way. They are going to require some time to get into. I like being mysterious and disguising my intentions.

*   *   *

Robert Smithson, "Fragments of an Interview with P.A. Norvell, April, 1969" (edited by L.R.L. and R.S.; a few additions made by the artist):

RS: An interesting thing to start with would be the whole notion of the object, which I consider to be a mental problem rather than a physical reality. An object to me is the product of a thought; it doesn't necessarily signify the existence of art. My view of art springs from a dialectical position that deals with whether something exists or doesn't exist. I'm more interested in the terrain dictating the condition of the art. The pieces I just did in the Yucatan were mirror displacements. The actual contour of the ground determined the placement of the twelve mirrors. The first site was a burnt-out field which consisted of ashes, small heaps of earth and charred stumps; I picked a place and then stuck the mirrors directly into the ground so that they reflected the sky. I was dealing with actual light as opposed to paint. Paint to me is matter, and a covering, rather than light itself. I was interested in capturing the actual light on each spot, bringing it down to the ground. I did this different ways with different kinds of supports—sometimes raw earth, sometimes tree limbs or other materials existing on the site. Each piece was dismantled after it was photographed. I just wrote an article on that trip [see *Artforum*, September, 1968]. It is a piece that involves travel. A lot of my pieces come out of the idea of covering distances. There is a certain degree of unmaking in the pieces, rather than making; taking apart and reassembling. It is not so much a matter of creating something as de-creating, or denaturalizing, or de-differentiating, decomposing. . . .

Earlier work has had to do with site and nonsite. I first got interested in places by taking trips and just confronting the raw materials of the particular sectors before they were refined into steel or paint or anything else. My interest in the site was really a return to the origins of material, sort of a dematerialization of refined matter. Like if you took a tube of paint and followed that back to its original sources. My interest was in juxtaposing the refinement of, let's say, painted steel, against the particles and rawness of matter itself. Also it sets up a dialogue between interior exhibition space and exterior sites. . . . It seems that no matter how far out you go, you are always thrown back on your point of origin. . . . You are confronted with an extending horizon; it can extend onward and onward, but then you suddenly find the horizon is closing in all around you, so that you have this kind of dilating effect. In other words, there is no escape from limits. There is no real extension of scale taking place simply by spreading materials inside a room.

In a sense my nonsites are rooms within rooms. Recovery from the outer fringes brings one back to the central point. . . . The scale between indoors and outdoors, and how the two are impossible to bridge. . . . What you are really confronted with in a nonsite is the absence of the site. It is a contraction rather than an expansion of scale. One is confronted with a very ponderous, weighty absence. What I did was to go out to the fringes, pick a point in the fringes and collect some raw material. The making of the piece really involves collecting. The container is the limit that exists within the room after I return from the outer fringe. There is this dialectic between inner and outer, closed and open, center and peripheral. It just goes on constantly permuting itself into this endless doubling, so that you have the nonsite functioning as a mirror and the site functioning as a reflection. Existence becomes a doubtful thing. You are presented with a nonworld, or what I call a nonsite. The problem is that it can only be approached in terms of its own negation, so that leaves you with this

Robert Smithson. *Asphalt Rundown.* Executed near Rome, October, 1969. Courtesy John Weber Gallery, New York, and L'Attico, Rome.

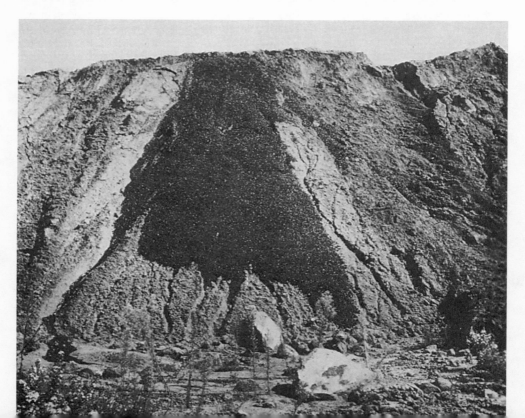

very raw material that doesn't seem to exist. . . . You are faced with something inexplicable; there is nothing left to express. . . .

Photographs are the most extreme contraction, because they reduce everything to a rectangle and shrink everything down. That fascinates me. There are three kinds of work that I do: the nonsites, the mirror displacements, and earth maps or material maps. The mirrors are disconnected surfaces. The pressure of the raw material against the mirrored surface is what provides its stability. The surfaces are not connected the way they are in the nonsites. The earth maps, on the other hand, are left on the sites. For instance, I have a project pending in Texas that will involve a large oval map of the world that existed in the Cambrian era. Like the map of a prehistoric island I built on quicksand in Alfred, New York. The map was made of rock. It sank slowly. No sites exist at all; they are completely lost in time, so that the earth maps point to nonexistent sites, whereas the nonsites point to existing sites but tend to negate them. The mirror pieces fall somewhere between the edge and the center. The photograph is a way of focusing on the site. Perhaps ever since the invention of the photograph we have seen the world through photographs and not the other way around. In a sense, perception has to decant itself of old notions of naturalism or realism. You just have to deal with the fundamentals of matter and mind, completely devoid of any anthropomorphic interests. That is also what my work is about—the interaction between mind and matter. It is a dualistic idea which is very primitive. . . . I consider the facile unitary or gestalt ideas part of the expressive fallacy, a relief after the horrors of duality. The apparent reconciliation seems to offer some kind of relief, some kind of hope. . . .

People are convinced they know what reality is, so they bring their own concept of reality to the work. . . . They never contend with the reality that is outside their own, which might be no reality at all. The existence of "self" is what keeps everybody from confronting their fears about the ground they happen to be standing on. . . . The sites show the effect of time, sort of a sinking into timelessness. When I get to a site that strikes the kind of timeless chord, I use it. The site selection is by chance. There is no wilful choice. A site at zero degree, where the material strikes the mind, where absences become apparent, appeals to me, where the disintegrating of space and time seems very apparent. Sort of an end of selfhood . . . the ego vanishes for a while.

PN: It is all a very self-contained system, once the site is selected.

RS: It is like a treadmill. There is no hope for logic. If you try to come up with a logical reason then you might as well forget it, because it doesn't deal with any kind of nameable, measurable situation. All dimension seems to be lost in the process. In other words, you are really going from some place to some place, which is to say, nowhere in particular. To be located between those two points puts you in a position of elsewhere, so there's no focus. This outer edge and this center constantly subvert each other, cancel each other out. There is a suspension of destination. I think that conceptual art which depends completely on written data is only half the story; it only deals with the mind and it has to deal with the material too. Sometimes it is nothing more than a gesture. I find a lot of that written work fascinating. I do a lot of it myself, but only as one side of my work. My work is impure; it is clogged with matter. I'm for a weighty, ponderous art. There is no escape from matter. There is no escape from the physical nor is there any escape from the mind. The two are in a constant collision course. You might say that my work is like an artistic disaster. It is a quiet catastrophe of mind and matter.

PN: What about limits in art?

RS: All legitimate art deals with limits. Fraudulent art feels that it has no limits. The trick is to locate those elusive limits. You are always running against those limits, but somehow they never show themselves. That's why I say measure and dimension seem to break down at a certain point. . . . Like there are the people of the middle, lawyers and engineers, the rational numbers, and there are the people of the fringe, tramps and madmen, irrational numbers. The fringe and the middle meet when somebody like Emmett Kelly sweeps light into a dustpan.

PN: Jack Burnham feels we are going from an object-oriented society to a systems-oriented society.

RS: System is a convenient word, like object. It is another abstract entity that doesn't exist. I think art tends to relieve itself of those hopes. Jack Burnham is very interested in going *beyond,* and that is a utopian view. The future doesn't exist, or if it does exist, it is the obsolete in reverse. The future is always going backwards. Our future tends to be prehistoric. I see no point in utilizing technology or industry as an end in itself, or as an affirmation of anything. That has nothing to do with art. They are just tools. If you make a system you can be sure the system is bound to evade itself, so I see no point in pinning any hopes on systems. A system is just an expansive object, and eventually it all contracts back to points. If I ever saw a system or an object, then I might be interested, but to me they are only manifestations of thought that end up in language. It is a language problem more than anything else. It all comes down to that. . . . As long as art is thought of as creation, it will be the same old story. Here we go again, creating objects, creating systems, building a better tomorrow. I posit that there is no tomorrow, nothing but a gap, a yawning gap. That seems sort of tragic, but what immediately relieves it is irony, which gives you a sense of humor. It is that cosmic sense of humor that makes it all tolerable. Everything just vanishes. The sites are receding into the nonsites, and the nonsites are receding back to the sites. It is always back and forth, to and fro. Discovering places for the first time, then not knowing them. . . . Actually it is the mistakes we make that result in something. There is no point in trying to come up with the right answers because it is inevitably wrong. Every philosophy will turn against itself and it will always be refuted. The object or the system will always crush its originator. Eventually he will be overthrown and be replaced by another series of lies. It is like going from one happy lie to another happy lie with a cheerful sense about everything. An art against itself is a good possibility, an art that always returns to essential contradiction. I'm sick of positivists, ontological hopes, and that sort of thing, even ontological despairs. Both are impossible.

Street Works I. March 15, 24 hours, between Madison Avenue and Sixth Avenue, 42nd and 52nd Streets, New York City. Organized by Hannah Weiner, Marjorie Strider, John Perreault. Some of the works published in *0–9,* supplement to no. 6, July, 1969. Participants: Acconci, Arakawa, Battcock, Burton, Byars, Castoro, Costa, Creston, Giorno, Kaltenbach, Levine, Lippard, B. Mayer, Monk, Patterson, Perreault, Strider (Rep.), Mr. T., Waldman, H. Weiner. Reviewed by John Perreault, *Village Voice,* March 27, 1969. Included:

John Perreault, Street Music I:

From one o'clock in the afternoon until ten minutes after three, beginning at 42nd Street and Madison Avenue, criss-crossing back and forth between Madison and Sixth all the way up to 52nd Street, I . . . made telephone calls from one telephone booth to another, letting the phone ring three times each time. The work was invisible and for the most part inaudible. . . . Street Music II, executed for Street Works II,

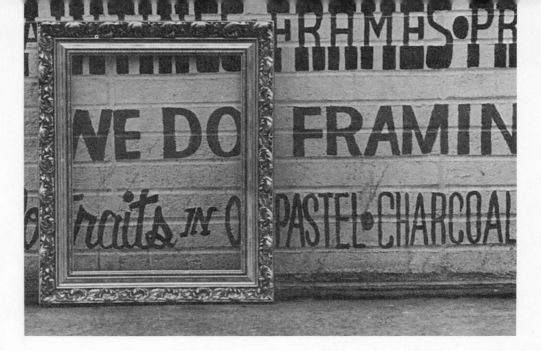

Marjorie Strider. *Street Work.* 1969.

Street Works I . . . . 30 empty picture frames were hung in the area, to create instant paintings and to call the attention of passers-by to their environment. March 15. (Above)

Street Works II . . . . I performed the same work in a different area. In both these works, most of the frames were taken home by people on the streets. April 18.

Street Works III . . . . A large felt banner (about ten feet long) on which was lettered the word PICTURE FRAME, was hung in the area. May 25.

Street Works IV . . . . (Sponsored by the Architectural League of New York). A 10′ x 15′ picture was placed in front of the entrance to the Architectural League, forcing people to walk through the picture plane. October.

Street Works V . . . . Taped frames were placed on the sidewalk, creating more picture spaces for people to walk through. December 21.

Friday, April 18,1969, between five and six o'clock, telephone booth located on 14th Street between Fifth and Sixth Avenues in New York City. I made phone calls to all the telephone booths I had used in Street Music I, retracing my route by telephone. As in Street Music I, I let each telephone ring three times and then hung up. Street Music III was also done the same day. There are two sets of phone booths on 14th Street between Fifth and Sixth Avenues. I made telephone calls from one booth to another. From telephone booth A to telephone booth D and from telephone booth C to telephone booth B, leaving the receivers off their hooks so that the telephones rang continuously. Hardly anyone noticed. . . . Street Music IV consisted of the following: from your own home telephone, ring all the telephone numbers I collected during Street Music I and reused for Street Music II. (Numbers listed; maps of phone patterns included.)

Robert Huot. Paula Cooper Gallery, New York, March 29–April 25, 1969. Fifteen-page catalogue, primarily photographs of tape and other architectural detail pieces executed in private houses. Exhibition consists of: *Two Blue Walls (Pratt & Lambert #5020 Alkyd)*; *Sanded Floor Coated with Polyurethane; Shadows Cast by Architectural Details and Fixtures Using Available Light.* (Rep.) Reviewed by Don McDonagh, "Oh, Wall," *Financial Times* (London), July 16, 1969 (also covers Siegelaub's January show).

Brøegger, Stig. *21. Marts 1969/ March 21, 1969.* Forty-page book, primarily photographs; 1969 edition, 3 xerox copies; 1970 edition, 500, published by Jysk/Kunstgalerie, Copenhagen.

Donald Burgy. Bennett College Art Gallery, Millbrook, N.Y., March 5–25. Artist's statement:
Art cannot be the source of new art. Art is exhibiting signs of historical pattern exhaustion. Therefore, art appearances, media, techniques, and designs cannot be the concern. Art cannot assume a life of its own; it must reaffirm its vitality by being in the world.

Objective information about selected aspects of the natural world and samples of those aspects are being presented by Donald Burgy. . . .

This information is presented as mathematical, verbal and visual statements. The samples are natural. The work exists as a relationship formed by the observer in his understanding of the information and his experiences of the samples.

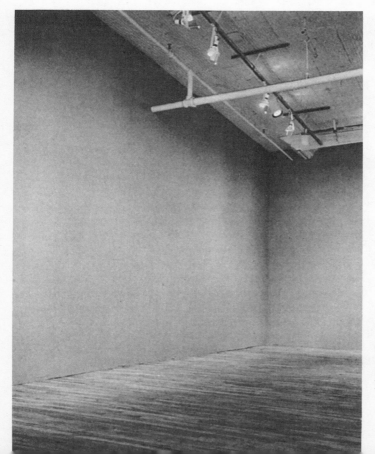

Robert Huot. *Two Blue Walls (Pratt and Lambert # 5020 Alkyd), Sanded Floor Coated with Polyurethane.* March–April, 1969. Paula Cooper Gallery, New York.

Joseph Kosuth, Robert Morris. Bradford Junior College, Bradford, Mass., March, 1969. Organized by Seth Siegelaub and Douglas Huebler. Seminar March 25.

Kosuth:
1. II. Relation (Art as Idea as Idea) 1968 [one of a series of works taken from the categories of Roget's *Thesaurus*]:
   Consisting of 3 parts:
   A. Absolute Relation
   B. Partial Relation
   C. Correspondence of Relationship
Each part will appear separately in 3 local publications.

* * *

Morris:
1. There are two temperatures: one outside, one inside. 1969.

Robert Morris: Aluminum, Asphalt, Clay, Copper, Felt, Glass, Lead, Nickel, Rubber, Stainless, Thread, Zinc. Leo Castelli, March 1–22, 1969.
These and other materials (including chemicals, dirt, water) were changed each day of the show in the morning and were open to the public in the afternoon, the artist choosing to use the gallery as his studio. Each day the changes were photographed, and after about a one-and-a-half-day time lag, the photographs were posted in the gallery. The materials underwent drastic changes during the show, but the results were less important to the artist than the fact of change and his three-week commitment to continue those changes. The end of the show consisted of the removal of all the material (well over a ton), which was tape-recorded. On the last day, the gallery held only the photographs and the sound of the piece's ultimate destruction, reversing the procedure of Morris's influential "Box with the Sound of Its Own Making" (1961).

John Latham (pieces mailed to L.R.L. March 24, 1969): Initial Premise: That "material" is steadystate idea, i.e., "habit."

In the given material:	*The Sculpture:*
Preconceptions about value	Persuade industrialists to take artists into their organizations and pay them as *opposition to dollar accountancy.* (Copyright APG London, 1965.)
Preconceptions about words	Review a dictionary without using words.
Preconceptions on physics	Define the least.
Preconceptions about economics	Account in units of attention.

art and economics (2): I am systematically not paid for work.

Ashton, Dore. "New York." *Studio International,* March, 1969.

Constable, Rosalind. "The New Art: Big Ideas for Sale." *New York,* March 10, 1969.

Dorfles, Gillo. "Arte concettuale o arte povera." *Art International,* March, 1969.

Hamilton, Richard. "Photography and Painting." *Studio International,* March, 1969.

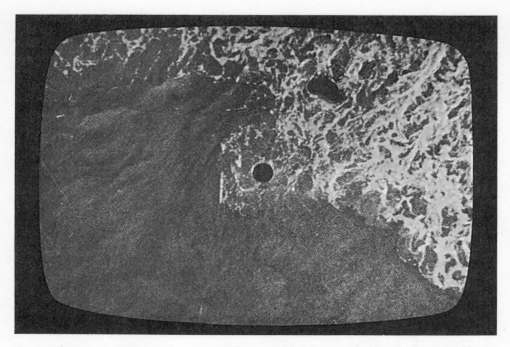

Barry Flanagan. *Hole in the Sea*. Still from the TV film. Scheveningen, Holland. February, 1969. Courtesy Videogalerie Gerry Schum, Düsseldorf.

"It's not that sculpture can be seen as more things and in new ways within an expanding convention, but that the premise of sculptural thought and engagement is showing itself as a more sound and relevant basis for operation in the culture." (Feb., 1969)

"I prefer working with the essential stuff of sculpture rather than my own 'ambitions' for it. This way I hope to find things. . . . What I like to do is to make visual and material inventions and propositions. I don't like the idea of inventing a rationale to accompany the work. The tradition is only a collection of rationales. I don't like to invent an involvement or the terms of an involvement; I prefer to fabricate the sculptures." (1971)

"I was interested in typical, general visual configurations that command our attention. This for me was the fabrication of a formal involvement." (1971)

Land Art. Fernsehgalerie Gerry Schum, Cologne. Catalogue of films commissioned by the gallery from Long (*Walking a Straight 10 Mile Line*), Flanagan (*Hole in the Sea*) (Rep.), Oppenheim (*Time Track*), Smithson (*Fossil Quarry Mirror*), Boezem (*Sandfountain*), Dibbets (*12 Hours Tide Object with Correction of Perspective*), de Maria (*Two Lines, Three Circles on the Desert*), Heizer (*Coyote*); transmitted on German television April 15. Documentation, reproductions, biographies, texts by the artists and by Schum:

The TV gallery exists only in a series of transmissions. . . . One of our ideas is communication of art instead of possession of art objects. . . . This conception made it necessary to find a new system to pay the artists and to cover the expenses for the realization of art projects for the TV show. Our solution is that we sell the right of publication, a kind of copyright, to the TV station.

Street Works II. 13th–14th Streets, Fifth and Sixth Avenues, New York, 5–6 p.m., April 18.

Original participants plus a great many others, including Arakawa, Burton, Gins, Graham, Kosuth, Piper, Venet, L. Weiner. Reviewed by John Perreault, *Village Voice,* May 1, 1969.

Hannah Weiner arranged a meeting with another woman whose name was the same as hers; Scott Burton walked around the block dressed as a female shopper and was totally unrecognized. Steve Kaltenbach's piece was a "Guide to a Metropolitan Museum of Modern Art," a map of the block with numbers directing attention to 36 found "works."

18'6'' × 6'9'' × 11'2¹/₂'' × 47' × 11'³/₁₆'' × 29'8¹/₂'' × 31'9³/₁₆''. San Francisco Art Institute, April 11–May 3, 1969. Organized by Eugenia Butler. Asher, Barry, Baxter, Byars, Butler, Huebler, Kaltenbach, Kienholz, Kosuth, Le Va, Oppenheim, Orr, Rudnick, Watts, Weiner.

Invisible Painting and Sculpture. Richmond Art Center, Calif., April 24–June 1, 1969. Organized by Tom Marioni.

Robert Barry/ Inert Gas Series/ Helium, Neon, Argon, Krypton, Xenon/ From a measured volume to indefinite expansion/ April 1969/ Seth Siegelaub, 6000 Sunset Boulevard, Hollywood, California, 90028/213 HO 4-8383 (full text of poster). Gallery is only a phone number. The gases were released by the artist on the beach, in the desert, in the mountains, etc., around Los Angeles. (Rep.)

George Brecht: *The Book of the Tumbler on Fire; Selected Works from Volume I,* Los Angeles County Museum of Art, April 15–May 18, 1969:

"*The Book of the Tumbler on Fire* is a continuing work begun in Spring of 1964. It now consists of fourteen chapters which, with 35 footnotes, an index, and a title page, will comprise the first volume. The book might be called a research into the continuity of un-like things; of objects with each other, of objects and events, of scores and objects, of events in time, of objects and styles, etc." (Brecht.)

7. (to Chapter VIII, page 1) Unpainted wooden chair with infrared lamp. "The

Robert Barry. *Inert Gas Series: Argon.* Photo showing gas returning to the atmosphere. Pacific Ocean, Santa Monica, California. 1969.

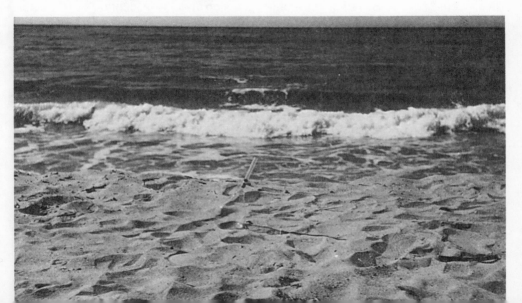

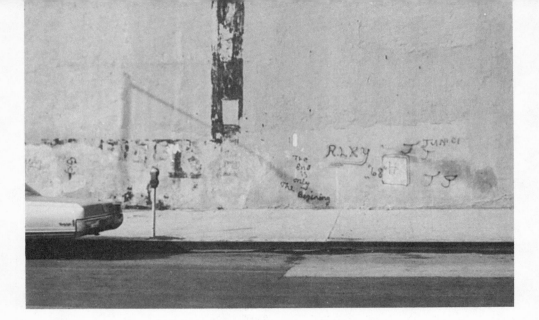

Richard Artschwager. *Blp.* New York City. 1969.

smallest colony in the world is Pitcairn Island with an area of 1.5 square miles."

10. (to Chapter VI, frame 85) Green chair with leash and brush. "The duration record of sitting in a tree is 55 days from 10 A.M. 22 July to 10 A.M. 15 Sept. 1930 by David William Haskell (born 1920) on a 4 foot by 6 foot platform up a backyard walnut tree in Wilmar (now Rosemond) California, U.S.A.

Scott Burton. *Four Changes.* April 28, 1969, Hunter College, New York:
    A performer faces the audience, stage center, wearing a shirt and a pair of pants the same color, color A. He removes the shirt, revealing under it an identical shirt of color B. He removes the pants, revealing under them an identical pair of color B. He removes the shirt, revealing an identical shirt of color A. He removes the shirt, revealing an identical shirt of color B. He removes the pants, revealing an identical pair of color B.

5 Works by Lawrence Weiner. NSCAD, Halifax, April 7–27, 1969:
    2. A wall pitted by a single air rifle shot
    4. Two common steel nails driven into the floor one directly in line with the other at points determined at the time of installation

Lee Lozano. *I Ching Piece,* started April 21, 1969, and continuing (Rep.):
Chart I. (April 21–October 29, 1969)—Hexagrams, time.
    Total no. of questions asked: 3,087.
        Total no. of days on which questions asked: 165.
        Average no. of questions asked per day: 18.7.
        Hexagram most frequently ret'n'd: H.33 (Withdrawal), (117) times.
        Hexagram least frequently ret'n'd: H.15 (Modesty), (60) times.

Chart 2. (April 21–November 20, 1969)—Changing Lines.
  Changing line most frequently ret'n'd: H.23, line 2, (24) times.
  Changing line least frequently ret'n'd: H.63, line 6, (2) times.
Chart 3. (April 21–November 20, 1969)—Subject Matter of Questions.
  Subject A: H.33, (17) times.
  Subject B: H.47, (26) times.
  Subject C: H.18, (15) times.
Chart 4. (Started December 11, 1969 and continuing). Old Yang, Young Yang,
  Young Yin, Old Yin lines.
(More information available from the artist.)

Lee Lozano. One page from notebook of *I Ching Charts*. 1969.

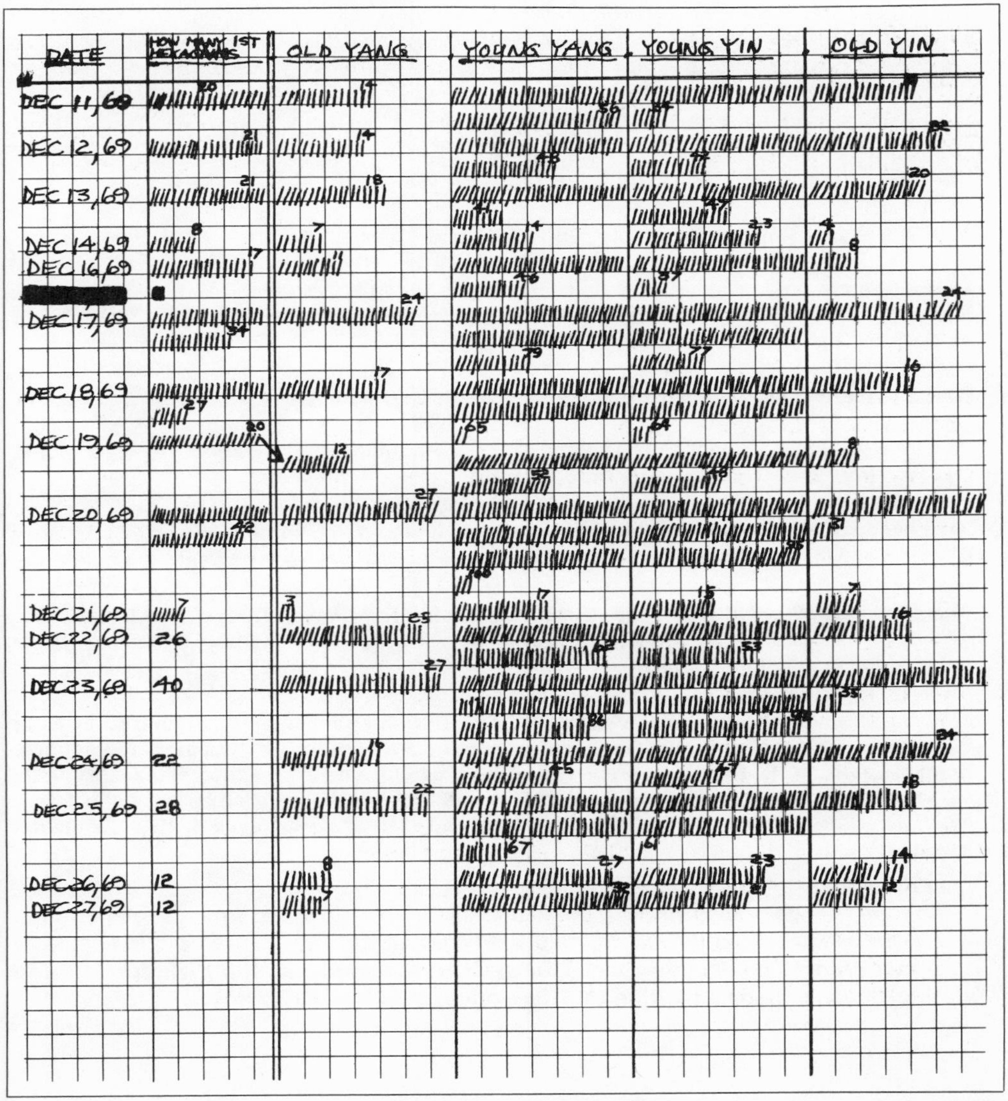

DATE	HOW MANY 1ST HEXAGRAMS	OLD YANG	YOUNG YANG	YOUNG YIN	OLD YIN
DEC 11, 69					
DEC 12, 69					
DEC 13, 69					
DEC 14, 69					
DEC 16, 69					
DEC 17, 69					
DEC 18, 69					
DEC 19, 69					
DEC 20, 69					
DEC 21, 69	7				
DEC 22, 69	26				
DEC 23, 69	40				
DEC 24, 69	22				
DEC 25, 69	28				
DEC 26, 69	12				
DEC 27, 69	12				

Lee Lozano, *Dialogue Piece:*

Call, write or speak to people you might not otherwise see for the specific purpose of inviting them to your loft for a dialogue.

In process perpetually from date of first call (April 21, 1969). Date of first interest in dialogues—1948. Date of decision to pursue (i.e., extend) investigation of dialogues —April 8, 1969.

Note: The purpose of this piece is to have dialogues, not to make a piece. No recordings or notes are made during dialogues, which exist solely for their own sake as joyous social occasions. (More information available from the artist.)

Lozano's "conceptual" work, conceived simultaneously with the end of a large series of paintings on wave phenomena, combine art and life to an extreme extent. Unlike most "instruction" or "command" pieces, for example, Lozano's are directed to herself, and she has carried them out scrupulously, no matter how difficult to sustain they may be. Her art, it has been said, becomes the means by which to transform her life, and, by implication, the lives of others and of the planet itself.

"Boezem—Ger van Elk." *Museumjournaal,* April, 1969. A dialogue.

Chandler, John Noel. "More Words on Curnoe's Wordly World." *Artscanada,* April, 1969.

Morris, Robert. "Notes on Sculpture, Part 4: Beyond Objects." *Artforum,* April, 1969.

Reise, Barbara, ed. "Minimal Art." Special issue of *Studio International,* April, 1964; includes Reise, "Untitled 1969: A Footnote on Minimal Stylehood," Smithson, "Aerial Art," "An Opera by Carl Andre," and LeWitt, "Drawing Series 1968 (Fours)."

Restany, Pierre. "Le redoutable pauvreté de l'antiforme." *Combat,* April, 1969.

Van Schaardenburg, Lieneke. "Kunstpromotor Seth Siegelaub: Jedereen Kan nu Kunst maken." *Het Parool* (Amsterdam), April 12, 1969.

Art-Language: The Journal of Conceptual Art, no. 1, May, 1969: Introduction by editors Terry Atkinson and Michael Baldwin; contributions by LeWitt, Graham, Weiner, Bainbridge, Baldwin.

The New York Graphic Workshop at the Manufacturers Hanover Trust's Safe Deposit Box #3001. New York, May 1–June 20, 1969. Camnitzer, Porter, Castillo, Plate. Exhibition visible only by documentation in mailer.

Simon Fraser Exhibition, May 19–June 19, 1969. Burnaby (Vancouver). Organized by Seth Siegelaub. Atkinson and Baldwin (Art-Language), Barry, Dibbets, Huebler, Kaltenbach, Kosuth, LeWitt, N. E. Thing Co., Weiner. Symposium held June 17 at Simon Fraser University via telephone hook-up from New York, Ottawa, and Burnaby. Reviewed by Charlotte Townsend, *Vancouver Sun,* May 30, 1969; Joan Lowndes, *The Province,* June 6, 1969. Exhibition includes:

Robert Barry:

Telepathic Piece, 1969. (During the exhibition I will try to communicate telepathically a work of art, the nature of which is a series of thoughts that are not applicable to language or image.) At the conclusion of the exhibition the information about the work of art was made known in this catalogue.

Stephen Kaltenbach:

POSTULATE: University administrations are set to function in certain patterns which allow very minimal latitude for response.

COMMUNICATIONS PROCEDURE:

Act 1. Offer problems which cannot be dealt with through existing (postulated) channels.

Act 2. Determine which aspects of the system were responsible for failures produced by Act #1.

Act 3. Address criticism toward these areas.

---

81 Greene Street
New York, N.Y. 10012
22 May 1969

Iain Baxter
N. E. Thing Co. Ltd.
c/o National Gallery of Canada
Ottawa 4, Ontario -CANADA-

Dear Iain,

 Will you please aid me in the delivery of my work for the May 19 to June 19 show at Simple Simon U.? My first two attempts malfunctioned at your end putting be in a bind.

 I'll explain: My first proposal was a request for 200 dollars for a piece, the nature of which could not be disclosed. This proved unᴸ acceptable to S. S. U. because the money available for the show had to be spent through normal University channels.

 The second proposal was that the university place the following ad in the Vancouver Sun for the duration of the show.

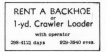

RENT A BACKHOE
or
1-yd. Crawler Loader
with operator
298-4121 days   929-3940 eves.

The universities counter-proposal that they run the Ad in the college paper would have radically altered the nature of the original art action. for the following reasons:

 1. The ad is a duplicate of an existing ad in the Vancouver Sun.
 2. The company which runs the (original) ad belongs to my brother.
 3. He would have removed his ad when Simple Simon U. placed their's causing no net physical visible change.
 4. The revalation of reasons 2 and 3 whould have radically altered this art action.

 My third proposal is that you determine to the best of your ability who or what was responsible for these failures and deliver from me to them or it a severe tongue-lashing. You may organize the exact text of this tirade but I would offer the following words as possibilities: narrow-minded, penny-pinching; provincial perhaps. You may use foul language.

 Sincerely yours,

 Stephen Kaltenbach

What I will make available sometime is that I had planned the entire thing when I was approached to make a communication piece. I tried to think of an aspect of the university itself that I could communicate or talk about or expose; the set up in schools, even the School of Visual Arts, for handling things like this is generally pretty rigid and there isn't much latitude for accepting things, so that is what I decided to expose. I made a couple of proposals that I specifically felt would be unacceptable for one reason or another to expose that unacceptability. Of course, one of them might have been accepted, which would have drowned my whole plan, but it worked out very nicely. That kind of mystery-story thing, keeping the real ending until last, is something I have always liked in literature, and I like it in my own work too. (Kaltenbach, in interview with P.A. Norvell; see above, pp. 84–87).

Number 7. **Paula Cooper Gallery, New York, May 18–June 15, 1969. Organized by Lucy R. Lippard.**

The large room of the gallery, apparently "empty," contained works by Barry (a magnetic field), Weiner (pit in wall from one shot of air-rifle), Wilson (oral communication), Kaltenbach (secret), Haacke (air currents from small fan by door), Huot (existing shadows), Artschwager (black blip inside, one visible from the window, and others in the street), and a very fragile lead cable piece by Andre. (Rep.) The smaller room contained a floor sculpture of tree branches by Bollinger, a Bochner measurement, a LeWitt wall drawing, Kosuth's Investigation (from Art as Idea as Idea) on wall labels, photographs by Smithson and Kirby, a de Maria text, an uncompleted Serra lead spatter piece, a Castoro wall cracking. (Rep.) All of the other participants were

Left: Carl Andre. Untitled. Cut cable wires, 108″. 1969. Paula Cooper Gallery, New York. *Right:* Rosemary Castoro. *Room Cracking #7.* May, 1969. Paula Cooper Gallery, New York.

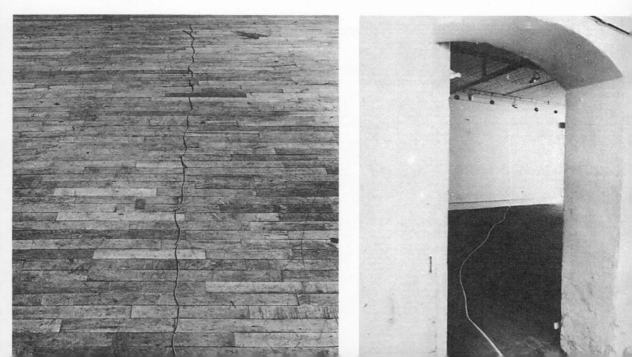

Donald Burgy.
From *Lie Detector.*
1969.

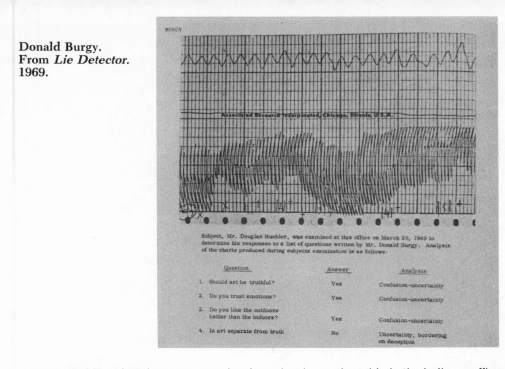

Subject, Mr. Douglas Huebler, was examined at this office on March 20, 1969 to determine his responses to a list of questions written by Mr. Donald Burgy. Analysis of the charts produced during subjects examination is as follows:

Question	Answer	Analysis
1. Should art be truthful?	Yes	Confusion–uncertainty
2. Do you trust emotions?	Yes	Confusion–uncertainty
3. Do you like the outdoors better than the indoors?	Yes	Confusion–uncertainty
4. Is art separate from truth	No	Uncertainty, bordering on deception

represented by printed matter—notebooks or books on the table in the hallway-office (Art & Language, Barthelme, Beery, Borofsky, Burgy (Rep.), Darboven, Dibbets, Graham, Huebler, Kaltenbach, Kawara, Kinmont, Kozlov, Long, Lozano, Lunden, Morris, Nauman (a tape recording), N. E. Thing Co. (a Telex machine and results of its operations during the show), N.Y. Graphic Workshop, Piper, Ruppersberg, Ruscha, Venet, Weiner. Reviewed by John Perreault, Village Voice, June 5, 1969. Following two works from the show:

Christine Kozlov: 271 Blank Sheets of Paper Corresponding to 271 Days of Concepts Rejected. February–October, 1968.

*   *   *

Lee Lozano, *Grass Piece* (April 2, 1969) [Footnotes at end of the piece.]:

Make a good score, a lid or more of excellent grass. Smoke it "up" as fast as you can. Stay high all day, every day. See what happens. (April 1, 1969)

One thing that happens is that it takes more and more grass to get feelin good. Immunity building up? (April 17, 1969)

The amount of grass needed to get high has stabilized itself. Tonight I started to smoke the last container of cleaned shit. When that is gone there are twigs to smoke and a lot of seeds which I'll eat.* (This has been a scintillating piece but I'd like to finish it in a flash.) Decided on next piece: Go without grass for the same amount of time.

> "Seek the extremes,
> That's where all
> The action is."   (April 24, 69)

I get more tired every day. This feeling wasted might be from smoking so much grass, or from working so hard, which I've been doing, or from the monotonousness of my days.† (April 29, 1969)

I'll end the *Grass Piece* with a fanfare: a cap of mescaline Kaltenbach gave me.° (May 2, 1969)

Not high anymore, just numb.● Finished grass, twigs and seeds△ about an hour ago. (May 3, 1969)

NOTE: Aside from when I woke up (down) in the morning there were two occasions when I wasn't stoned on grass during this piece, about a couple of hours each.○

---

*Nuthin happened from eating seeds. Nothing *could* happen: seeds can't make you high and only give headache. Do not smoke or eat seeds.

†Due to *General Strike Piece* during which I stay home almost all the time. (In process, as of May 16, 1969)

°This was postponed due to circumstances beyond my control. Finally took mescaline: May 11, 1969. It blanked out, must've been a dull pill, a bad cap.

● I believe this piece is a good example of Heisenberg's "Uncertainty principle," applied quantum mechanics: *The act of observing something changes it.* The piece made me numb, not the grass.

△Not feeling any effect from eating seeds might have been due to being so stoned from smoking twigs? Wrong.

○ And after No Grass Piece, only a few days when I haven't been stoned since (not including the week I spent in Halifax. My investigation of grass continues. . . . (January 21, 1971)

The Appearing/Disappearing Image Object. **Newport Harbor Art Museum, Balboa, California, May 11–June 28. Organized by Tom Garver. Baldessari, Le Va, Ruppersberg, Edge, Cooper, Rudnick, Asher.**

Street Works III. **May 25, Between Prince and Grand, Greene and Wooster Streets, New York, 9 p.m.–midnight. This show was entirely open; everyone was invited to do works.**

Language III. **Dwan Gallery, New York, May 24–June 18, 1969.**

Perreault, John. "Para-Visual." *Village Voice,* **June 5, 1969. Review of** *Language III* **and** *Number 7.*

Ecologic Art. **John Gibson, New York, May 17–June 28, 1969. Andre, Christo, Dibbets, Hutchinson, Insley, Long, Morris, Oldenburg, Oppenheim, Smithson.**

Anti-Illusion: Procedures/Materials. **Whitney Museum of American Art, New York, May 19–July 16, 1969. Organized by Marcia Tucker and James Monte. Texts by the editors and the artists, bibliography. Andre, Asher, Bollinger, Duff, Ferrer, Fiore, Glass, Hesse, Jenney, Le Va, Lobe, Morris, Nauman, Reich, Rohm, Ryman, Serra, Shapiro, Snow, Sonnier, Tuttle. Reviewed by Peter Schjeldahl,** *Art International,* **September, 1969.**

Mel Bochner, Measurements. **Galerie Heiner Friedrich, Munich, May 9–31, 1969 (Rep.):**

All works made in Munich during the week of May 1–May 8, 1969. Exhibition to include all and only those works possible to make in one week with material available.

Three Procedural Groups to be Worked From:

Group A: Exteriorated measurements—any stable object, material or place oriented to a system outside itself (declaration of position) *coordinated.*

Group B: Situated measurements—the measurements of a stable object or place mark directly onto it (Super-imposed).

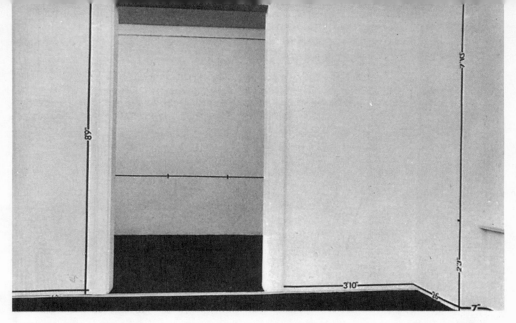

Mel Bochner. *Measurement Series: Group B 1967.* Black tape on wall. Installation: Galerie Heiner Friedrich, Münich. 1969.

Group C: Comparative measurements—any stable object, material of place related to pre-determined given standard (Sectioned).

The measurement series, continuing to the present, began with two sketches in 1967 that were seriously developed from the summer of 1968 on. The theme is one that has engaged "idea artists" from Duchamp's standard stoppages to Jasper Johns's paintings and Robert Morris's lead reliefs; Bochner's concerns are theoretical rather than metaphorical, his focus being on actual measurement and its direct implications rather than on the indirect and accumulative references used in previous art.

"On May 9 (Friday), May 12 (Monday) and May 30 (Friday), 1969, at 3:00 Greenwich Mean Time (9:00 EST) Jan Dibbets will make the gesture indicated on the overside at the place marked X in Amsterdam, Holland." Mailing "exhibition"—a picture postcard of the artist, thumb cryptically raised, on a balcony in Amsterdam; published by Seth Siegelaub. Dibbets won a national prize for this work and was awarded a trip to New York. Reviewed by Louwrien Wijers, "Wereldtentoonstelling per briefkaart," *Algemeen Handelsblad,* May 29, 1969.

Ammann, Jean-Christophe. "Perspective Corrections." *Art International,* May, 1969 (on Dibbets).

This Way (Stanley) Brouwn, Art and Project Bulletin, no. 8, May 31–June 25, 1969. Documentation, biography, bibliography of Brouwn's work.

May 14, London: Gilbert and George serve David Hockney "The Meal" before an audience at Ripley House, as a work of art. For an account, see *Studio International,* May, 1970.

David Lamelas, Galerie Yvon Lambert, Paris, May, 1969: A five-minute interview between Marguerite Duras and Raoul Escari was held and filmed on April 26. Ten photos were taken at irregular intervals during the interview and ten phrases were chosen from the interview; the combination constitutes the piece.

John and Barbara Latham, eds., NOIT NOW (with *APG news,* no. 1), London, May, 1969:
"In 1965 the art gallery appeared to be folding, or to be no longer relevant in London except insofar as it could further the series one called art—which went along by pressure of anti-art. The APG (Artists Placement Group) probe . . . was never a scheme for helping artists, or for raising money, for that matter. . . . Art was to scrub off—all kinds of stuff, systems, things, science, painting, ideas, love, boredom, politics, whatever it was, art was to defy it—maggots. Art was your actual opposition. [APG proposed, among other things] that industrial concerns, whose materials and equipment are of special interest to the artists we put forward, should incorporate within their salaried staff a practicing free artist, or graduate from an Art College, or even a small group of two or three."

In 1970, APG proposed to "set up under the auspices of the Ministry of Technology a body whose function would be to examine and cultivate *methods of raising levels of attention throughout the community* and of reducing problems brought about by redundant information." The idea is to insert an artist into the conventional mechanism, or habits, of industry as interruptive (not destructive) factor that would stimulate or generate new attitudes. "*Motivation* and *Structure* have become one and the same." (John Latham.)

Goldin, Amy. "Sweet Mystery of Life." *Art News,* May, 1969. On Kaltenbach, Oppenheim, Morris, etc:
Esthetic experiences are easier and purer than art *because* they're less consequential. Unlike art, the embodiment of an esthetic idea is informal. It sets no constraints on the idea and offers no clue to its human significance. . . . To deny this work the status of art is to claim that art is defined by a special kind of structure which this art lacks. You can refuse that premise and take the alternative one, defining art as a special sort of intention and response. Then this work is simply a new kind of art. I believe that art *is* a kind of structure and, consequently, that artistic value is beside the point here. The esthetic situation is pre-artistic, which is not to deny that some of this work is interesting, intriguing and delightful. At its most inventive, it has the mystery and charm of life itself. It is the toughness of art that is lacking.

Shirey, David. "Impossible Art." *Art in America,* May–June, 1969.

Arte Povera 1967–69. **Galleria La Bertesca, Genoa, June 25–30, 1969. Anselmo, Boetti, Icaro, Merz, Pistoletto, Prini, Zorio. Text by Germano Celant.**

Look at the N. E. Thing Company/ Voyez La Compagnie N. E. Thing. **National Gallery of Canada, Ottawa, June 4–July 6, 1969. Primarily reproductions and documentation of pieces done elsewhere before the show.**

N. E. Thing Co. Report on the Activities of the N. E. Thing Co. of North Vancouver, British Columbia, at the National Gallery of Canada, Ottawa, and other locations, June 4–July 6, 1969. **In French and English; biography, bibliography, list of projects, ACTS, ARTS, photos of exhibition environment and conference held in June at the museum. Among the participants in the conference were Iain and Elaine Baxter (presidents of NETCo.), Anne Brodszky, David Silcox, Greg Curnoe, John Chandler, Lucy Lippard, Seth Siegelaub, Brydon Smith, Mark Whitney, etc.:**

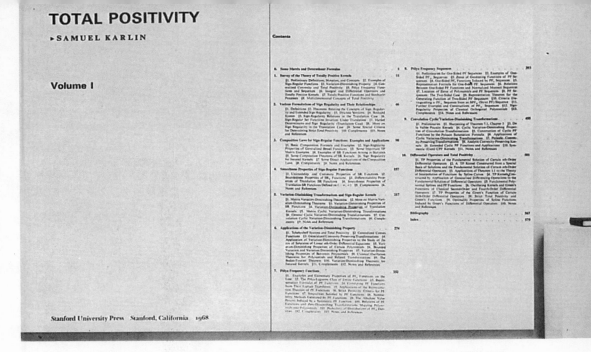

Bernar Venet. *Total Positivity*. Presentation of the book with enlargement of title page and contents. 1969.

Baxter: The thing that really interests me is that there are all kinds of information around—liquid information. IBM is interested in multiplying and collating information. Xerox is interested in copying information and there are also guys around who handle information purely for its own sake, and that's what I call visual informers. We call what we do Visual Sensitivity Information because it's a different way of looking at what the word "art" is. It gets at a broader area. Like you can start talking to a guy in the street or a businessman and if I say art he says, oh, Rembrandt. . . .

Siegelaub: It doesn't present you with speculations but with fact, and that's a critical difference. A painting is identical to its presentation, but now there's a body of work where the original of the art, the fact of the art, is not the presentation of the art. How you become aware of something is not what the thing is about. They are two different things. In other words, Iain can put something on the wall but it's not about something on the wall, it's about something that might be on the north coast of Southeast Asia. . . . Iain can be drawing attention to a very specific pile of rubbish and he's not even touching it; he's doing as little as possible to tell you it exists.

Summer: NETCo. executes a series of "landscapes" by erecting signs along roads in the countryside, appropriately spaced, and reading: "You will soon be passing by a $^1/_3$ mile N. E. Thing Co. Landscape"; "Start Viewing"; "You are now in the middle of the N. E. Thing Co. Landscape"; "Stop Viewing."

Lippard, Lucy R. "Iain Baxter: New Spaces." *Artscanada, June 1969. Special issue on "The Elements" also includes John Chandler, "Hans Haacke: The Continuity of Change."*

Gassiot-Talabot. "La Proposition de Buren." *Opus International,* no. 12, June, 1969.

June 4, Slade School of Fine Art, London: "Gilbert and George the Sculptors Present 'Underneath the Arches' (the most intelligent, fascinating, serious and beautiful art piece you have ever seen)."

Luis Camnitzer, Liliana Porter. The New York Graphic Workshop, Museo Nacional de Bellas Artes, Santiago de Chile, June 20–July 6, 1969. Text by Camnitzer and "algunas lineas por Lucy Lippard."

Sea Works. "Twelve days of Sea Works to be performed by Schuldt, Savannah, Georgia, 20 June 1969–2 July 1969, Antwerp. . . . The due performance of the programme is subject to maritime conventions, safety and security regulations, weather and the conditions set out by the vessel's owners."

Smithson, Robert. "Toward the Development of an Air Terminal Site." *Artforum,* June, 1969.

Mellow, James R. "Art Beyond Art." *New Leader,* June 23, 1969.

Millet, Catherine. "Petit Lexique de l'art pauvre." *Les Lettres Françaises,* June 4, 1969.

Tilson, Joe. "5 Questions Answered." *Art and Artists,* June, 1969. (On photography and words in art.)

July, 1969, Art Press, New York: Untitled periodical including contributions from Burn, Piper, Ramsden, Cutforth, Kaltenbach, LeWitt, Nelson (published by The Society for Theoretical Art & Analyses). Excerpt from Ian Burn's "Dialogue":
1. Language suggests, through idea and viewer, a kind of dialogue or "conversation."
2. This creates an actual area of the work.
3. Participating in a dialogue gives the viewer new significance; rather than listening, he becomes involved in reproducing and inventing part of that dialogue.

July–August–September, 1969. Organized by Seth Siegelaub. Catalogue of exhibition taking place simultaneously in eleven different locations all over the world. (See below, p. 125.) Andre (The Hague), Barry (Baltimore), Buren (Paris), Dibbets (Amsterdam), Huebler (Los Angeles), Kosuth (Portales, N.M.), LeWitt (Düsseldorf), Long (Bristol, England), N. E. Thing Co. (Vancouver), Smithson (Yucatan), Weiner (Niagara Falls). Reviewed by Howard Junker, "Idea as Art," *Newsweek,* August 11, 1969.

Conception-Perception. Eugenia Butler Gallery, Los Angeles, July 1–25, 1969.

Letters. Long Beach, N.J., July 11–31, 1969. Organized by Phillip M. Simkin; text by Lenore Malen. Loose pages in a box; projects complete and incomplete, documentation, photographs by Bollinger, Christo, Ferrer, Fulton, Heizer, Hutchinson, Insley, LeWitt, Morris, Oppenheim, Ruthenbeck, Serra and Glass, Smithson, Sonnier. This catalogue provides an illustration of the difficulties and variety involved in such a loosely knit show. Included:

Richard Serra and Philip Glass: *Long Beach Island, Word Location,* June, 1969:
In a 30-acre area of marshland and coastline 32 polyplanar speakers were placed in chosen locations so as to cover the site.
The word *is* was recorded on a 15-minute tape loop and became the sound source for the speakers. The volume was controlled so that the speakers did not interrelate, but could only be heard within their proximity. In other words, two speakers could not be heard in the same area. Each sound dissolved in a given space.

The placement of a specific word in location points to the artificiality of a language. The imposition of the word as symbol negates the experience of the place. Conversely the experience of the place denies itself in relation to the word. (For by defining itself in relation to language it denies its meaningfulness independent of definition.)

Wall Show. Ace Gallery, Los Angeles, summer, 1969. Bochner, Ryman, LeWitt, Weiner, Huebler, Huot, consecutively executed wall pieces.

Joseph Beuys. Kunstmuseum, Basel, July–August. Texts by Josef Vander Gritten, Dieter Koepplin.

Darboven, Hanne. *6 Manuscript '69 (Kunstzeitung,* no. 3). Düsseldorf, Michelpresse, July, 1969. "Miscellaneous constructions derived from the dates of the year 1969."

Summer, 1969: Sullivan County, New York: Agnes Denes begins her "Dialectic Triangulation: A Visual Philosophy":
Rice was planted to represent life/growth, *trees* were chained to represent interference with life/growth (obstruction of cambium regeneration can result in mutation or death) and *Haiku* was buried to represent the idea/thought, absolute, abstract, etc.
Since this time, Denes's research into tri-grouping has led her into an infinite number of disciplines, including philosophy, ethics, psychography, anatomy, religion, botany. Excerpts from her text on the project follow:
Dialectic Triangulation is a simplification and systematic re-building of complexes on any subject or matter through various methods such as re-evaluation, regrouping or division, at times beginning with a single proposition, at others searching for the mean between two extremes. It is a building of progressive trichotomies, failing and succeeding in a dialectic method, each time arriving at a better thesis on a higher level—like changing scientific theories, which always advance and develop in complexity. . . . One can create oppositional theories or "span-balances," and from them form a third, derived from the first two on a higher plane and on to successive trichotomies (e.g., the art of yesterday re-evaluated by the art of today, preparing the road for the art of tomorrow, which in turn will be re-evaluated by future disciples). . . . It is an art process which exhibits the workings of hypotheses instead of hiding them behind symbols, juxtaposition of color and elimination or complication of form. The activating forces of triangulations apply differently to pure idea groups, for they are never animate. Pure ideas lie in wait at all times to be activated by an argument, or an opportunity. (Rep.)

Restany, Pierre. "Hyper avantgarde." *Le Nouveau planète,* July–August, 1969. (Also printed in *Pianeta,* September–October, 1969.)

Morris, Robert. *Earth Projects.* Announcement with text by the artist of a series of ten color lithographs made at the Detroit Workshop, summer and fall, 1969. Projects include Dust, Steam, Temperatures, Vibrations, Waterfall, Mounds and Trenches, Burning Petroleum.

Burton, Scott. "Time on Their Hands." *Art News,* summer, 1969.

Kostelanetz, Richard. "Inferential Art." *Columbia Forum,* summer, 1969.

Meyer, Ursula. "De-objectification of the Object." *Arts,* summer, 1969.

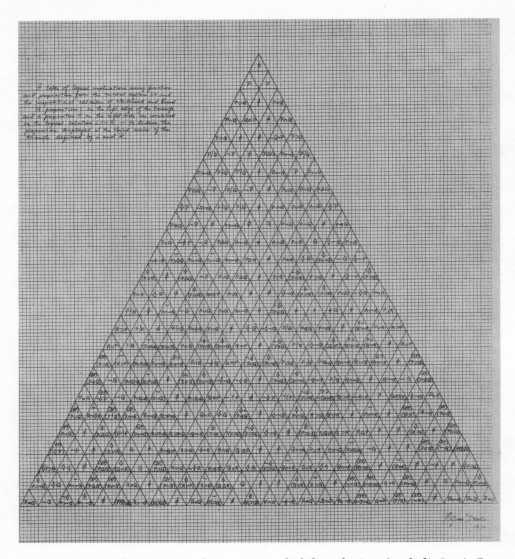

Agnes Denes. *Dialectic Triangulation: A Visual Philosophy into Symbolic Logic.* Part of the project: Exercises in logic. 1970.

A table of logical implications using functions and propositions from the modal system S8 and the propositional calculus of Whitehead and Russell. A proposition L on the left edge of the triangle, and a proposition R on the right side are combined in the logical relation L R, to deduce the proposition displayed at the third vertex of the triangle defined by L and R.

This triangle lists all logical human arguments, cutting the triangle vertically in half to produce a so-called Truth Table and Lie Table.

Wasserman, Emily. "Peter Hutchinson." *Artforum,* summer, 1969.

Late summer, Oxford, England: Student-organized exhibition in the garden of Christ Church College, Oxford University, includes Harvey, Flanagan, McLean, Lamelas, Long, Louw, Arnatt, Latham. Notebook on show is in the possession of Michael Harvey, New York.

Carl Andre. Gemeentemuseum, The Hague, August 23–October 5, 1969. Texts by Enno Develing, Hollis Frampton, and the artist.

"The Energy of a Real English Breakfast Transformed into Breaking a Real Steel Bar by the Artists Jan Dibbets and Reiner Ruthenbeck, London, August, 1969." Photographic piece on mailer from Konrad Fischer, Düsseldorf.

August, 1969: Gilbert and George perform as "living sculpture" and sing "Underneath the Arches" at the International Jazz Festival, Plumpton Race Course, Sussex.

Haber, Ira Joel. *Radio City Music Hall.* New York, August, 1969. List of films shown at the Music Hall from 1933 to 1969; pictures, plans, postcard, Christmas program (December 5, 1946), and billboards:

1937	1947
Lloyds of London	*The Yearling*
The Plough and the Stars	*The Sea of Grass*
On the Avenue	*The Late George Apley*
When You're in Love	*The Egg and I*
Fire Over England	*Great Expectations*
Wings of the Morning	*The Ghost and Mrs. Muir*
When's Your Birthday	*The Bachelor and the Bobby-Soxer*
Seventh Heaven	*Down to Earth*
Quality Street	*Song of Love*
The Woman I Love	*Cass Timberlane*
A Star is Born	*Good News*
Shall We Dance	
This Is my Affair	
Woman Chases Man	
Another Dawn	
Ever Since Eve	
New Faces of 1937	
Knight Without Armor	
The Toast of New York	
Stella Dallas	
Vogues of 1938	
The Prisoner of Zenda	
Lost Horizon	
Stage Door	
Victoria the Great	
The Awful Truth	
Stand In	
Nothing Sacred	
I'll Take Romance	
Tovarich	

August, Buenos Aires: New York Graphic Workshop sends four mail exhibitions from the Instituto Torcuato di Tella.

Celant, Germano. "La Natura e inserta." *Casabella,* August–September, 1969.

Free Media Bulletin, no. 1, Vancouver, 1969, Duane Lunden, Jeff Wall, Ian Wallace, eds. Loose texts and documents xeroxed from miscellaneous sources. "Contributors": Artaud, Burroughs, Duchamp, Eastlake, Huelsenbeck, Lunden, Reinhardt, Schwarz, Soleri, Toche, Trocchi, Vazan, Wall, Wallace.

Place and Process. Edmonton Art Gallery, Alberta, September 4–October 26, 1969. Organized by Willoughby Sharp and William Kirby. Andre, Dibbets, Heizer, Long, Morris, Weiner, N. E. Thing Co., Graham, van Saun, etc. Film made by Schley and Fiore. Discussed by Sharp in *Artforum,* November, 1969; see also *Artscanada,* October, 1969.

Projects Class. Nova Scotia College of Art and Design, Halifax, September, 1970. Organized by David Askevold. 12 cards, each of which outlines a project submitted to the class in the fall of 1969 by Barry, Bochner, Dibbets, Graham, Huebler, Kosuth, LeWitt, Lippard, N. E. Thing Co., Smithson, Weiner.

557,087. Seattle Art Museum (World's Fair Pavilion, Seattle Center), sponsored by The Contemporary Arts Council, September 5–October 5, 1969. Organized by Lucy R. Lippard. Catalogue consists of 95 4″ × 6″ index cards in random order; one card each designed by the artists themselves, 20 text cards by Lippard, 3 bibliography cards, list of films shown (Barry, Frampton, Gehr, Huot, Jacobs, Landow, Schum, Serra, Sharits, Snow, Wieland and *Land Art*).

Left: Gene Beery. *Note . . . (Planning for the Endless Aesthetic Visualization).* Acrylic, canvas. 5′ × 5′. 1969. This painting echoes Beery's roughly executed word paintings made in New York in the early 1960's and shown at the Iolas Gallery, New York, February–March 1963, the anti-estheticism of which seemed at the time to be aimed at the dominating "formalist" approach to art, "self-criticism," art about art, "valid and invalid" approaches to "high" art. Examples: "Sorry This Painting Temporarily OUT OF STYLE Closed for Updating Watch for Aesthetic Reopening," "Death in the Family. Painting CLOSED Till Further Notice." The Iolas show included painting-signs such as "The Exhibition Continues Around the Corner," etc. *Right:* Allen Ruppersberg. *Hay at the Ambassador.* Table, chair, hay, glass, hotel stationery. 1969.

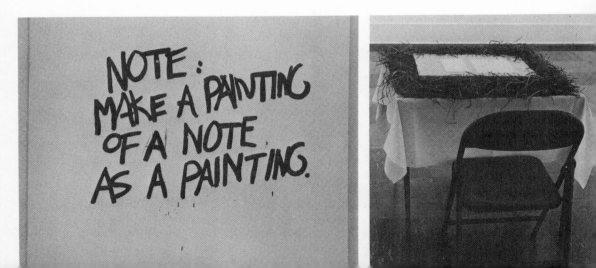

Artists: Acconci, Andre, Arnatt, Artschwager, Asher, Atkinson, Baldessari, Baldwin, Barry, Barthelme, Baxter, Beery (Rep.), Bochner, Bollinger, Borofsky, Burgy, Buren, Castoro, Darboven, de Maria, Dibbets, Ferrer, Flanagan, Graham, Haacke, Heizer, Hesse, Huebler, Huot, Kaltenbach, Kawara, Keinholz, Kinmont, Kosuth, Kozlov, Latham, Le Va, LeWitt, Louw, Lunden, McLean, Morris, Nauman, N.Y. Graphic Workshop, Nikolaides, Oppenheim, Perreault, Piper, Rohm, Ruppersberg (Rep.), Ryman, Ruscha, Sandback, Saret, Sawchuk, Serra, Sims, Smithson, Sonnier, Wall, Weiner, Wilson. (Rep.)

Reviewed by John Voorhees, *Seattle Times,* September 5; Thomas Albright, *San Francisco Examiner & Chronicle,* September 21; William Wilson, *Los Angeles Times,* September 21, and Peter Plagens, *Artforum,* November, 1969. The following paragraph is from Plagens's article:

557,087 . . . will be recalled generically as the first sizable (i.e. public institution) exhibition of "concept art," but it is in fact an amalgam of nonchromatic work running a gamut from late, funky Minimal to a point at which art is replaced, literally, by literature. The show is a bellwether, consolidated enough to necessitate sifting high-grade bullshit Canal Street art-thinking from genuinely dangerous, substantial material. . . . There is a total style to the show, a style so pervasive as to suggest that Lucy Lippard is in fact the artist and that her medium is other artists, a foreseeable extension of the current practice of a museum's hiring a critic to "do" a show and the critic then asking the artists to "do" pieces for the show. . . . In its parts, *557,087* emerges from manifold sources of varying degrees of relevance ("relevance" depends on belief in "issues" in current art, as opposed to endless refinement; *557,087* is about issues). . . . The single most pertinent source is, I think, an almost Puritan, moralistic concern with the threatening, nagging, perverse presence of "art" and, as subsource, anti-technology.

Actually, this show was conceived as an exercise in "anti-taste," as a compendium of varied work so large that the public would have to make up its own mind about ideas to which it had not been previously exposed. It was not a "concept art" show; had it been, it would most certainly not have included the work of artists like Andre, Bollinger, Hesse, Ryman, Serra, etc. When it originated, in the fall of 1968, "concept art" had not yet crystallized, and by the time the list was completed, in the early spring of 1969, I was particularly concerned not to be providing a new category in which disparate artists would be lumped. I didn't see how anyone could possibly lump "minimal art," "outdoor art," "idea art," etc., into any single new lump. The title was derived from the population of the city in which it was shown. (The present book constitutes yet another attempt to emphasize fragmentation, variety, and disparity of intention.) In any case, it was the first show I know of in which the work was spread out not only from indoors to outdoors but for a radius of some fifty miles around the city. Though maps were provided at the museum, it seems safe to say that no one but myself and museum assistant Anne Focke ever saw the whole show. Bollinger's giant (several tons) log was right in front of the museum, but Artforum's reviewer never noticed it. Imagine, therefore, the fate of Louw's white pole piece understatedly following the contours of a nearby hill, Baxter's mirrors reversing an isolated landscape, Sims's white-sprayed arc on the edge of a forest along a country road, George Sawchuk's pipes through a small grove of trees, etc. Several pieces were not executed in Seattle because of money, lack of help, my own inadequacy, or whatever. Everything was attempted; three pieces (Andre's, Flanagan's and Rohm's) were done wrong; Serra never got there to make his work; the pieces by LeWitt and Dibbets were never completed because of bad carpentry and weather conditions. Heizer's piece, both at Seattle and Vancouver, took an immense amount of time and never did get executed. It amazes me, in retrospect, that we got as much of the work done as we did, given my tremendous naiveté as to the effort involved in making even one piece. All in all, it was an experience I'd have to be crazy to repeat, but one that taught me more about the nature of the art involved than all the words that had gone under the bridge over the preceding two years.

The randomly read catalogue cards tended to romantic oversimplification, on which I look back with distaste. Because some of the ideas offered were, for better or worse, current at the time, excerpts follow:

- Deliberately low-keyed art often resembles ruins, like neolithic rather than classical monuments, amalgams of past and future, remains of something "more," vestiges of some unknown venture. The ghost of content continues to hover over the most obdurately abstract art. The more open, or ambiguous, the experience offered, the more the viewer is forced to depend upon his own perceptions.

- The visual artist uses words to convey information about sensorial or potentially perceptible phenomena; his current preoccupation with linguistics, semantics and social structures, as exposed by anthropology, is not surprising. The fact that it is indeed structural patterns which are the basis of these fields brings them into visual range.

- If the insistent physical presence of the primary structure is a time-stopping device that resists the modern world's flux by creating new, frontal, static monuments to the present, most of the work here deals with energy, animation, non-sequential and relatively irrational lines of time and material. It can, however, be speculatively concrete, even when it is invisible. Despite deceptively scientific or pragmatic presentations, the artists generally accept and are involved with the unknown on a different level than scientists. Artists do not analyze circumstances with "progress" in mind so much as expose them, making themselves and their audience aware of things previously disregarded, information already in the environment which can be harnessed into esthetic experience. And what can't be?

- An artist can make his own or his environment's presence felt by dropping a point, a line, an accent, a word, into the world, embracing all or parts of any area or period at any place or time. Concurrently, the area's or period's importance can be neutralized until the art becomes more abstract than ever, even when it is virtually inseparable from life. The implication is that what we now consider art will eventually be unrecognizable. On the other hand, the boundaries of seeing, like the perceptible aspects of nature or outer space, seem to extend as infinitely as man's experience and experiments can take them.

- Experience and awareness are, after all, shared by everyone. Art intended as pure experience doesn't exist until someone experiences it, defying ownership, reproduction, sameness. Intangible art could break down the artificial imposition of "culture" and at the same time provide a broader audience for a tangible, object art.

Among works in the show:

Robert Barry:

All the things I know but of which I am not at the moment thinking—1:36 P.M.; 15 June 1969, New York.

Sol LeWitt (executed in Vancouver by Glenn Lewis):

On a wall, using a hard pencil, parallel lines about ⅛″ apart and 12″ long are drawn for one minute. Under this row of lines, another row of lines are drawn for 10 minutes.

Under this row of lines another row of lines are drawn for one hour.

John Baldessari and George Nicolaidis:
"Boundary: A section of a city, especially a thickly populated area inhabited by minority groups often as a result of social or economic restrictions." (Text of a small silver and black label affixed to telephone poles, street signs, etc., along the boundary of the ghetto in Seattle.)

Other Ideas. **Detroit Institute of Art, September 10–October 9, 1969. Text by Samuel Wagstaff, Jr.: Andre, de Maria, Heizer, Smithson, etc.**

The Return of Abstract Expressionism (Procedurism). **Richmond Art Center, California, September 25–November 2, 1969. Organized by Thomas Marioni. Anderson, Crawley, Fish, Fox, Goldstein, Henderson, Kos, Linhares, N. E. Thing Co., Oppenheim, Stewart, TeSelle, Veres and Gnazzo, Woodall.**

Prospect '69. **Kunsthalle, Düsseldorf, September 30–October 12, 1969. Organized by Konrad Fischer and Hans Strelow. B. and H. Becher, Beuys, Boetti, Brouwn, Buren, Butler, Byars, Calzolari, Cotton, Darboven, D'Armagnac, Dekker, Dibbets, Haacke, Heizer, Kounellis, LeWitt, Long, Marriacci, Oppenheim, Orr, Penone, Prini, Raetz, Ruthenbeck, Ryman, Schnyder, Smithson, Zaj. Reviewed by Margit Staber, *Art International,* January, 1970. Interviews with Barry, Huebler, Kosuth, and Weiner from catalogue.**

Robert Barry:
Q: What is your piece for *Prospect '69?*
RB: The piece consists of the ideas that people will have from reading this interview.
Q: Can this piece be shown?
RB: No, but language can be used to indicate the situation in which the art exists. For me, art is about making art, not about someone being aware of it.
Q: How can these ideas be known?
RB: The piece in its entirety is unknowable because it exists in the minds of so many people. Each person can really know that part which is in his own mind.
Q: Is the "unknown" an important element in your other work also?
RB: I use the unknown because it's the occasion for possibilities and because it's more real than anything else. Some of my works consist of forgotten thoughts, or things in my unconscious. I also use things which are not communicable, are unknowable, or are not yet known. The pieces are actual but not concrete; they have a different kind of existence.
Q: How would you characterize your control over the elements of your piece?
RB: My control is indefinite, but, to a certain extent, I influence the form of the ideas. How much conscious control does any artist have over his art? The situation, this interview, also conditions the nature of the piece to be the natural result of this time and place.
Q: Does this piece in fact exist?
RB: It does exist if you have any ideas about it, and that part is yours. The rest you can only imagine.

*   *   *

Joseph Kosuth:
Q: Since I've known you, your interest in philosophy has been an involvement close to your art; in recent months, however, your work seems to have even less resemblance to anything we previously considered art. . . . Do you still think of yourself as an artist?

JK: I would certainly say yes—in the sense that my thinking is always related to a very abstract context which I feel in my time has become the postulate for a sense of the meaning of the word "art." I would also add, though, that my work has a lot less to do with cubism than cubism had to do with Ingres. By that I mean to say that I feel that I am perhaps the first artist to be out of the grip of the nineteenth century. Of course I couldn't have done it without the benefit of "American *art*" since Pollock—although "American *art*" as a context is irrelevant now. That's new with my generation, too. . . .

Previously when an artist worked within a tradition he therefore could maintain a kind of cultural placement. That just isn't real now. Nationalism of that sort is very alien to the young artists working today. To work in a tradition now is artistic timidity, and nothing more. My work is a continual kind of investigation with no one particular part any more important or final than any other. I try to keep away from thinking of works as individual "pieces"—which is a kind of thinking left over from sculpture; specific and more or less iconic. I continually try to keep my work general because that's the sphere of the abstract. As it is generally known, I have subtitled all of my work "art as idea as idea" since early 1966. The reasons that led me to want my art to exist only as ideas are manifold. And they all sort of occurred simultaneously. It answered specific formal problems—very personal ones—in my work which came out of painting/sculpture activities. It seemed to be much more what my time was about; it answered desires of mine toward a very complete abstraction—my primary concern has been with abstraction—and all of these things coincided with certain revelations I had about the history of art and philosophy. With my dictionary definition works it became evident to me that the form of presentation (photostats) were often considered "paintings" even though I continually attempted to make it clear that the photostats were photostats and the art was the idea. After that series I began to use obvious media (newspapers, magazines, billboards, bus and train advertising, television) as the form of presentation. I felt this made it clear that the art is conceptual and not experiential. . . .

The synopsis of [Thesaurus] categories series, which I refer to as "investigation 2" was conceptually completed last year when I began the presentation phase of the work. All my work exists when it is conceived because the execution is irrelevant to the art—the art is for an art context only—and when it is presented via media, it is for "mankind" not particularly men—I mean I'm not interested in changing anyone's life in the way, say, Walter de Maria would be. Anyway, the "investigation" series is about a two- or three-year project consisting of forty-three "works" with 190 separate sections. I'm over half finished with it, although I think of it now as old work.

*   *   *

Lawrence Weiner:

Q: You are exhibiting a work at *Prospect* that requires seven years to make. Is this exhibited as a work in progress?

LW: No. The work "Floatable Objects Thrown into Inland Waterways One Each Month for 7 Years" is a complete work at the time of exhibition. The idea of a series of floatable objects thrown into inland waterways is what is being exhibited, not any specific series.

Q: Why is this piece being constructed, and how does this affect its sale?

LW: The work is public freehold. I myself am the receiver and have chosen to have it constructed. It is not for sale, whereas the information of its existence is made public. I have been requesting assistance from people, *Prospect* itself, to aid me in constructing the work.

Q:You have previously referred to Art that gave directions as esthetic fascism. How do you condone people building work at your direction?

LW: They are not building work at my direction, only aiding me in its construction. Their aid does not in any way constitute participation in or involvement in the Art itself, nor is this construction necessary, for appreciation. Whether they build it or not in no way affects the work. My request is sufficient to satisfy myself that the piece is being built.

Q: Why seven years?

LW: Perhaps because seven years is the statute of limitations for many crimes in the United States.

Q: Why are all your works, no matter how complex, within the realm of possibility?

LW: If they were not possible to be built, they would negate the choice of the receiver as to whether they were built or not.

Q: What are the implications of thrown as opposed to dropped, flung, etc.?

LW: An object that is thrown is not necessarily dropped. An object that is dropped is not necessarily thrown.

Stanley Brouwn at Prospect '69. Art and Project Bulletin, no. 11, September 30–October 12, 1969:
Walk during a few moments very consciously in a certain direction; simultaneously an infinite number of living creatures in the universe are moving in an infinite number of directions.

September, 1969: Buren and Toroni are invited to the Paris Biennale. Having obtained major space, they cede it to a third painter—Ristori.

New Alchemy: Elements, Systems, and Forces in Contemporary Art. Haacke, Ross, Takis, Van Saun. Art Gallery of Ontario, Toronto, September 27–October 26. Organized by Dennis Young; discussed by him in Art and Artists, February, 1970.

FRARMRROREEROFIBSEATERLR (Robert Morris, Rafael Ferrer). C.A.A.M., University of Puerto Rico, Mayagüez, April, May, September, 1969. See account in Revista de Arte, no. 3, December, 1969 (Crespo, Angel, "Los Eventos Morris en el campus de Mayagüez").

Morris's section of the show consisted of sculpture and a day (September 2) of unannounced events, among them: The transplanting of a group of subtropical trees with a lifespan of exactly twenty-five years; placement of a circle of military helmets around a large rock; as an air hammer dented the rock, the helmets were removed one by one and the names of all the countries in Latin America were shouted out; a systematic rock-throwing event; a dancelike action with gasoline in a tarpaulin; the painting of brown palm-tree trunks brown; and a near disastrous combination of random-formal movement by some forty people carrying huge torches and accompanied by two dozen aerial bombs set off by Ferrer. Some of this work related to earlier performance pieces by Morris.

N.E. Thing Company. Trans VI Connection NSCAD-NETCO. Nova Scotia College of Art and Design, Halifax, 1970. "A word is worth 1/1000th of a picture" (Iain Baxter). A Record of an Exhibition September–October 5, 1969: "The connection consisted of an exchange of information between the Nova Scotia College of Art and Design Ltd. and the N. E. Thing Co., via telex, telecopier and telephone. The N. E. Thing Co. initiated propositions and the college community responded with some appropriate activity. The transmissions from the exhibition are arranged chronologically with evidence of response following each."

N. E. Thing Co., Ltd. *1970–71 Calendar.* Separate part of the catalogue for the Canadian representation at the 10th São Paulo Bienal, September, 1969–January, 1970. Each two-month page includes an ACT and an ART (see above, pp. 66–67).

September 24–27: Lawrence Weiner, N. E. Thing Co., and Harry Savage go to Inuvik, Northwest Territory, within the Arctic Circle, to execute Weiner's piece, *An abridgement of an abutment to on near or about the Arctic Circle,* and other works, accompanied by Bill Kirby (director of the Edmonton Art Gallery, Alberta, under whose auspices the trip is being made), Virgil Hammock, and Lucy Lippard. Account by the latter published as "Art Within the Arctic Circle," *Hudson Review,* winter, 1969–70.

Rosenstein, Harris. "The Bollinger Phenomenon," *Art News,* September 1969. Includes 1968 rope and wire pieces, 1969 dust and paint pieces. (Rep.)

Smithson, Robert, "Incidents of Mirror Travel in the Yucatan," *Artforum,* September, 1969.

Lawrence Weiner. Art and Project Bulletin 10, September, 1969:
  A translation from one language to another.

Burnham, Jack. "Real Time Systems." *Artforum,* September, 1969.

Claura, Michel. "Extremisme et rupture," Parts I and II. *Les Lettres Françaises,* September 24 and October 1, 1969.

Kundry, Kiki. "Neuestern's Ultimate Non-Act." *Art News,* September, 1969. (A parody.)

Lynton, Norbert. "Impossible Art—Is It Possible?" *New York Times,* September 21, 1969.

Bonito-Oliva, Achille. "America Antiforma." *Domus,* September, 1969.

Rosing, Larry. "Barry Le Va and the Non-Descript Description." *Art News,* September, 1969. Discusses pieces made from sifted flour (1969), distributions of oil-soaked paper toweling and

Bill Bollinger. *Graphite.* Bykert Gallery, New York. 1969.

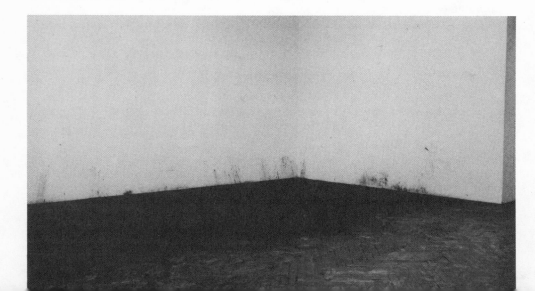

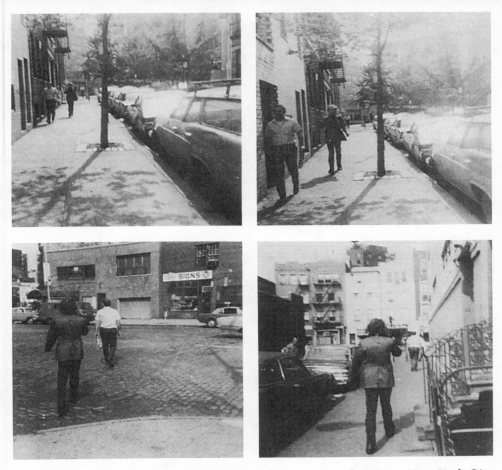

Vito Acconci. *Following Piece.* Activity, 23 days, varying durations. New York City ("Street Works IV," Architectural League of New York), John Gibson Commissions, Inc. 1969.

   Choosing a person at random, in the street, any location, each day. Following him wherever he goes, however long or far he travels. (The activity ends when he enters a private place—his home, office, etc.)

flour (1968), and gray cement powder spread in shapes on the snow (February, 1969, River Falls, Wisconsin).

Street Works IV. New York, October 3–25. Sponsored by the Architectural League. Acconci (Rep.), Arakawa, Burton, Costa, Kaltenbach, Levine, Lubelski, B. Mayer, Perreault, Strider, H. Weiner.

Christo. *Wrapped Coast: One Million Square Feet.* Minneapolis, Contemporary Art Lithographs, 1969. Book of photographic documentation (by Shunk-Kender) of Christo's work on the South Australian Coast, October 28, 1969. A film was also made of the event.

Burgin, Victor. "Situational Esthetics." *Studio International,* October, 1969.

Kosuth, Joseph. "Art After Philosophy." *Studio International,* **October, November, December, 1969. Correspondence and answers by Kosuth in issues of January, February, 1970.**

Bourgeois, Jean-Louis. "Dennis Oppenheim: A Presence in the Countryside." *Artforum,* **October 11, 1969.**

Allan Ruppersberg. "Al's Cafe" in Los Angeles. October 9–November 13.

Art by Telephone. **Museum of Contemporary Art, Chicago, November 1–December 14, 1969. Organized by Jan van der Marck. Catalogue is a 12″ LP record of artists stating or performing their pieces. Album text by van der Marck. Exhibition inspired by Moholy-Nagy's ordering art fabricated by telephone in 1922 to prove that "the intellectual approach to the creation of a**

Richard Long. October, 1969.

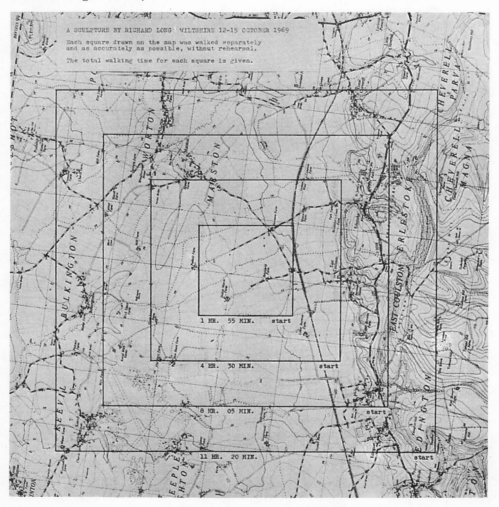

work of art is in no way inferior to the emotional approach." Artists: Armajani, Arman, Artschwager, Baldessari, Baxter, Bochner, Brecht, Burnham, Byars, Cumming, Dallegret, Dibbets, Giorno, Grosvenor, Haacke, Hamilton, Higgins, Huot, Jacquet, Kienholz, Kosuth, Levine, LeWitt, Morris, Nauman, Oldenburg, Oppenheim, Serra, Smithson, Thompson, Uecker, Vanderbeek, Venet, Viner, Vostell, Wegman, Wiley.

Konzeption/Conception. Städtische Museum, Leverkusen, October–November, 1969. Organized by Rolf Wederer and Konrad Fischer. Text: Sol LeWitt, "Sentences on Conceptual Art"; bibliographies. Arnatt, Baldessari, Barry, Baxter, H. and B. Becher, Bochner, Boetti, Broodthaers, Brouwn, Buren, Burgin, Burgy, Butler, Calzolari, Cotton, Darboven, Dibbets, Fulton, Gilbert and George, Graham, Huebler, Jackson, Kawara, Kosuth, Lamelas, LeWitt, McLean, Penone, Polke, Prini, Raetz, Ruppersberg, Ruscha, Sandback, Sladden, Smithson, Ulrichs, Venet, Weiner, Zaj. Some of the works shown:

Emilio Prini, *Magnet* (1968–69):
Free movements and variation of relations between unfixed bodies now. Free sounds and sound variations between unfixed bodies now. Groups of unfixed telepathic impulses *now.* (Documentation/film Dossier/ recorded tape/ Biological Duration.)

Magnet (2):
Cancel references on map. Cancel references in the universe. Cancel references to the universe. Be seen around.

Texts of Gilbert and George's catalogue piece at Leverkusen (each accompanied by a photograph of one of the sculptors):
We would honestly like to say how happy we are to be sculptors; It is our intention to bring to everyone a realization of the beauty and necessity of our sculpture; It is important for new sculptors to come to terms with the modern limitations of sculpture, apparent only through the feeling of the eye; With the tears streaming down our faces we appeal to you to rejoice in the life of the world of art.

October 11–18, 1969: Keith Arnatt's *Self-Burial,* executed earlier in the year in Tintern, England, is transmitted on German television under the auspices of Gerry Schum. The piece consists of nine photographs showing Arnatt progressively descending into the earth. Each one was shown twice each day for two seconds, cut into the daily television programming, with no introduction or commentary.

Glusberg, Jorge. "Argentina: Art and Dissolution." *Art and Artists, October, 1969. (On Rosario group in Tucuman.)*

Buren, Daniel. *Mise en Garde (Warning, Vorsorglicher Hinweis),* A379089, Antwerp, November, 1969. Buren's entry for the Leverkusen catalogue published as a trilingual booklet.

Pläne und Projekte als Kunst/Plans and Projects as Art. Kunsthalle, Bern, November 8–December 7, 1969. Catalogue in a newspaper format; text by P. F. Althaus.

A Report—Two Ocean Projects. Museum of Modern Art, November 1–30, 1969. Documents of works made by Oppenheim and Hutchinson in the waters off Tobago in August. One of Hutchinson's pieces was *Arc,* plastic bags at intervals on a 50-foot rope; the bags contained coral rocks and decomposing calabashes. The weight of the rocks counterbalanced the bouyant gas released from the decomposing fruits, maintaining the work's arc shape. Reviewed by William Johnson, *Art News,* November, 1969; Anthony Robbin, *Arts,* November, 1969.

Groups. School of Visual Arts Gallery, New York, November 3–20. Organized by Lucy R. Lippard. Among the artists: Barry, Borofsky, Gianakos, Huebler (Rep.), A. Katz, Miller, Moyer, N. E. Thing Co., Piper, Puente, Robbins, Tangen, Weiner, Zapkus.

A project was sent out to about thirty artists in October, 1969, requesting that they follow a series of instructions from which would emerge a verbal-visual experiment in repetitive photographs of a group of people and written descriptions of the photos. From the twenty-two responses received, the exhibition, Groups, was formed. I chose the participants almost at random, except that I wanted their own work to span a broad range of media and styles. I realized, after the fact, that the project itself was unnecessarily complicated and could have been practically anything (as subsequent experiments in placing artists in "situations" have indicated). I had insisted on groups of people because of personal preoccupations that turned out to be far more psychological than those of the responding artists. I was interested in the gaps and overlappings occurring when very differently oriented artists executed the same neutral project. The results were far more provocative than any conclusions that could have been drawn from them. The photographs and texts in this show were, in most cases, not considered "Art" by me or by the artists concerned. It was an "exhibition" only because that context presented itself as a vehicle for the experiment. Sections of the show were published in Studio International (inaccurately and often illegibly) in March, 1970, with a text by me of which the above is a synopsis.

Technical Data. Advanced Ceramics Class, Nova Scotia College of Art and Design, Halifax, November, 1969. Samples of the Pleistocene fluvial or marine clay from the west side of the Shubenacadie River at Elmsdale, Nova Scotia, and a technical data sheet sent to nineteen potters internationally; their responses comprise the booklet.

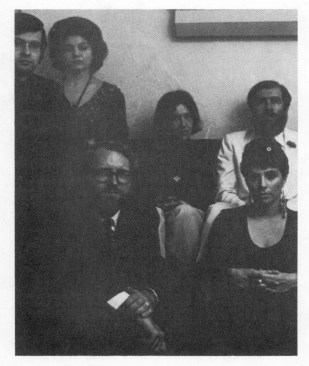

Douglas Huebler. *Duration Piece #14.* Bradford, Mass. May 1, 1970.

About 6 p.m. for seven consecutive days (October 5–11, 1969), a group of people assembled to have a single photograph made as they assumed nearly the same pose and relative position. They wore, each evening, the same clothes and accessories—even holding similar drinks in order to give the appearance that the photographs had been made in rapid succession during one sitting.

A sign was flashed to the group before each photograph was taken: each person was instructed to think of nothing other than *one* of the two words printed on the sign but in no way to allow that thought be expressed on his, or her, face. The photograph was made exactly 5 seconds after the words were flashed.

The photographs are presented, numbered, in the order that they were made. The words are listed below in no sequential order, as they were actually shown to the group by a person other than the artist and their order was not revealed to him.

NOTHING	SCREWING	BIRTH
ANYTHING	EATING	DEATH

FREE CHOICE

PEACE	MONSTER	HATE
WAR	KITTEN	LOVE

Seven photographs and this statement constitute the form of this piece.

Sharp, Willoughby. "An Interview with Joseph Beuys." *Artforum,* **November, 1969:**

WS: Has your teaching at the Dusseldorf Art Academy for the last eight years been an important function for you?

JB: It's my most important function. To be a teacher is my greatest work of art. The rest is the waste product, a demonstration. If you want to explain yourself you must present something tangible. But after a while this has only the function of a historic document. Objects aren't very important for me any more. I want to get to the origin of matter, to the thought behind it. Thought, speech, communication—and not only in the socialist sense of the word—are all expressions of the free human being.

WS: Would you say, then, that your goal is to make man freer and stimulate him to think more freely?

JB: Yes, I am aware that my art cannot be understood primarily by thinking. My art touches people who are in tune with my mode of thinking. But it is clear that people cannot understand my art by intellectual process alone, because no art can be experienced in this way. I say to experience, because this is not equivalent to thinking: it's a great deal more complex; it involves being moved subconsciously. Either they say, "yes, I'm interested," or they react angrily and destroy my work and curse it. In any event I feel I am successful, because people have been affected by my art. I touch people and this is important. In our times, thinking has become so positivist that people only appreciate what can be controlled by reason, what can be used, what furthers your career. The need for questions that go beyond that has pretty much died out of our culture. Because most people think in materialistic terms, they cannot understand my work. This is why I feel it's necessary to present something more than mere objects. By doing that, people may begin to understand man is not only a rational being. . . .

WS: How does art involve life?

JB: Art alone makes life possible—this is how radically I should like to formulate it. I would say that without art man is inconceivable in physiological terms. There is a certain materialist doctrine which claims that we can dispense with mind and with art because man is just a more or less highly developed mechanism governed by chemical processes. I would say man does not consist only of chemical processes, but also of metaphysical occurrences. The *provocateur* of the chemical processes is located outside the world. Man is only truly alive when he realizes he is a creative, artistic being. I demand an artistic involvement in all realms of life. At the moment, art is taught as a special field which demands the production of documents in the form of art works. Whereas I advocate an esthetic involvement from science, from economics, from politics, from religion—every sphere of human activity. Even the act of peeling a potato can be a work of art if it is a conscious art.

WS: What do you think about your present situation within the context of art?

JB: I think the crux of the matter is that my work is permeated with thoughts that do not originate in the official development of art but in scientific concepts. You know, to begin with I wanted to be a scientist. But I found that the theoretical structure of the natural sciences was too positivist for me, so I tried to do something new for both science and art. I wanted to widen both areas. So as a sculptor I tried to broaden the concept of art. The logic of my art depends on the fact that I have had one idea which I have obstinately worked with. Actually, it's a problem of perception.

WS: Perception?

JB: (After a long hesitation.) In the simplest terms, I am trying to reaffirm the concept of art and creativity in the face of Marxist doctrine. The Socialist movements in Europe which are now strongly supported by the young constantly provoke this question. They define man exclusively as a social being. I wasn't surprised by this development, which led to the confused political conditions not only in Germany but also in America. Man really is not free in many respects. He is dependent on his social circumstances, but he is free in his thinking, and here is the point of origin of sculpture. For me the formation of the thought is already sculpture. The thought is sculpture. Of course, language is sculpture. I move my larynx, I move my mouth and the sound is an elementary form of sculpture. We ask: "What is sculpture?" And reply: "Sculpture." The fact that sculpture is a very complex creation has been neglected. What interests me is the fact that sculpture supplies a definition of man.

WS: Isn't this rather abstract?

JB: My theory depends on the fact that every human being is an artist. I have to encounter him when he is free, when he is thinking. Of course, thinking is an abstract way of putting it. But these concepts—thinking, feeling, wanting—are concerned with sculpture. Thought is represented by form. Feeling by motion or rhythm. Will by chaotic force. This explains the underlying principle of my "Fettecke" [corners of fat]. Fat in liquid form distributes itself chaotically in an undifferentiated fashion until it collects in a differentiated form in a corner. Then it goes from the chaotic principle to the form principle, from will to thinking. These are parallel concepts which correspond to the emotions, to what could be called soul.

Carlo Cremaschi/Giuliano della Casa. *Geiger Sperimentale,* no. 14, Turin, November, 1969: "This booklet is the documentation and assemblage of an experiment concluded in Modena between 1967 and the early months of 1969 in a non-existent cultural climate; most of these works were never exhibited and were born precisely as a means to be shown without the medium of a gallery." Primarily outdoor pieces.

Hans Haacke. *Chickens Hatching.* Forsgate Farm, New Jersey. April 14, 1969.

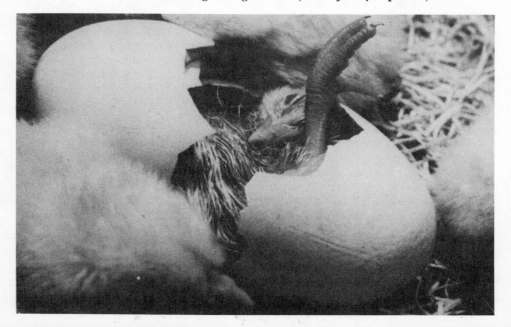

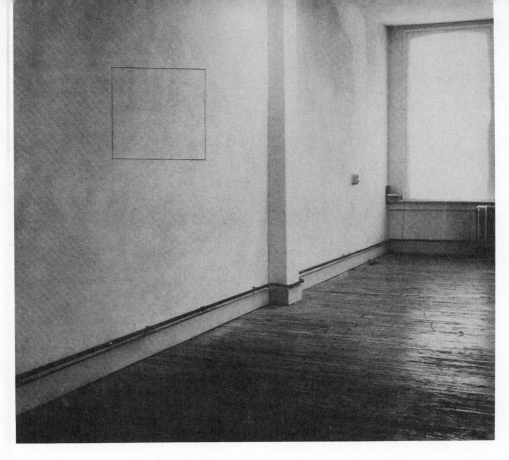

Jan Dibbets. *Corrected Perspective* on studio wall, Amsterdam. 1969.

Gino de Dominicis. L'Attico, Rome, November, 1969. Text by the artist.

Jan Dibbets. Art and Project Bulletin 15, November 26–December 16, 1969: "Send the right page of this bulletin by returning post to Art and Project; each returned bulletin will be marked on the world map by a straight line from your home to Amsterdam." Results of this piece published in *Studio International,* July–August, 1970.

Hans Haacke. Howard Wise Gallery, New York, November 1–29, 1969:
   The working premise is to think in terms of systems; the production of systems, the interference with and the exposure of existing systems. Such an approach is concerned with the operational structure of organizations, in which transfer of information, energy and/or material occurs. Systems can be physical, biological or social. They can be man-made, naturally existing or a combination of any of the above. In all cases verifiable processes are referred to. (H.H.) (*Rep.*)

On Karawa. One month from a series of daily postcards of New York scenes sent to L.R.L. for four months (and at different times to other friends), stating the date, the time the artist got up that day, his name and address, and L.R.L.'s address, all in rubber-stamped letters (Rep.):

```
Nov - 1 1969    I got up at 4.28 P.M.
Nov - 2 1969    I got up at 3.13 P.M.
Nov - 3 1969    I got up at 1.15 P.M.
Nov - 4 1969    I got up at 1.54 P.M.
Nov - 5 1969    I got up at 12.17 P.M.
Nov - 6 1969    I got up at 1.44 P.M.
Nov - 7 1969    I got up at 2.35 P.M.
Nov - 8 1969    I got up at 6.25 P.M.
Nov - 9 1969    I got up at 12.45 P.M.
Nov 10 1969    I got up at 1.22 P.M.
Nov 11 1969    I got up at 2.18 P.M.
Nov 12 1969    I got up at 12.10 P.M.
Nov 13 1969    I got up at 2.51 P.M.
Nov 14 1969    I got up at 2.17 P.M.
Nov 15 1969    I got up at 12.53 P.M.
Nov 16 1969    I got up at 4.51 P.M.
Nov 17 1969    I got up at 1.21 P.M.
Nov 18 1969    I got up at 2.52 P.M.
Nov 19 1969    I got up at 11.21 A.M.
Nov 20 1969    I got up at 8.10 A.M.
Nov 21 1969    I got up at 1.15 P.M.
Nov 22 1969    I got up at 2.54 P.M.
Nov 23 1969    I got up at 2.59 P.M.
Nov 24 1969    I got up at 3.59 P.M.
Nov 25 1969    I got up at 3.54 P.M.
Nov 26 1969    I got up at 3.52 P.M.
Nov 27 1969    I got up at 6.28 P.M.
Nov 28 1969    I got up at 11.08 P.M.
Nov 29 1969    I got up at 6.40 P.M.
Nov 30 1960    _____
Nov 31 1969    [no card arrived]
```

Joseph Kosuth. Art and Project Bulletin 14, **November 22–30, 1969. "Art as Idea as Idea." Light (Thesaurus category).**

Perreault, John. "Systems." *Village Voice,* **November 20, 1969.**

November, 1969, New York: Seth Siegelaub interviewed by Ursula Meyer for her projected book on anti-art (excerpts):

SS: Communication relates to art three ways: (1) Artists knowing what other artists are doing. (2) The art community knowing what artists are doing. (3) The world knowing what artists are doing. Perhaps it is cynical, but I tend to think that art is for artists. No one gets turned on by art as artists do. Of course, a person's approach to an artist's work is necessarily subjective. This is where I come in. The point is to "objectify" the work of the artist. And that is a question of numbers. It's my concern to make it known to multitudes.

UM: Which means are most suitable?

SS: Books and catalogues. The art that I am interested in can be communicated with books and catalogues. Obviously most people become acquainted with art via

On Kawara. Postcard from "I got up" series. 1969.

illustrations, slides, films. Rather than having the direct confrontation with the art itself, there is a secondhand experience, which does not do justice to the work—since it depends upon its physical presence, in terms of color, scale, material and context—all of which is bastardized and distorted. But when art does not any longer depend upon its physical presence, when it has become an abstraction, it is not distorted and altered by its representation in books and catalogues. It becomes *primary* information, while the reproduction of conventional art in books or catalogues is necessarily *secondary* information. For example, a photograph of a painting is different from a painting, but a photograph of a photograph is just a photograph, or the setting of a line of type is just a line of type. When information is *primary,* the catalogue can become the exhibition *and* a catalogue auxiliary to it, whereas in the January, 1969, show the catalogue was *primary* and the physical exhibition was auxiliary to it. You know, it's turning the whole thing around.

UM: Have you arranged any exhibitions where catalogues were dealt with in a more conventional sense?

SS: Yes, I have. For the Summer Show, the show called "July, August, September, 1969," eleven artists each made one work of art at eleven different locations throughout the world. The catalogue is more like a traditional museum's exhibition catalogue in the sense that it documents the works as a standard guide to the exhibition, the only difference being that instead of walking into, say, the Whitney Annual, where the catalogue makes reference to all the displayed work, here you have the whole world and not just a building for housing an exhibition. That is part of the reason why the catalogue is in three languages.

UM: Was all the work displayed at the same time?

SS: Yes, within the three-month period. In some cases, works were instantaneous, and in other cases they were only available to be seen part of the time. And then there were works which could be seen forever. They are still there.

UM: Tell me about your books.

SS: Books are a neutral source. In this sense, film is not quite neutral. It is an art medium in its own right. Books are "containers" of information. They are unresponsive to the environment—a good way of getting information into the world. My books are printed in three languages to further global communication, rather than limited and limiting local distribution.

UM: Will this art in your books be similar to the art shown previously?

SS: I don't know. I cannot possibly answer that.

UM: What do you think about Anti-art?

SS: Much of the Anti-art attitude in terms of anti-establishment is sheer cliché. An anti-establishment attitude of the vanguard is self-evident. Yet any form of art which becomes established becomes establishment. We all know that. It's a question of power. I may choose to deal with power in terms more interesting to me than those existing at present in the art world. For me, power is the ability to get things done—for example, by means of swift global communication. Lag in information is unfortunate. An art has its time and should be seen in its time. My idea of power has to do with reaching a lot of people quickly, not just a circumspect small art audience. . . . Fortunately, the time is getting shorter between when an artist does something and when the community becomes aware of it. Whereas it took years to get a work to Europe or California, now it takes a telephone call. These are significant differences. The idea of swift communication implies that no one has anything.

UM: How do you mean that?

SS: Physically. There is nothing a person could covet and hold on to.

UM: No object?

SS: Well, "object" you would say when you talk about any art thing. But when you become aware of something, it immediately becomes part of you. It's not something you have to wait to see until it comes to you. The idea of getting information to people quickly is a much different idea from getting a painting quickly—to say nothing about the logistics of sending a painting as opposed to sending a Barry or a Weiner. My interest in art transcends the present establishment's limited art-collector scope of communications. . . . For me, power is not recorded in dollars and cents. This is very important. It does not have to do with things I control but has to do with things I am in a position to *make happen.*

Alloway, Lawrence. "Arakawa." *Arts,* November, 1969. Reprinted in Yvon Lambert catalogue, Paris, 1970, with statement by the artist.

Josef Beuys: Werke aus der Sammlung Karl Ströher. Kunstmuseum, Basel, November 6–January 4, 1970. Statements and interview with the artist.

Christopher Cook. "Actuals." Shown at the University of New Hampshire, November 7–30, along with a "minimal replica" of the room where Czar Nicholas and his family were assassinated. (Cook's contribution to the 1970 *Information Show* at MOMA was the exact times of several assassinations.):

In general, I have been interested in objects or fragments ("actuals") supported with words (labels) to produce a mini-event. The fragment (actual) intensifies the experience which the words (label) recount, i.e., actual bullet from—etc., etc. The object-reinforced statement (mini-event) acts as a catalyst to refocus the viewer's mind on a major event.

Excerpt from *An Actual Autobiography of Christopher Cook* (1965):
1955: Actual pieces of bad checks and bird-seed.
1956: Actual pieces of thread worn by A.H., who departed from Hungary at 2 a.m., Nov. 22nd.
1957: Actual piece of wood from a crate used to ship a painting which was subsequently destroyed.
1958: Actual pieces of toys given to the children's ward, St. Elizabeth Hospital, Urbana, Illinois.
1959: Actual piece of a broken-down farmhouse and hard times.
1960: Actual piece of the last painting by Franklin Jesperson.

Jappe, Georg. "Revision in Sachen Konzept-Kunst." *FAZ,* November, 1969.

Michelson, Annette. *Robert Morris.* Corcoran Gallery of Art and Detroit Institute of Art, November 24–December 29, 1969, and January 8–February 8, 1970. Bibliography and biography.

November 2, 1969, WBAI-FM, New York, "Art Without Space." A symposium moderated by Seth Siegelaub with Lawrence Weiner, Robert Barry, Douglas Huebler, and Joseph Kosuth; program initiated by Jeanne Siegel, Art Programs Director of WBAI. Excerpts follow:

SS: What we will hopefully be concerning ourselves with is the nature of the art whose primary existence in the world does not relate to space, not to its exhibition in space, not to its imposing things on the walls. These men are not primarily concerned with the nature of making objects, perhaps, nor are they involved with the nature of performing with things. . . . Larry?

LW: I disagree wholeheartedly that there could ever be an art without space per se. It's just another catchall. Anything that exists has a certain space around it; even an idea exists within a certain space.

DH: I would agree altogether. Whatever you do involves space. I think the essential thing is that we are not concerned (*I* am not concerned; I should speak for myself) with the specific space wherein the so-called art image exists. There doesn't have to be a museum, gallery, or anything for what I do, because the environment does not affect what I do and it is not affected by what I have done.

RB: I honestly think there isn't an artist here whose work in some way doesn't have to do with some kind of spatial experiences. For instance, if an art is involved in objects—say there is a tangible three-dimensional object, then it is implied that there is space around it, or that it is *in* space. In fact, space is really defined by the objects that are in it. The object determines the nature of the space that it is in, and you can't really think about absolute space or space without objects. If we are not in close proximity to the object, that doesn't mean that we can't project ourselves. Say Lawrence does something in the Arctic Circle; there is obviously a space between me and the Arctic Circle and that space is very important. Maybe we are just dealing with a space that is different from the space that one experiences when confronting a traditional object.

JK: The point is, of course, that we are talking about space in the context of art. In other words, an artist using space as conceptually relevant to whatever his artistic proposition is. I would separate myself from what has been said already because space really has absolutely nothing to do with my work (unless I do a work that is *about* space and then, of course, there are subsequent questions about that). When

Douglas Huebler. *Location Piece #1.* New York–Los Angeles. February, 1969.

In February, 1969, the airspace over each of the thirteen states between New York and Los Angeles was documented by a photograph made as the camera was pointed more or less straight out the airplane window (with no "interesting" view intended).

The photographs join together the East and West coasts of the United States as each serves to "mark" one of the thirteen states flown over during that particular flight.

The photographs are not, however, "keyed" to the state over which they were made, but only exist as documents that join with an American Airlines System Map and this statement to constitute the form of this piece.

you are talking about something as rarefied as art is, you begin to realize that words like space have very functional meanings, and when we bring up space in the context of art, considering twentieth-century sculpture and other kinds of interest in space (and the word space, of course, in the fifties was very much part of the terminology of art), I think the subject is loaded. It has to do with physical objects and the place for them. I don't find those the issues. It's just not relevant to the work I'm doing.

RB: I use the word space in two specific senses; one, as an interest or subject matter of the work and, two, which is how I meant it, the space as a condition for the awareness of the work, in other words, a space in which you become aware of the work. For instance, Doug Huebler says he is involved with space. He has tried to document it, distances, time space, things of this nature, but by space I refer to the lack of space.

LW: I don't understand how you can think that something that is a fact of life is not germane. To use Joseph's term—rarefied atmosphere of art, etc.—you may be able not to concern yourself with the spatial problem in making art. You may not consider space an art material, but the fact that you are occupying a certain amount of space in a pure physical sense means that you are dealing with space whether you want to or not. Like you can say, I am not terribly interested in oxygen, but you are breathing it.

JK: But we are talking in the context of art. You conjecture that everything is relevant to art. I don't agree with that. It is very clear that in the nature of art, beginning with the twentieth-century, there was a shift in the visual experience from morphological to conceptual. Once you start realizing the implications of that, then you begin to realize that art doesn't have any subject matter; it has only what the artist uses in it.

SS: Gentlemen, do you have any feelings about how your work relates to the community at large, to the other art that is being made?

RB: Part of the nature of art is that it *is* out there in the community, part of what it is in other people's minds, so that it has to be out there. . . . My own art actually exists in the minds of other people as part of its very nature. Once I present my art, I don't have much control over what other people think of it, but certainly that's part of reality.

JK: I think that obviously the way art lives is through influencing other artists, but not by the physical residue that exists in museums. Some places exhibit the palettes with the paintings, with an equal amount of pride, because they are both just residues of an artist's activities. . . . One could make a case for artists just existing conceptually.

DH: I tend to agree and disagree with what Bob said about not being able to affect what happens to the work once it goes out. Some very bad interpretations are made, and you can't help that, but at the same time when the work gets out there again and again, if it is in any way unfamiliar or has any kind of strength, or resonance, it begins to condition that community, which is kind of what I think Joseph is saying. It is an additive process. . . . The thing that does tie us together in some way is that we are making art that doesn't have an object as the residue. What we call art is not visual, so it can exist in a number of contexts, for some of us at least.

RB: Yes. We all make objects that don't have any space around them except the personal experience of space, which is more subjective than our experience of color which registers directly on our eyes. We have to learn about depth and space, make judgments about it. Music is a very spatial experience. I think we can experience space in a less physical way and that's the kind of space I'm talking about.

LW: You bring up a very strange problem here. You bring in the subjective. Space for me would be almost an energy, since it doesn't matter to me whether my works are built or not built, or whether I build them or somebody else builds them. It is all exactly the same work, once it is presented or communicated. I believe the work itself *produces* a certain amount of energy, which in turn displaces a certain amount of space. . . . The only thing is, they don't have any way yet of determining this objective space, walking over it and chalking it out and saying this is the space that Weiner's idea in 1968 took up.

RB: I think space would be more frightening if it were found to be very objective. Maybe there is too much objective art around. People try to get away from their art, depersonalize it, dehumanize it, have someone else make it, or they try to take away any kind of humanistic elements. In my own work I don't. I try to put myself into it, or I try to realize the fact that art is something that is made by human beings, and when I present it, I present it to other human beings, and that is really what it is about.

LW: As I see it, it's an imposition to impose my personal life on the art which attempts to present something to people that is not just about me. It is all about materials, and it is about the world they live in, perhaps, but it is not about themselves, their own personal, everyday lives, which is what I try to take out of my art.

SS: I would like to ask each of you what exactly you consider your work to be about, the subject matter of your art.

LW: I really believe the subject matter of my art is—art.

SS: What separates your art from Douglas Huebler's?

LW: The fact that I made it and he didn't.

DH: I think everything is available as subject matter and I really mean everything. I concern myself with time, space, and things that are going on in the world, and everything. Not in the sense of trying to restate or interpret or express anything, but to take something out of the world just long enough and use just enough of that to throw something out, bring something back, that I can call an image. The way what is brought back is *presented* is just the package. The act of perceiving is what concerns me rather than what is perceived, because it is more interesting to find out what it is we do when we do perceive.

RB: I have always considered the viewer. Art is about man himself. . . . It is about myself, about the world around me. And it is also about things that I don't know, about using the unknown.

JK: I don't think art is about man any more than it is about the fact that it is made by man. There are other issues. My own art, my own attempt is to deal with abstraction in a way which is real for me and not a metaphoric kind of abstraction or one that grew morphologically out of traditional art, but an abstraction in what abstraction really means.

SS: Much of the work you men are involved in concerns itself with the use of language, which is a radical condition of the art. I'd like to know how you think about it and particularly in reference to how it differs from poetry or literature.

LW: This is a major problem with me because sharing my work could be done by publishing a book, just the statements *per se* of the work. It would be just as good as if the work were built. As for poetry, poetry is inherently involved in the medium of language as well as the content. I may utilize the medium in an attempt to get across *only* the content, in the most concise package I'm capable of at that moment. Inherent beauty or exciting ramifications of the language don't terribly interest me, but I don't see how you can differentiate poetry from art without the proper information. First you might see it as a poem, but with the correct information, you would accept it as it is intended. Perhaps the art I make and the art the rest of the gentlemen sitting here make differs from previous art in that it relies upon information, whereas previously the art was just presented. Nobody even knew terribly much about the art, how to cope with it.

DH: The language as information is absolutely necessary. Getting back to the space thing. The person who sits and looks at a TV set in any room and watches the man in the spacecraft, or stepping on the moon, makes a literal spatial jump that goes beyond any perceptual frame he could possibly have. Then there is the information that tells him that that picture is not contained in that frame; that picture is like 240,000 miles away, or however far the moon is, and it absolutely demands language. I

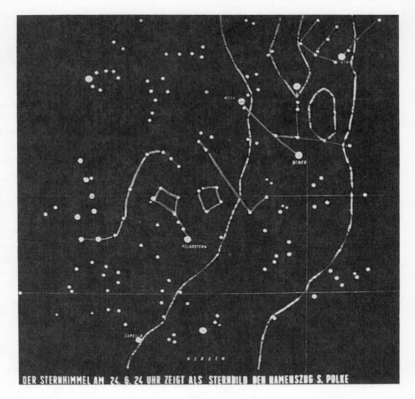

Polke. *The Starry Sky on 24/6, 24:00h the ...re of S. Polke.* May,

don't think any of us jumping over into language are interested in pure information, or pure poetry, but it would be a kind of McLuhan world where we do transcend the space that we can ordinarily perceive.

RB: In my work the language itself isn't the art. It doesn't even describe or detail the art much. I use language as a sign to indicate that there is art, the direction in which the art is, and to prepare someone for the art . . . to communicate your ideas through language.

JK: Yes, when you deal with language you deal with it conceptually, and when you deal with things conceptually, you deal with them in a most general way. My recourse is a way of making it clear that I'm using language to go beyond language. One begins to realize that if one uses language, as a medium it becomes invisible, so that you don't focus on any specifics, which implies a sort of stance, a kind of philosophy. Composition and taste are specific but language is very neuter because it is used in so many ways.

DH: If I might pose this: the idea of words as a convention and by extension the popular use of them as a more general condition, doesn't that parallel the use of the picture frame for sixty thousand years in which the rectangular painting became a convention? Isn't it subject to the same changes and pressures? What are you laughing about, Weiner?

LW: Well, the ease with which you throw that out on the table belies what you are saying, because the picture-frame convention was a very real thing. The painting stopped at that edge. When you are dealing with language, there is no edge that the picture drops over or drops off. You are dealing with something completely infinite. Language, because it is the most nonobjective thing we have ever developed in this world, never stops.

JK: Your analogy works better for poetry, in the sense that poetry has as much to do with words as *material.* I think that's why most of the concrete poets are now starting to do theater and getting out of concrete poetry [Acconci, Perreault, Hannah Weiner, etc.]. They realize the sort of decadence that follows from that sort of materialism. They are trying to say things about the world that are illogical in terms of language.

SS: One becomes very much aware of the speed with which this art travels, of the way it is rapidly transferred from continent to continent or city to city, by virtue of its portability, more quickly than other art.

RB: I haven't found that people understand it any faster even though it is able to get around a lot.

LW: I don't have that trouble because I'm working within the realm of complete generalities. There can be no misreadings. If somebody chooses, when they receive a piece, to build it themselves, they can't do it wrong. They can do it in a way that might displease me personally but not esthetically. They can't do it wrong.

JK: Conceptually.

LW: Not conceptually. They just can't do it wrong. You like the word conceptual. For you, it's fine. It fits you. I don't really see it fitting me. I don't think there is a preconceived concept because the material is so erratic.

JK: If you make a statement, say your work is so much paint poured; if you follow

Jan Dibbets. *Shadow Piece.* **Installation: Haus Lange, Krefeld. 1969.**

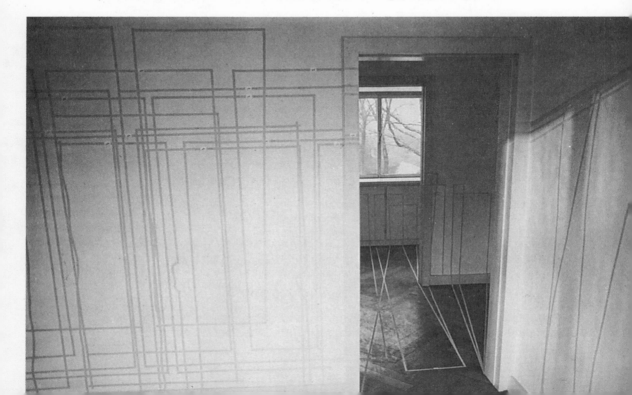

that concept, you can't do anything wrong because you are following that concept, right?

LW: Well, the concept is not necessarily a conceptual situation.

JK: I mean the conceptual has to do with the fact that you can deal with what I'm saying, and that those words have meanings; those words are the conception. I wasn't making any rarefied art-context use of the word conceptual. I was just using the word's standard meaning. You use language, so conceptual is applicable, whether you like it or not, baby.

Spaces. Museum of Modern Art, December 30–March 1, 1970. Text by Jennifer Licht and statements by some of the artists: Asher, Bell, Flavin, Morris, Pulsa, Walther.

Art in Process IV. Finch College Museum of Art, December 11–January 26, 1970. Statements by the artists: Andre, Benglis, Bochner, Bollinger, Ferrer, Flanagan, Hesse, Morris, Nauman, Ryman, Van Buren, Weiner.

Photo Show. Student Union Building (SUB) Gallery, University of British Columbia, Vancouver, December. Organized by Illyas Pagonis and Christos Dikeakos. Barthelme, Burgy, Dikeakos, Graham, Haacke, Huebler, Kinmont, Kirby, Nauman, N. E. Thing Co., Pagonis, Ruscha, Smithson, Wall, Wallace, etc. Reviewed by Charlotte Townsend, *Artscanada,* June, 1970.

Robert Barry. Art and Project Bulletin 17, December 17–31, 1969: "During the exhibition the gallery will be closed." This piece also executed at the Eugenia Butler Gallery, Los Angeles, March 1–21, 1970.

Jan Dibbets: Audio-Visuelle Dokumentationen. Museum Haus Lange, Krefeld, Germany, December 14–January 25, 1970. Introduction by Paul Wember. Includes maps, photos, documentation, and a phonograph record ("the sound of driving a car on a straight road with a constant speed of 100 km. an hour").

Jan Dibbets. *24 minutes: TV as a Fireplace.* "For 24 minutes Jan Dibbets transformed the TV set into an electronic fireplace. For this time pure fire was transmitted, no introduction, no commentary. TV as a Fireplace. Transmitted December 24–31, 1969. Video Gallery Gerry Schum."

"The Art of Michael Heizer." *Artforum,* December, 1969. Photodocumentation.

Müller, Grégoire. "Michael Heizer." *Arts,* December, 1969–January, 1970. Also Perreault, John, "Critique: Street Works."

Reise, Barbara. "Sol LeWitt Drawings, 1968–1969." *Studio International,* December, 1969.

"On Exhibitions and the World at Large, Seth Siegelaub in conversation with Charles Harrison, September, 1969." *Studio International,* December, 1969.

15 Locations 1969/70 Joseph Kosuth Art as Idea as Idea. The show took place all over the world by means of publication of selected categories from the Thesaurus in advertising boxes in local newspapers and magazines. Poster.

Walther, Franz Erhard. *Tagebuch Museum of Modern Art, New York, December 28, 1969–March 1, 1970.* Cologne, Heiner Friedrich, 1970: A diary-report of observations, reactions, reflections, written during or after Walther's participation in the MOMA *Spaces* show with his instrument objects.

1970

BOOKS

Ader, Bas Jan. *Fall.* Claremont, Calif., 1970. Photo documents of two falls, one in Los Angeles, one in Amsterdam.

Barry, Robert. Untitled book ("It has . . ." "It is . . ."; for a later version of this continually refined piece, see p. 250). Sperone, Turin, 1970.

Becher, Hilla and Bernhard. *Anonyme Skulpturen: Eine Typologie technischen Bauten.* Düsseldorf, Art-Press Verlag, 1970. A book of photographs of lime kilns, cooling towers, blast furnaces, winding-towers, water towers, gas holders, silos. Photos exhibited at the Konrad Fischer Gallery, December, 1970. (Rep.)

Burchman, Jerrold. *Reductions/Removals.* Los Angeles, 1970. Photos, some "found."

Buren, Daniel. *Limites Critiques.* Yvon Lambert, Paris, 1970.

Beuys, Joseph. *Ja Ja Ja Nee Nee Nee.* L.P. record, edition of 500; Galleria Colophon, Milan.

Bas Jan Ader. *I'm Too Sad to Tell You.* 1970.

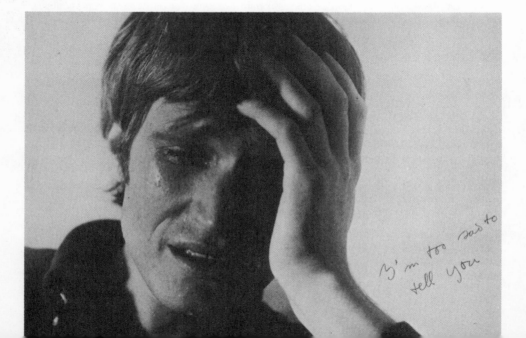

Hilla and Bernhard Becher. *Cooling Towers.* Corrugated concrete and steel. Mounted photo, 60″ x 40″. 1959–1972. Courtesy Sonnabend Gallery, New York.

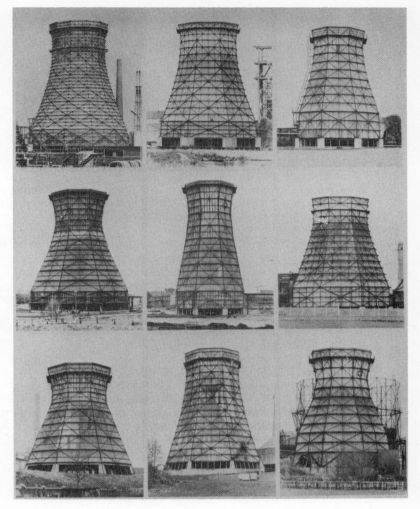

Brouwn, Stanley. *tatvan.* Aktionsraum 1, Munich, 1970.

———. *Atlantis.* Utrecht, 1970. Unique copy.

———. *durch kosmische strahlen gehen.* Städtisches Museum, Mönchengladbach, September 4–25, 1970. Unique copy of book for the show.

Burgy, Donald. *Art Ideas for the Year 4000.* Addison Gallery of American Art, Andover, Mass. Introduction by Jack Burnham:

Time-Information Idea # 2

Select, at random, seven different things, events or ideas.

Study the seven selections until you discover one factor common to all.

Record that factor.

Repeat this process once each day for one week, without ever repeating a selection or a common factor.

Reduce this group of seven to one common factor.

*   *   *

Inside-Outside Exchange # 1 (July, 1969)

Put some of your inside outside.
Take that outside back inside.
Put some inside far outside.
Take that outside back inside.
Increase the distance of exchange
each time until finished.

Burn, Ian, and Ramsden, Mel. *From the "Notes on Analysis" Book.* **New York, 1970:**

1. Rather than add to the chain of almighty art-icons some purported "analytic" art is intent only on advancing bases for analysis. Other merely indicates some areas of investigation.

2. The outcome of much of the "conceptual" work of the past two years has been to carefully clear the air of objects. One no longer feels obligated to materialize constructs and, perhaps of more consequence, one no longer feels the pressure to replace such constructs with specific "ideas," "proposals," etc.

The formulation of a set of art-constructs does not require justification through, nor is it contingent on, material productivity. It is now justifiable as a form of activity.

Amongst the earlier contentions of the conceptual cum analytic work was that no object contains any "magical" artness which may be said to individuate it as an art-object. Given that there are no such determinable characteristics within an art object and that, furthermore, the puzzle is how such and such an art-object is picked out as an art-object, then the area of attention must, arguably, shift away from the object itself. Individuation might then be held to come about by falling back upon various contextual and behavioral prescriptions. There is an obvious need to study such prescriptions since they provide the bases for individuation and must be known prior to individuating activity.

The contention here is that the area of attention is shifting from single iconic elements (art-objects, art-works) to comprise a whole continuum of these elements in a sign-process (semiosis).

3. Now in order to set up within an interpreter the disposition to react in a special way, a sign must have some known fixtures. Thus one might contend that only objects with known art-object fixtures could be picked out as signs of "the presence of art." But since we have already denied the existence of such internal fixtures, then it is tenable to suggest that no art-object can itself qualify as a sign of "art." In which case art-objects must be signified by falling back upon the norms and prescriptions of a known language and, since they are designated from this language, one picks the objects out through this language (and not by suddenly being struck dumb by whatever usage that language may have been put to).

So, analytic art may not be concerned with the proliferation of designated signifieds, but with the abstract structure of this designation: the semiosis.

Now the artist's traditional line of business has been with usage (practice) rather than with sorting out the terms of the semiosis itself. He has accordingly been more preoccupied with the material ramifications of single iconic elements than with the sub-structure or continuum determining the status of these elements. Increasing abstraction means decreasing iconicity. Analytic art seeks to formulate connections

136

between the "grammatical" parts of this semiotic mosaic—in other words, the analytic construct explains its line of business and does not merely act from that line of business.

Now we can call upon some cautious, if logically contentious, remarks about this sign-process.

4. Initial investigation ought to manifest (*i*) what would be the situation of the conventional iconic art-object in the sign-process, and (*ii*) what could be the situation (if any) of an analytic art-construct itself within this process?

i) If C (sign) sets up in D (interpreter) the reaction to E (signification), then it can be argued that C is the context or prescriptions that D must know to enable the bringing about of E: thus C displays the characteristics for D individuating E. Now if this latter event E were to stand for an art-object then it is as a significant designated by C. One might almost regard C as the language norms or "dictionary" learnt by D and then E is an instance of this language "spoken."

Given this, that conventional significants (E) are designated, then such a designation obeying all the contextual and syntactical dimensions of C, need only be observable; i.e., E might conceivably be anything on the face of this planet.

Such formidable spatio-temporal possibilities might be seen as the semantic proliferation of the designative sign-process. However, the abstract structure of such a process might be more rewardingly studied through its syntactic and pragmatic dimensions.

ii) Under the circumstances outlined in (*i*), it would be dumb to insist on nominating an analytic art-construct (i.e., this paper) as an "artwork." The contention is that the analytic construct occurs elsewhere in the semiosis.

So instead of seeking to parallel the conventional signification, an analytic construct may conceivably reproduce in itself the state of a sign: i.e., be "language" but not "usage," be prescription but not practice. Rather than be designated by a set of prescriptions, this construct would itself seek to state those prescriptions. Thus its meaning might be "read out" instead of "read in."

Consider then: C as a sign which sets up in D the disposition to react in a special way E. An analytic construct C need not designate any material element but rather the hope from D of a certain behavior E. It therefore need not be thought that something is "missing" when material elements are not included in the sign-process—rather, it is that the sign C is no longer semantically designative but has moved into the pragmatic mode: it is now prescriptive in that it signifies conduct E—not designative in nominating object E.

Finally, one can't loose material conditions by simplistic "dematerialization." Objects disappear because of fundamental procedural changes in the semiotic or conceptual sign-structure of the continuum itself. The apprehension of analytic art could lie in gaining an awareness of such abstract strategies.

Cook, Christopher C. *A Book of Instants* (Autobiographic Actuality). Andover, Mass., 1970.
First five pages:

November 21, 1844, 9:40 a.m.	June 26, 1875, 4:02 a.m.
June 30, 1875, 6:15 a.m.	March 2, 1883, 2:00 p.m.
December 22, 1883, 6:04 p.m.	June 11, 1906, 1:40 p.m.
May 28, 1932, 2:05 a.m.	April 1, 1933, 7:00 p.m.
January 28, 1935, 5:15 a.m.	August 17, 1938, 1:50 p.m.

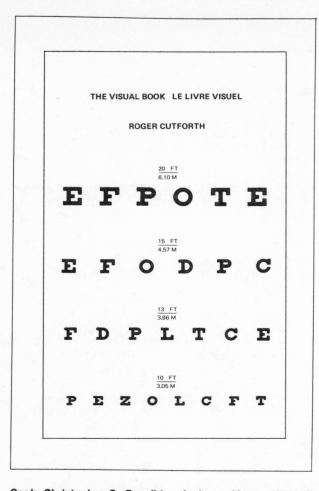

Roger Cutforth. Section from *"Long Distance Vision" Card* (cover of *The Visual Book*). 1970.

Cook, Christopher C. *Possibles.* **Andover, Mass., 1970. "The following exhibitions may possibly be produced at the Addison Gallery of American Art, Andover, Massachusetts." The artist directs the gallery.**

Cutforth, Roger. *The Visual Book.* **New York, 1970; in French and English. (Rep.)**

Dibbets, Jan. *Robin Redbreast's Territory/Sculpture 1969.* **Seth Siegelaub, Gebr. König, New York, Cologne, 1970. Documentation of piece executed April–June, 1969, Amsterdam:**
Sculpture/drawing territory redbreast

At the beginning of March, 1969, I decided to change a robin's territory, so that the bird would fly and control my sculpture-drawing. This sculpture-drawing can never be seen in its entirety; only through its documentation can the viewer reconstruct its form in his mind. In order to achieve this—I only suspected it was possible—I read a number of books (among others: Robert Ardrey, *The Territorial Imperative,* Dell, N.Y., 1968, and David Lack, *The Life of the Robin,* Pelican, London, 1953) until I had gathered sufficient insight into the possibilities. I planned to measure the territory, photograph the intervention, etc. The idea was to change, to enlarge the territory into a form that pleased me. I am not interested in biological facts; the idea arose from a concern with the frontiers of the visual arts. When everything was ready, I laid out the form of the new territory with small poles, like a drawing on the ground. The sculpture was comprised by the movements of the bird between the erected poles. This work is one of a series involving the visualization of ecological systems and was conceived and realized in 1969. (Rep.)

Dikeakos, Christos. *Instant Photo Information* **(October 8, 1970). National Film Board of Canada, Ottawa, 1970.**

Ferguson, Gerald. *Landscape.* **Halifax, 1970. Xerox.**

Gilbert and George. *A Message from the Sculptors Gilbert and George.* **Art for All, London, 1970. Booklet, loose photographs, and "sculptors' samples": "Gilbert and George have a wide range of sculptures for you—singing sculpture, interview sculpture, dancing sculpture, nerve sculpture, café sculpture, and philosophy sculpture. So do contact us."**

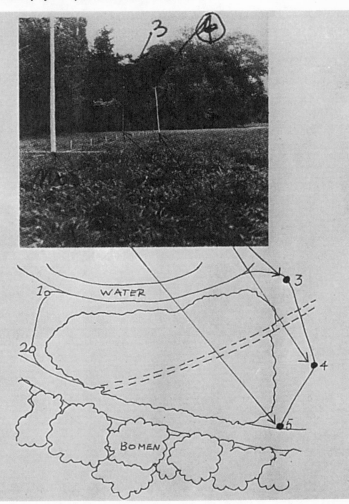

Jan Dibbets. Photo from *Robin Redbreast's Territory.* 1969.

————. *The Pencil on Paper Descriptive Works of Gilbert and George the Sculptors.* Art for All, London, 1970.

Graham, Dan. *Some Photographic Projects.* John Gibson, New York.

————. *1966.* John Gibson, New York.

Groh, Klaus. *"If I Had a Mind."* International Editions, Tübingen, Milan, New York, 1970.

Grieger, Scott. *Impersonations* [Los Angeles, 1970?]. Photographs of the artist impersonating art works by other artists.

Haber, Ira Joel. *36 Houses.* New York, March, 1970.

————. *Survey.* New York, 1970.

Huebler, Douglas. *Duration.* Sperone, Turin, 1970. The book consists of "Duration Piece 1, Torino, Italy, January, 1970"; 61 photographs made according to eight different systems in time.

Jarden, Richards. [*Seven Photo Series*]. Halifax, Nova Scotia, 1970: Cinderella, Traffic Jam, Facial Angle, Running in Place (Simulation), Falling. High Tide (Simulation), Sunset (Simulation). The first three plus Growth Rate (Girls) and Growth Rate (Boys) published earlier in slightly larger photographic booklets instead of in envelopes. (Rep.)

————. *Active and Passive States,* Halifax, 1970. A double photo.

Richards Jarden. *Facial Angle:* "The angle formed on the face by two straight lines drawn from the base of the nose, the one to the base of the ear, the other to the most projecting point on the forehead. In antique statues the facial angle is usually 90°. As a general principle it may be said that intelligence is proportional to the facial angle. It is at any rate an incontestible fact that the lower one descends in the human race the more the facial angle diminishes."—Jules Adeline, *The Adeline Art Dictionary* (New York: Frederick Ungar, 1966), p. 15.

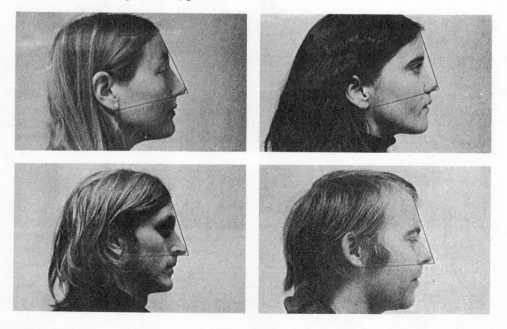

Jacks, Robert. *Twelve Drawings.* New York, 1970.

Kinmont, Robert. *Measuring Some of My Friends* (color) and *Just About the Right Size.* San Francisco, 1970.

Kosuth, Joseph. *Function/Funzione/Función/Fonction/Funktion.* Sperone, Turin, 1970. "This is from the sixth investigation of 'Art as Idea as Idea.'"

Maloney, Martin. *Fractionals.* Press Works, Brattleboro, Vt., 1970, and *Integuments,* n.d.

Merz, Mario. *Fibonacci 1202.* Sperone, Turin, 1970.

Morris, Michael. *Alex and Rodger, Rodger and Alex.* National Film Board of Canada, Ottawa, 1970.

Olsen, Richard. *Sixteen Sentences.* San Francisco, 1970.

Piene, Otto. *More Sky (Things to Do and Wind Manual).* Cambridge, Mass., 1970.

Ruppersberg, Allan. *23 Pieces* and *24 Pieces.* Sunday Quality, Los Angeles, 1970.

Ruscha, Edward. *Real Estate Opportunities.* Los Angeles, 1970.

Sanéjouand, J. M. *Introduction to Concrete Space.* Paris, Editions Mathias Fels, 1970.

Wall, Jeff. *Landscape Manual.* Fine Arts Gallery, University of British Columbia, Vancouver, 1960. Fifty-two-page booklet, text and photos "from and for a work in progress."

Weiner, Lawrence, *Tracce/Traces.* Sperone, Turin, 1970. Each of the following words, with its Italian translation, is one page of the book:

Reduced Flushed Marred Ruptured Greased Mashed Fermented Notched Smelted Smudged Painted Mined Bracketed Cabled Locked Mucked Mixed Bleached Demarked Thrown Breached Secured Turned Removed Tossed Sanded Poured Transferred Glued Ignited Diverted Affronted Abridged Cratered Shattered Pitted Placed Spanned Dug Displaced Sprayed Stained Translated Bored Dragged Folded Split Shored Strung Obstructed

Honnef, Klaus. *Concept Art.* A special edition of *Kunst,* vol. 10, no. 38, qu. 2, 1970. Text, chronology, bibliography, selected words, and "Zehn Fragen zur Concept Art"—a discussion between Dibbets, Fischer and Siegelaub in person, Jurgen Harten on the phone, and Brouwn, Groh and Ulrichs in writing.

Tucker, Marcia. *Robert Morris.* New York, Whitney Museum of American Art and Praeger Publishers, 1970.

Artists and Photographs. Multiples Gallery, New York, 1970. Text by Lawrence Alloway (reprinted in *Studio International,* April, 1970); large box of works by Bochner, Christo, Dibbets, Gormley, Graham, Huebler, Kaprow, Kirby, LeWitt, Long, Morris, Nauman (the book LAAIR), Oppenheim, Rauschenberg, Ruscha, Smithson, Venet, Warhol. Excerpts follow from Michael Kirby, "A Statement, May 10, 1969," to accompany cardboard models of photographic sculpture (Rep.):
    The primary use of photographs in my work is to "embed" the piece of sculpture in the space around it. Pictures are taken either "through" the piece—by taking two

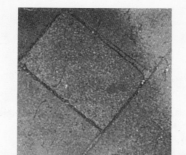
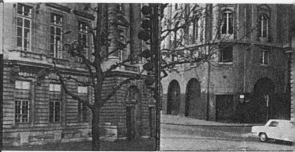
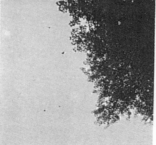

Michael Kirby. *Pont Neuf: The Construction of a Tetrahedron in Space.* 1970. Courtesy Multiples, Inc., New York.

photographs, one with the sculpture in position and one with it removed, this is possible even with a solid structure—or, with the camera perhaps lying on the sculptural surface, directly away from it. The latter procedure gives what I call a "mirror" photograph: a direct "reflection" of the space. When mounted in the completed structure, the photographs refer the piece outward to its environment. The information in the photographs relates to its real counterparts, "embedding" the work so that it cannot be moved from its exact location without destroying its psychological and esthetic content.

If a photograph and its subject are both presented to consciousness, a connection exists between them. Since the photographs in my embedded sculpture are "aimed" at their subjects, I conceptualize the relation as a straight line or a ray (somewhat like the invisible beam of an infrared searchlight) joining the two. To me the physical structure of the piece is composed of these mental elements; its shape is, in part, intangible. *Window Rectangle,* for example, consists of only the four corners of a rectangle, two mounted outside my apartment and two inside; mirror photographs on the truncating faces of each corner show the opposite corner as well as the detail

142

behind it and complete the four metal sides of the rectangle, two of which pass through the windows.

Thus photographs may make connections and draw lines in space, but they may also bridge distance in a more intellectual way by referring to that which is not present. When used systematically, this kind of relationship can, for example, join two sections of the same piece that are a great distance apart and beyond the range of visual context.

In all of my embedded pieces, the actual physical object is used to create a much larger, partly cerebral structure. The sculpture is a machine or instrument to be used by the conceptual mind rather than a mass or shape merely to be looked at. Just as an instrument such as a yardstick or a microscope must be actively used before it provides results, these pieces must be used as visual instruments before they can be understood. This operation takes time, and I consider my work to be basically contemplative. . . .

Another aspect of photography that interests me is its relationship to time. A photograph, as they say, "captures" an instant of the continuum. As soon as it has been taken, it is "out of date." In some situations and relationships, this fact can be exploited. A picture can refer not only to another point in space but to another time. Often, for example, the things represented in the photographs of my embedded sculpture are moved or new things added; the photo no longer matches the environment. This is one of several ways that time is directly represented in the work.

Strike Work, 1/70, 2/70, 3/70. School of the Art Institute of Chicago, 1970. Three booklets of work by students and artists associated with the school.

Statements, no. 1, January, 1970. David Rushton, Philip Pilkington, eds. Coventry, England, Analytical Art Press. "This magazine is to be produced twice yearly to contain work by students at present in their first year of the Fine Art Faculty [of Lanchester Polytechnic]. These articles either were written on topics set or developed from work that was begun within the five areas of study covered by the course: Art Theory, Audio Visual, Epistemology, Romanticism, and Technos." Contributors: S. Beeby, K. Lole, G. Mileson, P. Pilkington, D. Rushton, C. Willsmore.

955,000. Vancouver Art Gallery and Student Union Building Gallery, University of British Columbia, Vancouver, January 13–February 8, 1970. Continuation of Seattle *557,087* (September, 1969; see p. 110). Forty-two catalogue cards added; three artists added: Christos Dikeakos, Alex Hay, Greg Curnoe; two bibliography cards added. As in Seattle, the work was widely distributed over the city and nearby environs as well as in the two indoor locations. Reviewed by Ted Lindberg, *Artscanada,* June, 1970; Joan Lowndes, *Vancouver Province,* January 12, January 16, January 19; Charlotte Townsend, *Vancouver Sun,* January 2, January 14, January 16.

Tabernakel. Louisiana Museum, Humleboek, Denmark, January, 1970. Special issue of *Louisiana Revy,* vol. 10, no. 3, on the exhibition, edited by Per Kirkeby and John Hunov (in Danish). Artists include Beuys, Dibbets, Long, Panamarenko. Texts: Mauer, Strelow, and Christiansen on Beuys; texts or photo-sections by the other artists; text by Beuys on his student program (1968).

Trini, Tommaso. "Mutare le attitudini concettuali in practica." *Gennaio 70,* Bologna, January, 1970 (for the Biennale di Bologna).

January 1, 1970: At this point, The Great Griswold's work and its far-reaching implications surfaced. It was evident that He anticipated in His scientific perfectology program the convoluted implications of conceptual and dematerialized works made later in His manner. His work is continuously and carefully overlooked as was the traditional manner of the totem builders.

Frederick Barthelme. Two Works from January–February, 1970:

Date: February 2, 1970

RE: Sequence

____3____ individual work(s):

1. Being, in the physical and/or mental condition____hungry_____.
2. Being, in the physical and/or mental condition____eating_____.
3. Being, in the physical and/or mental condition____not hungry_____.

OMIT 4. Being, in the physical and/or mental condition_____
OMIT 5. Being, in the physical and/or mental condition_____
OMIT 6. Being, in the physical and/or mental condition_____.

       Each work includes and accepts but does not determine everything that occurs in duration of the specific condition.

       Each work can only be accomplished personally, and in that way exists as a field of potential delimited by the specified condition.

F. Barthelme, excerpt from a text of February 4, 1970:

Instead of presenting information to be perceived, most of my recent work locates the presentation-perception process in the individual. But so that it can be said that I am making art or anything else, some presentation is required. Because any presentation contains information, each of those presentations contains information. But the information is such that it declines the central role of object or object-substitute. In the "being" pieces the information is either peripheral (facing north, facing south, etc.), or it is hopelessly central and unavoidable (tired, refreshed, etc.). Thus it is not the type of information that can successfully accept serious study. The "art" or "meaning" of the work does not come directly from the represented information, but must be inferred individually by each audience member. In these works I am not interested in presenting anything for people to see, experience, or think about. I am interested in suggesting conditions which, defining an art context, allow the inference of any meaning.

DATE: February 6, 1970
SUBSTITUTION: 15

INSTEAD OF MAKING ART I ___filled___
out this form.

_____

_____

Frederick Barthelme. *Substitution 15.* February 6, 1970.

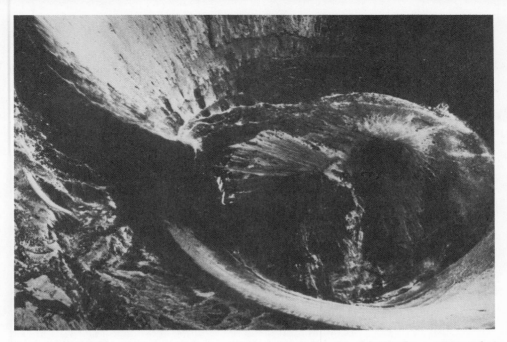

Peter Hutchinson. *Paricutin Volcano.* 450 lbs. of bread and mold, 250′ long. 1970. John Gibson Commissions, Inc.

Hutchinson, Peter. "Paricutin Volcano," January, 1970. Offset text accompanying exhibition of an "Ecologic Work" at John Gibson, New York, February 14–March 31. Account of making his bread and colored-mold piece in the volcano's crater (Rep.):

My project was to lay the bread, wet it once and let the steam and the heat of the rocks and sun do the rest. I expected mold to grow in large quantities and, I hoped, in patches large enough to show in the photographs I would make. I would cover the bread with plastic in the interim, which would condense the water on its surface and make a super-saturated environment in which mold likes to grow. This, in effect, would make a greenhouse environment in surroundings which hitherto had been practically sterile, and certainly unable to support molds or even lichens. . . .

It is not extraordinary to grow mold on bread. I was not doing so in any scientific sense. I was attempting several other things—to juxtapose a microorganism against a macrocosmic landscape, yet in such amount that the results would be plainly visible through color changes. I also chose an environment that, although having the necessary elements for growth, needed a subtle alteration on utilization to make growth possible. Volcanic ground in a sense is new material, sterilized and reorganized then thrown out from the deeper crust of the earth. It is similar to the earliest earth landscapes and related to the early geological periods such as the Precambrian when molds and algae played the dominant role on dry land that today belongs to the higher mammals and insects. Today, when volcanoes appear from the sea, they are first colonized by bacteria, molds, and algae. The conditions of early history are continually duplicated.

Ferguson, Gerald. Proposal: *A Dictionary for Concrete Poets;* **twenty-eight sections, each section devoted to words (alphabetized) of the same length. Halifax, January 28, 1970.**

January 12–29, School of Visual Arts Gallery, New York: Sol LeWitt directs an exhibition in which he asks Hollis Frampton and Michael Snow to record separate sequential studies of dance motion; homage to Muybridge.

Meyer, Ursula. "How to Explain Pictures to a Dead Hare." *Art News,* January, 1970. Based on conversations with Joseph Beuys:

In How to Explain Pictures to a Dead Hare, Beuys covered his head with honey and gold-leaf, transforming himself into a sculpture. He cradled the dead hare in his arms and took it "to the pictures and I explained to him everything that was to be seen. I let him touch the pictures with his paws and meanwhile talked to him about them. . . . I explained them to him because I do not really like explaining them to people. Of course there is a shadow of truth in this. A hare comprehends more than many human beings with their stubborn rationalism. . . . I told him that he needed only to scan the picture to understand what is really important about it. The hare probably knows better than man that directions are important. You know the hare can turn on a dime. And actually nothing else is involved."

Claura, Michel. "Conceptual Misconceptions." *Studio International,* January, 1970.

Lipman, Jean. "Money for Money's Sake." *Art in America,* January–February, 1970.

Primarily on money works by Kienholz (lettered Watercolor *series sold for $1 to $10,000), Morris ($50 investment loan piece for Whitney* Anti-Illusion *show), and Les Levine ("Profit Systems One," profit or loss on 500 shares of stock); Lee Lozano's* Cash Piece *(giving money to visitors to her studio and recording their reactions) and* Investment Piece *(investing a grant she received December, 1968) were among earlier money works (April 3, 1969, and January 15, 1969). Douglas Huebler has made money works that continue operating into the distant future.*

Millet, Catherine. "L'Art Conceptual." *L'Art Vivant,* January, 1970.

Rosenberg, Harold. "The Art-World: De-Aestheticization." *New Yorker,* January 24, 1970.

***Art-Language,* no. 2, February, 1970, Coventry. Contributions by Kosuth (American editor), Atkinson, Bainbridge, Baldwin, Barthelme, Brown-David, Burn, Hirons, Hurrell, McKenna, Ramsden, and Michael Thompson, "Conceptual Art: Category and Action":**

It is an astonishing but inescapable conclusion that we have reached; namely, that the seemingly erudite, scholastic, neutral, logical, austere, even incestuous, movement of conceptual art is, in fact, a naked bid for power at the very highest level—the wresting from the groups at present at the top of our social structure, of control over the symbols of society.

Joseph Kosuth, "Introductory Note by the American Editor":

Current American art activity can be considered having three areas of endeavor. For discussion purposes, I call them: aesthetic, "reactive," and conceptual. Aesthetic or "formalist" art and criticism is directly associated with a group of writers and artists working on the east coast of the United States (with followers in England). It is, however, far from limited to these men, and as well is still the general notion of art as held by most of the lay public. That notion is that, as stated by Clement Greenberg: "aesthetic judgments are given and contained in the immediate experience of art. They coincide with it; they are not arrived at afterwards through reflection or thought. Aesthetic judgments are also involuntary: you can no more choose whether or not to like a work of art than you can choose to have sugar taste sweet or lemons sour."

In terms of art, then, this work (the painting or the sculpture) is merely the "dumb" subject-matter (or cue) to critical discourse. The artist's role is not unlike that of the valet's assistance to his marksman master: pitching into the air of clay plates for targets. This follows in that aesthetics deals with considerations of opinions or perception, and since experience is immediate, art becomes merely a human ordered base for perceptual kicks, thus paralleling (and "competing" with) natural sources of visual (and other) experiences. The artist is omitted from the "art activity" in that he is merely the carpenter of the predicate and does not take part in the conceptual engagement (such as the critic functions in his traditional role) of the "construction" of the art proposition. If aesthetics is concerned with the discussion of perception and the artist is only engaged in the construction of the stimulant, he is thus—within the concept "aesthetics as art"—not participating in the concept formation. In so far as visual experiences, indeed aesthetic experiences, are capable of existence separate from the art, the condition of art in aesthetic or formalist art is exactly that discussion or consideration of concepts as examined in the functioning of a particular predicate in an art proposition. To restate: the only possible functioning as art aesthetic painting or sculpture is capable of, is the engagement or inquiry around its presentation within an art proposition. Without the discussion it is "experience" pure and simple. It only becomes "art" when it is brought within the realm of an art context (like any other material used within art).[1] [Footnotes appear at end of article.]

A discussion of what I call "reactive" art will be necessarily brief and simplistic. For the most part "reactive" art is the scrap-heap of 20th century art ideas—cross-referenced, "evolutionary," pseudo-historical, "cult of personality," and so forth; much of which can be easily described as an angst-ridden series of blind actions.

This can be explained partially via what I refer to as the artist's "how" and "why" procedure. The "why" refers to art ideas and the "how" refers to the formal (often material) elements used in the art proposition (or as I call it in my own work, "the form of presentation"). Many disinterested in and often incapable of conceiving of art ideas (which is to say: their own inquiry into the nature of art) have used notions such as "self-expression" and "visual experience" to give a "why" ambient to work which is basically "how" inspired.

But work that focuses on the "how" aspect of art is only taking a superficial and necessarily gestural reaction to only one chosen "formal" consequence—out of several possible ones. As well, such a denial (or ignorance) of art's conceptual (or "why") nature follows always to a primitive or anthropocentric conclusion about artistic priorities.[2]

The "how" artist is one that relates art to craft, and subsequently considers artistic activity "how" construction. The framework in which he works is an externally provided historical one, which takes only into account the morphological characteristics of preceding artistic activity. This reactionary impetus has left us with a kind of involuted artistic inflation.

Thus the only real difference between the formalists and the "reactive" artists is that the formalists believe that artistic activity consists in closely following the "how" construction tradition; whereas the "reactive" artists believe that artistic activity consists in an "open" interpretation (and subsequent reaction to) not as much the "how" construction of "long range" (or traditional) "how" construction, but the "short range" or directly preceding "how" constructions. But both readings of "how" construction still—in a more or less sophisticated form—are concerned with the morphological characteristics, rather than the functional aspects, of artistic propositions.

Art propositions referred to by journalists as "anti-form," "earthworks," "process art," etc. comprise greatly what I refer to here as "reactive" art. What this art attempts is to refer to a traditional notion of art while still being "avant-garde." One support is securely placed in the material (sculpture) and/or visual (painting) arena, enough to maintain the historical continuum while the other is left to roam about for new "moves" to make and further "breakthroughs" to accomplish. One of the main reasons that such art seeks connections on some level to the traditional morphology of art is the art market. Cash support demands "goods." This always ends in a neutralization of the art proposition's independence from tradition.

In the final analysis such art propositions become equivocated with either painting or sculpture. Many artists working outside (deserts, forests, etc.) are now bringing to the gallery and museum super blown-up color photographs (painting) or bags of grain, piles of earth and even in one instance a whole uprooted tree (sculpture). It muddles the art proposition into invisibility.

At its most strict and radical extreme the art I call conceptual is such because it is based on an inquiry into the nature of art. Thus, it is not just the activity of constructing art propositions, but a working out, a thinking out, of all the implications of all aspects of the concept "art." Because of the implied duality of perception and conception in earlier art, a middleman (critic) appeared useful. This art both annexes the functions of the critic, and makes a middleman unnecessary. The other system—artist-critic audience—existed because the visual elements of the "how" construction gave art an aspect of entertainment, thus it had an audience. The audience of conceptual art is composed primarily of artists—which is to say that an audience separate from the participants doesn't exist. In a sense, then, art becomes as "serious" as science or philosophy, which don't have "audiences" either. It is interesting or it isn't, just as one is informed or isn't. Previously, the artist's "special" status merely relegated him into being a high priest (or witch doctor) of show business.[3]

This conceptual art, then, is an inquiry by artists that understand that artistic activity is not solely limited to the framing of art propositions, but further, the investigation of the function, meaning, and use of any and all (art) propositions, and their consideration within the concept of the general term "art." And as well, that an artist's dependence on the critic or writer on art to cultivate the conceptual implications of his art propositions, and argue their explication, is either intellectual irresponsibility or the naivest kind of mysticism.

Fundamental to this idea of art is the understanding of the linguistic nature of all art propositions, be they past or present, and regardless of the elements used in their construction.[4]

This concept of American "conceptual" art is, I admit, here defined by my own characterization, and understandably, is one that is related to my own work of the past few years. Yet it is here at the "strict and radical extreme" where agreement is reached between American and British conceptual artists—at least in the most general aspects of our art investigations—as diverse as the "choice of tools" or methodology or art propositions may be.

There is a considerable amount of art activity between the "strict and radical extreme," and what I call "reactive" art earlier. My contributions by artists working on the American continent will be relatable—whenever possible—to the former, though unfortunately the quantity of such activity makes the sole consideration of such contributions impossible.

NOTES [*Three have been omitted by the artist for this version.*]

1. One begins to understand the popularity among critics of such mindless movements as expressionism, and the general disdain toward "intellectual" artists such as Duchamp, Reinhardt, Judd, or Morris.

2. In recent years artists have realized that the "how" is often purchasable and that purchasability of the "how" (and the subsequent "de-personalization" of "how" construction) is negatively impersonal only when the "how" is functioning for a "personal touch" "why" construct.

3. An aspect of this problem is that which was fundamental to our earlier discussion of formalist and "reactive" art. That has to do with the supervisory, even "parental" role critics have taken in the 20th century toward artists; the institutionalized condescension engaged in by museum and gallery personnel; and the peculiar ability artists themselves have to romanticize intellectual bankruptcy and opportunism.

4. Without this understanding a "conceptual" form of presentation is little more than a manufactured stylehood, and such art we have with increasing abundance.

Art-Language (Atkinson, Baldwin, Bainbridge, Hurrell). "Status and Priority." *Studio International,* **February, 1970. In two parts; excerpts from Part II follow:**

"It makes no difference to the thought whether I use the word 'horse' or 'steed' or 'carthorse' or 'mare.' The assertive force does not extend over that in which the words differ. . . . It is just as important to neglect distinctions that do not touch the heart of the matter as to make distinctions which concern what is essential. . . .

"Thoughts are by no means unreal, but their reality is of quite a different kind from that of things. And their effect is brought about by an act of the thinker without which they would be ineffective, at least, as far as we can see. And yet the thinker does not create them, but must take them as they are."—Gottlieb Frege, "The Thought: A Logical Inquiry," A. M. and M. Quinton, trans. (*Mind,* vol. 65, 1956, p. 296 and p. 311.)

This might look like an arm's-length-away attempt to get to a respectable multiple object theory. Keeping "Occam's Razor" in mind, one will only engage in entity multiplication as necessary.

If it is a matter of history at all, then it is more than a simple Taine-like one that some critics, particularly the so-called formalists, are guilty (in their "analytical" maunderings) of uttering zeugmas (or, at least, some kind of category mistakes). It might be that they just make intentionally biased semantic errors, i.e., not just mistakes in the counting of class members.

The assumption that there are "effective" decisions as to categorical commitment is central to most constructural edifices: in a sense, it adds a "practical" significance to theoretical, historical and evaluative thinking. Also, it adds a significance to a position's categorical commitment, which it otherwise would lack. The determination of virtual "practicabilities"[1] includes the determination of categorically informed as well as "empirical" possibilities. ("Empirical" is used here legitimately insofar as one is faced at times with things to observe and interpret.) One's evaluation of constructual possibilities presupposes that some of them are categorically "practicable." . . .

There has been little analysis of the relation between *ad hoc* categorical thinking and its theoretical convolutions. One of the difficulties, met half submerged, is a notion of indistinguishability (*qua* categories) which is not transitive. . . .

A lot of critics and artists are disposed to take seriously mere assertions of class membership which disguise specious operationism. The point is that the onto-logical-categorical status of a work of art may vary *mutatis mutandis* with the onto-categorical commitment of significant (*qua* art) operations and theorizing; hence, one has the "range" of (loosely) "application" of "work of art."

There isn't much of a problem created by the upshots of this: it doesn't matter if one can't helpfully sort works of art into the same substitution class (or semantic category). Neither is it particularly unhelpful if works of art be treated as virtual entities only. But virtuality does not alone inform one of categorical complexity: the concept ". . . of art" or "art . . ."[2] is as operable when works of art (etc.)are only talked of nominally—i.e., when they are thought of as merely having an intentional structure and as only indirectly referred to (*Sunnybank,* Terry Atkinson's essays, etc.) as it is when they are regarded as pretty clear-cut extensional entities. One may well take the "formalists" to task for an insistence on a reistic, physicalistic "object" commitment, which, so far, seems to disclose a species of creeping essentialism.[3] . . .

Ad Reinhardt's dictum[4] (which is perhaps the locus classicus of a lot of mutually irreconcilable theories) must be one of the few genuine tautologies of natural language:[5] it seems odd that it's treated as a revelation. . . .

One does not, as a linguistic agent, just learn to apply a term ostensibly: as Professor Quinton pointed out, in a purely ostensive situation, there would be hardly any intelligible distinction to be made between coextensiveness and synonymy: definition itself would be a problem.[6]

It is not just a matter of appealing to the obviousness of an equivocation when a description is misused (i.e., here, "confused"—applied to two things of different types in the same sentence). It is pretty obvious that for a concept to be regarded as operable, then it must have some range of application in the appropriate context. If every hypothesis, etc., which employed or applied it were a category mistake, then apart from just syntactical application, it would not be considered as of any cognitive value.

Pedantic category confusions aren't consistent or inconsistent, although, again, they may retain some syntactic operability. What is appropriate in the context of art-objects, etc., is some procedure of clarification . . . a procedure which might well disclose the multiple complexity of the situation in which a notion of a priority which is not just couched in terms of qualitative analogy might be significant. One would have to have some theory of category correctness. In the present context, one has not the choice of dealing with violations (there are usually two)—here a mismanaged sequence never comes up for the count, it's not even a matter of throwing it out. Clarification on this level is taxonomically—or if you like the long-range 8 by 75 term, ontologically—revealing. That indicates something else, namely that constructural and conceptual edifices are isomorphic with taxonomic ones. . . .

The class of operationally significant art objects is restricted to the class of entities—which, with respect to a corpus of theory, etc., can mistakenly be said to be art objects.

This is not just a way of holding off, or of circumlocuting prerogative questions, neither is the matter just one of pleading for language strata: the assertion is, rather, that constructs, etc., and evaluation procedures are not examined by the inspection of one paradigm of significance. Echoing Frege, one has some action but little interaction.

NOTES [*One has been omitted in this version.*]

1. "Practicabilities" is intended to convey something like "operationally and theoretically significant possibilities."

2. Fill in, for the former, "work of . . .", for the latter, ". . . object," etc.

3. A sort of weakened "essentialism" may well be acceptable where it is viewed as a sort of operationalism. And the upshot of this might be that no corpus of art constructs, etc., can deny, or be denied by, Joseph Kosuth's "analyticity" metaphor.

4. Quoted by, among others, Joseph Kosuth in a recent article.

5. Something informative usually lurks in apparent "tautology" in natural language.

It would be helpful when a sort of operationalism ("different operations define different concepts"; cf. Pap, *Semantics & Necessary Truth,* etc.) is revealed that it be noted for what it is: sculpture of the 70's ideology disguises it in a flabby dialectic.

6. A. M. Quinton (in *P.A.S.,* vol. 64, 1963–64, p. 54) has noted that "It is not inconceivable that ostensively learnt terms with the same extension should differ in meaning . . . a learner might connect two such co-extensive terms with different recurrent aspects or features of the common stock of situations with which they were co-related."

*   *   *

I don't understand a good deal of what is said by Art-Language, but I admire the investigatory energies, the tireless spade-work (not calling one one), the full commitment to the reestablishment of a valid language by which to discuss art, and the occasional humor in their writings. The chaos inherent in their reason fascinates me, but it is also irritating to be unequipped to evaluate their work. I don't know how it is or if it is evaluated by adepts in philosophy as philosophy, but I find it infuriating to have to take them on faith. I agree with their goal of clearing the air around the "pseudo mystique" of art and artists, their demand that observers stop being "good catholics." If only they could exorcise the Jesuit in themselves at the same time. In the land of Quine and Rroses inhabited by A-L, "direct experience" doesn't exist until it has been made indirect, often in loco parentheses. If the air were cleared, what would they use to make art? For all their distaste for formal or "esthetic" or "reactive" art, it seems to me that A-L's work in itself constitutes a kind of formalism, inasmuch as it approaches given conditions analytically (what is more "esthetic" than "an inquiry into the nature of art" or into the nature of "natural sculpture"?); as well as reactively, inasmuch as words, thought, tortuous systems are their material, and they emphasize this material and its inherent properties as much as, say, Carl Andre emphasizes his. My main questions are: Why must art as language be considered the replacement for all other art intentions? Are A-L's own intentions primarily to function critically? Does art fundamentally opposed to A-L's ideas have to "stand up to an analysis" on A-L's grounds? Is A-L justified in raking anyone else over the coals for lack of clarity? They have set up a situation within which the obsessive beauty of their abstractions can only continue to be interesting, but their position is considerably weakened when they leave their semantically-sustained and self-imposed isolation for the arena of ephemeral art world (as opposed to art) issues, and just when they seemed to be out of reach of "the artist's dependence on the critic or writer on art to cultivate the conceptual implications of his propositions and argue their explication." A-L is at its best when it is self-referential, when it operates within its own hypothetical domain of analogue, when it sticks to its own rejection of "all outside experience," its characterization of its "typed material" as "nothing over and above theoretical considerations." Having arrived early (1966) and radically at that stage, the danger now is not that A-L will be surpassed at their own game, so much as that they may become the critics they are trying to make obsolete. (From an unpublished review by L.R.L. of *Idea Structures*, June, 1970.)

Rosemarie Castoro. Excerpt from *Love's Time*, February 26, 1970, 6:15 P.M.–March 1, 1970, 3:30 P.M.:

Minutes	Activity
0–22/7	From history thinking to over compensation
0–42/14	From leaving stoned out of my mind to look for someone to buy me a whip
0–13	From the search for a whip to the finding of a friend
0–34/24$^1/_2$	From an unorganized sense of order to putting something there
0–20/7	From breathtaking to slandering and cursing
0–135/15	From starting to make time at St. Adrian's to arousing into the day and somehow being carried
0–31/28	From an uplift to the start of work
0–165/53	From vacuuming to splitting
0–12/50	From entering and exiting to the arrival of the IRT local
0–54/5	From leaving in taxi after seeing likenesses of drawings of mine in hair of movie
0–27/28	From onward to no answer
0–9$^1/_2$/57	From needing to go away to still being here
0–63/20	From leaving through frippery of musical comedy war movie to sitting in St. Adrian's
0–5/26	From ordering white wine to reading over "Love's Time" and improving the legibility of my quick handwriting
0–55	From clarity and legibility to what kind of poetry do you write

A receiver in which the incoming signal is mixed with a locally generated signal to produce an intermediate frequency that is then amplified and detected a second time **to produce the audio frequency, University of British Columbia, Vancouver, Fine Arts Gallery (director: Alvin Balkind), February 25–March 14, 1970. Audio and visual potentialities, sound compositions, display situations of tape recorders as objects. Organized and installed by the students of Fine Arts 438.**

Four Artists: Tom Burrows, Duane Lunden, Jeff Wall, Ian Wallace. Fine Arts Gallery, University of British Columbia, Vancouver, February 3–18.

Harrison, Charles. "Notes Towards Art Work." *Studio International,* February, 1970.

February 2–28: The four members of the OHO group (Andraš Šalamun, Dávid Nez, Milenko Matanovic, Marco Pogačnik), two of them in Ljubljana, Yugoslavia, and two in New York, "simultaneously looked at the sun and dropped from the height of 10 cm. one matchstick on a piece of paper" and made a piece combining the results. In April–May, they worked between the New York Museum of Modern Art's *Information* show and the 4th Jugoslavanski Trienale in Belgrade. The group is primarily concerned with systems relationships between locations, time, structures. In May, 1970, they did projects along the Zarica Valley of the River Sava at Drulouka, in relation to historical locations (Neolithic settlement, Celtic mounds, Slovanic graves, medieval church). A piece by Dávid Nez deals with "drawings documenting vibrations of travel during the artist's trip from Ljubljana to Washington, D.C.: (1) drawing begins with placing of felt pen in the center of the paper; (2) artist's control is limited to confining the pen within the boundary of the page." (Rep.)

Milenko Matanovic (OHO group). *String Bending Wheat.* 1970.

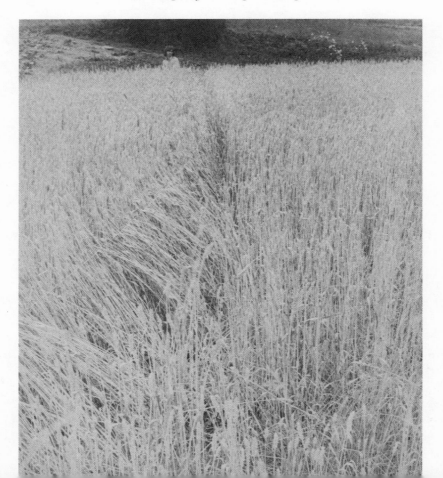

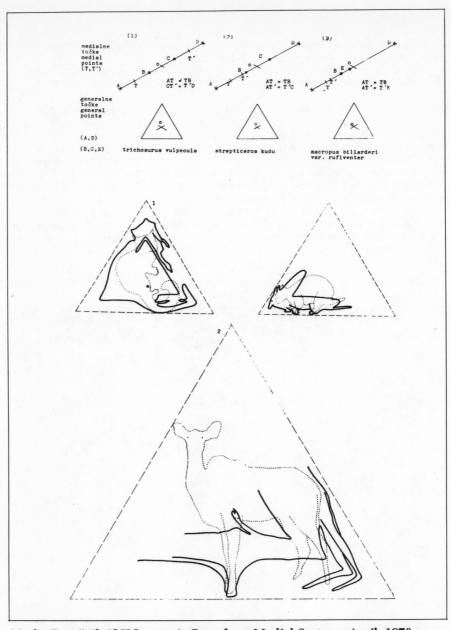

Marko Pogačnik (OHO group). *Page from Medial Systems.* April, 1970.
A piece concerning the time and space relations between "Even Points" (photograph of the *lynx pardellus* from the book *Die Tiere der Erde;* sign of the lynx based on medial systems; rock on the Sava River with engraved medial sign; cat sitting on the rock with the engraved medial sign of the lynx) and "Odd Points" (Albin Pogačnik, 1890–1933, first owner of the book *Die Tiere der Erde;* the lynx alive at the moment of taking photograph for the book; physical process of engraving the sign; geographical location of the rock); all based on a spherical grid.

February–April: Art & Project of Amsterdam moves its activities to Tokyo. Since the "gallery" is usually the *Bulletin,* they function as easily in Japan as in Holland.

Stanley Brouwn. *La Paz.* Book published on occasion of show at the Stedelijk Museum, Schiedam, February 14–March 16, 1970.

February–May: Ian Milliss sends "mailing pieces" from Sydney, Australia.

Los Angeles: "Society for the Preservation and Prevention of Art" founded by Allen Ruppersberg.

Alloway, Lawrence. "Arakawa Annexed: Interview." *Arts,* February, 1970.

Honnef, Klaus. "Jan Dibbets." *Das Kunstwerk,* February, 1970.

Robbin, Anthony. "Peter Hutchinson's Ecological Art." *Art International,* February, 1970.

Arato, G. "Arte povera e rivoluzione." *Secolo XIX,* February 25, 1970.

Brikcius, Eugen. "Happenings in Prague." *Studio International,* February, 1970. In particular: Zorka Saglova's "Hommage à Gustav Obermann."

Burnham, Jack. "Alice's Head: Reflections on Conceptual Art." *Artforum,* February, 1970.

Bongartz, Roy. "It's Called Earth Art—and Boulderdash." *New York Times Magazine,* February 1, 1970.

McNay, M. "Art Povera: Conceptual, Actual or Impossible Art?" *Design,* February, 1970.

Millet, Catherine. "Conceptual Art." *Opus Internationale,* February, 1970.

VH-101, Paris, no. 1, March, 1970. Editors: Otto Hahn and Françoise Essellier. Includes Daniel Buren, "Mise en Garde No. 3".

March 8, WBAI-FM, New York. Symposium moderated by Lucy R. Lippard with Douglas Huebler, Dan Graham, Carl Andre, Jan Dibbets; program initiated by Jeanne Siegel, Art Programs Director, WBAI. Excerpts follow:
  LL: I want to talk about the word in relationship to the physical object, the physical sensation, and physical experience. These are four visual artists who have used words one way or another.
  CA: I'm a disciple of Brancusi and I don't know what I'm doing here.
  LL: He's here because he is a sculptor who also writes poetry. Dan, you've been called a poet and a critic and a photographer. Are you an artist now?
  DG: I don't define myself, but whatever I do, I think, is defined by the medium. I did printed matter about three or four years ago. Things in print, things for magazines, things that use photography. I've done things in all the areas that other people have worked in and I think they define themselves.
  LL: I suppose one thing we'll have to talk about is the lack of distinction between the various media. . . .
  CA: I distinguish among media as severely as anyone. I think the so-called art object has always been part of an open system.
  DG: I agree one hundred per cent. Something is defined by the reader and the

context it is placed in. The artist is defined by the product he makes, but not necessarily by himself. I was interested in a system that is tied into a medium rather than in my saying I am an artist.

LL: A sort of giver and receiver situation.

DG: That's very important. The recipient effect is as important as the giver part. The object is just a cause.

CA: I think the object is just a locus, embodying some sort of transaction which is between all those things we are talking about—the reader, the recipient, the sender, the social situation, the art, whatever.

LL: But the experience is different. When you experience an object it tends to be, if not necessarily a static experience, at least more physically involved than when you experience words. Or does it?

DH: I just came in on an airplane and I was thinking about what we were going to do. While I was looking out the window, it hit me that I was measuring off things, that I could *see* where I had been. I saw the last place I'd stayed, in Brooklyn, and the Statue of Liberty for the first time in all these years, and an area where I thought Lucy lives. Anyway, I realized that I was measuring sense impressions against conceptual knowledge, the conceptual knowledge being maps. I knew that this physical reality could be translated into language or into words that were very much like the words on a map. So as Dan and Carl, I think, are pointing out, there is much more flexibility between what is an object and what registers in the head as the experience of the object than the kind of separation that we all seem to be objecting to.

LL: But maybe words are a better vehicle for a certain kind of experience. . . .

DH: No, not necessarily. Just a recognition that they are perhaps more a part than an embarrassed byproduct, which is what art historians have always made of them.

CA: I want to give you the three phases of art as I know it. There was a time when people were interested in the bronze sheath of the Statue of Liberty, modeled in the studio. And then there came a time when artists were not really concerned with the bronze sheath but were interested in Eiffel's iron interior structure, supporting the statue. Now artists are interested in Bedloe's Island.

DG: I'd like to question the use of the terms "words" as opposed to "objects." I think what Doug was talking about has more to do with something reduced to schematic information. Just perceiving an object—the way the eye works, the way our senses work—in terms of schematic information. It is not a word-object dichotomy, but really what is the nature of information, i.e., how we perceive things. This is a very complicated process and in part that is what the art, or whatever you call it, is about. I'm also interested in the reading process that is so relevant to the reader rather than to the impetus of the object.

LL: Isn't it also for capturing something that has hitherto been considered uncapturable by art because of the time-space factors? Jan, when you did your territorial piece with the robin [see *p. 139*], why did that have to be called a "drawing-sculpture"?

JD: It doesn't matter to me what I'm called. I just use the work, what is there. I think I did it because people call me an artist and so I had to call it sculpture and drawing.

CA: I have spent part of my life working as a poet and I distinguish between poetry, which is hard work, and sculpture, which is hard work. I don't really know what conceptions are. I don't have any ideas about art and poetry. I have *desires.*

LL: You acknowledge that when you call yourselves artists. You are pushing something, making some art that didn't exist before, something you *want* to exist.

DH: I am having it make itself, in a sense, or having other people make it. I want to put it in a situation or context where it will be happening not only now but later. I just start it.

CA: People in Halifax kept bugging me because I refused to say that I had ideas for my work, and finally I said, look: i have very few ideas but I have some strong desires. I want what is not yet in the world. Ideas are a dime a dozen. I agree with Dr. Guillotine that all ideas are the same except in execution. You can't cut off desires except painfully. George M. Cohan once said that anybody who believed they had thought of something new was either a liar or a fool.

DG: I agree about conception. I don't think I am doing conceptual art.

LL: Whether you like it or not, Carl, you have an idea—whether or not it is articulated. You are talking about people who write down their ideas as their art, but you can't make a distinction between idea and doing something.

CA: I can make a distinction between Lucy Lippard as an idea and Lucy Lippard as a desire, believe me. . . . I have a great anger against so-called conceptual art because the great beauty of art, of the physical arts now, and even many kinds of poetry, is the simple fact that art is close to nature, and the trouble with conceptual art is that it is not close to nature. If abstract art is art as its own content, then conceptual art is pure content without art. Following Reinhardt, I desire art-as-art, not art-as-idea.

LL: I don't know how you can say that, but let's not get into defining conceptual art, because it seems like an awful dead end. Certainly there are at least twenty people using either words or written things as vehicles for their art, but there is a distinction between concrete poetry, where the words are made to *look* like something, an image, and so-called conceptual art, where the words are used only to *avoid* looking like something, where it doesn't make any difference how the words look on the page or anything. Maybe Larry Weiner bridges some of that. . . .

CA: Larry is a good poet.

LL: Or else as an artist he's taken poetry further than poetry can ever take itself.

CA: Not at all. He is just into something which in the English language has not been done much before, a more intense poem. Larry Weiner doesn't say "take a ball to Niagara Falls and throw the ball into Niagara Falls." Larry Weiner does a thing that doesn't even exist— "a ball thrown into Niagara Falls." Now that is a suddenness that we don't know in the Western language, except in a very few poets. I must also say that the few language works which Larry Weiner has actually executed have also been good, so I think there is a poet there and some fragment of an artist. Actually he says he has no desire to see a ball thrown in Niagara Falls. He says he doesn't care whether it is done by him or by somebody else, or not done at all.

LL: I think it's nonsense to say there's no desire there. He's probably just as much a physical, or *visual,* artist as Doug and you. . . . His pieces can be done a million times and never be done. I think the difference between poetry and something like Larry's pieces, or those by any of you who use words primarily, is the isolation of a single visual experience. In poetry the words form continuing relationships. Anyway, one thing I like about a lot of so-called conceptual art is that while it communicates itself, or else it doesn't, just as objects do or don't, it gets *transmitted* much more rapidly. Print, photos, documents get out faster and more people see them. Then critics become unnecessary because the primary experience is their audience's own. The responsibility lies with the audience instead of an intermediary. Maybe that's what people don't like about it. The public likes everything explained for it, sorted out for it, value judgments made, which is why all this quality bullshit is dominant. They say, Gee, I don't have much time to look at or think about or enjoy art, so you just tell me ten things I should see, the ten masterpeices this year. Art transferrable by word is forcing people to do some work on their own.

DG: I think art has to have some kind of content. It can't be programmed à la Jack Burnham into everybody's consciousness as adult education.

LL: Doug, is it any part of your work that it can reach more people, or is that just a by-product?

DH: I think objects probably reach more people than art that uses words, because such work still has to be either published or seen. It has to exist *somewhere.*

JD: Well, I don't see so much difference between a written work and any other kind of object. When I do something it has to do with something which is feasible, with what is there. When you have an idea or write something down it has no physical body; then there is nothing.

LL: When you taped a car ride, so what is heard are the miles marked off by voice, and the miles marked off in real space on a map and imaginary head space, and in time, is the visible *map* more important than the other imagined or heard part?

JD: I don't see so much difference between a car driving a certain length and seeing a map.

DH: They are saying now that noise itself is a pollutant. They are giving it a material aspect. Jan's linear recording of noise might be seen as much as a "desire in substance."

LL: Once you communicate a physical sensation to anybody, you have gotten it into the world, and just as physically as if you had put a timber piece or a turd on the ground. You are giving somebody a physical sensation of an experience of an object. There is a very weird dividing line. Like I have a piece of Carl's that is eighty something small pink paper squares; that is pretty damn dematerialized. People tend not to trip over it, not to notice it, and so on. Now, Jan's tape-recorder piece, Doug's ten photographs and statement that I have are far more visible in the house than your sculpture. And they both have to do with physical experience. Doug's piece has to do with sound; it involves birds singing in each photograph. Yours has to do with being there in that place on the floor, but I'm not sure there is any tremendous degree of difference.

CA: I'm not sure there is a difference, but I'm sure that I know what I want to do, and a lot of the pieces that I'm doing now are ephemeral and cannot be recovered, because they return to the state of nature. Salvation in art has always been a struggle between grace and good works.

DG: I think I'm interested in fusing something in the present without documentation. I was never interested in words or syntax in poetry, but more in information. I wanted the things I did to occupy a particular place and be read in a particular present time. The context is very important. I wanted my pieces to be about place as in-formation which is present.

DH: For me, my whole sense of minimal or primary art has to do with the experience of the percipient in the situation I was working with. I always felt that the work was meant to launch the person viewing into a "real-life" experience. The first thing that I did differently from those works was a spontaneous act. . . . I took a road map: it was almost like, "Christ, why not *this*!" I just drew random trips with a magic marker as on an AAA map, and I wrote on those things and gave a number of them out. I wrote something like, "Take the trip or don't take the trip, but if you do take the trip, you better take *my* trip, but it doesn't really matter," and so forth. What you *get,* then, in that work, is everything you see.

LL: Jan, with the photographic perspective-correction pieces—where you stretched a rope out on the ground in a shape that was not a square, but when it was photographed became a square—you had replaced the *seen* perspective with the *photographed* perspective. Did the works themselves have any importance to you or just the photographs?

JD: Only the photographs. In fact, only the negatives.

Evidence on the Flight of Six Fugitives. Museum of Contemporary Art, Chicago, March 27–May 10, 1970. Photographic records of projects by Heizer, Oppenheim, de Maria, Hutchinson, Smithson, Long.

Art Concepts from Europe. Bonino Gallery, New York, March, 1970. Organized by Pierre Restany. "The gallery not as exhibition hall but as bank of ideas"; contributions were filed in drawers and available on request. Discussed by Restany in *Domus* 487, June, 1970.

World Works. March 31, 1970, noon. "Artists and people everywhere are invited to do a street work in a street of their choice. A street work does not harm any person or thing." Documentation sent to H. Weiner, J. Perreault, M. Strider for a book, as yet unpublished.

March 18: Founding by Tom Marioni (Allan Fish) of the Museum of Conceptual Art, San Francisco. At the opening, buckets of white paint were given to visitors with which to paint the walls. On April 30, *Sound Sculpture As,* an exhibition of ten sound events, described in *Avalanche,* no. 1.

March 11, 18, 25: *Hannah Weiner at Her Job,* A. H. Schrieber Co., Inc., New York. "My life is my art. I am my object, a product of the process of self awareness."

Buren, Daniel. "Beware!" *Studio International,* March, 1970. Written July, 1969, and January, 1970; published as "Mise en Garde" in catalogue of Leverkusen *Concept Art* show; see above, November, 1969. Also, "Comment (on Buren's Text)," by Michel Claura.

Burgy, Donald. "Checkup." *Art in America,* March–April, 1970. *Self,* a piece executed in January, 1969, in which data of all kinds on the artist's body and body processes were tested over several days in the hospital devoted to the making of this work.

March 10, 1970: Don Celender, from *Preliminary Statement.* St. Paul, Minnesota:
Realizing that art, as it is experienced currently, reaches only a small portion of the public, my conceptual movements were initiated to explore the realm of the impossible in order to stimulate innovative and creative approaches to bringing art to the masses. Synectics and brainstorming, two techniques which expand normal thought processes, were basic to formulation of the movements. In addition to the concept of art dissemination, these movements were motivated by the desire to survey the attitudes about art held by individuals and organizations occupying key positions in American society.

About twenty-five chief executive officers of major organizations were contacted in each of the four movements listed below. The organizational head received, in addition to his own proposal, copies of proposals sent to the other principals included in the movements so that each would be aware of the scope of the concept.

A brief comment about the intent of the individual movements follows:

Corporate Art Movement
This movement, launched on December 18, 1969, was initiated with business corporations, whose practical orientation was challenged by art concepts which proposed impractical extensions of the products or services of these companies.

Cultural Art Movement
This movement, launched on January 12, 1970, was directed at the museum profession in order to encourage museum officials to disseminate art more widely than at present using unorthodox innovative techniques.

Mass Media Art Movement
This movement, launched on February 18, 1970, was conceived to involve mass media in the process of developing art awareness by bringing art to the masses through their respective media.

Organizational Art Movement
This movement, launched on March 4, 1970, was designed to explore the reactions of divergent groups such as the Ku Klux Klan and Black Panthers to conceptual art proposals. Furthermore, the organizational character of this movement permits art interaction on a grass-roots level involving people from all segments of society.

Celender's "Movements" have since been followed by the *Political Art Movement* (April 1, 1971) and the *Religious Art Movement* (July 1, 1971) with the *Heads of State Movement,* the *Affluent Art Movement,* and the *Militant Art Movement* projected.

Mr. Sherman E. Lee, Director   January 12, 1970
Cleveland Museum of Art
1150 East Boulevard
Cleveland, Ohio

Dear Mr. Lee:

Your museum has been selected for inclusion in my Cultural Art Movement. I would like you to execute, to the best of your ability, the following proposal:
>Assemble 1,000 of the best Far Eastern
>artifacts from your permanent collection
>and place them into a weather balloon.
>Fly the balloon across the state of
>Alabama releasing a work of art (attached
>to a parachute) every thirty seconds until
>the supply has been exhausted.

Please reply at your earliest convenience and describe the method you intend to use to expedite my proposal. Thank you.
Enclosures.

Sincerely,
Don Celender
Cultural Art Movement
Saint Paul, Minnesota 55110

Mr. Don Celender
15 Duck Pass Road
St. Paul, Minn. 55110

Dear Mr. Celender:

I have your letter of January 12 with its enclosures relating to the Cultural Art Movement and the Corporate Art Movement.

May I first congratulate you on the amount of time, research, imagination, and wit which has been so tellingly combined to produce the letters included in the Cultural Art Movement portfolio.

Since all art is in the mind of the beholder, I am told, then this obviously is the means I propose to use in expediting your proposal. I have mentally performed the proposal for Cleveland and despite the exhaustion attendant upon unaccustomed rigorous use of my imagination, I can report that the mission has been accomplished. How fortunate for Alabama!

Sincerely yours,
Sherman E. Lee
Director, The Cleveland Museum of Art

Jan Dibbets. Gegenverkehr, Aachen, Zentrum fur aktuelle Kunst, Kat. 3/70, March 12–April 4, 1970. Photo-documentation of a tide piece, text by Klaus Honnef, biography, bibliography.

Gilbert and George. Art and Project Bulletin 20, March, 1970. Two drawings: "George by Gilbert" and "Gilbert by George."

"Nineteen Stills from the Work of Richard Long." *Studio International,* March, 1970.

Matsuzawa, Yutaka. Art and Project Bulletin 21, March, 1970, Tokyo: "You! fill the frame of the diamond-world mandala with water and drink to satisfy your thirst."

Alphons Schilling. Richard Feigen Gallery, New York, March 7–28, 1970. Catalogue is book of photographic portraits ("my mailman," "my grocer," "my neighbor to the left," "my love," etc.).

Sharp, Willoughby. "Nauman Interview"; Calas, Nicolas, "Wit and Pedantry of Robert Morris"; Alloway, Lawrence, "American Stock Exchange Transactions" (Bernar Venet); and von Bonin, Wibke, "Germany: The American Presence," *Arts,* March, 1970.

Burnham, Jack. "Robert Morris: Retrospective in Detroit." *Artforum,* March, 1970.

Lawrence Weiner. Yvon Lambert, Paris, March 19–26, 1970:
1. Something old something new something borrowed something blue
2. Lead tin and mercury roasted till ready
3. Earth to earth ashes to ashes dust to dust
4. A stone left unturned
5. The peace of the Pyrenees over and out

18 Paris IV. 70. Exhibition selected and catalogue written by Michel Claura, organized by Seth

Siegelaub at 66 rue Mouffetard, Paris, April, 1970. Wilson, Weiner, Toroni, Ryman, Ruscha, Lon, LeWitt, Lamelas, Kawara, Huebler, Guinochet, Gilbert and George, Dijan, Dibbets, Buren, Brouwn, Broodthaers, Barry. Catalogue includes an introduction and a postface by Claura, explaining the concept and outcome of the show's organization: "On November 20th, twenty-two artists were invited to participate in the exhibition. . . . On January 2nd, all the projects received were sent to each of the invited artists, who were asked to send back, up to February 1st, what would be their definitive participation in the exhibition (that is to say, their first project again, or with modifications, or something completely different, etc.)."

18 Paris IV. 70 reviewed or discussed by Claura and René Denizot, "La limite du concept," *Opus International,* no. 17, April, 1970, and translated in *Studio International*; François Pluchart, "Journiac lessive les conceptualistes," *Combat,* April 13; Georges Boudaille, "18 Paris IV. 70: L'avant-garde à la Mouffe," plus reply by Claura, *Lettres Francaises,* April 22, 1970; Gassiot-Talabot, "Concept non Concept," *La Quinzaine Littéraire,* May 1–15, 1970. Three of the catalogue entries follow:

Ian Wilson:
   I. My project will be to visit you in Paris, April, 1970, and there make clear the idea of oral communication as artform.
   II. Ian Wilson came to Paris in January 1970 and talked about the idea of oral communication as artform.

Sol LeWitt:
   I. On a wall (smooth and white if possible) a draftsman draws 500 yellow, 500 gray, 500 red and 500 blue lines, within an area of 1 square meter. All lines must be between 10 cm. and 20 cm. long and straight.
   II. Delete the first project.

On Kawara:
   I. [Texts of telegrams]: I am not going to commit suicide—Don't worry. 5 December 1969. On Kawara.
   I am not going to commit suicide—Worry. 8 December 1969. On Kawara.
   I am going to sleep—Forget it. 11 December 1969. On Kawara.
   II. One postcard sent each day since January 1st 1970. (Sample: Jan. 4 1970 I got up at 2.47 p.m.)

Conceptual Art and Conceptual Aspects. New York Cultural Center, New York, April 10–August 25, 1970. Organized by Donald Karshan. Art-Language, Barthelme, Barry, Baxter (NETCo.), Bochner, Buren, Burgy, Burn, Byars, Cutforth, Dibbets, Haacke, Huebler, Kaltenbach, Kawara, Kozlov, Society for Theoretical Art & Analyses; quotations by artists in and not in the exhibition; biographies, bibliographies, text by Karshan, "The Seventies: Post-Object Art." Reviewed by Peter Schjeldahl, *New York Times,* August 9, 1970.

Art in the Mind. Oberlin College, Oberlin, Ohio, April 17–May 12, 1970. Organized by Athena Tacha Spear. Acconci, Armajani, Asher, Baldessari, Barry, Barthelme, Beckley, Bochner, Borofsky, Brecht, Burgin, Burgy, Burton, Byars, Camnitzer, Castoro, Celender, Cone, Cook, Costa, Cummings, Dendler, Dunlap, Eisler, Feke, Ferrer, Gladstone, Graham, Haber, Jarden, Kawara, Kirby, Kos, Kosuth, Lau, Le Va, Levine, Lewis, LeWitt, Maloney, McLean, Nauman, NETCo., Oldenburg, Ostrow, Pechter, Perreault, Piper, Rea, Ruppersberg, Shannon, Society for Theoretical Art & Analyses (Burn, Cutforth, Ramsden), Strider, Van Saun, Venet, Wall, Wegman, H. Weiner, L. Weiner. From the catalogue:

Bruce Nauman:
Drill a hole into the heart of a large tree and insert a microphone. Mount the

amplifier and speaker in an empty room and adjust the volume to make audible any sound that might come from the tree. (September, 1969)

Drill a hole about a mile into the earth and drop a microphone to within a few feet of the bottom. Mount the amplifier and speaker in a very large empty room and adjust the volume to make audible any sounds that might come from the cavity. (September, 1969)

Eduardo Costa:

A piece that is essentially the same as a piece made by any of the first conceptual artists, dated two years earlier than the original and signed by somebody else. (January, 1970)

Robert Barry:

Dear Athena Spear—I recommend the following artist for inclusion in the *Art of the Mind* "exhibition": James Umland 1139 Calhoun Ave. Bronx, New York 10465 212-TA9-5672. You may consider this my contribution. Robert Barry 27 Mar. 70

Bernar Venet: *Against Leisure:* For the duration of the exhibition at the Allen Memorial Art Museum, any extra effort* by the students of Oberlin College, in all disciplines, will be part of my proposition.

———

*Didactic function is a part of my work. The power to create is not different from the ability to analyze.

Siah Armajani:

A FAIRLY LARGE NUMBER
OR A 350,000 (Computer, 1969) DIGIT NUMBER[1]

---

1. Total number of atoms in the universe is 3×10^{74} or a 75 digit number.
   Total number of protons and electrons is $N = 3/2 \times 136 \times 2^{256} = 2.5 \times 10^{79}$
   Total number of sand grains to fill up the universe[2] is 10^{100} or 1 and 100 zeros or 101 digit number.

---

2. The visible universe (as far as the telescope can penetrate).

Conceptual Art. **Protetch-Rivkin, Washington, D.C., April, 1970.**

KCTS-TV, Seattle, transmits *TV Gallery,* directed by Anne Focke; art works made for the program by Bauer, Garner, Manolides, Scott, Teeple, etc, April, 1970.

Battcock, Gregory. "Documentation in Conceptual Art." *Arts,* April, 1970. Works by Buren, Bochner, LeWitt, Weiner.

Buren, Daniel, "It Rains, It Snows, It Paints." *Arts,* April, 1970.

James Byars speaks at the Nova Scotia College of Art and Design, Halifax, April 21, 1970:

I was invited on a Carnegie Grant out to the University of California to do a project which involved the diffusion of fine arts in all communications. My project was specifically to get my Ph.D.-fic. They offered for me to go and simply experience the circumstance. Can you, for example, out of 1,500 people in the university, gather all of the areas of hypotheses in general intellectual talk that would be intelligible to an eighteen-year-old student? . . . That was the beginning of a serious interest in the idea of *question.* I wondered if there was such a thing as a chronology of a person's feelings. And then I began to wonder, well, maybe we instantly arrive at some understanding intuitively, or somehow in quanta, of how someone feels about us. Why do you like certain people? Finally the reasons are incredible, and they seem to be instantaneous, so maybe time really doesn't matter. Then I started thinking things like, maybe there's something like ubiquity rather than simultaneity, and then I thought maybe it doesn't take 100 sentences. Maybe you do it in one. So I started thinking things like, can you write a single-sentence autobiography? Or maybe if it isn't even verbal. So I set up things like mile-long situations where two people look at each other on Fifth Avenue not knowing who's at the other end, or just the proposition that you know somebody's at the other end looking at you. . . .

So then I began to wonder if I asked someone for a question that was pertinent to them in regard to the evolution of their knowledge of their own discipline, if that would be a sensible sort of synthesis of that personality, So I started the World Question Center on that premise. I had an interview by the Rand Corporation and places like that in regard to the possibility of total informational synthesis . . . . I went up to the Hudson Institute and the first thing that Herman Kahn said in an introductory seminar was "What is the question?," which was Gertrude Stein's death sentence . . . . I thought, I'm really in the right place. So I asked for a world telephone and for *Who's Who* and for a little room, and I started. I called up more than 2,500 people around the world. To establish my credentials, I would say "I'm James Byars, Hudson Institute, running The World Question Center, and I wonder if you'd be interested in trying to offer the hypotheses in regard to your discipline, for the evolution of your own knowledge of that, in general intellectual language?"

Some of the individual experiences were extraordinarily interesting. For example, it is not unfeasible to think of science as publicly verifiable information. But I was getting from people in all of the sciences and certainly in the arts things like, "I have questions but why give them away?" or "My questions are not intended for uninitiated ears." Or "This is an absolute menace to the idea of both art and technology." It became increasingly difficult for me to understand why it was so difficult to try to collect questions. . . . So I took two months off from my project and I went to the public library, where I thought I would do research on the history of question. And the greatest surprise came when I looked in the index of the Encyclopaedia Britannica and found to my amazement that there's no mention of question in the Encyclopaedia Britannica, and there's no book listed as question.

I found then that my pursuit had to take even more exotic levels of calling and going to places like the Princeton Institute for Advanced Studies. . . . And I called Alvin Weinberg, the director of American Atomic Energy. And I said, "What questions are you asking yourself?" And he said, "Can you invent an axiology for all of science?" And I said, wow I don't know what axiology means. He said he just learned it last week himself and it means the study of all value systems. And I said that's incredible. That's such an elegant question. Can you ask me another? And he said, sure, "Can you on *a priori* terms assess all technology?"

But that's very rare, believe me. There was usually the general blush—"I don't have any questions and that's embarrassing," or "What do you mean, questions?" I got that from some very famous people. . . . Then I began to wonder *can* you ask a direct question? Why is it so hard to make questions? I started wondering about the prejudice against question in schools. What does a question mean? We're discouraged generally by schools. I mean, there are questions where you're taught the answer before the question, and then you're asked the question and you raise your hand and the teacher thinks that's a big deal. That kind of question is defeating. And so I wondered—Is all speech interrogative?

Douglas Huebler, Art and Project Bulletin 22. "Location Piece No. 8, Amsterdam, Holland," April 25–May 8, 1970.

Poppy Johnson. *Earth Day, April 18, 1970.* Yearly planting of garden and list of previous yield at Greenwich and Duane Streets, New York; similarly "ephemeral garden site" by James Turrell and Choyashi Kawai in Venice, Calif., spring, 1970.

Kosuth, Joseph. "A Short Note: Art, Education, and Linguistic Change," *The Utterer* (School of Visual Arts), April, 1970.

April 7: Jeanne Siegel, Interview with Joseph Kosuth, WBAI, New York, unpublished.

Jouffroy, Alain. "David Lamelas." *Opus International,* April, 1970. (Same issue, Claura and Denizot on *18 Paris IV. 70* exhibition.)

Roelof Louw. X-One, Antwerp, April 9, 1971. A tape-recorder piece.

Morris, Robert. "Some Notes on the Phenomenology of Making: The Search for the Motivated." *Artforum,* April, 1970.

April, Salt Lake, Utah: Robert Smithson makes his earthwork *The Spiral Jetty* and a 35-minute color film on the subject, shown at the Dwan Gallery October 31–November 25, 1970.

O? (Byars.)

Townsend, Charlotte. "N. E. Thing Co. and Les Levine." *Studio International,* April, 1970.

Tokyo Biennale '70: Between Man and Matter. Tokyo Metropolitan Art Gallery, May 10–30. Two-volume catalogue, anonymous text and, in vol. 2, photographs of the works and "After the Exhibition" text. Albrecht, Andre, Boezem, Buren, Christo, Dibbets, van Elk, Enokura, Fabro, Flanagan, Haacke, Horikawa, Inumake, Kaltenbach, Kawaguchi, Kawara, Koike, Kolibal, Koshimizu, Kounellis, Krasinski, LeWitt, Louw, Matsuzawa, Merz, Narita, Nauman, Nomura, Panamarenko, Penone, Raetz, Rinke, Ruthenbeck, Schnyder, Serra, Shoji, Sonnier, Takamatsu, Tanaka, Zorio. Reviewed by Joseph Love, *Art International,* summer, 1970; Yoshiuki Tono, *Art and Artists,* June, 1970.

Projections: Anti-materialism. La Jolla Museum of Art, May 15–July 5, 1970. Introduction by Lawrence Urrutia; foreword by Buckminister Fuller. Barry, Deutsch, Emerson, Le Va, (see below), LeWitt, Thompson. Reviewed in *Art International,* January, 1971. Excerpt from Fuller text:
More than 99.9 percent of all the physical and metaphysical events which are evolutionarily scheduled to effect the further regeneration of life aboard our spaceship earth transpire within the vast non-sensorial reaches of the electromagnetic spectrum. The main difference between all our yesterdays and today is that man is now intellectually apprehending and usefully employing a large number of those 99.9 percent invisible energetic events. Humanity has therefore created for itself a new set

165

of responsibilities requiring a ninety-nine fold step-up in its vision and comprehension. This calls for an intuitive revision of humanity's aesthetical criteria, philosophical orientation, conscious action, cooperation and initiative in accommodating evolution's inexorable drive to have mind comprehend and surmount every physical eventuality. Intuition and aesthetics automatedly trigger us into consciousness of the existence of opportunities to consider and selectively initiate alternative acts or position-taking regarding oncoming events, potential realizations or unprecedented breakthroughs in art, technology and other human productivity.

Today's epochal aesthetic is concerned almost exclusively with the invisible, intellectual integrity manifest by the explorers and formulators operating within the sensorially unreachable, yet vast, ranges of the electro, chemical and mathematical realms of the physical and metaphysical realities. Their invisible discoveries and developments will eventuate as sensible instruments, tools, machines and automation, in general.

Barry Le Va (*Velocity Piece # 1* was executed at Ohio State University, fall, 1969, and lasted 1 hour 43 minutes):

Velocity Piece #2
(Impact Run)
Movable Object Against Immovable Interior Boundary

In this case:
Object 1—170 pounds—human body
Interior Boundary—2 walls (opposite)
Distance—50 feet wall to wall
Action—Running
Speed—Fast as possible
Duration—As long as physically possible

Using Walls (Indoors). **Jewish Museum, New York, May 13–June 21, 1970. Introduction by Susan Tumarkin Goodman, bibliographies, statements by the artists: Artschwager, Bochner, Bollinger, Buren, Diao, Gourfain, LeWitt, Morris and Kauffman, Rothblatt, Ryman, Tuttle, Weiner, Yrisarry, Zucker.**

Keith Arnatt. Art and Project Bulletin 23: 1220400-0000000. **May, 1970:**
An exhibition of the duration of the exhibition by the following means: A digital countdown system (time related to Amsterdam time) will count down the duration of the exhibition in seconds . . . exhibition time may be purchased at $1.00 per unit. . . .

Bochner, Mel. "Elements from Speculation (1967–1970)." *Artforum,* **May, 1970; excerpts:**
A fundamental assumption in much recent past art was that things have stable properties, i.e., boundaries. This seemingly simple premise became the basis for a spiraling series of conclusions. Boundaries, however, are only the fabrication of our desire to detect them . . . a trade off between seeing something and wanting to enclose it. . . . The problem is that surrendering the stability of objects immediately subverts any control we think we have over situations. Consider the possibility that the need to identify art with objects is probably the outgrowth of the need to assign our feelings to the things that prompt them. . . .

The line above is rotating on its axis at a speed of one revolution each day
Douglas Huebler. 1970.

The root word "image" need not be used only to mean representation (in the sense of one thing referring to something other than itself). To re-present can be defined as the shift in referential frames of the viewer from the space of events to the space of statements or vice versa. Imagining (as opposed to imaging) is not a pictorial pre-occupation. Imagination is a projection, the exteriorizing of ideas about the nature of things seen. It re-produces that which is initially without product. . . . My disagreement with [the term] dematerialization goes beyond a squabble with terms. There is no art which does not bear some burden of physicality. To deny it is to descend to irony. . . . It is misleading to the intentions of artists finding different ways for art to come into being . . . and both how and how long it stays there.

Christopher Cook. Bradford Junior College, Laura Knott Gallery, May 1–18, 1970. "Autobiographic Compression Series #1"—"a kind of 'information profile' of the college."

Gilbert and George. "Art Notes and Thoughts." *Art and Project* (unnumbered Bulletin), May 13–23, 1970. May 12: 2 hours of "living sculpture."

Moynihan, Michael, "Gilbert and George," *Studio International,* May, 1970.

Graham, Dan. "Eleven Sugar Cubes." *Art in America,* May–June, 1970.

Douglas Huebler. The Addison Gallery of American Art, Andover, Mass., May 8–June 14, 1970. (Rep.)

THE WORK ORIGINALLY INTENDED FOR THIS SPACE HAS BEEN WITHDRAWN.
THE DECISION TO WITHDRAW HAS BEEN TAKEN AS A PROTECTIVE
MEASURE AGAINST THE INCREASINGLY PERVASIVE CONDITIONS OF FEAR.
RATHER THAN SUBMIT THE WORK TO THE DEADLY AND POISONING INFLUENCE
OF THESE CONDITIONS, I SUBMIT ITS ABSENCE AS EVIDENCE OF THE
INABILITY OF ART EXPRESSION TO HAVE MEANINGFUL EXISTENCE UNDER
CONDITIONS OTHER THAN THOSE OF PEACE, EQUALITY, TRUTH, TRUST
AND FREEDOM.

(Adrian Piper, May, 1970)

William Wegman. *3 Speeds, 3 Temperatures,* performed in the faculty men's room at the University of Wisconsin, Madison, May, 1970. Three faucets running progressively warmer and harder.

Lawrence Weiner. **Gegenverkehr, Aachen, Zentrum fur Aktuelle Kunst, Ka. 5/70., May 1970. Text by Klaus Honnef, biography, 10 pieces in English and German:**

> to the sea
> on the sea
> from the sea
> at the sea
> bordering the sea
> to the lake
> on the lake
> from the lake
> at the lake
> bordering the lake

Calas, Nicolas, "Documentizing"; Müller, Grégoire, "The Scale of Man"; and Sharp, Willoughby, "Elemental Gestures: Terry Fox." *Arts,* **May, 1970.**

What's to all thought? (Byars.)

Camnitzer, Luis, "Contemporary Colonial Art." In *Marcha* **(Uruguay), mid-1970; excerpt:**
It is strange that the phrase "Colonial Art" is filled with only positive connotations and that it only refers to the past. In reality it happens in the present, and with benevolence it is called "international style". . . . As with Commerce, Art is above stingy political games: "it helps the communication and understanding of the people," "it is a common denominator for understanding," "The world is smaller every day," and under the rug of this phrase is swept the constantly growing difference between the cultural needs of economically developed countries and those underdeveloped or developing. . . .
I believe the possibilities for change are two:
The first one, moderate, is to continue to use the system of reference pertaining to certain forms capable of being related to art, not to produce cultural products, but rather to inform about data toward a culture. . . . We can call it perceptual alphabe-

tization. It implies economical underdevelopment as cultural stimulus, without relative value judgments. What may be negative in economic terms is only factual in cultural terms. At this moment, a huge percentage of inhabitants of the underdeveloped areas are starving to death. But artists continue to produce full-belly art.

The second possibility is to affect cultural structures through social and political ones, applying the same creativity usually used for art. If we analyze the activities of certain guerrilla groups, especially the Tupamaros and some other urban groups, we can see that something like this is already happening. The system of reference is decidedly alien to the traditional art reference systems. However, they are functioning for expressions which at the same time as they contribute to a total structure change also have a high density of aesthetic content. For the first time the aesthetic message is understandable as such, without the help of the "art context" given by the museum, the gallery, etc.

The urban guerrilla functions in conditions very similar to those with which the traditional artist is confronted when he is about to produce a work. There is a common goal: to communicate a message and at the same time to change with the process the conditions in which the public finds itself. There is a similar search to find the exact amount of originality which, using the known as a background, allows the message to be stressed toward notoriety for its effectiveness, sometimes signaling the unknown. But by going from the object to the situation, from the elitist legality to subversion, new elements there appear. The public, a passive consumer, by suddenly passing from object to situation, has to participate actively to be part of the situation. Passing from legality to subversion, the need appears to find a minimum stimulus with a maximum effect—an effect that through its impact justifies the risk taken, and pays for it. During certain historical periods, at the level of the object, this meant dealing with and creating mysteries. At the level of situations, and in this case, it means the change of the social structure.

It's too and both? (Byars.)

Celant, Germano. "Conceptual art." *Casabella,* May, 1970.

Štembera, Petr. "Events, Happenings, Land-Art, etc., in Czechoslovakia," May–June 1970 (written for *Revista de Arte,* Puerto Rico). Excerpts follow:
"Thanks" to the unpropitious cultural politics of the country in the 50's, Czechoslovak modern art lagged behind world development for many years. One of the few personalities of Czech artistic life in these years unafraid to make experiments was indubitably Vladimír Boudník. . . . In the early years after World War II, Boudník walked the pavements of Prague in search of crumbling walls, on which he made drawings of fantastic and abstract shapes before the eyes of passers-by. . . . In 1949–50 Boudník only framed the damaged walls with empty frames. He issued endless numbers of manifestations . . . but remained purposely misunderstood by the cultural institutions and was even proclaimed mentally retarded. . . .

A number of years later news trickled into Czechoslovakia about the work of . . . Allan Kaprow and the Fluxus group. Now, after a period of ten years the influence of A. Kaprow seems of basic importance in the work of Milan Knížák, the leader of Czech happening art [who traveled to America in 1968]. The Aktual group—Milan group—Milan Knížák, Soňa Šveceva, the Mach brothers, Robert Wittman, Jan Trtílek—entered the public eye in 1964, at a time when non-socialist-realist art activity was permitted officially in Czechoslovakia. . . . In early 1966 they realized a "Topical Event for One House" in Prague-Dejvice. They sent the inhabitants of this house, chosen quite at random, large numbers of bulky parcels . . . and secretly decorated the various floors of the apartment building. . . . Robert Wittman's best-known project was the "Exhibition of Street Reality" in which a little street in Prague was hung with empty picture frames in such a way as to present scenes from life itself. . . . A similar atmosphere was achieved in his "Panel," where he placed a panel with a view-square cut out on the busy crossroads on Jungmann Square in Prague, through which many spectators were able to view the life of the city. Also well known are his "Landscape Frames" from the same period. [In 1964 Mel Ramsden, in Australia, constructed a huge open rectangular "frame" outdoors, as a sculptural viewing framework; Richard Long, unacquainted with the former, made a similar piece in England some years later as did Jan Dibbets in Holland; Marjorie Strider did a series of street and slide works in New York in 1969, utilizing empty frames. *(See p. 91.)*]

Eugen Brikcius founded the Presentological Society with Rudolph Němec in 1968. The first public meeting of this society was realized on a town square in Prague in May, 1968, and during this event Němec outlined the shadows of the participants onto an enormous roll of paper that was spread over the whole area of the square. Eva Kmentová arranged a one-day exhibition in April 1970 in the Prague Špálova gallery—an event called "Footprints." There was a trail of the artist's footprints that led from the entrance of the gallery onto the first floor—plaster casts—followed by all exhibition participants. In the evening the artist gave the footprints away. Zorka Ságlová arranged her first event in the summer of 1969—with a group of friends she threw a great number of balls onto the water of the Pruhonice pond near Prague. . . . In the autumn of 1969 Ságlová placed mounds of hay and straw in the Špálova gallery, with which the spectators could play according to their own wishes. Her third large event was "Hommage à Gustav Obermann" near Humpolec in Bohemia, where she lighted 19 great bonfires on a snow-bound plain. . . . Petr Štembera stretches out sheets of polyethylene between trees in a snow-covered landscape, stretches textile ribbons in a single color, paints rocks, etc." (Rep.)

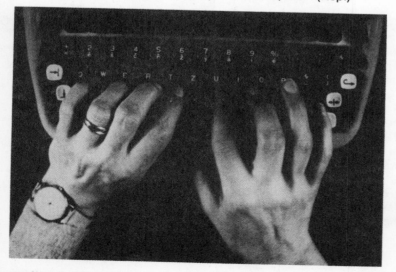

Petr Štembera. *Handpieces: Daily Activities, Typewriting.* 1971–72.

Idea Structures. Camden Arts Centre and Central Library, Swiss Cottage, London, June 24–July 19. Organized by Charles Harrison. Catalogue contains full pieces by each artist: Art and Language, Arnatt, Burgin, Ed Herring, Kosuth. The following works are from the show. The italicized notes are part of an unpublished review by L.R.L., summer, 1970.

Victor Burgin:

1
All Substantial Things Which Constitute This Room
2
All The Duration Of 1
3
The Present Moment And Only The Present Moment
4
All Appearances of 1 Directly Experienced By You At 3
5
All Of Your Recollection At 3 Of Appearances Of 1 Directly Experienced By You At Any Moment Previous To 3
6
All Criteria By Which You Might Distinguish Between Members Of 5 And Members Of 4
7
All Of Your Recollection At 3 Other Than 5
8
All Bodily Acts Performed By You At 3 Which You Know To Be Directly Experienced By Persons Other Than Yourself
9
All Bodily Acts Directly Experienced By You At 3 Performed By Persons Other Than Yourself
10
All Members Of 9 And All Members Of 8 Which Are Directed Towards Members Of 1
11
All Of Your Bodily Acts At 3 Other Than 8
12
All Of Your Bodily Sensations At 3 Which You Consider Contingent Upon Your Bodily Contact With Any Member Of 1
13
All Of Your Bodily Sensations At 3 Which You Consider Contingent Upon Any Emotion Directly Experienced By You
14
All Criteria By Which You Might Distinguish Between Members Of 13 And Members Of 12
15
All Of Your Bodily Sensations At 3 Other Than 13 And 12
16
All Of Your Inferences From 9 Concerning The Inner Experiences Of Any Person Other Than Yourself
17
Any Member Of 16 Which You Consider In Whole Or In Part Analogous With Any Member Of 13

Any Member Of 16 Which You Consider In Whole Or In Part Analogous With Any Member Of 12

The vehicles for Burgin's systems are linguistic, while their implications are perceptual and behavioural. One's recognition of the system remains the same while one's experience of it alters when the work is exhibited in different spaces, as at Camden and Swiss Cottage, and as printed in the catalogue. That experience is, however, very abstract, in the sense that it is constantly referred back to mental processes by the physical conditions it imposes. Burgin has posited esthetic objects that are "located partly in real space and partly in psychological space" with the result that "an immaterial object is created which is solely a function of perceptual behaviour but yet which inducts attributes of physicality from its material setting." Thus at Camden, where the piece appeared as sheets of paper on the walls of a large empty room, with several yards between each page, these "situational cues" existing in an "extended present" were converted into invisible structures between certain areas and certain (anonymous, accidental) people and their thoughts, which filled that place. The behaviouristic energy is regulated by internal cross-references which provide the time-frame (subsequent to X and previous to XL, etc). Taken singly, they would escape into the less specific energies of generalization (as do, intentionally, those of Robert Barry, whose language but not intent is recalled by Burgin's recent work); together, they form their own context.

The catalogue piece in this show referred to abstract elements ("criteria") where the exhibited piece referred to physical and mental experience of the relationships between the space, the people and the objects in it, and the viewer, thus taking into consideration the different forms of presentation. In the latter case the artist's demand that the gaps (white paper, space, and inter-thought time) be filled by the viewer took on a literally physical cast, in terms of the energy released by the cross-reference structure. I found the references to what other people in the room might be thinking and feeling when confronted by the piece and by my own invisible unnoticed experience the real core of the work. Rick Barthelme and Jon Borofsky come to mind as American proponents of this branch of so-called "conceptual art," in which logical complex systems are imposed on loose illogical situations.

*   *   *

Keith Arnatt. "Is It Possible for Me to Do Nothing as My Contribution to This Exhibition?":

To put forward the idea "I have done nothing," as my contribution to this exhibition would appear to be slightly unreasonable. Moreover, the request to utilize a certain amount of gallery space in which "to do nothing" seems to compound this unreasonableness. Nevertheless, in putting forward the above idea as my contribution to this exhibition, it becomes necessary to examine the implications of such a decision.

The questions that come immediately to mind are: In the context of this exhibition am I simply putting forward the idea "I have done nothing" as an idea (abstraction), or, am I claiming to have fulfilled what is asserted by the statement, namely, that I have done nothing (here implying, that I have done nothing as my contribution to this exhibition). If the latter is the case, what do I mean by "I have done nothing"?

Leaving aside a more general semantic issue, i.e., does the statement "I have done nothing" make any kind of sense (any sentence containing the word "nothing" seems to raise difficulties), how is this statement likely to be taken in the context of this exhibition?

It might be taken to mean that I have done no special work of which there is evidence (of one kind or another) in the exhibition. But such an interpretation would have to exclude the means whereby the idea "I have done nothing" is communicated. This written material itself is evidence of having done something.

Let us suppose then that this written information does not exist. This simply raises the question, How would it be known that I put forward the idea "I have done nothing" as my contribution to this exhibition?

In the absence of this written information, supposing the question were put to me, "What have you done as your contribution to this exhibition?" Would the reply, "I have done nothing" be meaningful?

The question would not have been asked in the first place unless the questioner had assumed that I was making a contribution. This would presuppose some prior knowledge on the part of the questioner which must refer back to an initial agreement on my part to contribute to this exhibition. Could such an agreement (the evidence of which might be only my name, printed in the catalogue, with no other information) be construed as having done something (if only to agree to having my name printed)?

The interpretation put upon the statement "I have done nothing," which might be taken to mean that I have done no special work for this exhibition, might well include the making of decisions that in any way relate to the exhibition as part of a definition of "special work."

It would seem then, as a contributor to this exhibition, I can put forward the idea "I have done nothing" as my contribution to the exhibition, as an idea only. My interest, however, is in implementing any possibility of doing nothing (meaning "no special work") as my contribution to this exhibition.

What if I change the statement "I have done nothing" to "I will do nothing"? Is it

Keith Sonnier. *Dis-Play.* Video tape with Sony. 1969.

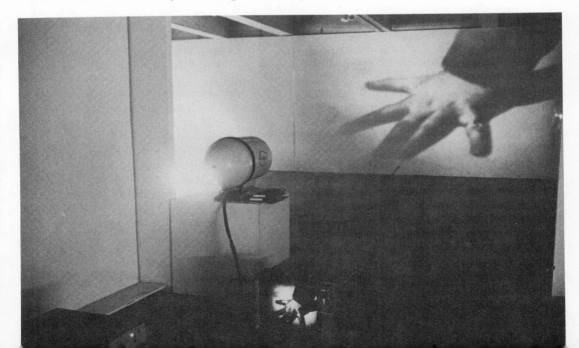

possible to fulfill the claim made by the modified statement which could be taken to mean "I will do no special work for this exhibition"?

Does the claim "I will do nothing" necessarily imply that I have done nothing in the context of this exhibition? Any claim to have done nothing for this exhibition has already been shown to be false.

One might object to the claim "I will do nothing" on the grounds that it calls for a decision that has to be effective throughout the duration of the exhibition and is, as a decision, a special case of doing something for the exhibition. The difference here is that there is and can be no concrete evidence that would make any kind of sense in relation to the claim. The statement "I will do nothing," at any given time, always refers to the future.

To sum up: The claim "I have done nothing," made at any time throughout the duration of the exhibition would be false for the reasons already given. The claim "I will do nothing," made at any time throughout the duration of the exhibition, implies intention only and as such would further imply temporal and spatial considerations.

If, as a contributor to this exhibition, my intention is to do no special work for the exhibition (as my contribution), I must, during the period of the exhibition, be doing something else.

If I'm doing something else I must be doing it somewhere.

Somewhere might be anywhere.

Anywhere might include the location of this exhibition.

The location of this exhibition might include this gallery.

If I do something in this gallery (meaning in the future course of this exhibition), it does not necessarily follow that whatever I do is to be taken as having done some "special work" for this exhibition.

Arnatt comes to "idea art" via process or behavioral land art (a consistent interest in hermeticism and holes) and a something-to-nothing development. In Camden, for instance, a little machine on the wall clicked away the number of seconds in the entire exhibition: 2188800-0000000, as an "exhibition of the duration of the exhibition," a pretty simple idea that has a mesmerizing physical effect, a terrifying associational effect, and a dramatic ending. When the row of zeros is about to strike, one has the feeling of teetering on the brink of time itself; what happens when there are no more seconds?

The Nothing piece is an exercise in mental gymnastics. The idea of doing nothing has a long art-historical pedigree by now, running from Picabia and Duchamp to Yves Klein, Buren, Barry, and the N. E. Thing Co. and Christine Kozlov, a specialist in the reduction of complex intentions to rejection. Arnatt answers his unanswerable question with a (double) negative by doing something and covering himself in the last sentence, an instance of the provocative tension in which he works between the countdown and a reverse generosity of both ends and means. [A related work appeared in the catalogue of the Lisson Wall Show, January, 1971, entitled "Did I Intend to do This Work?"; see also p. 225 for a third omission piece by Arnatt].

* * *

Joseph Kosuth. "Special Investigation":
1. A LOGICIAN, WHO EATS PORK-CHOPS FOR SUPPER, WILL PROBABLY LOSE MONEY;
2. A GAMBLER, WHOSE APPETITE IS NOT RAVENOUS, WILL PROBABLY LOSE MONEY;

3. A MAN WHO IS DEPRESSED, HAVING LOST MONEY AND BEING LIKELY TO LOSE MORE, ALWAYS RISES AT 5 A.M.;
4. A MAN, WHO NEITHER GAMBLES NOR EATS PORK-CHOPS FOR SUPPER, IS SURE TO HAVE A RAVENOUS APPETITE;
5. A LIVELY MAN, WHO GOES TO BED BEFORE 4 A.M., HAD BETTER TAKE TO CAB-DRIVING;
6. A MAN WITH A RAVENOUS APPETITE, WHO HAS NOT LOST MONEY AND DOES NOT RISE AT 5 A.M., ALWAYS EATS PORK-CHOPS FOR SUPPER;
7. A LOGICIAN, WHO IS IN DANGER OF LOSING MONEY, HAD BETTER TAKE TO CAB-DRIVING;
8. AN EARNEST GAMBLER, WHO IS DEPRESSED THOUGH HE HAS NOT LOST MONEY, IS IN NO DANGER OF LOSING ANY;
9. A MAN, WHO DOES NOT GAMBLE, AND WHOSE APPETITE IS NOT RAVENOUS, IS ALWAYS LIVELY;
10. A LIVELY LOGICIAN, WHO IS REALLY IN EARNEST, IS IN NO DANGER OF LOSING MONEY;
11. A MAN WITH A RAVENOUS APPETITE HAS NO NEED TO TAKE TO CAB-DRIVING, IF HE IS REALLY IN EARNEST;
12. A GAMBLER, WHO IS DEPRESSED THOUGH IN NO DANGER OF LOSING MONEY, SITS UP TILL 4 A.M.;
13. A MAN, WHO HAS LOST MONEY AND DOES NOT EAT PORK-CHOPS FOR SUPPER, HAD BETTER TAKE TO CAB-DRIVING, UNLESS HE GETS UP AT 5 A.M.;
14. A GAMBLER, WHO GOES TO BED BEFORE 4 A.M., NEED NOT TAKE TO CAB-DRIVING UNLESS HE HAS A RAVENOUS APPETITE;

COMPLETE CONTENTS OF ADVERTISEMENT

(SECTION TWO)—FRENCH
(SECTION TWO)—AS IS
(SECTION TWO)—GERMAN
(SECTION TWO)—ITALIAN

INTO FRENCH

UNIVERSAL "MEN"; A—EARNEST; B—EATING PORK-CHOPS FOR SUPPER; C—GAMBLERS; D—GETTING UP AT 5; E—HAVING LOST MONEY; H—HAVING A RAVENOUS APPETITE; K—LIKELY TO LOSE MONEY; L—LIVELY; M—LOGICIANS; N—MEN WHO HAD BETTER TAKE TO CAB-DRIVING; R—SITTING UP TILL 4.

ENGLISH AS IS

UNIVERSAL "MEN"; A—EARNEST; B—EATING PORK-CHOPS FOR SUPPER; C—GAMBLERS; D—GETTING UP AT 5; E—HAVING LOST MONEY; H—HAVING A RAVENOUS APPETITE; K—LIKELY TO LOSE MONEY; L—LIVELY; M—LOGICIANS; N—MEN WHO HAD BETTER TAKE TO CAB-DRIVING; R—SITTING UP TILL 4.

INTO GERMAN

UNIVERSAL "MEN"; A—EARNEST; B—EATING PORK-CHOPS FOR SUPPER; C—GAMBLERS; D—GETTING UP AT 5; E—HAVING LOST MONEY; H—HAVING A RAVENOUS APPETITE; K—LIKELY TO LOSE MONEY; L—LIVELY; M—LOGICIANS; N—MEN WHO HAD BETTER TAKE TO CAB-DRIVING; R—SITTING UP TILL 4.

INTO ITALIAN

UNIVERSAL "MEN"; A—EARNEST; B—EATING PORK-CHOPS FOR SUPPER; C—GAMBLERS; D—GETTING UP AT 5; E—HAVING LOST MONEY; H—HAVING A RAVENOUS APPETITE; K—LIKELY TO LOSE MONEY; L—LIVELY; M—LOGICIANS; N—MEN WHO HAD BETTER TAKE TO CAB-DRIVING; R—SITTING UP TILL 4.

The "Investigations" are more interesting in themselves than anything Kosuth has done so far, unless you count his life and interaction with other people and situations as his art, which of course he would just as soon you didn't, or his ideas, and now writings, as his art, rather than their materializations, about which he seems rather more ambivalent (his "entry" in the Oberlin Art of the Mind show is a reprint of an article from Art-Language). And he seems finally to have come to terms with his "form of presentation" problems. An earlier investigation was typed on small gummed labels and stuck across a 20-foot wall. The Thesaurus classification series see pp. 72–73) has, over a period of 2 years, moved from newspaper ads to billboards to bus-posters to such improbable manifestations as the "powerhouse" in Nova Scotia (subheads of "Power" on the roof of a barn) or the recent piece in Turin—a white-on-black banner across the street. Before that, the dictionary definitions series was presented as 4' × 4' negative photostatic blow-ups, which although not strictly paintings, lacking paint, remain large flat depictive surfaces hung on the wall. The reason given for this potentially gimmicky distribution of one idea over so many media has been to assure no undue emphasis on presentation per se, or as formal "style"; medium nevertheless does become confused with pure idea when it is so varied. With the xeroxed "Investigations" in booklet form, Kosuth has finally made the crucial decision to let the work stand or fall on the internal linguistic-artistic relationships. The "Investigations" in this show refer to Wittgenstein more interestingly than previous work and the introduction of proper names changes one's expectations, and therefore the context, providing witty pseudo-narrative feedback most certainly not intended by the artist to be as provocative as it is. Kosuth's ideas have been important since 1966, but this seems to me the first time that he has produced a conceptual art that is, in his own words, "an inquiry by artists who understand that artistic activity is not solely limited to the framing of art propositions, but furthers the investigation of the function, meaning, and use of any and all [art] propositions and their considera- tion within the concept of the general term 'art.'" (See pp. 146–49.) The "Investiga- tions" are not "original" any more than his previous material has been, but they are original art, whoever made up the riddles and then collected and printed them.

Conceptual Art, Arte Povera, Land Art. Galleria Civica d'Arte Moderna, Turin, June–July, 1970. Organized by Germano Celant. "Texts" by Celant, Lippard, Malle, Passoni; statements by some of the artists, bibliography. Andre, Anselmo, Baldessari, Barry, Beuys, Bochner, Boetti, Calzolari, Christo, Darboven, de Maria, Dibbets, Fabro, Flavin, Fulton, Gilbert and George, Haacke, Heizer, Huebler, Kaltenbach, Kawara, Klein, Kosuth, Kounellis, LeWitt, Manzoni, Merz, Morris, Nauman, Oppenheim, Paolini, Pascali, Penone, Pistoletto, Prini, Ryman, Sand- back, Serra, Smithson, Sonnier, Venet, Weiner, Zorio.

June 20. Washington, D.C.: *Lookout,* an event organized by Douglas Davis and Fred Pitts, in which inhabitants of the city were asked to scrutinize their environments and report their findings by phone or in person to the Corcoran Gallery of Art.

Fox, Christopher. "Interview with Edward Ruscha." *Studio International,* June, 1970.

Michael Snow/Canada. XXVe Biennial Exhibition of Art, Venice, June 24–October 31, 1970. Texts by Brydon Smith and the artist. Reviewed by Barry Lord, *Art and Artists,* June, 1970.

Tuchman, Phyllis. "An Interview with Carl Andre." *Artforum,* June, 1970.

James Collins. *Postals,* June, 1970–April, 1971. #1: "Introduction Pieces," June, 1970; #2,

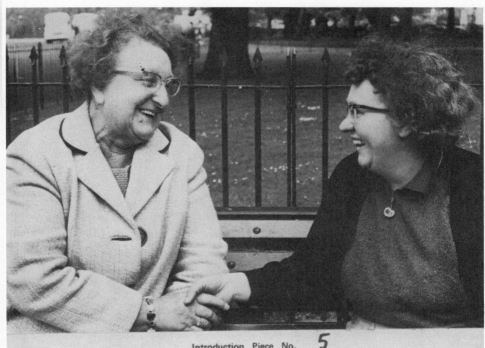

Introduction Piece No. 5

This is to certify that James Collins is a complete stranger to me and that he approached me :

Location *Hyde Park*

Time *2.20 p.m.*

Date *29th May '70*

and I agree to participate in an art work where I'm introduced by James Collins to a complete stranger.

This piece would be documented by a photograph showing this meeting taking place.

Signed *E. Marsden*

No 8 of "Strangers"

This is to certify that James Collins is a complete stranger to me and that he approached me :

Location *Hyde Park*

Time *2.20*

Date *29th May '70*

and I agree to participate in an art work where I'm introduced by James Collins to a complete stranger.

This piece would be documented by a photograph showing this meeting taking place.

Signed *F. Vincent.*

No 8 of "Strangers"

James Collins. *Introduction Piece No. 5.* 1970.

"Introduction Pieces Proposal," July; #3: "Delegation Proposal 1," August; #4, "Interim Travel Proposal," September; #5, "Set' Piece 3," October; #6x "Semiotic Aspects," February; #7, "Contexts," March (see below, pp. 225–26); #8, "Contexts 2," April. (Rep.)

Wijers, Louwrien. "Gesprek met Sol LeWitt." *Museumjournaal,* June, 1970.

Eugene Goossen. "The Artist Speaks: Robert Morris." *Art in America,* May–June, 1970.

Gina Pane: Acqua Alta/Pali/Venezia. Galerie Rive Droite, Paris, June 11–July 20, 1970. Text by Pierre Restany (a "conceptual environment: concerning the rising waters of Venice").

Information. Museum of Modern Art, New York, July 2–September 20, 1970. Organized by Kynaston McShine; text by him, "recommended reading" bibliography; page for each artist: Acconci, Andre, Armajani, Arnatt, Art & Language, Art & Project, Artschwager, Askevold, Atkinson, Bainbridge, Baldessari, Baldwin, Barrio, Barry, Barthelme, H. & B. Becher, Beuys, Bochner, Bollinger, Brecht, Broegger, Brouwn, Buren, Burgin, Burgy, Burn and Ramsden, Byars, Carballa, Cook, Cutforth, D'Alessio, Darboven, de Maria, Dibbets, Ferguson, Ferrer, Flanagan, Group Frontera, Fulton, Gilbert & George, Giorno Poetry Systems, Graham, Haacke, Haber, Hardy, Heizer, Hollein, Huebler, Huot, Hutchinson, Jarden, Kaltenbach, Kawara, Kosuth, Kozlov, Latham, Le Va, LeWitt, Lippard, Long, McLean, Meirelles, Minujin, Morris, NETCo., Nauman, New York Graphic Workshop, Newspaper, Group OHO, Oiticica, Ono, Oppenheim, Panamarenko, Paolini, Pechter, Penone, Piper, Pistoletto, Prini, Puente, Raetz, Rainer, Rinke, Ruscha, Sanejouand, Sladden, Smithson, Sonnier, Sottsass, Thygesen, van Saun, Vaz, Venet, Wall, Weiner, Wilson.

Reviewed by Gregory Battcock, "Informative Exhibition at the MOMA," *Arts,* summer, 1970; David Shapiro, "Mr. Processionary at the Conceptacle," *Art News,* September, 1970.

Works in the exhibition:

David Askevold:

	SHOOT	DON'T SHOOT
SHOOT	DEATH FOR BOTH	DEATH FOR ONE
DON'T SHOOT	DEATH FOR ONE	LIFE FOR BOTH

Robert Barry. *Art Work,* 1970:

It is always changing. It has order. It doesn't have a specific place. Its boundaries are not fixed. It affects other things. It may be accessible but go unnoticed. Part of it may also be part of something else. Some of it is familiar. Some of it is strange. Knowing of it changes it.

Yoko Ono. *Map Piece:*

Draw an imaginary map. Put a goal mark on the map where you want to go. Go walking on an actual street according to your map. If there is no street where it should be according to the map, make one by putting the obstacles aside. When you reach the goal, ask the name of the city and give flowers to the first person you meet. The map must be followed exactly, or the event has to be dropped altogether. Ask your friends to write maps. Give your friends maps. (Summer, 1962.)

N. E. Thing Co. *Nomenclature* (1966–67):

VSI—Visual Sensitivity Information (term NETCo. uses instead of "art")
SI—Sensitivity Information (all cultural information)
SSI—Sound Sensitivity Information (music, poetry [read], singing, oratory, etc.)

MSI—Moving Sensitivity Information (movies, dance, mountain climbing, track, etc.)

ESI—Experimental Sensitivity Information (theatre, etc.)

**—It should be recognized that there are categories where certain types of sensitivity information are combined with others to provide their form, but for the most part the categories above have been established because the "arts" tend to have a particular emphasis on one kind of information characteristic.

—We find that by setting up a new set of definitions like this that people are better able to see the cross-relationship between the "arts" and in doing so can become much more involved and supportive of the new types of "arts activity"—Sensitivity Information—SI—that are going on.

—The idea of comprehending "all arts as information handled sensitively" breaks the historical chains that keep them apart from each other and grossly misunderstood.

All questions are ubiquitous? (Byars)

July/August Exhibition. Special edition of *Studio International,* July–August, 1970, edited by Seth Siegelaub. Also published as a hardcover book without advertising, backmatter, etc. All texts in English, French, German. A magazine exhibition in which six critics were asked to fill an eight-page section without writing anything themselves; each critic chose any number of artists to fill their space: David Antin (Graham, Cohen, Baldessari, Serra, Eleanor Antin, Lonidier, Nicolaides, Sonnier); Germano Celant (Anselmo, Boetti, Calzolari, Merz, Penone, Prini, Pistoletto, Zorio); Michel Claura (Buren); Charles Harrison (Arnatt, Art-Language, Burgin, Flanagan, Kosuth, Latham, Louw); Lucy R. Lippard (Barry, Kaltenbach, Weiner, Kawara (Rep.), LeWitt, Huebler, NETCo., Barthelme; each artist was asked to pass on to the next a situation within which to work); Hans Strelow (Dibbets, Darboven).

Visions, Projects, Proposals. Nottingham Festival, July 11–August 2, 1970; organized by the Midland Group Gallery. Text by Tim Turelfall. Askevold, Dee, Dibbets, Hall, Herring, LeWitt, Long, Morris, Smithson, among others.

John Baldessari. July 24, 1970, San Diego: "Notice is hereby given that all works of art done by the undersigned between May, 1953, and March, 1966, in his possession as of July 24, 1970, were cremated on July 24, 1970, in San Diego, California." Notarized document published in the newspaper as a general affidavit. Photo album and plaque shown in *Software* (see p. 191).

Summer, 1970: Gerald Ferguson, Relational Sculpture:

(1) a point in Halifax, Nova Scotia, 44°38′47.41″ north latitude, 63°34′48.21″ west longitude. (2) a point on Gerald Ferguson, tattoo, left forearm. (3) a point as yet to be determined. "Upon initiation the sculpture exists as an indeterminate relationship; upon the artist's death the sculpture exists as a determinate relationship."

Robert Barry Presents a Work by Ian Wilson, July, 1970. The work: "Ian Wilson."

Ian Wilson and Robert Barry on Oral Communication, July, 1970, Bronx, N.Y.:

[Note: Ian Wilson has been concerned with Oral Communication as a way of making art for the past four years. This part of a discussion between him and Robert Barry was recorded in July, 1970. The interview grew out of the compatibility of the artists' positions at that time and can be considered a part of Robert Barry's "presentation of artists" series.]

RB: This question will be based on my observations of your use of oral communication over the last couple of years, from the first time you came to my old studio and

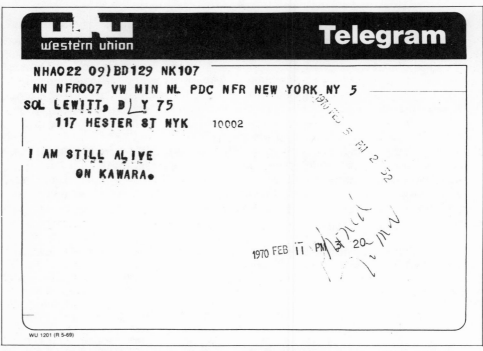

On Kawara. *Confirmation.* Telegram sent to Sol LeWitt, February, 1970.

Weiner's "instructions" to Kawara were: "Dear On Kawara, I must apologize but the only situation I can bring myself to impose upon you would be my hopes for your having a good day. Fond Regards, Lawrence Weiner." Kawara's telegram constituted his piece as well as the situation passed on to Sol LeWitt, who in turn made 74 permutations on the telegram's message for his piece.

said that oral communication was your art. It seemed to me at that time and shortly thereafter, whenever we met, you said to me that you were using oral communication as an art form, then you would stop it; there would be a period where oral communication wasn't your art, and so forth. In other words, later on it seemed to me that the *concept* of oral communication became the art rather than oral communication being the means of making individual works of art. Is that accurate?

IW: Well, first of all I had to take the object or the idea of oral communication out of its natural context, put it into an art context. And I had to speak it to do that, right? It was more logical for me to speak it, but having done that it became a concept, naturally.

RB: I think when you say concept, you mean something you know that no longer needs to be said. It seems to me that you changed your use of oral communication so that everything embodied in that term became art, rather than using it as a material, using the actual periods of time when you were using oral communication as your art.

IW: Do you mean that my means of presenting my idea became less rigid, that the use of oral communication generally as art began at the "Time Panel," when it was recorded and put into print? That sort of contradicted the essential intention which was *oral* communication?

RB: No. What I'm thinking about is periods of time earlier on, when you were dealing with certain periods of time set aside when your oral communication was your art. Then later, time was no longer an element. In fact I noted that you don't really say that so much any more, that "oral communication is my art." It seemed to me that at first that phrase keyed the beginning of a work of art, whereas that phrase doesn't have the same function any more. Rather we are dealing with the *idea* of oral communication rather than individual instances.

IW: That's interesting. I never thought of that.

RB: You know, in the past this discussion might have started out by your saying "oral communication is my art." But it didn't. We are just talking about it now, about how you have used it, what it means.

IW: Would you say the difference also is that now I don't refer the idea of oral communication to myself? That now it's abstracted from myself? It is just an idea, part of the community now, an idea which can be used to illuminate a certain aspect of art.

RB: Partly, but what I really mean is that we were thinking about oral communication as a *thing* in itself, rather than specific examples, times, when you used oral communication.

IW: I see. There has been a change from a particular first instance at the introduction to the less "original" situation. The atmosphere of the original presentation is gone. In a way I often think of oral communication as existing really in that first day. Before that I was using time. . . .

RB: My first impression when you said oral communication was your art form was that you had discovered something very important in one way. It was like making art with an extension of yourself, which is essentially what oral communication is. It is an extension of ourselves out into the world, and it is like a painter discovering that he can make his art using vision rather than having to mess around with paint and other stuff. . . .

IW: What struck me as important with oral communication was that when a person makes something that he is attached to, and he wants to call it art, he has to *call* it art. To call anything anything, you have to either speak it or print it or use sign language, if you're deaf and dumb. These are the three alternatives.

RB: Well, you could put it in a certain place so it would be designated as art—an art gallery, an art museum, an art magazine.

IW: But that place would have to have been *called* too. . . . I am still trying to figure out why the hell I chose oral language instead of printed language and I think it must have been a very unconscious sort of . . . well, perhaps I was reacting to the static situation of the gallery, but I don't think that is justified because nothing is static, or everything is static, one way or another. Oral communication is perhaps a response to the anticipated question asked artists—What are you doing? I was able to answer "I am speaking to you." It was at the time an attempt to come to grips with the situation in which a person wants to be an artist and wants to present something as representative of his thinking. . . .

RB: How do you feel about putting all this into print?

IW: That's a big question. It makes a difference between now and what I did two years ago. Before, I would not consider print. Now, some two years later, I find the dichotomy, the dualism, extremely interesting.

RB: Would you say the art exists in the differences between oral communication and written communication?

IW: I would say that it was possible to disassociate myself from print. I don't accept the responsibility for print. But obviously I'd be naive to say that. The ambiguity of the word spoken and then printed is not displeasing. . . . But the protection of saying something is having it dissolve into an emotion, a security you don't have when something is printed.

RB: But if you take the quality of the medium that you had at the beginning, when you were first using oral communication. . . . I thought of it in terms of what I knew about art, about materials that artists use. I myself was using radio carrier waves which dissolve when I first heard about oral communication. I thought of it in those terms, or like the gas I was releasing into the atmosphere then, something that was gone, and you didn't have a chance to do anything with it. Something released.

IW: About the ambiguity of printing oral communication—it's possible to put something through a process not indigenous to itself and still be attached to the outcome. Even as we were releasing things—gas or spoken words or sound—something is still released from the printed page.

RB: There is a question of control there. Yours is a kind of situational art. When you said "oral communication is my art" you didn't consciously plan what you were going to talk about; you didn't have a program; you just continued the flow of conversation as it was going, although your statement may have influenced what was said after you said it.

IW: I was aware of that. I liked that. I still do.

RB: So that part of your art would have been conversation about something that wasn't oral communication, where later the art was only about oral communication.

IW: Maybe at the very beginning of oral communication I might have said that I was involved with timelessness and spacelessness. But later on I think perhaps I became more aware of the implied consciousness of the art situation in oral communication. That made it more specific. I don't know. I don't think I ever really made that difference very clear. I just wanted to say something else. Because I say something and know that it will be printed eventually doesn't mean that I have given up the idea of speaking. What it means is that I don't find this metamorphosis from oral into print as disturbing as I used to think it would be.

RB: It's no longer a problem?

IW: Beautiful. It's no longer a problem! . . .

RB: Is oral communication just language?

IW: No. Obviously not just language.

RB: Is it action?

IW: Language could be action, I suppose. Language is the grammar of behavior.

RB: You talked about a certain situation that arises when somebody asks what are you doing. This seemed to be very important.

IW: Oral communication is about language. Well I suppose it is. Perhaps not as directly as some artists are involved in language. I don't really know what oral communication is. Some kind of attempt to grapple with the problems of communication. Maybe having realized the artist is not a mystic but the opposite of a mystic in the sense that the artist by his nature communicates, whereas the mystic is someone who experiences and does not place importance on his experience being communicated. . . . Maybe a reason for this concentration on language as art is a more acute consciousness on the artist's part that he is really a part of the world . . . so the artist is talking about his ambiguous position. Dualism. Which is why Joyce is a good artist.

RB: I would also add to that a slight qualification, which is that he is also talking about possibilities. It goes back to Sol LeWitt's idea, where he says that all good art is a very simple idea. They are basically simple ideas, but the thing about them is that the potential implied in each idea is the possibility of each idea for those people who are willing to involve themselves with that idea.

Daniel Buren, July, 1970, Los Angeles: "There are visible alternate vertical stripes, white and blue, from July 15 to July 31st day and night on 50 bus benches" (plus list of locations).

Buren, Daniel; Claura, Michel; Denizot, René. *MTL Art/Critique*. Booklet printed but never distributed, with cover by Buren illustrating a show of his in Brussels (rue Armand Campenhout, June 13–July 1); texts by the two critics.

Hanne Darboven: Das Jahr 1970. **Konrad Fischer, Düsseldorf, July 3–30.**

Gilbert and George. *The Sadness in Our Art*. July 4, 1970, London. Artificially aged leaflet with two drawings; text of "Underneath the Arches."

Nirvana. **Kyoto Museum of Art, August, 1970.**

Sol LeWitt. **Gemeentemuseum, The Hague, July 25–August 30, 1970. Texts by the artist and by Andre, Atkinson, Bochner, Chandler, Develing, Flavin, Graham, Kapteyn-van Bruggen, Hesse, Kirby, Krauss, Ira Licht, Lippard, Van der Net, Reise, Strelow, Weiner.**

Richard Long Skulptures, England Germany Africa America 1966–1970. **Städtische Museum, Mönchengladbach, July 16–August 30, 1970. Book of photos of work, boxed; brief text by Long and one by Johannes Cladders.**

Baker, Elizabeth, "Traveling Ideas: Germany, England"; and Gendel, Milton, "Avant-Garde Milanese." *Art News,* summer, 1970.

Ratcliff, Carter. "New York Letter." *Art International,* summer, 1970.

Sharp, Willoughby. "Outsiders: Baldessari, Jackson, O'Shea, Ruppersberg." *Arts,* summer, 1970.

The likely real? (Byars.)

Burgin, Victor. "Thanks for the Memory." *Architectural Design,* August, 1970.

Burnham, Jack. "Dennis Oppenheim: Catalyst 1967–1970." *Artscanada,* August, 1970.

Avalanche, **no. 1, New York, fall, 1970. Lisa Béar and Willoughby Sharp, eds. Contents: Interviews with Carl Andre and Jan Dibbets; "Pace and Process" (documenting a horseback-riding photographic piece by Robert Morris, September, 1969); "Body Works" by Sharp; a photo essay by Shunk-Kender on Beuys; documentation of pieces by Long; discussions with Heizer, Smithson, and Oppenheim are excerpted below:**
Oppenheim: Gradually I found myself trying to get below ground level. Because I wasn't very excited about objects which protrude from the ground. I felt this implied an embellishment of external space. To me a piece of sculpture inside a room is a disruption of interior space. It's a protrusion, an unnecessary addition to what could be a sufficient space in itself. My transition to earth materials took place in Oakland a

few summers ago, when I cut a wedge from the side of a mountain. I was more concerned with the negative process of excavating that shape from the mountainside than with making an earthwork as such. It was just a coincidence that I did this with earth. . . . Andre at one point began to question very seriously the validity of the object. He began to talk about sculpture as place. And Sol LeWitt's concern with systems, as opposed to the manual making and placing of object art, can also be seen as a move against the object. These two artists have made an impact on me. They built such damn good stuff that I realized an impasse had been reached. Morris also got to the point where if he'd made his pieces a little better, he wouldn't have had to make them at all. I felt that very strongly and I knew there must be another direction in which to work. . . . The earth movement has derived some stimulus from minimal art, but I think that now it's moved away from their main preoccupations. . . . A good deal of my preliminary thinking is done by viewing topographical maps and aerial maps and then collecting various data on weather information. Then I carry this with me to the terrestrial studio. For instance, my frozen lake project in Maine involves plotting an enlarged version of the International Date Line onto a frozen lake and truncating an island in the middle. I call this island a time-pocket because I'm stopping the IDL there. So this is an application of a theoretical framework to a physical situation—I'm actually cutting this strip out with chain saws. Some interesting things happen during this process: you tend to get grandiose ideas when you look at large areas on maps, then you find they're difficult to reach so you develop a strenuous relationship with the land. If I were asked by a gallery to show my Maine piece [see p. 66], obviously I wouldn't be able to. So I would make a model of it . . . or a photograph. I'm not really that attuned to photos to the extent which Mike [Heizer] is. I don't really show photos as such. At the moment I'm quite lackadaisical about the presentation of my work; it's almost like a scientific convention.

Sharp: What would you say about the relationship between your work and photographs of it?

Smithson: Photographs steal away the spirit of the work. . . .

Oppenheim: One day the photograph is going to become even more important than it is now—there'll be a heightened respect for photographers. Let's assume that art has moved away from its manual phase and that now it's concerned with the location of material and with speculation. So the work of art now has to be visited or abstracted from a photograph, rather than made. I don't think the photograph could have had the same richness of meaning in the past as it has now. But I'm not particularly an advocate of the photograph.

Sharp: It's sometimes claimed that the photo is a distortion of sensory perception.

Heizer: Well, the experience of looking is constantly altered by physical factors. I think certain photographs offer a precise way of seeing works. You can take a photograph into a clean white room, with no sound, no noise. You can wait until you feel so inclined before you look at it and possibly experience to a greater depth whatever view you have been presented with.

Oppenheim has said, concerning one of his transfer-overlay pieces:

Altitude lines on contour maps serve to translate measurement of existing topography to a two-dimensional surface. . . . I create contours which oppose the reality of the existing land, and impose their measurements onto the actual site, thus creating a kind of conceptual mountainous structure on a swamp grid.

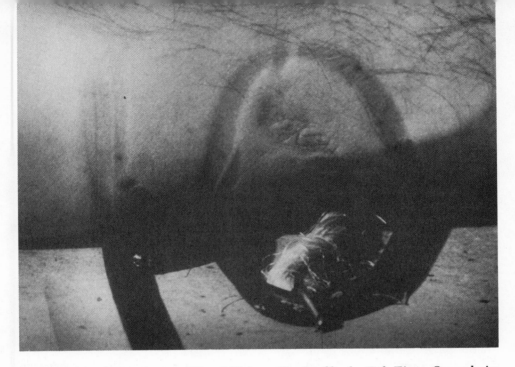

Dennis Oppenheim. *Arm & Wire.* Still from 16-mm. film by Bob Fiore. Oppenheim repeatedly rolled the underside of his right arm over some wires. 1969.

Willoughby Sharp on Oppenheim, in "Body Works":

In several works Oppenheim's body is created as a place. Generally the body as place acts as a ground which is marked in ways quite similar to those employed in earthworks. In *Wound 1* (1970) he transferred the configuration of his healing skin onto a small piece of land. In *Arm and Asphalt,* a film of 1969, he rolled his underarm over sharp bits of asphalt. Intercuts of a landmass related the action back to the original site of the earth material. It is not surprising then to find that Oppenheim's "concern for the body came from constant physical contact with large bodies of land." He also feels that working with land "demands an echo from the artist's body." This echo can literally be perceived in his *Reading Position for Second Degree Burn* (1970). Oppenheim went to a Long Island beach and exposed his body to the sun. He placed a large leather-bound book entitled *Tactics* over his chest. In this work, represented by two photos, one color shot shows the artist lying on the beach before the burn and the other after, without the book. An unburned rectangle occupies the place where the book was. A related work is *Hair Piece* (1970), in which Oppenheim exposed parts of his scalp to a video camera. In *Material Interchange* (1970), Oppenheim is concerned with intimate transactions between his body and the environment. The work consists of four photographs, two of which show the artist wedging a fingernail between floorboards, and the others the same finger into which a long splinter from the same floorboard has been introduced.

aux travaux d'analyse"; Otto Hahn, "Notes sur l'avant garde"; and works and statements by Barry, Bochner, Burgin, Huebler, Kosuth, Lamelas, Weiner.

"Four Pages—Joseph Beuys." *Studio International,* September, 1970. Statements by the artist and Per Kirkeby.

Mel Bochner. Art and Project Bulletin 27. "Excerpts from Speculation (1967–1970)," rough draft.

His product is fame? (Byars.)

Lamelas, David. *Publication.* Nigel Greenwood, London, September, 1970. Responses to three statements: "1. Use of oral and written language as an Art Form. 2. Language can be considered as an Art Form. 3. Language cannot be considered as an Art Form"—published as Lamelas's exhibition. Contributors: Arnatt, Barry, Brouwn, Buren, Burgin, Latham, Maloney, Reise, Weiner, Wilson, and (below) Claura, Lippard, Gilbert & George.
Michel Claura. *Outline of a Detour:*

Art is a kind of language. At least, this is what can be deduced from its adhesion to diverse means of communication. It is useless to ask questions about the value of this language, especially if it must be used to compare, or compete with, other forms of language. On the contrary, the central issue is to analyse this form of language called "art," in its function; a specific calling into question of a particular field.

Nevertheless, this preoccupation will not be ours in the present context, or rather will not be dealt with in this form.

The desire to approach the problem of spoken or written language in art, means the formulation of a given fact, namely: language (written or spoken) as an art form which is also a form of camouflage.

The mere fact that we should be obliged to specify that the language under discussion is spoken or written shows very well that confusion is recognised as such. Confusion between art as a form of language, and language (written or spoken) as an art form. We shall see later on that this fear of confusion is not justified.

In so far as it exists as a form of language differing from others, art must possess its own means of existence, a technique, a vocabulary, a "syntax," a "grammar" which characterises it.

As a means of communication, we find that art is false because its language is one of dissimulation, obedience to a basic law which requires one to "speak of something else." Communication is false because it is put forward as a screen with which it becomes merged.

As far as language is concerned (the grouping together of its productive elements), art can appear to pursue a certain truth which is the reality of its historic existence. It is precisely this which constitutes the mask of art. This mask is its form. Its form is its language.

Art is perpetuated under a diversity of formal adventures which always happen in such a way that their succession alters every approach to its calling into question. The use of spoken or written language as an art form can therefore be applied in the same way as the use of a painting or a hammer. The use of spoken or written language as an art form will be accepted as a necessity. The mere fact that it is present "in" art—and is therefore accepted—because it fulfills a function differing from an art form, a different art form which differs the moment the question of art appears as a necessity.

Nevertheless, as an art form, the use of spoken or written language runs the risk of becoming more quickly exhausted than another form. Indeed, it implies obedience to absolute laws constituting the written or spoken language to which obedience to the laws of art is added. This double yoke inevitably leads fairly soon to the observation of what is called an "academism." This is only a detail.

The artist is habituated to art. Art as a habit merges with the renewal of solutions which constitutes it. The habit of offering solutions means the avoidance of art as a question. It is in these conditions and for these reasons that the use of a spoken or written language as an art form will be judged as satisfactory.

At a given moment, it is the mask required for the perpetuation of dissimulation.

*   *   *

Lucy Lippard:

David Lamelas has asked me (presumably as part of his own art work) to "comment," along with other critics and artists, on three statements: 1) Use of oral and written language as an Art Form; 2) Language can be considered as an Art Form; 3) Language cannot be considered as an Art Form.

Douglas Huebler has sent me a piece of his (art) and asked me to send him something (implied art) in exchange.

I don't make art. But now and then I write about artists or use their work in such a way that I'm accused of making art. Accused because it's not necessarily a compliment since I'm a writer and not dissatisfied with being called a writer since I use words as a conventional Art Form called literature or criticism, Art in this case being used as a broad term meaning any sort of not necessarily visual framework imposed on or around real or imagined experience. I don't make pictures. I don't use pictures. I don't make patterns on the page with the words (or if I do, they're conventional, random, non-hierarchical patterns and only incidental to the intention of *writing* something). The only object I have any urge to make is a pile of paper covered with words, or the ordinary paperback book. (Hard covers are pretentious and usually too big to be carried in the pocket and will therefore be read pretentiously in a pipe-smoking rocking chair situation. Now I Will Read a Book; instead of an ongoing fragmented in and out of life and in and out of the book situation.)

Later I talked to Doug and he (mistakenly) told me he was going to publish the pieces he received in exchange as part of his exchange piece. I had thought of doing an Artificial Word Series from a book I'm writing or just a randomly chosen page of the (unreadable) first draft of the manuscript of the book I'm writing. But now I guess I'll give him a statement of some kind to this effect:

Conventional "Literature" (dictionary definition: "The profession and production of an author") unlike conventional visual art (first dictionary definition: "human ability to make things") is worth nothing per se before it is a book, and when it is a book it is worth maybe two bucks and is available to everybody with two bucks, or with a library, or a friend who has the book. Art can be traded and so can books, but if I trade a copy of my book for a painting or a sculpture or even for a print, the receiver of the book will probably feel cheated. My book should be traded, when and if it is printed, for a reproduction of a work of art. Maybe Doug's piece, existing in an "edition" of 50, is a reproduction? If so, what is it a reproduction of? Maybe Doug's piece is tradeable for a book printed in an edition of 50 copies and therefore "worth" two hundred instead of two bucks? Or is my book, published or unpublished, and Doug's piece, unique or multiple, "worth" whatever we can get for it? Or is it "worth" whatever is traded for it since that kind of open situation obviously has to do with the kind of piece he is making; and once our exchanges are incorporated into the piece, is it "worth" more as the sum of the parts than each part separately, or is it still worth two hundred bucks or a grand or whatever these things are "worth" on the market?

It's all getting distasteful. Obviously Doug doesn't care if it's an "equal" trade, only that the trade is accomplished. The point is not the monetary worth or the prestige worth of either Doug's piece or whatever I produce in return (I would like to make it a direct response to his piece rather than something that exists independently or was around before I got the request for an exchange). The point, anyway, lies in the differences between the media and their manipulability.

It's almost an oil-water problem. Can you trade art for literature? Or for cauliflowers? Are languages as a (visual) Art Form and language as a (written) Art Form, i.e. literature, interchangeable? If written (visual) art is a viable (visual) Art Form how do you distinguish it from literature? Is the only difference that one is made by an Artist and one by an Author? If an Artist makes up a story and tells it in book form is it Art? If an Author paints a pretty picture is it Literature? If I borrow (plagiarize, which originally meant to kidnap) a piece (Special Investigation, 1969/70) from Joseph Kosuth, who has presented it as (visual) Art after borrowing it from a riddle book by another "author," and use it in my book of "fiction," does it become Literature again? (And was it Literature in the riddle book?) Is it therefore no more a plagiarism than Joseph's original act of borrowing it was plagiarism? What price the ransom? If I put my book of fiction into an art show, *then* have I plagiarized Joseph's piece? A similar question came up several years ago when Erle Loran wanted to sue Roy Lichtenstein for making paintings after Loran's pedagogic diagrams after Cézanne. No conclusions were drawn. Does it make a difference if I add a footnote to my use of Joseph's piece that says "I would like to thank Joseph Kosuth for bringing this material to my attention"? Would it have changed Joseph's piece if he had acknowledged his source?

If that's confusing, consider this one. Is a curator an artist because he uses a group of paintings and sculptures in a theme show to prove a point of his own? Is Seth Siegelaub an artist when he formulates a new framework within which artists can show their work without reference to theme, gallery, institution, even place or time? Is he an author because his framework is books? Am I an artist when I ask artists to work within or respond to a given situation, then publish the results as a related group? Is Bob Barry an artist when he "presents" the work of Ian Wilson within a work of his own, the process of the presentation being his work and Ian's work remaining Ian's? If the critic is a vehicle for the art, does an artist who makes himself a vehicle for the art of another artist become a critic?

It's all just a matter of what to call it? Does that matter? It has to if Joseph Kosuth, for instance, is making "art as idea as idea" and not just idea as idea, if the Art and Language group are making language *about* art and calling it art. Clearly what it's called does matter, maybe more than what it is? As long as there are Art Shows and Books as Art Shows as distinguished from Books as Literature, and until it is possible to pick up a book-as-object and neither know nor care whether it's called art or literature or fiction or non-fiction, it matters. Artists want to be called artists. Writers want to be called writers. Even if it doesn't matter.

It's not the medium that counts, and it's not the message that counts, it's how either or both are presented, in what context, that counts. And artists who claim they are making non-art or anti-art should have the grace to stay out of art galleries and art museums and art magazines until those names have been obliterated. No art, no matter how much it resembles life, or literature, can call itself anything but art as long as it has been, is, or ever will be shown in an art context.

And writers who claim they are writers should stay in books and magazines and catalogues? But the catalogue part gets confusing now that there is art that may appear only in the catalogue of a show. When I wrote a critical text (not wholly recognizable as such) for the Museum of Modern Art's *Information* catalogue, it was put into the body of the book with the artist's contributions and I was listed with the artists. This confuses matters and I didn't know about it until too late. I rather like its confusing matters but I don't like to be listed as an artist. Public self-identity becomes important. Privately one tends not to bother. One of the few things I'm sure of is that I deal with words as a writer. I like them in long relatively sequential passages and I like words that refer to other words. I can't think of any (visual) artist who does this without calling it art (which makes it art). Or who does it without referring to its structural framework. No, that's not quite right. Kosuth's investigations when they are on the page (not on wall labels), Ian Wilson's oral communication, Lamelas' interview with Duras, and the Art and Language group, and its sidekicks, all prove that language is an art medium but has to be trapped firmly in the bounds of Art the container to be an Art Form. Is it habit that makes an artist keep his language within the bounds of Art? Or discipline? Is it possible that once language is not called art (or literature, whatever that is), it is no longer significant? Is it significant as art primarily because its isolation as art, its separation from life, makes people aware of language in an unexpected and therefore more powerful context? Just as painting and sculpture separate themselves from commercial art, decoration, and industrial design by that same act of self-upgrading? Are artists making their work significant as art because of a reluctance to participate (and compete) in the larger literary-academic world of language-usage? What difference is there between "This sentence has five words" and "this whole has five parts"?

Or is it all a synthetic dualism, a synthetic dilemma leading back simply to the problems of one's intentions to affect the world or not? And how? If I'm all in favor of a future in which the distinctions are confused and effaced, why, in the meantime, am I so concerned to retain my public identity as a writer? I'd like to do that mainly because confusing criticism with art dilutes the art still further than its third to twenty-ninth string does. At the same time I'll do as much as I can to confuse the distinction between writing and art writing, maybe eventually between art and art writings, and to generate circumstances in which these distinctions *are* obliterated. It probably is a synthetic dilemma, but what is there about art that isn't synthetic, when you come down to it, or writing either?

Everything written by me above and all rights to it belong to Douglas Huebler in exchange for his *Duration Piece # 8, Global*; only with the written permission of Douglas Huebler may it be printed in David Lamelas' book, which is also his exhibition.

Lucy R. Lippard, New York, 25 September 1970.

*　　*　　*

Gilbert & George:

Oh Art, what are you? You are so strong and powerful, so beautiful and moving. You make us walk around and around, pacing the city at all hours, in and out of our Art for

All room. We really do love you and we really do hate you. Why do you have so many faces and voices? You make us thirst for you and then to run from you escaping completely into a normal life—: getting up, having breakfast, going to the work-shop and being sure of putting our mind and energy into the making of a door or maybe a simple table and chair. The whole life would surely be so ease-ful, so drunk with the normality of work and the simple pleasures of loving and hanging around for our lifetime. Oh Art where did you come from, who mothered such a strange being. For what kind of people are you—: are you for the feeble-of-mind, are you for the poor-at-heart, are you for those with no soul. Are you a branch of nature's fantastic network or are you an invention of some ambitious man? Do you come of a long line of arts? For every artist is born in the usual way and we have never seen a young artist. Is to become an artist to be reborn, or is it a condition of life? Coming slowly over a person like the daybreak. It brings the art-ability to do this funny thing and shows you new possibilities for feeling and scratching at oneself and surroundings, setting standards, making you go into every scene and every contact, every touching nerve and all your senses. And Art we are driven by you at incredible speed, ignorant of the danger you are pushing and dragging us into. And yet Art, there is no going back, all roads go only on and on. We are happy for the good times that you give us and we work and wait only for these titbits from your table. If you only knew how much these mean to us, transporting us from the depths of tragedy and black despair to a beautiful life of happiness, taking us where the good times are. When this happens we are able to walk again with our heads held high. We artists need only to see a little light through the trees of the forest, to be happy and working and back into gear again. And yet, we don't forget you, Art, we continue to dedicate our artists-art to you alone, for you and your pleasure, for Art's-sake. We would honestly like to say to you, Art, how happy we are to be your sculptors. We think about you all the time and feel very sentimental about you. We do realise that you are what we really crave for, and many times we meet you in our dreams. We have glimpsed you through the abstract world and have tasted of your reality. One day we thought we saw you in a crowded street, you were dressed in a light brown suit, white shirt and a curious blue tie, you looked very smart but there was about your dress a curious wornness and dryness. You were walking alone, light of step and in a very controlled sense. We were fascinated by the lightness of your face, your almost colourless eyes and your dusty-blonde hair. We approached you nervously and then just as we neared you you went out of sight for a second and then we could not find you again. We felt sad and unlucky and at the same time happy and hopeful to have seen your reality. We now feel very familiar with you, Art. We have learned from you many of the ways of life. In our work of drawings, sculptures, living-pieces, photo-messages, written and spoken pieces we are always to be seen, frozen into a gazing for you. You will never find us working physically or with our nerves and yet we shall not cease to pose for you, Art. Many times we would like to know what you would like of us, your messages to us are not always easily understood. We realize that it cannot be too simple because of your great-complexity and all-meaning. If at times we do not measure up or fulfil your wishes you must believe that it is not because we are unserious but only because we are artists. We ask always for your help, Art, for we need much strength in this modern time, to be only artists of a life-time. We know that you are above the people of our artist-world but we feel we should tell you of the ordinariness and struggling that abounds and we ask you if this must be. Is it right that artists should only be able to work for you for only the days when they are new, fresh and crisp. Why can't you let them pay homage to you for all their days, growing strong in your company and coming to know you better. Oh Art, please let us all relax with you. Recently Art, we thought to set ourselves the task of painting a large set of narrative views descriptive of our looking for you. We like very much to look forward to doing it and we are sure that they are really right for you.

To be with Art is all we ask.

Ho Ho Ho is the same in all languages? (Byars.)

September 18, New York: Adrian Piper performs *Catalysis I* **in the third car of the first D train to pass the Grand Street Station after 5:15 p.m.; September 19, in Marboro Book Store, 8th Street, between 9 and 10 p.m. (see below, p. 235).**

Recorded Activities. **Moore College of Art, Philadelphia, October 16–November 19, 1970. Organized by Diane Vanderlip; "text" by Lucy Lippard. Statements or works by the artists: Acconci, Baldessari, Bochner, Findlay, Graham, Hutchinson, Johnson, Kosuth, Levine, Telethon, Nauman, Oppenheim, Snow, Van Saun, Venet, Smithson.**

October 18, Breen's Bar, San Francisco: First showing of *Body Works,* **a video exhibition (Acconci, Fox, Nauman, Oppenheim, Sonnier, Wegman). Coordinated by the Museum of Conceptual Art and Willoughby Sharp.**

October, 1970: Press release announces the opening of the "Jean Freeman Gallery," 26 W. 57th Street, New York; releases continue to announce one-man and one-woman shows of "process art" through March, 1971. See p. 223.

Network '70: NETCo. **Fine Arts Gallery, University of British Columbia, Vancouver, October 7–24, 1970. "A transcontinental telex-telecopier hook-up" to galleries and museums in New York, Los Angeles, Tacoma, Seattle, Halifax, North Vancouver, Vancouver. Visual Sensitivity Information.**

October 5–6, Halifax, Nova Scotia: Halifax Conference organized by Seth Siegelaub at the Nova Scotia College of Art and Design. Among participants: Andre, Beuys, Buren, Dibbets, Merz, Morris, NETCo., Serra, Smithson, Snow, Weiner.

Carl Andre. **Solomon Guggenheim Museum, New York, September–October, 1970. Bibliography, biography, poetry by the artist, text by Diane Waldman.**

Software. **Jewish Museum, New York, September 16–November 8, 1970. Organized by Jack Burnham. Texts by him, Karl Katz, Theodor Nelson. Among participants: Acconci, Antin, Baldessari, Barry, Burgy, Denes, Giorno, Goodyear, Haacke, Huebler, Kosuth, Kaprow, Levine, Weiner. Reviewed by Bitite Vinklers,** *Arts,* **September–October, 1970; Dore Ashton,** *Studio International,* **November.**

Paul Pechter, fall, 1970: *Proposal for Device entitled "Discriminations":* **This device is composed of many individual works; the one presented here is intended for insertion in a magazine:**

Take a 10-page section of page numbers and randomize their order. Example: pgs. 23–33; change order to: 26, 31, 29, 27, 24, 23, 32, 28, 33, 30. List in table of contents as follows: "Discriminations" by Paul Pechter . . . pgs. 23–33.

Device Intended to Function as an Art Device: Sheet of paper. One hundred and fifty of these devices total one pound. Sheet of paper: One hundred and sixty seven of these devices total one pound. Sheet of paper: One hundred and twenty-six of these devices total one pound.

Billy Apple, *VACUUMING:*

Second floor front and rear space, landing,
stairs, and entrance at 161 West 23rd Street [New York],
Beginning October 1, 1970 a continuous work
still in progress.

Vacuum Bags

Thursday, October 1, 1970 12:44 P.M.
Tuesday, October 20, 1970 1:15 P.M.
Monday, December 21, 1970 1:10 P.M.
Sunday, February 21, 1971 2:49 P.M.
Saturday, March 20, 1971 12:10 P.M.
Friday, April 2, 1971 4:39 P.M.
Saturday, May 1, 1971 1:33 P.M.
Saturday, June 5, 1971 12:07 P.M.
Thursday, September 9, 1971 3:32 P.M.
Thursday, November 4, 1971 3:58 P.M.
Saturday, December 11, 1971 5:54 P.M.

Daniel Buren. Bradford Junior College, Mass., October 11–29, 1970: "The thing to see is alternate white and gray vertical stripes of 8.7 cm. each whatsoever may be their place, number, author . . . " Artist in residence, October 11–16.

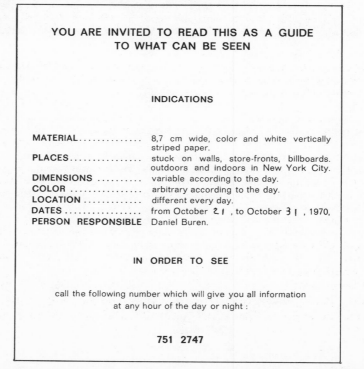

YOU ARE INVITED TO READ THIS AS A GUIDE TO WHAT CAN BE SEEN

INDICATIONS

MATERIAL . . . . 8,7 cm wide, color and white vertically striped paper.
PLACES . . . . stuck on walls, store-fronts, billboards. outdoors and indoors in New York City.
DIMENSIONS . . . . variable according to the day.
COLOR . . . . arbitrary according to the day.
LOCATION . . . . different every day.
DATES . . . . from October 2 1 , to October 3 1 , 1970,
PERSON RESPONSIBLE Daniel Buren.

IN ORDER TO SEE

call the following number which will give you all information
at any hour of the day or night :

751 2747

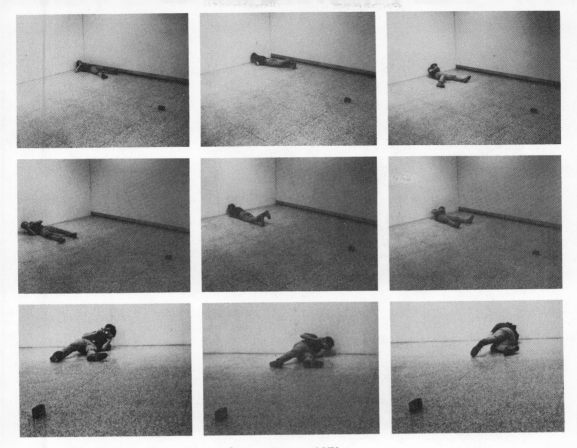

Dan Graham. *Roll.* 2 Super-8 Films on Loops. 1970.

Mute super-8 camera is placed just above, base parallel to the ground. After looking through viewfinder to determine left and right frames, I position my body at line (seen through viewfinder) on right frame—my feet facing the camera's view. Using a second super-8 camera as an extension of my eye, I roll slowly toward the left framing line trying to continuously orient my eye-camera view centering on the first placed camera's position. My legs–body extensions are in the foreground of the held camera's (my eye's) view and I observe their shifting alignment as *necessary feedback to achieving my orientation (image).*

In the past tense, the two films made are projected for viewing on opposite walls. One image the *spectator* sees is my view from inside my feedback loop extending from eye/camera to muscular adjustment (eye to brain to muscles to kinesthetic feeling of change of gravitational and postural orientation) to what my eye sees etc. . . . as I move: a continuous learning process to achieve—stabilize—the image which is the premise of the work. On the other end, the opposite image simultaneously shows the outside, objective view of the mute, placed camera: the performer's body as an object moving across the frame. Both views are mirror parity parallel and simultaneously define the other's eye level (and ground level) picture planes.

Dan Graham: 7 Performances. 16 Presentations. Obverse. **Nova Scotia College of Art and Design, Halifax, October 8–15, 1970; March 10–22, 1971. (Rep.)**

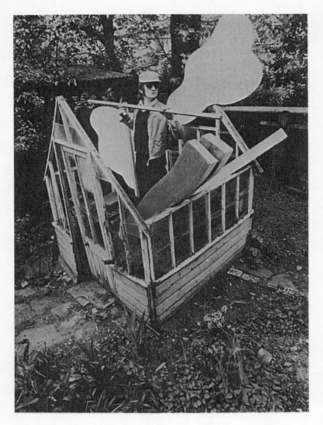

Bruce McLean. *People Who Make Art in Glass Houses.* 1970.

Bruce McLean. *King for a Day plus 99 other pieces incorporating "The Piece a Minute Show" and "The World's Fastest Piece in the World" piece–work thing.* Nova Scotia College of Art and Design, Halifax, October, 1970. Excerpt (full 1,000 pieces published in *Avalanche*, no. 2, winter, 1971) (Rep.):

109. Major breakthrough (piece) study.
110. Breakthrough 1.
111. Breakthrough 2.
112. Breakthrough 3.
113. Small art (study piece).
114. Small piece (for specific environment).
115. 10 part installation work for heads (specific).
116. 25 part installation work for hands (unfinished).
117. Work of the Decade thing.
118. Last piece of the decade (1970).
119. First piece of the Decade.
120. Memory piece.
121. Remember Alan Davie with his Poddle piece.
122. Remember Anthony Caro (piece work).
123. Portrait of artists' pub at lunchtime piece.

194

124. Collectors piece.
125. Song and dance action and piece work 4th version.
126. Eat work.
127. Laugh work.
128. Smoke work.
129. Wink work.
130. Talk (piece).
131. Fun art work.
132. Subterranean floataway piece.
133. Puddle piece. Wet and dry, work.
134. 150 ft. seascape (Largibeg).
135. Define a space with you (piece).
136. Define a space with friends. Piece.
137. Define a space with sticks, poles anything (stuff).
138. Getting into the gallery scene. Work.
139. Getting out of the Gallery scene piece.
140. Meeting people piece (friends of the Tate).
141. Mingle work/piece. Multimedia.
142. Multimedia thing/piece/work.
143. Revived 25 piece. From way back last month Piece.
144. People say I'm the life of the party, work.
145. Cloudscape, Nos. 1–24.
146. Shadow pieces (a selection).
147. Stepping into reality. Piece.
148. Working my way back to you piece.
149. Installation Barnes Pond Area.
150. Song/dance/joke/action Piece, work. 5th version.
150a. Piece with yellow chair, feather and Firework (work).
151. Gouache work paper/cut outs etc., piece.
152. Large studio piece.
153. Studio in the country work.
154. The artist and his wife work.
155. The artist and his model (second version) 1st state.
156. The green cupboard installation piece, for rooms.
157. Boy with a dustpan and brush. Art work. Transition (piece).
158. Transition. (piece).
159. Dancing girl piece.
160. Walking girl piece.
161. Portrait of the artist as a young man piece.
162. Documentation project piece, 20 photos of walls, archway, st.
163. Sand-pile revisited.
164. Pond at Barnes Reappraisal, work.
165. Glass on grass piece.
166. 4 part installation for 2 armchairs 1 sofa 1 room.
167. Wall/floor piece.
168. Guy Fawkes piece (smoke) etc.
169. Two part Kickaround.
170. Paint in your gutter piece.

171. Hoax art work for specific audience.
172. 3 part Lakescape for Lake Washington.
173. 10 part disposable piece Barnes pond area.
174. 2 hour walk and stand piece (specific location).
175. Song kick joke smile laugh, artwork 6th version.
176. Installation for specific part of the body, 1 underarm.
177. Installation for specific part of the body, 2 crutch.
178. Installation for specific part of the body, 3 mouth.
179. Installation for specific part of the body, 4 ear.
180. Installation for specific part of the body, 5 nose.
181. Installation for specific part of the body, 6 arse.
182. Installation for specific part of the body, 7 hair. (public?).
183. Installation for specific part of the body, 8 eyes.
184. Edible art work.
185. Drinkable art work.
186. Poem piece (rhyming).
187. Super duper star at work. 2nd version.
188. Dance piece for Ballrooms (spotlights).
189. Instruction piece for Ballrooms (RF forward and across in PP).
190. Participation piece.
191. Latest offering piece, art work.
192. McLean in the boys' Gym.
193. Touch piece, grip grope grab art work.
194. An evergreen memory piece. Art work.
195. "There Grassy Places" art work.
196. Erotic porno piece, art work.
197. Hopscotch (Anthony Caro) executed (art work).
198. Etching (a day in the life of an etcher) piece.
199. Acquisition piece, thing.
200. Song/dance joke laugh cough. Art piece/work etc. 7th version.
201. Fresh look at the last 200 pieces (piece).
202. Think piece.
203. Installation for super duper markets. (work).
204. Retrospective art piece.
205. Art as object (work).
206. Climb every mountain (piece).
207. Walk every highway (piece).
208. Climb every rainbow (piece).
209. Mickey Mouse cultpiece.
210. Jimmy Young (edible piece).
211. My love sculpture grows where my Rosemary goes (piece).
212. Heavy rock/jazz (sound installation work).
213. Moving around the Tate (art work).
214. Everybody's talking about it (oral piece).
215. Dig your garden (work).
216. Mow your lawn (work).
217. Cut your grass (work).
218. Edge your lawn (work).

219. Dig that crazy rhythm, piece.
220. The artist as a baker (work).
221. The artist as a bricklayer (work).
222. The artist as an artist (piece).

McLean, Bruce. "Not Even Crimble-Crumble." *Studio International,* October, 1970.

NETCo. *North American Time Zone Photo-V.S.I. Simultaneity, October 18, 1970.* West Vancouver, B.C., West Coast Publishing Ltd. Folio of 18 prints of 14 subjects (Time, Nude, Still Life, Cityscape, Earth, Air, Fire, Water, North, South, East, West, Shadow, Self-Portrait) photographed simultaneously in Vancouver, Edmonton, Winnipeg, London (Ont.), Halifax, Mt. Carmel (Newfoundland), each of which is in a separate time zone (PDT, MDT, EDT, ADT, NDT). Message from the presidents—Ingrid and Iain Baxter. (Rep.)

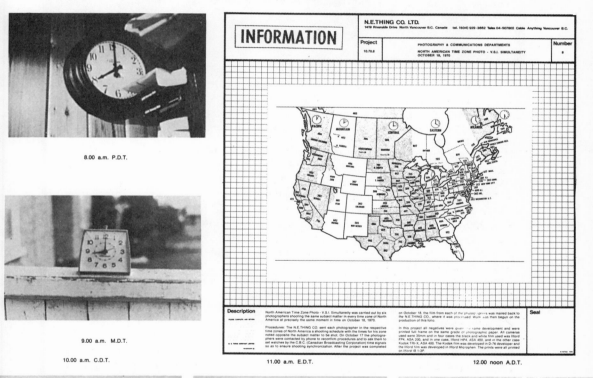

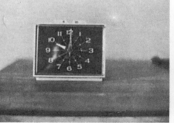

8.00 a.m. P.D.T.

9.00 a.m. M.D.T.

10.00 a.m. C.D.T.

11.00 a.m. E.D.T.

12.00 noon A.D.T.

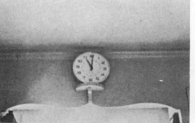

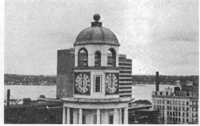

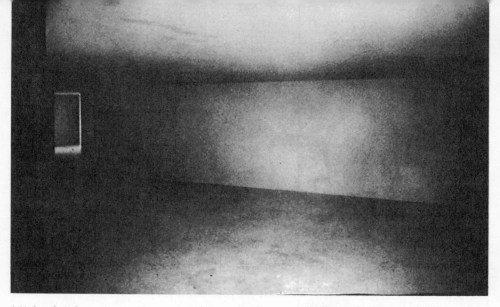

Michael Asher. An environmental project. Pomona College. February, 1970.

Cameron, Eric, "Drawing Lines in the Desert: A Study of North American Art," and Munger, Barbara, "Michael Asher: An Environmental Project" (excerpts below). *Studio International,* **October, 1970 (Rep.):**

One large irregular-shaped area appears to be two adjoining rooms; the rooms, one much larger than the other, are in the form of right triangles; the triangular rooms converge and flow into one another at their narrowest point, beginning a short passageway connecting the two rooms. One wall of each room has a corresponding parallel wall and corresponding angle in the other room, and both rooms are positioned so they are the reverse of each other. This interior architecture is Michael Asher's project that was constructed February, 1970, over a period of a month of development. It was one in a series of one-man exhibitions organized by Hal Glicksman for the Pomona College Art Gallery. . . .

Sound of traffic, of people walking past the gallery—sounds of vibrations of the day that vary from minute to minute, hour to hour—all enter the project. Being exposed to outdoor conditions, the first small room transmits sounds through the pathway into the back room. They are amplified as they pass into the first room, but are further intensified as they enter the second larger room. High-frequency sounds are greatly intensified to a degree where they are louder in the back room than at their places of origin. Sound is considered to be acoustically thin (rather than acoustically thick) in the areas where it is more reverberant—in the passageway and along the back wall. For example, a visually dark area appears to be more dense, more weighty than a visually light area; a darkly lit room appears to be almost impenetrable as one gropes his way through it. In the same way, the acoustically thick areas seem to be more dense, allowing for noise absorption, while the thin areas seem to act as a vacuum that draws in and intensifies sound. These thick and thin areas form a spatial pattern perceived as one experiences it.

Light fills and saturates the first small room which, in turn, generates much less light into the second. All interior surfaces, except the inner back wall, are exposed to a subtle gradation of light, from bright to dark, becoming darker towards the back wall. Softly glowing, the back wall itself reflects the most amount of light.

Light entering the project will vary, depending upon the sun's location in the sky. Since the project is open twenty-four hours a day, night light, as well as daylight, enters. At night, the moon is the main source of illumination for the two rooms. However, the shadows upon the walls of the first room are softened by a blending together of two other light sources: a seventy-five watt light covered with clear and blue Plexiglas, having two fibreglass diffusers in between (flushed up to the portico ceiling), and the street lights. As a result, dark blue coloring is mixed into the night light of the project. . . .

A spatial phenomenon is created and defined by light and sound as objects of perception, rather than by the bordering interior architecture of walls, floor, and ceiling. Light gives the space a brilliant yellowish color during the day and a deep, dense blue at night.

Sound is responsible for the acoustically thick and thin areas within the space, that, although not visual, can be sensed as one passes through them. All surfaces appear to dissolve, as they are overwhelmed by the space. They evade detection of their location. For example, the ceiling is so ambiguous that few ever know its proper height (6 ft 4 in.); it is so low that it can be touched if one were to lift one's arms above one's head. As the space exists independently from the existing architecture, it becomes a boundless space extending toward infinity.

Statements, no. 2, November, 1970. Contributors: Pilkington, Richings, Willsmore, Rushton, Dove.

Concept-Théorie. Galerie Deniel Templon, Paris, November 3–21.

Christo, Barry Flanagan. CAYC, Buenos Aires. Folio catalogue, biographies, texts by Flanagan, Jorge Glusberg in English and Spanish.

November 24, 1970. Kunstakademie, Düsseldorf: *Isolation Unit* executed by Joseph Beuys and Terry Fox, "after spending four hours alone together in the cellar of the school." A phonograph record of the last 13 minutes is part of the catalogue *Fox, Fish, Kos* (see p. 222).

MacKintosh, Alastair. "Beuys in Edinburgh." *Art and Artists,* November, 1970.

Identifications, a television exhibition organized by Gerry Schum for Sudwestfunk, Germany. Anselmo, Beuys, Boetti, Calzolari, de Dominici, Dibbets, Gilbert and George, Merz, Rückriem, Ruthenbeck, Weiner, Zorio.

November, Sydney, Australia: Founding of Inhibodress, an artist's loft cooperative gallery, by Peter Kennedy, Tim Johnson, Mike Parr. Early shows include Kennedy's sound piece *But the Fierce Blackman,* Johnson's *Installation as Conceptual Theme,* Parr's *Word Situations.*

$E = mc^2$, next? (Byars.)

Eleanor Antin, Four New York Women. Shown at the Hotel Chelsea, New York, November, 1970. Object biographies, for which the texts alone follow; when exhibited the work consists of the objects alone, or photographs and texts, or texts alone, depending on the circumstances:
Naomi Dash: Ruth Moss used to live in an old house on Cornelia Street. There were still slave quarters rotting in the backyard. Whenever she heard the fire engines

(usually in the middle of the night) she would grab Rasputin with one hand, her box of sterling with the other and still dressed in her night clothes rush down the 5 flights to the street.

Margaret Mead: She is a great Optimist. Once she put a scarf over her eyes and walked around her house for a week tapping with a cane. She reported afterwards that being blind wasn't so bad. One got used to it.

Yvonne Rainer: Rochelle said Yvonne was plump and bosomy in the old days. She and Al used to scream and throw things at each other like Anna Magnani. She came from a family of Italian anarchists. Carlo Tresca was a relative. Another uncle attended a Bund rally in Yorkville and got so angry he had a heart attack and died.

Carolee Schneemann: Carolee told Rochelle that she always took whatever she wanted from department stores and never got caught. The first time Rochelle tried it she was stopped at the door of Bloomingdales but demanded, "How dare you handle me, you German. My husband is a college professor!"

APG (Artists Placement Group). "INN₇O." *Studio International,* November, 1970. A magazine collage of printed information from various sources.

David Askevold: *Videotape, film and amplified tuning fork installations.* Nova Scotia College of Art and Design, Halifax, November 16–30.

Hanne Darboven. *Art and Project Bulletin* 28, November 10–December 11, 1970:
00/366 - 1.
99/365 - 100. On exhibition: 100 Book 00–99.

Gerald Ferguson: *Provincial Illustration.* Art Gallery, Dalhousie University, Halifax, Nova Scotia, November 17–December 17, 1970.

Sol LeWitt. Pasadena Art Museum, November 17, 1970–January 3, 1971:
The draftsman and the wall enter a dialogue. The draftsman becomes bored but later through this meaningless activity finds peace or misery. The lines on the wall are the residue of this process. Each line is as important as each other line. All of the lines become one thing. The viewer of the lines can see only lines on a wall. They are meaningless. That is art. (From Pasadena catalogue.)

The artist conceives and plans the wall drawing. It is realized by draftsmen. (The artist can act as his own draftsman.) The plan, written, spoken or a drawing, is interpreted by the draftsman.

There are decisions which the draftsman makes, within the plan, as part of the plan. Each individual, being unique, given the same instructions would carry them out differently. He would understand them differently.

The artist must allow various interpretations of his plan. The draftsman perceives the artist's plan, then reorders it to his own experience and understanding.

The draftsman's contributions are unforeseen by the artist, even if he, the artist, is the draftsman. Even if the same draftsman followed the same plan twice, there would be two different works of art. No one can do the same thing twice.

The artist and the draftsman become collaborators in making the art.

Each person draws a line differently and each person understands words differently.

Neither lines nor words are ideas. They are the means by which ideas are conveyed.

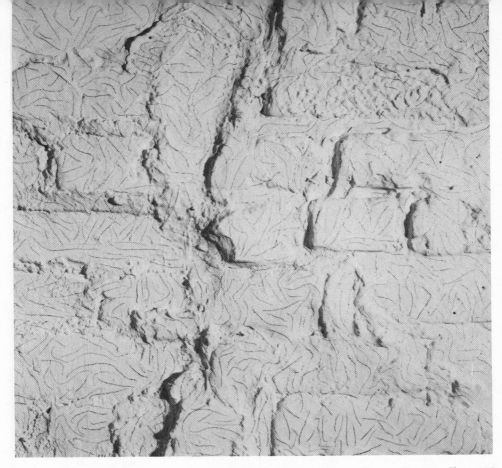

Sol LeWitt, *Wall Drawing, Lines not Touching.* Close-up of pencil on wall at 138 Prince Street, New York. 1971.

The wall drawing is the artist's art, as long as the plan is not violated. If it is, then the draftsman becomes the artist and the drawing would be his work of art, but art that is a parody of the original concept.

The draftsman may make errors in following the plan without compromising the plan. All wall drawings contain errors. They are part of the work.

The plan exists as an idea but needs to be put into its optimum form. Ideas of wall drawings alone are contradictions of the idea of wall drawings.

The explicit plans should accompany the finished wall drawing. They are of importance. (from *Art Now,* vol. 3, no. 2, 1971.)

***Lines, not short, not straight, crossing and touching, drawn at random, using four colors (yellow, black, red and blue), uniformly dispersed with maximum density covering the entire surface of the wall* (plan for LeWitt wall drawing at the Guggenheim International Exhibition, 1971; executed by David Schulman, whose notes on the process are quoted below):**

Started Jan. 26, having no idea how long it would take to reach a point of maximum density (a very ambiguous point at that). Being paid $3.00 per hour, trying to let my financial needs have little effect on the amount of time I worked. . . . I was exhausted after 3 days of working without the slightest intimation of density. Having only one mechanical pencil, even the energy expended changing leads had an accumulative tiring effect. . . . I pushed to get the lines down faster while keeping them as not short as not straight and as crossing, touching and random as possible. I decided to use one color at a time, and use that color until it reached a point I considered one quarter "Maximum Density." . . . Signals of discomfort became an unconscious time clock determining when I would stop and step back from the drawing. Walking up the ramp to look at the drawing from a distance provided momentary relief from the physical strain of the drawing. From a distance, each color had a swarming effect as it slowly worked its way across a portion of the wall. . . . The drawing in ways was paradoxical. The even density and dispersement of the lines took on a very systematic effect. Once the individual difficulties of each color were determined, any thought as to how the lines were going down in relation to lines previously drawn gradually diminished until there was no conscious thought given to the lines being drawn. Doing the drawing I realized that totally relaxing my body was only one way of reaching a deep level of concentration. Another was in the mindless activity of doing the drawing. Keeping my body totally active in an almost involuntary way—in a sense, totally relaxed my mind. When my mind became relaxed, thoughts would flow at a smoother and faster pace.

John Latham: Least Event, One Second Drawing, Blind Work, 24 Second Painting. **Lisson Gallery, London, November 11–December 6, 1970. Documentation of past and present works. Invitation to show (in toto):**

"John Latham/ The Lisson Gallery does not exist for 100 years/ Time Sculpture/ ADMIT ONE."

"During the third week of the exhibition the gallery will be at places other than Bell Street, for short periods, probably not much more than a minute at any place, and the show there will be recorded on video or film. The places and times indicated below are likely to be chosen—check with Lisson 262-1539." Places listed: The Insect House, Regent's Park; The Tate Gallery; The Stock Exchange; Fiona's Shoe; Junk Farm, Winkfield; Inside Encyclopedia Britannica. See also Latham's "Least Event as a habit . . . how basic is physics? " *Studio International,* December, 1970.

Ulrich Rückriem: Steine und Eisen. **Museum Haus Lange, Krefeld, November 15, 1970–January 10, 1971. Text by Paul Wember, biography.**

Lawrence Weiner: Beached. **Fernsehgalerie Gerry Schum, Baden-Baden, November 30, 1970. "On 16 August 1970 in Holland Lawrence Weiner built 5 examples of Beached."**

Ian Wilson. Art and Project Bulletin **30, November 30, 1970. (Completely blank.)**

Nemser, Cindy. "An Interview with Stephen Kaltenbach." *Artforum,* **November, 1970.**

"Willoughby Sharp Interviews Jack Burnham." *Arts,* **November, 1970:**
   WS: So you think art is at an impasse?
   JB: Yes, in terms of breaking rules . . .
   WS: Do you see art dissolving into nothingness in the near future?
   JB: No, it's dissolving into comprehension. The reason art exists in the first place is that it's a mystery.

Antin, David. "Lead Kindly Blight." *Art News,* **November, 1970.**

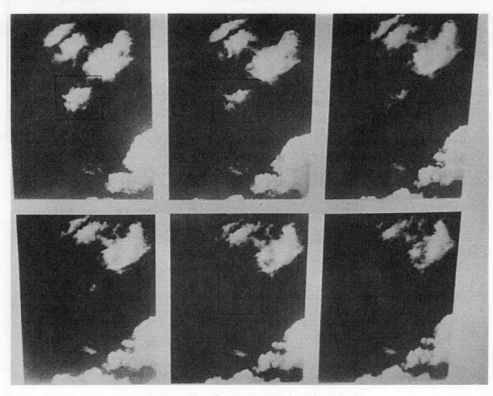

Peter Hutchinson. *Dissolving Clouds.* Aspen, Colorado. 1970.

Using Hatha yoga technique of intense concentration and pranic energy it is claimed that clouds can be dissolved. I tried it on cloud (in square) in photographs. This is what happened. "This piece happens almost entirely in the mind."

Develing, Enno. "Sculpture as Place." *Art and Artists,* November, 1970.

Harrison, Charles. "A Very Abstract Context." *Studio International,* November, 1970.

2,972,453. CAYC, Buenos Aires, November, 1970. Organized by Lucy R. Lippard as an unofficial continuation of *557,087* Seattle (1969) and *955,000* Vancouver (1970) shows; none of the artists were in the previous shows; catalogue on forty-three 4″ x 6″ index cards misprinted by the CAYC in defiance of the organizer's and artists' wishes; English and Spanish. Text by Lucy R. Lippard, note by Jorge Glusberg. Antin, Armajani, Askevold, Brouwn, Burgin, Calzolari, Celender, Collins, Cook, Gilbert & George, Haber, Jarden. Some works in the show follow:

Calzolari:

        1 e 2 giorno come gli orienti sono due
        3 The Picaro's day
        Fourth day as 4 long months of absence
        5 Contra naturam
        6th day of reality
        7—Seventh—with usura-contra naturam.

*   *   *

Siah Armajani. A number between 2 and 3, computer, 1970:
    A number between two numbers or there are infinite numbers between any two numbers. The infinity of all numbers is as large as the infinity of even numbers.
    Or there are as many points on a line one inch long as there are points in the entire universe. An infinite class has the unique property that the whole is not larger than some of its parts.

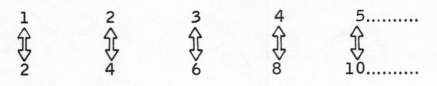

    Or what is obvious for the finite is false for the infinite.

Three works by David Askevold:
    Let A, B, and C be the three alternatives, and 1, 2, and 3 the three individuals. Suppose individual 1 prefers A to B and B to C (therefore A to C), individual 2 prefers B to C and C to A (and therefore B to A), and individual 3 prefers C to A and A to B (and therefore C to B). Then a majority prefer A to B, and a majority prefer B to C. But in fact a majority of the community prefer C to A.

*   *   *

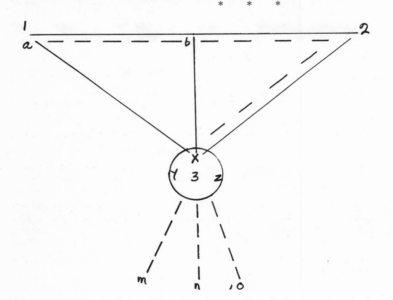

1.   Hall remembered that officer Willis had gone through Piedmont
earlier in the evening --a. just a few minutes before the disease
broke out --b. He had gone through without stopping   2.   and had gone
mad later on --x. connection? --y. he wondered --z. there might be.

3.   Certainly, he could see many similarities --m. Willis had an ulcer,
--n. had taken asprin and --o. had, eventually, committed suicide.

David Askevold.
1970.

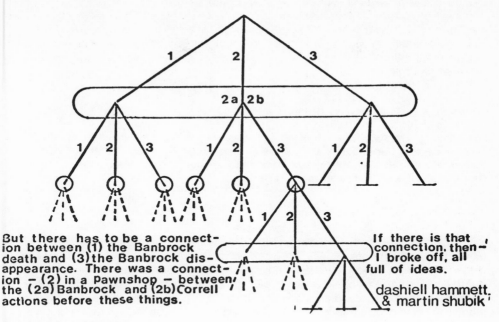

But there has to be a connection between (1) the Banbrock death and (3) the Banbrock disappearance. There was a connection — (2) in a Pawnshop — between the (2a) Banbrock and (2b) Correll actions before these things.

If there is that connection, then — I broke off, all full of ideas.

dashiell hammett & martin shubik

David Askevold. 1970.

Robert Barry. Galleria Sperone, Turin; Galleria San Fedele, Milan; Art and Project, Amsterdam (April 10, 1971); Yvon Lambert, Paris; Paul Maenz, Cologne (December–April, 1971):
 Some places to which we can come, and for a while "be free to think about what we are going to do" (Marcuse).

Buren, Daniel. *Limites/Critiques.* Yvon Lambert, Paris, December, 1970. Booklet plus colored illustrations.

Cook, Christopher C. *A Poem System.* Andover, Mass., December, 1970. 114 3″ x 5″ index cards.

Graham, Dan. *Performance 1.* John Gibson, New York, 1970. "Performance 1" was presented live at New York University, December 14, 1970. Booklet contains several pieces and commentaries as well as four articles on (and as) "entertainment."

Haber, Ira Joel. *Films,* no. 1, December, 1970. "A list of some of my favorite films (1947–1970) and the New York Theatres where they premiered."

Alain Kirili, Côtes de Finlande. Galerie de la Salle, Vence, December 19–January 10, 1971. Text in French and English.

LeWitt, Sol. "Ruth Vollmer: Mathematical Forms." *Studio International,* December, 1970.

Sanéjouand, *Plans d'organizations d'espaces,* Galerie Mathias Fels, Paris, December 3, 1970–January 10, 1971.

Lawrence Weiner. **Galleria Sperone, Turin, December 14, 1970:**
1. over the edge
2. around the bend
3. beside itself
4. under the line
5. over the hill
6. beside the point

He said yes before I asked? (Byars)

December 1, 1970, Paris: Ian Wilson presents his work ("Oral Communication") at the Café de la Monnaie; also December 12 at the Albergo Rosa, Milan. Organized by Michel Claura. Tucker, Marcia. "PheNAUMANology." *Artform,* **December, 1970. Excerpt below: Bruce Nauman, work and notes, early 1970:**

Dance Piece

You might hire a dancer to perform the following exercise each day of the exhibition for 20 minutes or 40 minutes at about the same time each day. The dancer, dressed in simple street or exercise clothes, will enter a large room of the gallery. The guards will clear the room, only allowing people to observe through the doors. Dancer, eyes front, avoiding audience contact, hands clasped behind his neck, elbows forward, walks about the room in a slight crouch, as though the ceiling were 6 inches or a foot lower than his normal height, placing one foot in front of the other, heel touching toe, very slowly and deliberately.

It is necessary to have a dancer or person of some professional anonymous presence.

At the end of the time period, the dancer leaves and the guards again allow people into the room.

If it is not possible to finance a dancer for the whole of the exhibition period a week will be satisfactory, but no less.

My five pages of the book [exhibition catalogue] will be publicity photographs of the dancer hired to do my piece, with his name affixed.

Manipulation of information that has to do with how we perceive rather than what.

Manipulation of functional (functioning) mechanism of an (organism) (system) person.

Lack of information input (sensory deprivation)-breakdown of responsible systems Do you hallucinate under these circumstances? If so, is it an attempt to complete a drive (or instance) (or mechanism)?

*   *   *

Pieces of information which are in "skew" rather than clearly contradictory, i.e., kinds of information which come from and go to unrelated response mechanism. Skew lines can be very close or far apart. (Skew lines never meet and are never parallel. How close seems of more interest than how far apart. How far apart-Surrealism?

Withdrawal as an Art Form
activities
phenomena

Sensory Manipulation
  amplification
  deprivation
Sensory Overload (Fatigue)
Denial or confusion of a Gestalt invocation of physiological defense mechanism (voluntary or involuntary). Examination of physical and psychological response to simple or even oversimplified situations which can yield clearly experienceable phenomena (phenomena and experience are the same or undifferentiable).
  Recording Phenomena
    Presentation of recordings of phenomena as opposed to stimulation of phenomena. Manipulation or observation of self in extreme or controlled situations.
    ● Observation of manipulations.
    ● Manipulation of observations.
    ● Information gathering.
    ● Information dispersal (or display).

Graham, Dan, ed. *Aspen,* December, 1970–January, 1971. Includes contributions by Graham, LaMonte Young, Steve Reich, Yvonne Rainer, Ruscha, Antin, Serra, MacLow, Oppenheim, Smithson, Morris, and Jo Baer.

Millet, Catherine. "Bernar Venet: La Fonction Didactique de l'art conceptuel." *Art International,* December, 1970.

1971

BOOKS

Ackerman, Cara. "Post-Esthetic Art." Unpublished paper written for the Whitney Museum Study Program and Vassar College, 1970–71.

Aue, Walter. *P.C.A.: Projects, Concepte, und Actionen.* Cologne, DuMont Schauberg, 1971. A huge unpaged collection of reprinted works and reproductions, primarily European and German; brief text.

Aycock, Alice. *An Incomplete Examination of the Highway Network/User/Perceiver System(s).* Unpublished Master's thesis for Hunter College, New York, 1971, under Robert Morris. Also the basis for a work consisting of "approximately 180 transactions conducted with various agencies in obtaining maps of network systems."

Barry, Robert. *One Billion Dots 1969.* Published in an edition of one, 25 volumes, Sperone, Turin, 1971.

————. *30 Pieces as of 14 June 1971.* Gerd de Vries in association with Paul Maenz, Cologne, 1971.

Mel Bochner. Milan, Editore Toselli, 1971.

Bowles, Gerry G., and Russell, Tony, eds. *This Book Is a Movie.* New York, Dell (Delta), 1971. Anthology. Includes among others: Acconci, Arakawa, Barry, Bochner, LeWitt, Lippard, Weiner.

Brouwn, Stanley. *1000 this-way-brouwn problems for computer I.B.M. 360 Model 95.* Gebr. König, Cologne–New York, 1971. Drawings collected February 25–26 on Dam Place, Amsterdam, from passers-by giving Brouwn directions. "I have become direction?" (S.B.)

————. *Steps.* Stedelijk Museum, Amsterdam, March 18–April 18, 1971.

————. *Steps* (IX–100X). Gallery MTL, Brussels, 1971.

Burgy, Donald. *Contexts, Completions, Ideas (Ideas para completar contextos).* CAYC, Buenos Aires, 1971. Spanish and English. Revised edition, *Context, Completion, Ideas* published by Schuring Galerie, Krefeld, 1971.

Burn, Ian, and Ramsden, Mel. *Unlimited Edition: subscription (per annum).* New York, 1971. A record of their works from 1964; to be continued.

Burnham, Jack. *The Structure of Art.* New York, George Braziller, 1971.

Jan Dibbets. *Art and Project Bulletin* 36. "A White Wall: 12 numbered photographs with different shutter speeds." (Rep.)

In 1963, Dibbets's Amsterdam mailbox was labeled "Jan Dibbets Dematerial-isateur." In 1970–71 he concentrated increasingly on film, slides, light: "That demater-ialization you are speaking about is going to be for me (in contrast to many other artists) more and more visual" (letter to L.R.L., September, 1971).

Ferguson, Gerald. *The Standard Corpus of Present Day English Language Usage* **arranged by word length and alphabetized within word length. Nova Scotia College of Art and Design, Halifax, 1971. Excerpt:**

KERYGMA KESTNER KETCHES KETCHUP KETOSIS KEYHOLE
KEYNOTE KEZZIAH KICKING KICKOFF KIDDING KIDNEYS KIEFFER
KIKIYUS KILHOUR KILLERS KILLING KILOTON KIMBALL KIMNELL
KIMPTON KINDEST KINDLED KINDRED KINETIC KINGDOM KINGPIN
KINSELL KINSHIP KIPLING KISSING KITCHEN KITCHIN KITTENS
KITTLER KIWANIS KLAUBER KLEENEX KLEIBER KLINICO KNEECAP
KNEELED KNIGHTS KNITTED KNOCKED KNOTTED KNOWETH
KNOWING KNUCKLE KOEHLER KOFANES KOLKHOZ KOMLEVA
KONISHI KOONING KOREANS KOSHARE KRAEMER KRASNIK
KREMLIN KRISHNA KROGERS KYO-ZAN LABELED LABORED
LABORER LABOTHE LACKEYS LACKING LACQUER LACTATE
LADGHAM LAGOONS LAMBERT LAMBETH LAMMING LAMPOON
LANCERT LANDING LANGUID LANTERN LAO-TSE LAOTIAN LAPLACE
LAPPETS LAPPING LAPSING LARAMIE LARCENY LARGELY LARGEST
LARIMER LARKINS LASHING LASTING LASWICK LATCHED LATCHES
LATERAL LATERAN LATTICE LAUCHLI LAUGHED LAUNDRY
LAURELS LAURITZ LAWFORD LAWLESS LAWSUIT LAWYERS LAXNESS
LAYERED LAYETTE LAYOFFS LAZARUS LAZZERI LB-PLUS LEACHES
LEADERS LEADING LEAFLET LEAGUES LEAGUER LEAGUES
LEAKAGE LEAN-TO LEANING LEAPING LEARNED LEASHES LEASING
LEASURE LEATHER LEAVING LEAVITT LECTURE LEDFORD
LEDGERS LEDYARD LEERING LEESOMA LEFTIST LEGALLY
LEGATEE LEGENDS LEGGETT LIPPMAN LIQUER LIQUIDS LISTING
LITERAL LITTERS LIVABLE LIZARDS LOADERS LOADING LOATHED
LOBBIED LOBBIES LOBSTER LOBULAR LOBULES LOCALES LOCALLY
LOCATED LOCATIN LOCKIAN LOCKIES LOCKING LODGING LOESSER
LOG-JAM LOGGING LOGICAL LOHMANS LOLLING LOLOTTE
LOMBARD LONGEST LONGING LONGISH LONGRUN LOOKING
LOOKOUT LOOMING LOOSELY LOOSENS LOOSEST LOOTING
LORELEI LORRAIN LOTIONS LOTTERY LOUDEST LOUNGED
LOUNGES LOUVERS LOVABLE LEGIONS LEHMANN LEISURE

Harvey, Michael. *White Papers.* **New York, 1971. Seventy-one 5″ × 8″ index cards. The following cards are random selections:**

GRANICUS, strategy—Alexander
                       all the fighting Persians form a line.
                       the strength of a line is its continuity.
                       therefore the Persians are weak when
                       the line is broken.

---

ekgreteffectmenwriteinplacelite;th'ententeisal,andnatthelettresspace

---

the practice comma art comma method comma or system
of inserting points or open single quote periods closed
single quote to aid the sense comma in writing or
printing semicolon division into sentences comma
clauses comma etc period by means of points or periods
period other punctuation marks comma e period g period
exclamation marks comma question marks comma refer
to the tone or structure of what precedes them period
a sentence can contain any of these symbols comma
its termination marked by a period period

you can lead a horse
a horse you can lead
can you lead a horse
lead a horse can you
a horse can lead you
can a horse lead you

this zeugma is written in black and white

still life; relative proximity

book eraser ruler pen pencil
eraser book pen ruler pencil
pen eraser pencil ruler book
pencil ruler pen book eraser
ruler pencil book eraser pen

Jan Dibbets. *White Wall.* 12 numbered photographs taken at different shutter speeds.
1971. Courtesy Art & Project, Amsterdam.

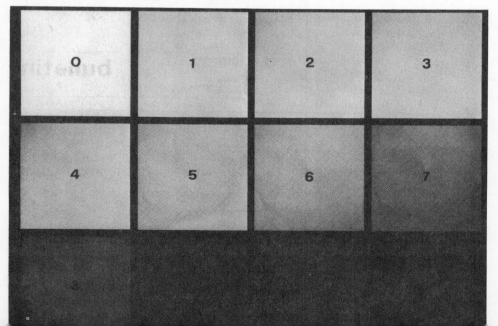

Jacks, Robert. *An Unfinished Work 1966–1971.* New York, 1971. Related work shown at the New York Cultural Center, winter, 1970–71.

Katz, Leandro. *Ñ (a'nyay).* New York, 1971.

Kawara, On. *One Million Years.* Konrad Fischer, Düsseldorf, 1971.

Kennedy, G. N. *Dedications.* Nova Scotia College of Art and Design, Halifax, 1971. "This collection of 100 dedication pages was chosen at random from the holdings of the library" at the NSCAD. Examples:
   To my husband whose many breakfasts included a look at the glass that had cooled in the night.
   For SMUDGE, my silent one-eyed critic, who helped more than he can say.
   To all those Artists and Laymen of the past and the present who have done their best to hold high the creative ideal of the true, the good, and the beautiful, This Volume is Dedicated.

La Rocca, Ketty. *In Principio Erat.* Centro di, Florence, 1971. "This volume was published for the exhibitions of Ketty La Rocca during 1971"; preface by Gillo Dorfles; brief texts and photographs of hands.

LeWitt, Sol. *Four Basic Colours and Their Combinations, 1971.* London, Lisson Publications, 1971.

———. *Art and Project Bulletin* 32, 1971. *Sol LeWitt/Ten Thousand Lines/Six Thousand Two Hundred and Fifty-Five Lines.*

Lippard, Lucy R. *Changing: Essays in Art Criticism.* New York, E. P. Dutton, 1971. Includes "The Dematerialization of Art," "Art in the Arctic Circle," "Absentee Information."

Richard Long. Art and Project Bulletin 35. "Reflections in the Little Pigeon River, Great Smoky Mountains, Tennessee (1970)."

Paul Maenz Köln Jahresbericht, 1971. Documents shows by Barry, Boyle, Burgin, Haacke, Knoebel, Kosuth, Louw, Maloney, Paolini, Roehr, Rückriem, Salvo, Visser.

Maloney, Martin. *Reject objects.* Paul Maenz, Cologne, 1971.

Murray, Ian. *Twenty Waves in a Row.* Strawbooks, "Canada," 1971.

Metz, Michael. *Blueprints for Performance.* Two booklets, Providence, R. I., 1971, and untitled book, 1971, containing "Notes" and sections from several earlier booklets.

Parr, Mike. *One Hundred Page Book,* Sydney, Australia, 1971; *Self-Circles,* Sydney, 1971, 17 pages:
   In an area of bush . . . sit on the ground among bushes. Draw a "self-circle" about yourself on the ground. Stay sitting in the circle (quietly) until the birds are back busy in the bushes about you.
   Above a pool . . . allow your body to fall feet first into the pool so that a ripple moves out in circles from the point where your body enters the water.
   A dream seems to be a result of one "imagining" without inhibition . . . without control. Before going to sleep . . . daydream and think consciously about your ambi-

tions. Do this every night . . . for a number of nights . . . before going to sleep . . . with the intention and the hope that these thoughts just prior to sleep will recur in your dreams.

Pazos, Luis; Puppo, Hector; and Gutierrez, Jorge de Lujan. *Experiencias.* CAYC, Buenos Aires, 1971 (in conjunction with the VII Biennale de Paris, September–November, 1971).

Ruppersberg, Allan. *25 Pieces.* 1971, unpublished. (Rep.)

Ruscha, Edward. *A Few Palm Trees.* Los Angeles, 1971.

———. *Records.* Heavy Industry Publications, Hollywood, 1971.

Salcedo, Bernardo. *What Is It?/Que Es?* CAYC, Buenos Aires, 1971. "Manual for the new avant-garde October 1971."

Vazan, William. *Worldline 1969–71.* Montreal, 1971. Documentation of a work consisting of taped lines on the floors of locations around the world. The tapes are envisaged as visible markers of an invisible line determined by time and calculated angled space. Executed simultaneously March 5, 1971. In January, 1970, Vazan had made a similar piece that "crossed Canada."

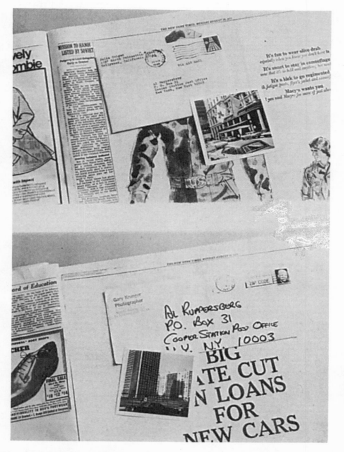

Allen Ruppersberg. 2 pages from *25 Pieces.* 1971.

Wall, Jeff. *Cine Text (Excerpt) 1971.* Vancouver, London, 1971; accompanied by Ian Wallace's photographs. Excerpt:

The building was constructed as follows: In a large high factory lit with streams of flourescent lighting, fibreglas sections covered in heavy corrugated cardboard wrapping are stacked in supply bays. There are separate supply bays for wall sections with window and door openings, floor and ceiling sections, and for window and door units and for electrical components. The factory floor is divided into five assembly lines of flatbed frames, large steel rectangles on wheels. Each frame is attached to small electric service cars which pull them from bay to bay along the line. The assembly bays connect to the supply bays via overhead conveyor delivery systems. Foremen with walkie-talkies relay orders between assembly and supply. The conveyor system is operated by a man at each terminal: one manipulates the units from the racks, raises them aloft, and directs them along the gleaming tracks 45 feet above the floor. At a point midway along the conveyor a switch transfers control to a man in a yellow booth above the assembly bay. He brings the unit, swaying slightly, and speckled with small glittering strokes from tubes on the ceiling, into position over the base frame standing in the bay and the assembly crew waiting below. 1 Bay: four men jockey floor sections into place as they are lowered by the crane. They lock them together and affix aluminium brackets securing the whole floor to the foundation frame.

The crew men wear heavy rubber-soled shoes, bright blue overalls and white caps with numbers stenciled on them. Their faces and hands, multiplying in gestures, are released into prominence, as in sudden close-up, by the clarity and evenness of the lighting. There is no glare and almost no shadow in the factory; the light is not hard and does not cut off sharply. It permeates hollows under

Move, see, touch, hear—lift, hoist, twist, pour, stack, lean, cut, balance—clip, nail, bolt, glue, rivet, mold, saw, melt, measure—build. (In the hot sunlight a trailer stands in front of the Safeway. The bright light slickers over its surfaces, the aluminium and plastic, rubber, glass and steel; across the vacu-formed S of Safeway in complex oily arcs, penetrates throughout the rancho grande rockwork, flows onto the sizzling asphalt flesh and glare off heavy latex painted lines on the parking lot. Nearby a radio station is having a booth built beside another long silver and glass trailer.) Allan Kaprow did a happening called "Work" in which some workmen painted a plywood room several times a week—as an Event. El Lissitzky mentioned that the 1917 revolution in USSR introduced the concept of art as a form of cultural labour (Russia: An Architecture for World Revolution, 1930). Labour incorporates in a determinate complex elemental, invisible acts. Cultural labour has as one of its critical factors its mode of relation with such acts. By its own logic, the process may become relatively dematerialized, aspects of information, etc. What is significant is not the engagement of macrophysical material at a low-density level, but the necessary congruence of limitations of material and of bodiless information (physical velocity limit of universe-nonphysical limit of immediacy of information, time function etc.). Dematerialization is the truth of materialism, whether naive ("doing more with less") or philosophical. Furthermore, mass production of physical results is the necessary and minimum condition for the dematerialization of effect; dissolution of physical uniqueness through technique.

* * *

In the largeness of the terms used in its description and analysis, the landscape machinery, the moving frames, scaffolding, between the components stacked together in the racks. Inside the building it is always a lovely morning. The sun can is the portrait of a critical terrain, it is its physical reality and its metaphor. At sites in this landscape are constructed events which are vast and pure as senseless

Weiner, Lawrence. *10 Works.* Yvon Lambert, Paris. English and French; also in Spanish and English. CAYC, Buenos Aires, July, 1971.

————. *Broken Off.* A public freehold piece shown in Los Angeles, East Berlin, Frankfurt, during 1971 (not a book).

————. *Causality: Affected and/or Effected.* Leo Castelli, New York, 1971. Excerpt:

AFFECTED AS TO PRESSURE AND/OR PULL
EFFECTED AS TO PRESSURE AND/OR PULL

AFFECTED AS TO HEAT AND/OR COLD
EFFECTED AS TO HEAT AND/OR COLD

AFFECTED AS TO EXPLOSION AND/OR IMPLOSION
EFFECTED AS TO EXPLOSION AND/OR IMPLOSION

AFFECTED AS TO CORROSION AND/OR VACUUM
EFFECTED AS TO CORROSION AND/OR VACUUM

AFFECTED AS TO NOISE AND/OR SILENCE
EFFECTED AS TO NOISE AND/OR SILENCE

Avalanche, no. 2, January, 1971. Interviews with Saret and Lew, Nauman, Fox, Acconci, and Oppenheim. Photo essays on or works by Acconi, Wegman, Rinke, McLean, Klein, Nauman, Serra, Oppenheim, van Saun, 112 Greene Street group. Excerpts from Fox follow ("Avalanche" is Liza Béar and Willoughby Sharp):

AV: What do you see as your earliest body work?

TF: The *Push Wall* piece. It was like having a dialogue with the wall, exchanging energy with it. I pushed as hard as I could for about eight or nine minutes, until I was too tired to push any more. I used to park my car every day in that alley and I always looked at those walls but never touched them. Then one day I touched one of the walls, felt its solidity, its belly. I realized we were both the same but we had had no dialogue, in a sense. We normally just walk by these things, not feeling connected to them.

AV: You could say that a lot of the new art is about looking at aspects of reality and realizing the unexpected energy they possess.

TF: Oh, sure. For me, in a performance, all the elements have exactly the same weight, including myself. Exactly. And dialogues can take place between them, psychically and physically. When I was pushing the wall, I felt it was somehow alive like a person.

AV: What other work came out of that realization?

TF: Pushing myself into a corner at Reese Palley in San Francisco. That was the negative of the *Push Wall* piece. A corner is the opposite of a wall. That was a short piece, it was hard to do. I was trying to push as much of my body as I could into the corner. My feet got in the way, I tried to stand on my toes, but it didn't work. You lose your balance.

AV: How do you see your works relating to body works by other artists?

TF: You know, I'm not sure what body works are, exactly. Everyone is doing them in a different way. . . . For me the most important aspect of it is treating the body as an element in its own right rather than as an initiator of some act. Instead of disregarding it in the making of sculpture, using it directly as a tool. The body is an element like any other, only a lot more flexible.

AV: You mentioned before that you saw Nauman's Palley show in 1969. What was it like?

TF: He had a half-hour film loop of himself painting his body all over in four different colors, one color at a time. It was really beautiful. Then at the back of the gallery there were two television monitors and a detective video camera. When you entered the space you could see yourself on the monitor, upside down and from the back. The first time I saw it I was put off. It seemed too simple and obvious. But then I realized that was the beauty of it in that space. There was nothing else. . . . What the Nauman show confirmed for me was the realization that I was an element equivalent to the others, that I could work with them without fear of interfering with their processes.

Lisson Wall Show. Lisson Gallery, London, January, 1971. Arnatt, Arrowsmith, Edmonds, Flanagan, Ginsborg, Hemsworth, Hilliard, Latham, Lew, LeWitt, Louw, Munro, Newman, Palermo, Rinke, Sirrs, Stezaker, Tremlett, Weiner, Wentworth; catalogue of projects. Included:

Sue Arrowsmith:

> a white frame
>
> a white frame being painted black
>
> a white frame being painted black
> a black frame being painted white
>
> a black frame being painted white .
>
> a black frame.

Formulations. Addison Gallery of American Art, Andover, Mass., January 8–February 14, 1971. Exhibition organized, or "suggested by," Konrad Fischer and Gianenzo Sperone. Atkinson, Boetti, Brouwn, Buren, Darboven, Dibbets, Fulton, Paolini, Penone, Salvo.

The Nature of Things. Harkus-Krakow Gallery, Boston. One-man shows by Sonfist, Hutchinson, and Oppenheim; January, February, March.

January, Toronto: Founding of A Space, "a non-profit corporation concerned with the flow of people and information relevant to visual art." Beginning May, 1971, an "information package" or newsletter is published approximately monthly, open to contributions from anyone. The focus so far is on video and performance pieces (Acconci, Oppenheim, NSCAD group, etc.). Co-directors: Stephen Cruise, Robert Bowers, John McEwen.

Opus International, no. 22, January 1971. Includes articles on LeWitt, Byars, Kirili, Ben.

January 26, New York: Public exhibition of the walls of BMT Subway Station at Times Square; photos of the walls had been unofficially hung in the MOMA *Information* show on August 25 (Lowell Zack).

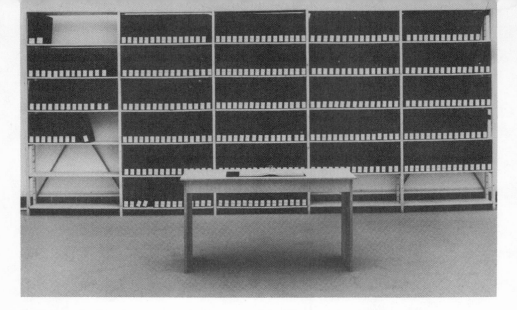

Hanne Darboven. *One Century in one Year.* 365 volumes of 100 pages each. Installation: Konrad Fischer Gallery, Düsseldorf. 1971.

Joseph Beuys. Aktioner Aktionen. Moderna Museet, Stockholm, January 16–February 28, 1971. Biography, Bibliography, interview with the artist.

Daniel Buren. Städtisches Museum, Mönchengladbach, January 28–March 7, 1971. "Vertical Colored and White Stripes Seen at the Same Time at . . .:" Locations in Aachen, Dortmund, Essen, Hamburg, Hannover, Cologne, Krefeld, Leverkusen, Mönchengladbach, Münster, Saarbrucken, Stuttgart. Text in catalogue by Buren, "Positions/Proposals," published as "Repères" in *VH-101,* no. 5, Spring, 1971, and as "Standpoints" in *Studio International,* April, 1971.

Hanne Darboven: One Century in One Year. January 1–December 31, 1971. Exhibition changing daily. Konrad Fischer, Düsseldorf. (Rep.)

Darboven says she hates to read and loves to write. Despite the apparently impersonal "conceptualism" of her drawings, they are in fact the intentionally visual results of a process, not accidental traces of mental procedures. She prefers to show them on film, or framed and hung, than in notebooks. Permutation—the basis of Darboven's work since 1966—provides the armature for her obsession much as the grid does for other artists. That obsession is not so much numbers as the physically (visually) experienced time span. As she fills page after page, book after book with her distinctive handwriting, with precisely rhythmic "waves," or with typed words and numbers, her personal calendar is synchronized with that of her work, as well as with that of the real world. For all the detachment implied by the use of systems, Darboven is closer to her art than almost any artist I can think of. The work comes from inside, from the artist's own needs and compulsions, which explains its mesmeric sincerity and vigor.

Lee Lozano: Infofiction, Nova Scotia College of Art and Design, Halifax, January 27–February 13, 1971. (For works included, see pp. 96–97, 98, 101–2)

Lee Lozano: Form and Content," July 19, 1971:

content   form
What happens   If . . .

I can't be interested in form for form's sake. Form is like mathematics: a model which might be applied to various sets of data.

Form is seductive; form can be perfect.

But there's no justification for form (in the Experiments & Investigations) unless it's used to expose content which has meaning. The result of an experiment is the meaningful content.

Information is content. Content is fiction.

Content is messy. Like the universe it's unfinished and, furthermore, it becomes obsolete so quickly when multiplied by time. Form is reduplicable, content is not reduplicable. Fiction has meaning, but only in a given instant of time.

Morris, Robert. "The Art of Existence. 3 Extra-Visual Artists: Work in Process." *Artforum,* **January, 1971. "Marvin Blaine," "Jason Taub," and "Robert Dayton."**

N. E. Thing Co., Ltd. **University of Alberta Art Gallery, Edmonton, January 15–February 10, 1971. Recent projects for radio and television; interview.**

Sondheim, Alan. *Resonances,* **Providence, R. I. (public domain), January–March, 1971.**

Ger van Elk, "Paul Klee-um den Fisch, 1926." *Art and Project Bulletin* **33, January 9–23, 1971.**

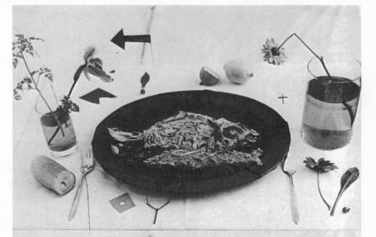

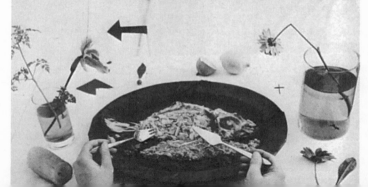

Ger van Elk. *Paul Klee—um den fisch, 1926.* 1970. Courtesy Art & Project, Amsterdam.

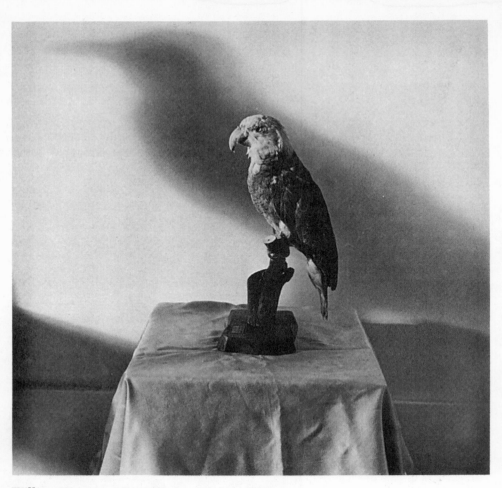

William Wegman. *Crow/Parrot.* October, 1970.

William Wegman: Videotapes, Photographic Works, Arrangements. Pomona College Art
Gallery, January 7–31, 1971. Biography, introduction by Helene Winer:

    The photographic works are either single or in series of two or more, and fall into
several categories. In the works that explore sameness vs. difference, Wegman
compares superficially identical items, or twins to emphasize the enormous subtle
differences that are naturally present. His works that deal with sameness vs. change
concentrate on manipulated differences. The changes are such that the composition
as a whole appears the same in all the photographs of a series. This is most surprising
in one set of photographs, using objects in the artist's studio, where the altered
details are extensive. Almost every item in the scene is in duplicate in one of the two
photographs. The comparison of "big and little" in Wegman's terms, involves the use
of objects whose only essential difference is size. One such work is a photograph of
the artist, posed with various tools. He is standing next to a larger man of some
resemblance who is holding the same but larger tools in a similar arrangement. The
shadow of a duck that appears to be cast on the wall by a crow, in another work,

represents the incongruities present in many of Wegman's single photographic pieces. (Rep.)

Lawrence Weiner. "Untitled." Art and Project Bulletin, **January, 1971. 20 works; also published in Spanish and English by CAYC, Buenos Aires, 1971:**

perhaps when removed
perhaps when replaced
perhaps when recharged
perhaps when rebounded
perhaps when reproduced
perhaps when reimposed
perhaps when reinserted
perhaps when redone
perhaps when readjusted
perhaps when refloated
perhaps when received
perhaps when repainted
perhaps when retranslated
perhaps when returned
perhaps when rebutted
perhaps when related
perhaps when reshaped
perhaps when rehung
perhaps when retransferred
perhaps when recanted

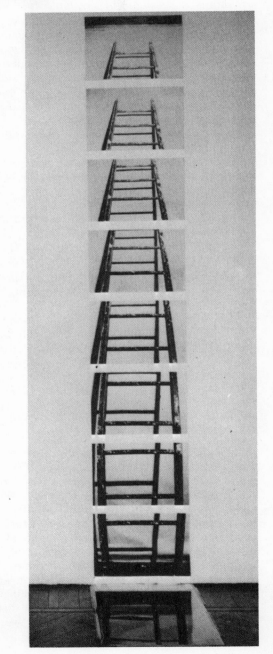

Michael Snow. *Of a Ladder.* **11″ x 14″ black-and-white photographs. 1971. Courtesy Bykert Gallery, New York.**

Excerpts from Mierle Laderman Ukeles's *Maintenance Art . . .* **proposal for an Exhibition "Care,"** © **1969, as cited in Jack Burnham, "Problems of Criticism, IX,"** *Artforum,* **January, 1971:**

In a prospectus for an exhibition of "Maintenance Art"—a most elegant and philosophically timely proposal—Mierle Laderman Ukeles explains art in a super patriarchal society. It begins with the heading "Ideas" and is worth quoting at length.

A. *The Death Instinct* and *The Life Instinct.*

The Death Instinct: separation, individuality, Avant-Garde par excellence; to follow one's own part to death—do your own thing, dynamic change.

The Life Instinct: unification, the eternal return, the perpetuation and maintenance of the species, survival systems and operation, equilibrium.

B. Two basic systems: *Development* and *Maintenance.*

The sourball of every revolution: after the revolution who's going to pick up the garbage on Monday morning?

Development: pure individual creation; the new; change; progress; advance; excitement; flight or fleeing.

Maintenance: Keep the dust off the pure individual creation; preserve the new; sustain the change; protect progress; defend and prolong the advance; renew the excitement; repeat the flight.

Show your work—show it again

Keep the contemporary art museum groovy

Keep the home fires burning

Development systems are partial feedback systems with major room for change.

Maintenance systems are direct feedback systems with little room for alteration.

C. *Maintenance is a drag;* it takes all the fucking time, literally; the mind boggles and chafes at the boredom; the culture confers lousy status and minimum wages on maintenance jobs; housewives = no pay.

Clean your desk, wash the dishes, clean the floor, wash your clothes, wash your toes, change the baby's diaper, finish the report, correct the typos, mend the fence, keep the customer happy, throw out the stinking garbage, watch out—don't put things in your nose, what shall I wear, I have no sox, pay your bills, don't litter, save string, wash your hair, change the sheets, go to the store. I'm out of perfume, say it again—he doesn't understand, seal it again—it leaks, go to work, this art is dusty, clear the table, call him again, flush the toilet, stay young.

D. *Art:*

Everything I say is Art is Art. Everything I do is Art is Art. "We have no Art, we try to do everything well." (Balinese saying à la McLuhan and Fuller.)

Avant-garde art, which claims utter development, is infected by strains of maintenance ideas, maintenance activities, and maintenance materials.

Conceptual and Process Art especially claim pure development and change, yet employ almost purely maintenance processes.

E. The exhibition of Maintenance Art, "CARE," would zero in on maintenance, exhibit it, and yield, by utter opposition, a clarity of issues.

Mierle Ukeles then proceeds to explain her three-part exhibition. "I am an artist . . . woman . . . wife . . . mother (random order). I do a hell of a lot of washing, cleaning, cooking, renewing, supporting, preserving, etc." Up to now she's also "done" art, but now Mierle Ukeles is willing to do all that drudgery in a museum on an exhibition basis. "I will sweep and wax the floors, dust everything, wash the walls (i.e., floor paintings, dust works, soap sculpture, wall paintings, etc.), cook, invite people to eat, clean up, put away, change light bulbs. . . . My working will be the work." Second, typed interviews with various people from maintenance professions and museum-goers concerning their views on the piddling but essential tasks of life would be presented. Finally, "Earth Maintenance," the last part, involves delivering refuse to the museum where it is "purified, depolluted, rehabilitated, recycled," and conserved by various technical (and/or pseudo-technical) procedures. . . . " Incidentally, this is an offer which Mierle Ukeles hopes some enterprising museum curator will consider; the offer *is* real.

Mrs. Ukeles is implying that avant-gardism amounts to running around in tighter and tighter circles, doing the same thing over and over again but trying to make it look and sound different; it seems that the mythic drive behind high art has run its course. The sudden transference of some avant-garde artists to politics stems from a desire to find a viable revolution, one providing the needed psychological surrogate. Presently avant-gardism can only mean revival, unacceptable iconoclasm, or the deliberate presentation of nonart.

Forge, Andrew. "Forces Against Object-Based Art;" Harrison, Charles, "Art on TV" (re: Gerry Schum Gallery). *Studio International,* January, 1971.

Thwaites, John Anthony. "Street Art: One-Hanover; Two-Minnesota; Three-Holland." *Art and Artists,* January, 1971.

Earth, Air, Fire, Water: Elements of Art. Museum of Fine Arts, Boston, February 4–April 4, 1971. Organized by Virginia Gunter. Two-vol. catalogue: (1) introduction by Gunter, text by David Antin, selected bibliography; (2) errata, addenda, photographs (published later). Bas-Cohain, Bollinger, Brain, Budelis, Burgess, Burgy, Christo, Dallegret, Dignac, Franklin, Goodyear, Graham, Grisi, Haacke, Harrison, Hayes, Heizer, Huebler, Hutchinson, Jenney, Kaprow, Kosice, Neustein and Batlle and Marx, Oppenheim, Piene, Puusemp, Rieveschl, Ross, Serra, Simons, Smithson, Sonfist, Sproat and Clark, Torffield, Uriburu, van Saun, Warhol, Wegman, Wixon. Reviewed by Kenneth Baker, *Artforum,* March, 1971.

Situation Concepts. Galerie im Taxispalais, Innsbruck, February 9–March 4. Organized by Peter Weiermair. Texts by Bochner, Kosuth, LeWitt, Weiermair, and Ricky Comi. Arakawa, Arts Agency, Baldessari, Bochner, Buren, de Dominici, Ernst, Fabro, Fazion, Gilbert & George, Germana, Gerz, Haacke, Heizer, Hollein, Hoeikawa, Huebler, Kawagachi, Kosuth, Kriesche, Jasci, LeWitt, Lindow, Matsuzawa, Nicolaides, Oberhuber, Ohmyia, Oppenheim, Paolini, Pisani, Raetz, Schult, Serra, Smithson, Tanaka, Ulrichs, Weiner.

Sixth Guggenheim International. Solomon R. Guggenheim Museum, New York, February 12–April 11, 1971. Organized by Diane Waldman and Edward Fry. Boxed catalogue with individual booklets, bibliography, texts by Messer, Fry, and Waldman. Andre, Burgin, de Maria, Buren, Darboven, Dias, Dibbets, Flavin, Heizer, LeWitt, Long, Judd, Kawara, Kosuth, Merz, Morris, Nauman, Ryman, Serra, Takamatsu, Weiner. Reviewed by Barbara Rose, *New York,* March 8, 1971; James Monte, *Artforum,* March, 1971. Buren's work was withdrawn from the show, following protests by other artists; see below, pp. 245.

45°30'N–73°36'W + Inventory. Organized by Arthur Bardo and Zoe Notkin at the Saidye Bronfman Center and by Gary Coward and Bill Vazan at the Sir George Williams University, Montreal, spring, 1971. Catalogue consists of c. 175 slips of paper with works, quotations, and miscellany. Reviewed by Normand Thériault, "de Chicago à Montreal," *La Presse,* Montreal, February 6, 1971.

Kaprow, Allan. "The Education of the Un-Artist, Part I." *Art News,* February, 1971: "To escape from the traps of art, it is not enough to be against museums or to stop producing marketable objects; the artist of the future must learn how to evade his profession."

Japp, Georg. "Interview with Konrad Fischer." *Studio International,* February, 1971.

Fish, Fox, Kos. De Saisset Museum of Art, University of Santa Clara, Calif., February 2–28, 1971. Catalogue includes visual, verbal, and recorded material.

February 19, New York: Video works from NSCAD by Askevold, Jarden, Robertson, Waterman, Zuck. Shown by W. Sharp at 93 Grand Street.

February, 1971, postcard from Protetch-Rivkin, Washington, D.C.: "Irby Benjamin Roy, formerly Lawrence Stephen Orlean, formerly Alva Isaiah Fost, formerly Ed McGowin."

Pier 18. New York, February–March, 1971. Organized by Willoughby Sharp and photographed by Shunk-Kender. Photos exhibited at the MOMA, June–August, 1971. Works were executed at an abandoned pier on the Hudson River, New York, by Acconci, Askevold, Baldessari, Barry, Beckley, Bochner, Buren, Dibbets, Fox, Graham, Huebler, Jaffe, Jarden, Matta, Merz, Morris, Oppenheim, Ruppersberg, Scanga, Serra, Snow, Sonnier, Stoerchle, Trakas, van Saun, Wegman, Weiner, and documented by photographs. Reviewed by Robert Pincus-Witten, "Anglo-American Standard Reference Works: Acute Conceptualism," *Artforum,* October, 1971.

> *Vito Acconci, Untitled (project for Pier 18),*
> 1971. Activity: deserted area, night, meet-
> ings, secrets. Pier 18, an abandoned pier at
> West Street and Park Place, New York.
> Twenty-nine nights; one hour each night:

—From March 27 to April 24, 1971, I will be at Pier 18 at 1 a.m. each night; I will be alone, and will wait at the far end of the pier for one hour.
—To anyone coming to meet me, I will attempt to reveal something I would normally keep concealed: censurable occurences and habits, fears, jealousies—something that has not been exposed before and that would be disturbing for me to make public.
—My intention is to meet each person individually, so that he alone will have possession of the information given.
—I will document none of the meetings. Each visitor, then, can make any documenta-tion he wishes, for any purpose; the result should be that he bring home material whose revelation could work to my disadvantage—material for blackmail.

February 9, San Diego: Eleanor Antin sends out the first postcard of a photographic mailing piece, *100 Boots Facing the Sea;* the continuing "100 Boots" series to be published in *Art in America,* accompanied by an interview with the artist by "Anna English." (Rep.)

Rubens Gerchman. Jack Misrachi Gallery, New York, February 9–March 6, 1971. Catalogue includes statement by the artist, biography.

Entwürfe, Partituren, Projekte: Zeichnungen. Galerie René Block, Berlin, March 5–31, 1971. Among others: Beuys, Darboven, Dibbets, Graham, LeWitt, Vostell.

At the Moment. March–April, 1971. Poster-catalogue for "conceptual art show" at "Doorway-

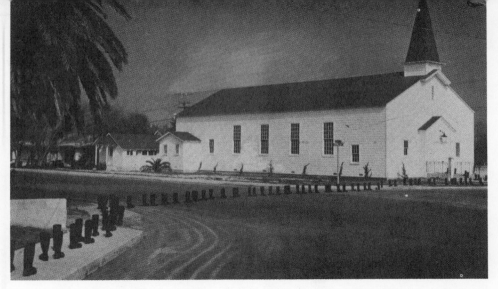

Eleanor Antin. *100 Boots on the Way to Church, Solana Beach, California, February 9, 1971, 11:30 a.m.* Mailing date, April 5, 1971.

Hall," Zagreb, Yugoslavia. Anselmo, Barry, Brouwn, Buren, Burgin, Dibbets, Dimitrijević, Flanagan, Eventstructure, Huebler, Kirili, Kounellis, Latham, LeWitt, Matanovic, Nez, Pognačnik, Šalamun (Oho group), Trbuljak, Weiner, Wilson.

For the People in Pasadena Exhibition, opened March 7, 1971, "never officially closed." Organized by "Whoever" (Frank Brown). Extensive catalogue recording all work and documents received in reply to posters sent out nationwide to artists, colleges, radio stations, etc., and posted, for this open and free exhibition.

Opus International, no. 23, March 11, 1971. Includes articles on Arte Povera and Land Art.

Baker, Elizabeth. "Critic's Choice: Daniel Buren." *Art News,* March, 1971

Fugate-Wilcox, Terry. "Force Art: A New Direction." *Arts,* March, 1971: Press release from the "Jean Freeman Gallery" via Terry Fugate-Wilcox: "26 West 57th St. does not exist." Nor did the gallery, which was Fugate-Wilcox's own work.

Beginning March 11, 1971, eight signed booklets mailed out by Gilbert & George (Art for All, London); each one consists of a scratchy pen and ink drawing on the cover (after photographs) and a brief text in couplets; each ends with "Goodbye for Now":

Lost Day 11 March 1971. [G & G leaning against the wall along the Thames, a lamppost to the right.] There were two young men who were tired/ They were tired and a little bit lost. They thought they were kings of their best/ and found out they were just like the rest. One day they went out for a day/ Though they risked falling down a drain. They smiled like two babies without fear/ As you will all be happy to hear.

Shyness 29 March 1971. [G & G sitting and learning against a large log in a quite densely drawn woodland setting.] There were two young men who were crooked/ They were crooked in the way you feel best. They gave them the answers to live/ And left them with heads full of fizz. But their friends they all left behind/ They became lonely, artistic and shy. Be aware of these silly old heads/Or you'll always look over the hedge.

Experience 2nd April 1971. [G & G facing each other, leaning against a railing overlooking a river; George's foot is raised onto the stone base of the railing; Gilbert's arms are crossed; a castle of sorts in the background; paving stones in the foreground] There were two young men who did laugh/They laughed at the people's unrest. They stuck their sticks in the air/ And turned them around with the best. Then with time they began to feel strange/For no longer it swung in their way. So to capture again that old thrill/They started to take the life-pill.

Worldliness 13th April 1971. [George standing just behind Gilbert; they both look to the left from under a tree in a sylvan setting over a small pond.] There were two young men from afar/Who travelled and met with no bar. They went up and down in their way/And attempted to make the world pay. There was no one at all they could blame/Because it just goes this way. They've had a few pokes in the eye/But like everyone else they're not blind.

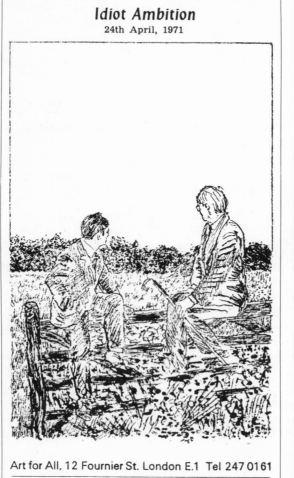

Idiot Ambition
24th April, 1971

There were two young men so polite
Polite in the way that they moved

Their mothers had told them to wait
But their chances, the boys felt, were great

Good-morning dear dad it is now time to rise
The two sweeties await your surprise

Whilst the birds whistle tunefully outside on the fence
The young men sleep on without sense.

Art for All, 12 Fournier St. London E.1 Tel 247 0161

Normal Boredom 1st May 1971. [G & G sitting under a stone archway on the ground; Gilbert leans over to look at a plant; rocks in the foreground; an unidentifiable band of water (?) at the top.] There were two young men with no heart and no peace/They thought to be free lying under a tree. And so they lay there from the dawn till dusk/Enjoying the air and the chickens and ducks. They thought to be nice and wave with their hands/ And so day after day they are under that tree. Counting the leaves and waiting for tea/They are as happy as can be.

Manliness 15th May 1971. [G & G seen as tiny figures in the distance on a country road with stippled foreground; house at the right, trees in the side-backgrounds.] There were two young men who were covered with blood/They are wounded and slashed and smeared with mud. They battle along singing a song/straining to be jolly though the journey's long. They think nothing of health or worry or care/Because their job is to do their share. So left leg out and away it goes/And where they go to nobody knows.

Artist's Culture 19th May 1971. [G & G sitting in close foreground on a tiled roof(?), they are smiling; George wears a striped tie.] There were two young men who were charming as sweets/They turned the heads of all in the streets. They looked at their ties and laughed and were pleased/Looking down to their socks they began to sneeze. The boys didn't mind as much as they might/For they were artists and that was their plight. The funny thing is they're really quite normal/ It's just that they seem of another order.

Proposition for New York, Beograd and Amsterdam. (Anonymous), three cards asking recipients in New York "to think of Amsterdam 12–2 p.m. March 3"; in Beograd "to think of New York 18–20 hrs. March 3"; in Amsterdam "to think of Beograd 6–8 p.m. March 3." Executed for an exhibition at the Museum of Modern Art, Belgrade.

Keith Arnatt, "Art as an Act of Omission." Postcard received March, 1971:
> A person is said to have omitted X if, and only if, (1) he did not do X, and (2) X was in some way expected of him.*
> . . . although it is the note of "being expected" which seems to mark off omissions from other not-doings, some not-doing statements refer to actions so completely unexpected that they would not count as not-doings in any but the most artificial sense.*
> *Eric D'Arcy, "Human Acts—An Essay in their Moral Evaluation."

> If art is what we do and culture is what is done to us [Andre]—what could culture do to us if art is what we didn't do?

Collins, James. *Contexts,* Postal 7, New York, March 1971:

AN ARTIST WILL INTRODUCE TWO STRANGERS AS AN ART WORK
It is a *relational* statement, and it could be said the relationship could be represented by R, and three people by *a, b,* and *c.* This gives R *abc,* and it doesn't essentially matter *what* replaces *a, b,* and *c* or who *a, b,* and *c* are replaced by.

AN ARTIST WILL INTRODUCE TWO STRANGERS AS AN ART WORK
. . . the elements of the sentence are brought together as a result of the *rules of language,* and not because they are in any way connected themselves.

AN ARTIST WILL INTRODUCE TWO STRANGERS AS AN ART WORK
Variations in the *order* and *context* of these signals correspond to a change of meaning in the behavior.

AN ARTIST WILL INTRODUCE TWO STRANGERS AS AN ART WORK
The progressive information context, acts as a *cultural re-locating device,* the information is increased, and the message *shifts* its context.

AN ARTIST WILL INTRODUCE TWO STRANGERS AS AN ART WORK
Questions of *intent,* and these notes, themselves a "metalanguage," change the *status* of semiotics, as an *unstated* and implicit support language in previous works, from that of predicate, to that of subject.

AN ARTIST WILL INTRODUCE TWO STRANGERS AS AN ART WORK
That the message functioned *disjunctively* culturally was employed as a device to re-align the recipients' relationship to the message, as a *theoretical construct* . . .

(All quotations are from *Semiotic Aspects* by the artist, Postal 6, February, 1971.)

Haber, Ira Joel. *Films No. 2,* New York, March, 1971. "The following is a random selection of films and the theatres and the locations I saw them at. The films are listed alphabetically and the dates denote the years the films were released and the years I saw them."

Jarden, Richards: "A 16mm continuous single surface 100p (möbius strip) made from a segment of film of the artist walking from the center of the room to the wall on the camera's left and back again. The ends of the film are joined with a half twist which cinematically allows the continuation of the activity of the opposite wall (November, 1970)," NSCAD, Halifax, March 1–8, 1971.

Johnson, Tim. *Installation as Conceptual Scheme.* 25-page text for exhibition, at Inhibodress, Sydney, Australia, March, 1971.

Peter Kennedy—Tape No. 1 (B): Piece of ten-minute duration also executed at Inhibodress: . . . Video and Audio Indefinition Transference:
    The video microphone is to be heavily bound with a number of pieces of transparent adhesive tape of varying lengths.
    The binding is to occur around the most sound-sensitive area of the microphone. A performer, in front of the camera, should commence to remove the pieces of adhesive tape one by one.
    Each piece, as it is removed, should be placed by the performer across the lens of the camera.
    It is intended that, as the work proceeds, the audio-definition should increase in direct proportion to the decreasing video definition.

Nemser, Cindy. "An Interview with Vito Acconci." *Arts,* March, 1971.

Bob Kinmont, Sculpture Photographs Films. Reese Palley, San Francisco, March 17–April 10, 1971 (booklet).

"Klaus Rinke: Between Spring and Ocean." *Studio International,* March, 1971.

Lovell, Anthony. "Lawrence Weiner." *Studio International,* March, 1971. Also a page of works by Weiner.

Martha Wilson. *Chauvinist Pieces;* Halifax, March, 1971:

Determined Piece: A woman determines her child on the basis of some arbitrary system (a row of sperm bottles marked with colors, the letters of the alphabet, numbers) according to what color, letter or number pleases her.

Astrological Piece: Couple with unexpected offspring are permitted to trade with couples whose children were born in a more sympathetic astrological sign to their own.

Color Piece: A dark-skinned couple (perhaps Negro), a medium-colored couple (perhaps Chinese) and a light-skinned couple (perhaps Anglo-Saxon) permutate sexually. The resultant nine children may be distributed in any emotionally comfortable manner.

Unknown Piece: A woman under ether has a child in a large hospital. When she comes to, she is permitted to select the child she thinks is hers from the babies in the nursery.

Chauvinist Piece: A man is injected with a hormone that produces the symptoms of motherhood.

Celant, Germano. "Information documentation archives, untitled." ***Domus,*** **March, 1971. Italian and English.**

Davis, Douglas. "Man of Parts" (Nauman). ***Newsweek,*** **March 1, 1971.**

April 1, New York: Thomas Messer, director of the Guggenheim Museum, cancels projected show by Hans Haacke (to have opened April 30) on the grounds that the documentary works included dealt with "specific social situations" not considered art.

Haacke's public statement follows; it was published, among other pieces, in the 9-page booklet of information handed out on the occasion of the Art Workers' Coalition's mass demonstration inside the museum on May 1, protesting art censorship:

Hans Haacke. *Business Office of Shapolsky, et al., Manhattan Real Estate Holdings—A Real Time Social System, as of Oct. 1, 1971.*

608 E 11 St Block 393 Lot 11

25' x 94' 1-story Store Building

Owned by 194 Ave. A Realty Corp., 608 E 11 St. N.Y.C.

Contracts signed by
  Sam Shapolsky, President ('58)
  Harry Shapolsky, President ('60)
  Alfred Fayer, Vice-President ('58)

Principal—Harry Shapolsky
Acquired 3/27/1963 from Surenko Realties, Inc., 608 E 11 St. N.Y.C.
Harry Shapolsky, President

No Mortgage (1971)
Assessed Land Value $8,500.
Total Value $24,000.

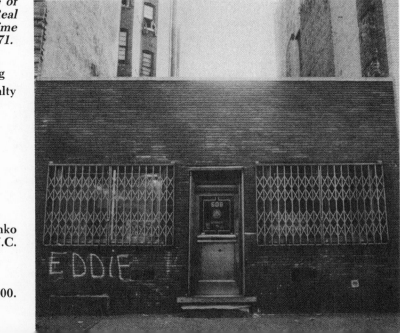

These questions and your answers are part of

Hans Haacke's VISITORS' PROFILE

a work in progress during "Directions 3: Eight Artists", Milwaukee Art Center,
June 19 through August 8, 1971.

Please fill out this questionnaire and drop it into the box by the door.
DO NOT SIGN.

1)   Do you have a professional interest in art,
     e.g. artist, student, critic, dealer, etc.?   yes   no
- -
2)   How old are you?   years
- -
3)   Should the use of marijuana be legalized,   legal   light   severe
     lightly or severely punished?   punishment
- -
4)   Do you think law enforcement agencies
     are generally biased against dissenters?   yes   no
- -
5)   What is your marital status?   married   single   div.   sep.   widowed
- -
6)   Do you sympathize with Women's Lib?   yes   no
- -
7)   Are you male, female?   male   female
- -
8)   Do you have children?   yes   no
- -
9)   Would you mind busing your child to integrate schools? yes   no
- -
10) What is your ethnic backround, e.g. Polish, German, etc.? _____
- -
11) Assuming you were Indochinese, would you
     sympathize with the Saigon regime?   yes   no
- -
12) Do you think the moral fabric of the US is strength-_____
     ened or weakened by its involvement in Indochina? strengthened weakened
- -
13) What is your religion?   _____
- -
14) In your opinion, are the interests of profit-oriented
     business usually compatible with the common good?   yes   no
- -
15) What is your annual income (before taxes)? $_____
- -
16) Do you think the Nixon Administration is mainly
     responsible for our economic difficulties?   yes   no
- -
17) Where do you live?   city/suburb   county   state
- -
18) Do you consider the defeat of the supersonic transport
     (SST) a step in the right direction?   yes   no
- -
19) Are you enrolled in or have graduated from college?   yes   no
- -
20) In your opinion, should the general orientation of the
     country be more conservative or less conservative?   more   less
- -

Your answers will be tabulated later today together with the answers of all
other visitors of the exhibition.   Thank you.

Hans Haacke. *Visitors' Profile.* **10 demographic, 10 opinion questions on current
socio-political issues posed to museum visitors. Answers tabulated, correlated,
and posted regularly throughout exhibition. Milwaukee Art Center version.
1969–70.**

Two of the three works are presentations of large Manhattan real estate holdings (photographs of the façades of the properties and documentary information collected from the public records of the County Clerk's office). The works contain no evaluative comment. One set of holdings are mainly slum-located properties owned by a group of people related by family and business ties. The other system is the extensive real estate interests, largely in commercial properties, held by two partners. The third work is a poll of the Guggenheim Museum's visitors, consisting of ten demographic questions (age, sex, education, etc.) and ten opinion questions on current socio-political issues ranging from "Do you sympathize with Women's Lib?" to "In your opinion, should the general orientation of the country be more or less conservative?" The answers are to be tabulated and posted daily as part of the piece. Following standard polling practices, I tried to frame the questions so that they do not assert a political stance, are not inflammatory, and do not prejudge the answers. . . . These pieces are examples of the "real time systems" which have constituted my work for many years. . . .

If I wanted to remain true to my philosophical premises, I could not comply with Mr. Messer's insistent demands to essentially modify or eliminate the three works. Verifiability is a major ingredient of the social, biological and physical systems which I consider as mutually complementary parts of an encompassing whole. . . . Mr. Messer is wrong on two counts: First in his confusion of the political stand which an artist's work may assert with a political stand taken by the museum that shows this work; secondly, in his assumption that my pieces advocate any political cause. They do not. Mr. Messer has taken a stand which puts him completely at variance with the professed attitudes of all the world's major museums, except for those located in countries under totalitarian domination, a stand which must put him in potential conflict with every artist who accepts an invitation to show his work at the Guggenheim Museum.

The affair received wide coverage by, among others, Jack Burnham, "Hans Haacke's Cancelled Show at the Guggenheim," *Artforum,* **June, 1971; Edward Fry (curator in charge of the Haacke show who was fired peremptorily for his actions in favor of the artist), "Hans Haacke, the Guggenheim: The Issues,"** *Arts,* **May, 1971:** *New York Times,* **April 17 and 27, May, July 4;** *New York Post,* **April 18, 24, 27;** *Newsday,* **April 19;** *Der Spiegel,* **April 26; Betsy Baker, "Artists vs. Museums,"** *Art News,* **May (plus letters, September); CBS radio and television interviews (April 25, May 2, April 27), etc.; Barbara Reise, "Which is in fact what happened: Thomas M. Messer in an interview," "A tale of two exhibitions: The aborted Haacke and Robert Morris shows," both** *Studio International,* **summer, 1971; "Gurgles Around the Guggenheim: Statements and Comments by Daniel Buren, Diane Waldman, Thomas Messer, Hans Haacke,"** *Studio International,* **June, 1971; Lawrence Alloway,** *The Nation,* **August 2.**

In Another Moment. **Studentski Kulturni Centar, Belgrade, 1971. Documentation of a three-hour exhibition held in the entry hall of an apartment building, April 23, 1971; organized by Braco and Nena Dimitrijević. Participants: Anselmo, Barry, Beuys, Brouwn, Buren, Burgin, Dibbets, Dimitrijević, Flanagan, Grupa/E KOD, Grupa OHO, Huebler, Kirili, Kounellis, Lamelas, Latham, LeWitt, Trbuljak, Weiner, Wilson.**

Summer, 1971. Agnes Denes, *Psychographic.* **From her continuing "Dialectic Triangulation" project:**

Psychograph is a truth approximation. It is a triangulation in search of truth. My initial probe [a questionnaire, which follows] prompting others to react plus their answers in various degrees of truth creates interactive triangulations such as in-

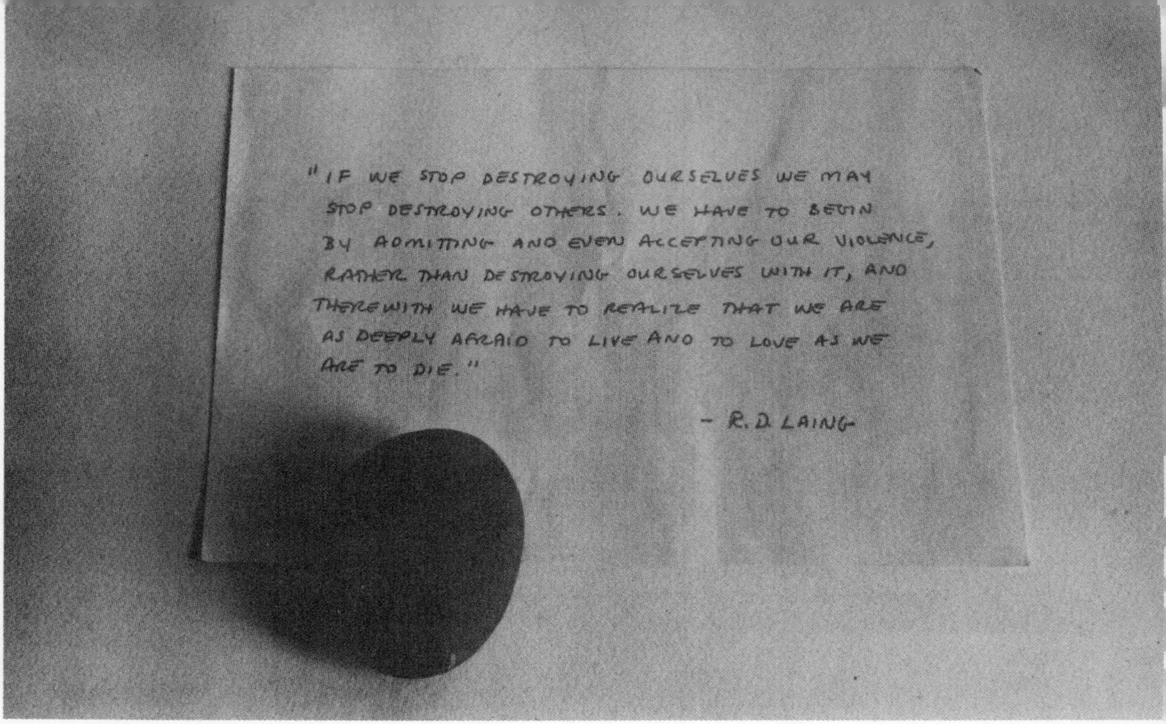

"IF WE STOP DESTROYING OURSELVES WE MAY STOP DESTROYING OTHERS. WE HAVE TO BEGIN BY ADMITTING AND EVEN ACCEPTING OUR VIOLENCE, RATHER THAN DESTROYING OURSELVES WITH IT, AND THEREWITH WE HAVE TO REALIZE THAT WE ARE AS DEEPLY AFRAID TO LIVE AND TO LOVE AS WE ARE TO DIE."

— R. D. LAING

LIGHTHOUSE TENDERS

VK   Roberts, Alyson
1012
R1

" One 'piece of information was a quotation
from R.D. Laing, 'who as everybndy knows
is a beacon of light to a whole generation
of young romantics. I categorized that one as
VK 1012, Lighthouse Tenders.'".

Eleanor Antin. "Lighthouse Tenders" from *Library Science,* one-woman exhibition at San Diego State Library. 1971.

terdependent or progressive ideas become effective through successive stages of advancement, threefold theories forming argumentative conclusions or pure idea groups activated by controversy. An ever deepening network of people and meanings is formed. [Results of the questionnaire are subjected to analyses on some twelve different levels and points of view to arrive at the final work.]:
DREAMS ARE . . . ; MY MIND . . . ; I ENJOY . . . ; I SUFFER . . . ; MY ART . . . ; I FAILED . . . ; I AM OBSESSED BY . . . ; I WANT TO KNOW . . . ; I MUST . . . ; MY PASSION . . . ; I WONDER WHY . . . ; I SUFFER . . . ; MY WORK . . . ; IT PAINS ME WHEN . . . ; IT IS A JOY TO . . . ; LOVE . . . ; HOME . . . ; IT IS SAD THAT . . . ; CREATING . . . ; MY LOVER . . . ; WOMEN ARE . . . ; MEN ARE . . . ; THE FUTURE . . . ; MONEY . . . ; I CAN'T . . . ; I FEEL . . . ; MY GREATEST

DREAM IS THAT . . . ; ARTISTS CREATE BECAUSE . . ; THE FUTURE OF ART IS . . . ; THE TRUE MEANING OF LIFE . . . ; GREATNESS CONSISTS OF . . . ; I SECRETLY . . . ; MY CHILDHOOD . . . ; IN THE YEAR 2050 ART WILL . . . ; IT WILL BE CREATED . . . ; MY GREATEST LOVE . . . ; IT WOULD KILL ME IF . . . ; WHAT PEOPLE REALLY NEED IS . . . ; WHAT REALLY HANGS PEOPLE UP IS . . . ; WHAT REALLY MAKES PEOPLE STRONG . . . ; THE DESTINY OF THE HUMAN RACE ON THIS PLANET IS . . .

Vito Acconci. *Pull,* **1971 (April 9). Performance (eyes, movement, "hypnotic force"); videotape record of the performance. Eisner and Lubin Auditorium, New York University. Thirty Minutes:**
An area ten feet square marked off with masking tape. One 500-watt bulb lights the area; the rest of the auditorium is dark. An activity for two performers, one female and one male.

1. The female performer, Kathy Dillon, functions as a center point; I walk in a circle around her; she rotates in the center—she follows my direction, or starts a direction of her own, which I follow (or refuse to follow).
2. The goal of each of us is to keep staring at the other, to keep his eyes bound to the other's eyes (to keep the other's eyes bound to his).
3. At any time, either of us can shift direction, change speed, etc.: either of us can control, exert pull on, the other. (Each decides whether he wants to control or be controlled; each tries to determine if he is controlling or being controlled.)
—Private circle: closed circle (the action combines the performers and separates them from the audience): performance as withdrawal.
—Private circle: circle of unity—subjective performance (one performer is subsumed in the other): performance as identification.

Eleanor Antin, *Library Science,* **April, 1971. First shown at the San Diego State College Library, April–May, 1971, and later at NSCAD, Halifax. February, 1972:**
Each participant in the exhibition of women artists was asked to provide me with a "piece of information" of any form that described or represented her self, her life, her work, or any aspect of herself that she felt appropriate at this time. Twenty-six participants responded. Each "piece of information" (object or document) was classified for subject as a book in accordance with the classificational system of the Library of Congress. . . . All of the "pieces of information" were exhibited beside their "subject catalog cards." (See article on Antin in *The American Librarian,* February, 1972.) (*Rep.*)

April 9, Berkeley, California: David Askevold's *Tuning Fork Show,* **transmitted on KPFA Radio FM, 11:00–11:17 p.m. (a 17-minute radio spot—5 tuning forks, 4 notes).**

Robert Barry Presents Three Shows and a Review by Lucy R. Lippard. **Yvon Lambert, Paris, April, 1971. The "review" follows:**
Robert Barry's current show at the Yvon Lambert Gallery in Paris is announced by a mailer that reads: "ROBERT BARRY presents three shows and a review by LUCY R. LIPPARD." Ms. Lippard is an American art critic. The show itself consists of this review and of a box of some 150 4 x 6 index cards which constituted the catalogues of three exhibitions organized by Ms. Lippard from 1969 to 1971, each titled according to the population of the city in which it was held: 557,087, Seattle U.S.A.; 955,000, Vancouver, Canada; 2,972,453, Buenos Aires, Argentina (several cards from the latter have been vehemently canceled because instructions were not followed in their printing).

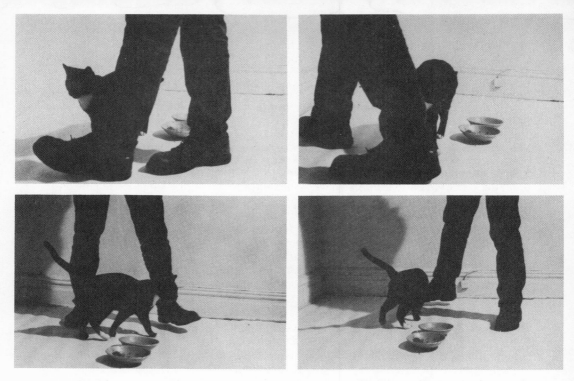

Vito Acconci. *Zone.* 30-minute performance. Eisner and Lubin Auditorium, New York University. April 9, 1971.

An area ten feet square marked off with masking tape. One 500-watt bulb lights the area; the rest of the auditorium is dark. An activity for one cat, one male performer.
1. The cat functions as a center point.
2. I walk around the cat, forming the periphery of a circle that encloses the cat.
3. When the cat moves, and tries to break away, I shift my circular movement: my goal is to keep the cat enclosed within the circle.
—Performance as point (the performance is a matter of "keeping to the point," preventing the cat from getting away from the point).
—The goal of the performance is to create a still point (unmoving cat): lull: charmed circle: performance as hypnosis.

From 1968, Barry has worked in almost invisible nylon cord, invisible but extant radiation, magnetic fields, radio carrier waves, telepathy, suppressed knowledge, non-specific qualifications defining undefined conditions. This exhibition is the third in a series of presentation pieces by Barry, the first two involving the work of artists James Umland and Ian Wilson. It is also part of another group, dating from 1969, which comments on the use of gallery space and the international gallery system for an art so dematerialized that it has no fundamental need of either one. The first of this group was a piece that announced: "During the exhibition the gallery will be closed." In January, 1971, Yvon Lambert showed a Barry piece that read: "Some places to which we can come, and for a while, 'be free to think about what we are going to do' (Marcuse)." "Read" is the wrong term; Barry does not work with words; he communicates conditions. The newer work indicates an overlap rather than a gap between art and life, in the sense that it attempts to define (again by circling around something) the place of the artist in the world, not socially (though social impact is implied), but as an art-maker rather than as a person. Perhaps the most important of the many questions raised by Barry's work are: Does the artist have a place in the world, and, if so, is it changing? Is he/she simply a questioner or is he/she the imposer of conditions upon the esthetic capacity of everyone else, without which the world would be quite a different place?

*

And I have some questions of my own. Is a review which is not published in a journal but constitutes part of an exhibition in itself a fake review? Can it view itself objectively? Or is it valid anyhow because people read it, because it does comment directly upon the show it is part of? Is the writer of such a review an artist even if he/she has not made art? If a writer calls what he/she does "criticism," can anyone else call it "art"? Is the artist who "presents" a writer's work as a minor part of his piece (the major part being the presentation per se) a critic himself? Is an artist ever not an artist if he/she says he or she is an artist? Does an artist have to make art? And, finally, it doesn't matter what this review says. Its potential is confirmed by its existence rather than by its contents.

Special Issue on Ben Vautier, *Flash Art*, no. 23, April, 1971.

Although Vautier's attitude and presentations have much more in common with the Fluxus group (with which he has long been associated), some of the ideas he has dealt with superficially or poetically relate to others in this book. For instance: in 1960 he signed (or claimed) money (rubles, dollars, francs, and marks) as art; he signed the deaths of Yves Klein and Piero Manzoni, also tombs, catacombs, mummies and "MY DEATH"; he made holes or removals, stating that "the hole is by essence an extraordinary thing." In 1961: "Destruction of my works of art as a work of art"; in 1962, he made two identical works and dated one 1952, the other 1966. In 1967: "To ask somebody for ideas and then sign the ideas with someone else's name"; in 1968, "to decide what is bad in art and do it," etc. Ben's major influence was clearly that of Yves Klein, whose mystical approach to non-object art affected all European "concept art" as well as most Fluxus actions and gestures. In 1960, Klein "signed the world."

***Mel Bochner/Notes on Theory.* University of Rhode Island, Kingston, April 26–May 14, 1971. Handwritten text and photos.**

***Stanley Brouwn.* Art and Project Bulletin 38, April, 1971. "The total number of my steps."**

Celender, Don. *Artball.* Five boxes containing one piece of sugarless bubble gum and 20 baseball cards with artists as players. Shown at OK Harris, New York, April 10–May 1.

Boston, April 9, 1971: "The Trustees of the Institute of Contemporary Art are pleased to announce the acquisition of a new work by Christopher C. Cook: Information Compression Series #4: LIAP 1":

I will become director of the I.C.A. for one year. During that period I will have the same responsibilities and opportunities as a regular director. I will energize the Institute in all possible ways, carry out a varied program and attempt to establish (workable) real communication between Boston cultural institutions. Any and all activities may/will be recorded for use in a comprehensive exhibition which will be the result of this year's activity. (C. Cook.)

April 15: Christopher Cook. *Tell Your Life in 25 Words, Autobiographical Compression series no. 2.*

Christine Kozlov. One page from *Neurological Compilation: The Physical Mind Since 1945 (Project 1: The Bibliography).* **Shown at "Twenty-six Contemporary Women Artists", Larry Aldrich Museum, Ridgefield, Conn., April, 1971:**
ELECTROENCEPHALOGRAMS FROM NEOCORTEX AND LIMBIC SYSTEM DURING
TEMPERATURE REGULATING RESPONSES OF THE RABBIT
BLOCKADE OF THALAMOCORTICAL AND PYRAMIDAL PATHWAYS BY STRIATAL
SPREADING DEPRESSION IN RATS
THE RELATIONSHIP OF OLFACTORY RECEPTOR STIMULATION TO STIMULUS
—ENVIRONMENTAL TEMPERATURE
MUSCLE POTENTIALS IN REACTION TIME
STUDIES ON THE ROLE OF NERVE IMPULSES AND ACETYLCHOLINE RELEASE
IN THE REGULATION OF THE CHOLINESTERASE ACTIVITY OF MUSCLE
THE SPINAL PATHWAY FOR SHIVERING
RESPONSE OF THE UNRESTRAINED CAT FOLLOWING ELECTRICAL STIMULATION
OF THE CINGULATE THALAMUS AND MESENCEPHALON
MUSCLE SENSE IN MAN
ELECTROTONIC POTENTIALS AT THE THORACIC LEVEL OF THE SPINAL CORD
THE EFFECT OF PREFRONTAL LESIONS AND FOOD DEPRIVATION ON RESPONSE
FOR STIMULUS CHANGE
EFFECTS OF DRUGS ON THE SPIKE COMPLICATION OF HIPPOCAMPAL FIELD
POTENTIALS
RETICULAR AND THALAMIC MULTIPLE UNIT ACTIVITY DURING WAKEFULNESS
SLEEP AND ANESTHESIA
EFFECT OF GLIAL-EPENDYMAL SCAR AND TEFLON ARREST ON THE REGENERATIVE
CAPACITY OF GOLDFISH SPINAL CORD
THERMAL RESPONSE PATTERNS OF SEPTAL AND PREOPTIC NEURONS IN CATS
PHYSIOLOGICAL AND HISTOLOGICAL CLASSIFICATION OF CEREBELLAR
NEURONS IN CHLORALOSE-ANESTHETIZED CATS
PATTERNS OF RESPONSE OF NEURONS IN THE CEREBRAL GANGLION OF
APLYSIA CALIFORNICA
THE ACQUISITION OF CONDITIONAL DISCRIMINATIONS IN BABOONS FOLLOWING
TEMPORAL AND FRONTAL LESIONS
NEURAL REGULATION OF ENZYMES IN MUSCLE FIBERS OF RED AND WHITE
MUSCLE
THE HYPEREXCITABLE NEURON: MICROELECTRODE STUDIES OF THE CHRONIC
EPILEPTIC FOCUS IN THE INTACT AWAKE MONKEY
EXCHANGE OF Y-GLOBULIN BETWEEN BLOOD CEREBROSPINAL FLUID AND BRAIN
IN THE CAT

Adrian Piper, section of an ongoing essay, January 1971; from *26 Contemporary Women Artists,* **Aldrich Museum, April, 1971:**
 Some ideas I've been working around: (1) I can no longer see discrete forms in art as viable reflections or expressions of what seems to be going on in this society. They refer back to conditions of separateness, order, exclusivity, and the stability of easily-accepted functional identities which no longer exist. For what a *posteriori* seems to be this reason, I'm interested in the elimination of the discrete form as art object (including communications media objects), with its isolate internal relation ships and self-determining esthetic standards. I've been doing pieces the significance and experience of which is defined as completely as possible by the viewer's reaction

234

and interpretation. Ideally the work has no meaning or independent existence outside of its function as a medium of change; it exists only as a catalytic agent between myself and the viewer. E.g. *Catalysis VIII,* which is a recorded talk inducing hypnosis. (2) Making artificial and nonfunctional alterations in my own bodily presence of the same kind as those I formerly made on non-art materials. Here the entire art making process *and* end product has the immediacy of being in the same time and space continuum as the viewer. This process/product is in a sense internalized in me, since I exist simultaneously as the artist and the work. This is not to be confused with life as art or my personality and tastes as art. The artifice of the work temporarily replaces or supersedes those characteristics which define me as a private individual. I define the work as the viewer's reaction to it: to me the strongest, most complex, and most interesting catalysis is the one that occurs in undefined and non-pragmatic human confrontation. The immediacy of a human presence as artwork/catalysis has greater impact; it confronts the viewer with a more powerful and more ambiguous situation than discrete forms or objects. E.g. *Catalysis IX,* in which I covered my face, neck and arms with feathers and attended the opening of the "Women Artists" show as an otherwise conservatively dressed spectator, and accompanied by a number of other people similarly altered. (3) Preserving the power and uncategorized nature of the confrontation. Not overtly defining myself to viewers as artwork by performing any unusual or theatrical actions of any kind. Actions tend to define the situation in terms of pre-established theatrical categories, e.g. "guerrilla theatre," "streetwork," etc. making viewer disorientation and catalysis more difficult. E.g. *Catalysis V,* in which I recorded loud belches made at five-minute intervals, then concealed the tape recorder on myself and replayed it at full volume while reading, doing research, and taking out some books and records at Donnell Library. For the same reason I don't announce most of these works, since this immediately produces an audience vs. performer separation. (4) Art contexts (galleries, performances) are becoming untenable for me. They are being overwhelmed and infiltrated by pieces of other disintegrating structures; political, social, economic. They preserve the illusion of an identifiable, isolable situation, much as discrete forms do, and thus a prestandardized set of responses. Because of their established functional identities, they prepare the viewer to be catalyzed, thus making actual catalysis impossible. Alternate contexts I've been using: public transportation, parks, Macy's, the Empire State Building Elevator, the Metropolitan Museum (as a spectator in *Catalysis VII,* in which I went to "Before Cortes" show while chewing wads of bubble gum, blowing large bubbles, and allowing the gum to adhere to my face and clothes). The exceptions to this are where the pieces depend only on their diffuse and unobtrusive presences regardless of context. E.g. *Catalysis VIII* (see 1, above) at the "Women Artists" show. (5) Eliminating as many decision-making criteria as possible. This has a psychological function for me. It decreases the separation between original conception and the final form of an idea; the immediacy of conception is retained in the process/product as much as possible. For this reason I have no way of accounting for the final form which an idea takes. It may be objected that all the ideas described above constitute decision-making criteria, but in fact just about everything I've written occurred to me *a posteriori,* including the idea expressed in this paragraph. Which may mean it's time to start doing something else.

April 29, New York: Guerrilla Art Action Group (Jon Hendricks, Jean Toche) sends letters to Nixon, Agnew, Hoover, Mitchell, Laird, Kissinger. To Nixon:

Guerrilla Art Action, to be performed every day, from May 1 through May 6, 1971, by Richard M. Nixon, President of the United States of America:

EAT WHAT YOU KILL

To Laird: Guerrilla Art Action, to be performed every day, from May 1 through May 6, 1971, by Melvin Laird, Secretary of Defense:

QUOTATIONS FROM THE WASHINGTON MEAT MARKET:
BRAINS: . . . . 79¢ per pound
TONGUES: . . . . 81¢ per pound
BLOOD: . . . . $2.50 per gallon
HEADS: . . . . 50¢ each
CAN YOU DO BETTER?

To Mitchell: Guerrilla Art Action, to be performed every day, from May 1 through May 6, 1971, by John B. Mitchell, Attorney General of the United States of America:

Sing "America the Beautiful" to the tune of "Dixie."

Benthall, Jonathan. "Bochner and Photography." *Studio International,* **April, 1971. Excerpts from the lecture given by Mel Bochner at the ICA, London, April, follow. "Problematic Aspects of Critical/ Mathematic Constructs in My Art":**

Any sort of information or re-formation can be divided by a set of externally maintained constants. Concentration on these constants, rather than on the information, results in the surfacing of the micro-structure. This forces a shift in consideration from formation as structure to structure as formation.

Thought is order.

When order is focused upon it, it reveals the inherent necessities of fixed procedures for realization. This mode of thinking immediately links one to certain areas of mathematical thought. Mathematical thinking is generally considered the antithesis of artistic thinking. This is one of the things that has led even art-lovers of good faith to resist certain works. At this point I want to underline the point that in my work there is no pretense to mathematics. That would lead to the conclusion that the work is about "something." At the same time, however, I am not "making" art. In the sense that it is an endeavor, I prefer to say that I am "doing" art. . . .

In what I am doing the synthesis is in the contradiction of the visible and the mental. This contradiction is central to any examination of recent art. What is the function of the visible element if the initial concentration is on the ideational aspect? Particularly if the artist is aware that art is *not* the illustration of ideas. I might add that this contradiction has not been resolved by artists who have abandoned the visible altogether. In fact, it remains specifically impossible to abandon visibility; to speak, as it were, only with the mental voice. I do maintain, however, that one can significantly alter the conventions of visuality to demonstrate entirely different modes of thinking. What I want my art to do is operate on the level of a proposition about the nature of things both thought and seen . . . to refrain from imperative. This work, or this, is not "how it must be," but rather, for these conditions, "how it might be" . . . situational, provisional, non-hierarchical.

Gopnik, Irwin, and Gopnik, Myrna. "The Semantics of Concept Art." *Artscanada,* **April–May, 1971.**

Poinsot, Jean-Marc. "Beuys à propos de quelques objets." *Opus International,* **May, 1971.**

VH-101, no. 5, Spring, 1971: Michel Claura, "Actualité" (on Buren, Mosset, Parmentier, and Toroni); "L'art didactique de Donald Karshan"; Phillippe Sollers, "Alain Kirili: Texte Aphoristique"; "Bernar Venet"; "Entretien de Lawrence Weiner avec Michel Claura."

The British Avant-Garde. New York Cultural Center, New York, May 19–August 29, 1971. Organized by Charles Harrison; catalogue in collaboration with ***Studio International*** (May issue). Texts by Harrison ("Virgin Soils and Old Land") and Karshan. Arnatt, Arrowsmith, Art-Language, Burgin, Crumplin, Dipper, Dye, Flanagan, Gilbert & George (Rep.), Long, Louw, McLean, Newman, Tremlett. Reviewed by Pincus-Witten, ***Artforum,*** October, 1971.

Art-Language (Terry Atkinson, Michael Baldwin). Excerpt from "De Legibus Naturae," in catalogue:
  Supposing that one of the quasi-syntactic individuals is a member of the appropriate ontologically provisional set—in a historical way, not just an *a priori* way (i.e., is historical); then a concatenation of the nominal individual and the ontologically provisional set is *Theories of Ethics* (according to the "definition"). But this is a bit odd; it suggests that the subjects of the unit relation in question are, respectively, the quasi-syntactic individual and the ontologically provisional set. This also suggests that one has a unit relation swanning around independent of its being part of (i.e., theorized about) the context it is said to be, i.e., *Theories of Ethics.* This is plainly silly. The declaration is a unity; the "unit relation" etc. are in that unity.
  There is no ontological commitment to a unit relation referred to. Neither is there any to any individual or congeries of them, or to any ontologically provisional set. One

Gilbert & George. Still from the film *The Nature of Our Looking.* 1971.

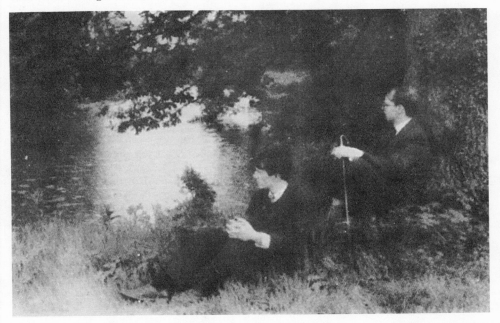

'Here in the country's heart where the grass is green life is the same sweet life as it ere hath been.' Gilbert & George
THE SCULPTORS

is talking about the "expressions" which "go into" a theory, ordered in some way. One does not either have to say that one has an illusion of "reference"—one has a way of speaking.

Because the "expressions" do refer *a priori* to the "individuals," one is only one remove from the "individuals." But one is two removes from them when one talks quasi-syntactically of an ontologically provisional set. The ontologically provisional set is one "individual," the expression which refers, *a priori,* to it is another, and in the end, the "ordering" on some "theoretical" basis (of the unit relation) is another. These are all ontological, and non-naturalistic, "provisions." One cannot say one's "object of 'reference'" is a unit relation; the order is sunk in the context which includes the declaration that the "expression" "is" it. One could, for example, think of the ordered pair (unit relation) obtained by concatenating the quasi-syntactic or nominal "individual" and the ontologically provisional set as actually having an "individual" as its first-order constituent. But this is wrong, because when one says that that unit relation is *Theories of Ethics,* one is talking quasi-syntactically. In actual fact one would be here talking about expression of the "object" theory (language) which designates them *a priori* instead.

In the context where one has the declaration as a part, it can be said that one is no more committed than to say that he talks about an "ontologically provisional (quasi) individual," an "ontologically provisional, ontologically provisional (quasi) set," and an "ontologically provisional (quasi), ontologically provisional unit relation" of that (those) "ontologically provisional individual" with that ontologically provisional (quasi), ontologically provisional set.

Theories of Ethics can now sustain a sort of "epoché."

One area in which one might well need a change is in the context where someone wants to make a distinction between "observations" (that sort of history) and theoretical predicates. One might want *Theories of Ethics* to be thought of solely in

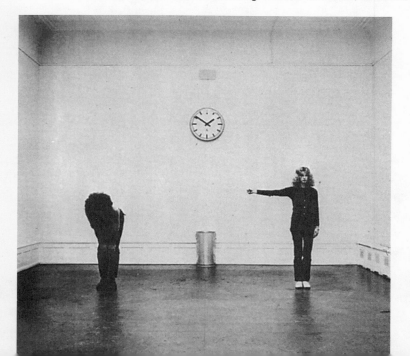

Klaus Rinke and Monika Baumgartl. *Primary Demonstration.* 1971.

terms of the former. Accordingly one would have to restrict one's theoretical discourse on *Theories of Ethics*—i.e., one's expressions for it. Now introducing *Theories of Ethics* this way satisfies most of the model desiderata. The point about the "thing" as "ethical" makes it more than just a semantic mechanism; the problem is what to make of the "pieces of paper." The above is addressed to this problem with the intention of avoiding the gratuitous celebration of semantic (i.e., Russell's) paradox.

Klaus Rinke and Monika Baumgartl. ***Primary Demonstrations*** **(Time-Space-Body-Actions). Kunsthalle, Baden-Baden, May, 1971 (Rep.):**

Time Measure/Time Position/body/head eyes ears nose mouth/neck/shoulder right left/arms elbows hands fingers/chest/back/spine/crotch/sex/legs right left/ thighs knees calves feet toes/.

to lie to run/to stand to sit/to go to lie/

standing turned away/standing turned towards/standing sidewards/ to look at each other/to look away/to overlook/to see each other not at all/to look on/to look round at/to look through/to look behind.

wall/floor/space.

distance/diagonals/center.

horizontal-vertical.

actions/gestures.

masculine-feminine:

    I   you

     we

   you   I

aggression/defensiveness/situation

transit/from starting point/to starting point.

past/present/future:

I you he she it we you they/will be are were.

One moment of the future.

To put a situation of today into the past, by which it becomes present in the future. from the spring to the ocean.

to go for water/to fill/to bring/to spout/to spill/to draw.

begin   end.

To walk a given path at different speeds.

one day lived—experienced.

past	present	future
I will be	I will be	I will be
I will be	I will be	I am
I will be	I am	I am
I will be	I will be	I will be
I am	I will be	I will be
I am	I am	I am
I am	I am	I was
I am	I was	I was
I was	I am	I was
I was	I was	I am
I was	I was	I was
past	present	future

Arte como idea en Inglaterra. CAYC, Buenos Aires, May, 1971. Organized by Charles Harrison. Folio catalogue in English and Spanish. Arnatt, Arrowsmith, Art-Language, Burgin, Dye, Woodrow.

Flash Art (Milan), no. 24, May, 1971. Works and texts by Acconci, Christo, Fabro, Graham, Griffa, Guarneri, Marriaci, Nagasawa, Oppenheim. *Flash Art* was founded in 1967 and is edited by Giancarlo Politi.

"Notebook: Vito Acconci on Activity and Performance." *Art and Artists,* May, 1971.

Ferguson, Gerald. *Four.* NSCAD, May, 1971. One-hour cassette recording from the *Standard Corpus of Present Day English Language Usage* (see p. 209) arranged by word length and alphabetized within word length. "A four letter word every 4 seconds for one hour = 900 fours. A 4-second tape loop—the same FOUR with the same interval is perceived as a different FOUR at different intervals, which is to say the viewer or listener cycle-needs is the issue."

Jeanne Siegel. "An Interview with Hans Haacke." *Arts,* May, 1971:
  Information presented at the right time and in the right place can potentially be very powerful. It can affect the general social fabric. Such things go beyond established high culture as it has been perpetrated by a taste-directed art industry. Of course I don't believe that artists really wield any significant power. At best, one can focus attention. But every little bit helps. In concert with other people's activities outside the art scene, maybe the social climate of society can be changed. Anyway, when you work with the "real stuff" you have to think about potential consequences. . . . Real-time systems are double agents. They might run under the heading "art," but this culturization does not prevent them from operating as normal. (H.H.)

Douglas Huebler. Art and Project Bulletin 39, May 22–June 11, 1971. "Variable Piece I (January, 1971)." Executed in the Netherlands, U.S., Italy, France,and Germany:
  Eight people were photographed at the instant exactly after each had been told: "you have a beautiful face" or "you have a very special face," or "you have a remarkable face." or in one instance, nothing at all. The artist knew only one person among the eight; it is not likely that he will ever again have a personal contact with any of the others. The eight photographs join with this statement to constitute the form of this piece.

Leandro (Katz) begins *The 21 Columns of Language,* May, 1971, New York. (Spanish and English).

Al's Grand Hotel. 7175 Sunset Blvd., Hollywood, Calif., May 7–June 12, 1971. Twelve-page catalogue of Allan Ruppersberg's hotel-show in which variously decorated and named rooms (The "B" Room, the Al Room, the Jesus Room, the Bridal Suite, etc.) were visitable or rentable for six weeks. Brochure and twelve-page catalogue.

Ruscha, Edward. *Dutch Details.* Octopus Foundation with Sonsbeek (see below); executed May, 1971.

Taylor, Thoss W. *Consider Your Confine.* NSCAD, May 2–13, 1971. Also "shown" at sixteen other locations in the U.S. in April, May, and June, including the Eugenia Butler Gallery, Los Angeles, which represents the artist. "#17 from an edition of 100 (photographic) pieces each approaching a definition of the concept of confine."

Waldman, Diane, "Holes Without History" (On Heizer); Bowles, Jerry G., "Can Epistemology Be Entertaining?" (on Arakawa). *Art News,* May, 1971.

Tim Johnson. *Erotic Observation (2).* **July 28, 1971: 3:50 p.m. Fisher Library, Sydney University, Australia:**
   A girl wearing a very short red, blue, and white striped dress is leaning with her elbows on a table. Because of the table's height (about 4 feet) her dress is partly pulled up over her bottom. There is a flight of stairs coming out just behind her so I go down these, then climb slowly back up. I do this six times observing the following:
   (1) Legs held together firmly. Cream coloured pants with wide lace. Fairly loose; (2) Legs relaxed, left hip pushed up causing bottom to stick out a little more and stretch pants off-center; (3) Rubbing legs together and opening and closing them a little; (4) Legs tightly crossed, pants pulled in and creased; (5) as for (4); (6) Not there.

Activity: Sonsbeek '71. **Sonsbeek Park, Holland, June 19–August 15, 1971. Organized by a "Working Committee" headed by W. A. L. Beeren. Two-volume catalogue including texts by Beeren, extensive documentation on the show, which was placed all over Holland, in the park itself, and in publications and films. List of related group exhibitions, bibliography, biographies. Reviewed in** *Arts,* **September–October, 1971;** *Artforum,* **October, 1971;** *Studio International,* **September, 1971. Participants: Acconci, Ader, Andre, Armagnac, Arschwager, Baillie, Bakker, Beuys, Bladen, Boezem, Brouwn, Buren, Christo, Conrad, Darboven, de Maria, Dekkers, Dibbets, van Elk, Engels, Enschede, E.R.G., Eykelboom, Flanagan, Fluxus, Frampton, Gehr, Graham, Grosvenor, Heizer, Huebler, I.C.W., Jacobs, Joepat, Judd, Kawara, Knoebel, Koetsier, Kraan, Kubelka, Landow, Lawder, LeWitt, Long, Mass, Matsuzawa, Merz, Moore, Morris, Nauman, Nelson, Noord-Brabant, Oldenburg, Oppenheim, Paik, Panamarenko, Philips, Prini, Rinke, Roehr, Rückriem, Ruscha, Sandback, Sanéjouand, Schippers, Serra, Sharits, Siegel, Smith, Smithson, Snelson, Snow, Stuyf, Tajiri, Tenjo and Yokoyama, Visser, Volten, Vries, Wechgelaar, Weiner, Wieland.**

Buren, Daniel. *Lettre ouverte à la revue Robho et à son comité de rédaction,* **June 25, 1971. Two-page mimeo.**

Collins, James. *Revision and Prescription.* **New York, June, 1971:**
   The "fixity" of art frameworks continue . . . on the "analytic" front, though supposedly against the mindless retinal activations of much "visual work." Philosophically it is suspect because it presupposes the need of a new art to have the same parallel physical appendages as previous art—for every object cancelled there has to be "something" in its place—the move becomes merely syntactic, from one sort of object to another—canvas and wood to paper, for example. That argument would mean that this essay is an art object, to be related formally to prior "art objects." The "art work" of this essay is contained in its semantic function. This essay is functional rather than formal. It's what it means that counts, not whether it challenges notions of what "art work" should look like.
   Reading and Walking are not the most sophisticated ways to receive information anyway (the same might be said of walking around objects). The indignity often compounded by "work" behind visual barriers with strong status quo implications like glass cases placed at ergonomically unhappy reading levels. Stooped and moving crabwise around a room, reading, is not good pragmatics (an undeniable aspect of any semiotic situation). But pragmatics aside, many artists aware of the paradox use the gallery system merely as a form of advertisement. To others, the placing of their work in situations with cultural and aesthetic implications as strong as the most

241

vaunted of art objects has meant a sort of conceptual stunting of its growth. The reason is obvious, for the feedback from the situation is physical and visual and explains the "conceptual exhibitionism" of spreading "reading matter" around walls and tables. The "handsomeness" of these works on the one hand relates them to "visual perusal" works, they "hold their own," but has an adverse effect on the other, of making "the concept" labored. The "concept" is "dressed up," or stretched to fit a visual form, so that its conceptual growth is always subservient to its container. The notion of displaying an essay on a wall, or series of "instructions for perception," or whatever, in a linear sequence, relates it directly to the form of prior art—serial sculpture—and perhaps explains its "optical philosophical" mannerism. The new work can never find its own identity when it uses "presentational forms" which have cultural and functional "fixations" of artists as diverse as Noland, whose paintings invite a retinal "journey" down their length, or Morris, where the spectator is "invited" to walk around the work.

Possibly it is a paranoia that stepping too far out of line with the existing rules of the game will make the work meaningless. This panders to the idea that the rules are unchanging and necessary; it is the old formalist argument in a different guise. Sticking to the rules (if the game analogy is even applicable) is only meaningful if the game is meaningful. What is being asked is, "Is the game worth playing?" not "How far do we tamper with the rules?" My contention is that the game has changed, it is not a predictable internal syntactic move like the one from football to rugby, that's a formalist example. Picking up the ball and running with it is the same kind of formalist strategy as, for example, the change from painting a stripe, to "walking" a stripe (Long). There is no significant difference between the two. There are richer more multi-layered "games" to play. If words are used as strategy and as antidote, it seems necessary to follow through the implications fully, and not seek cover in the status and warmth of familiar sustainers. . . .

In conclusion, if "Art-Language," Burn, Ramsden and others are at all correct in their commonly shared but rarely understood insights regarding the fundamental task of "analytic art" and its methodological demands, then the contention that the investigation into the art semiotic signals a fundamental revision into the artist's traditional mode of operation, may have profound consequences in both revisionary and prescriptive spheres. As we can only discover language with language, though, the question might be asked, can a system discover itself, or is there a lacuna?

June 21: Longest day of the year. Geoff Hendricks exchanges "sky and sky-related pieces with people around the world."

Kosuth, Joseph. *The Sixth Investigation (Art as Idea as Idea) Proposition II.* CAYC, Buenos Aires, 1971, in English and Spanish; Kosuth lectures at the CAYC June 18, in connection with his show there; catalogue with texts, bibliography, in addition to book.

Levine, Les. "The Information Fall-Out." *Studio International,* June, 1971. (Written as an insert for the catalogue of *Recorded Activities,* October, 1970.)

LeWitt, Sol. "Doing Wall Drawings." *Art Now,* June, 1971. (see excerpt, pp. 200–201).

Malloy, Mike. *Conference of the Society of Cemetery Aestheticians,* June 1, 1971 at the State Mutual Savings Building, Los Angeles. Sponsored by Eugenia Butler. Tape and report,

documentation, concerning the arbitrary subdivision into twenty-seven parts and sale of a cemetery lot in the Olivet Memorial Park, Los Angeles.

Michelson, Annette. "Toward Michael Snow, Part 1." *Artforum,* June, 1971.

Benthall, Jonathan, "David Bohm and the Rheomode"; Blotkamp, Carel, "Dutch Artists on Television." *Studio International,* June, 1971.

Pluchart, François. "Les Agressions d'Acconci." *Combat,* June 14, 1971.

Analytical Art, no. 1 (formerly *Statements*). Coventry, July, 1971. Contributors: Pilkington, Rushton, Lole, Atkinson, Baldwin, Howard, Burn and Ramsden, Smith, Willsmore.

Chandler, John Noel, and Maldavin, Allré. "Correspondences." *Artscanada,* June–July, 1971.

Flash Art, no. 25–26, June–July, 1971; work and texts by Kawara, LeWitt, Fulton, Arakawa, de Dominicis, Agnetti, Tremlett, Zini, Innocente.

Arte de Sistemas/Art Systems. Museo de arte moderno, Buenos Aires, July–August 22. Organized by Jorge Glusberg. Books published by Burgy, Kosuth, Weiner (2), and by Grippo, Pellegrino, and Portillos; "telephone book transformation" by Jochen Gerz, etc. Special issue *Arte informa* (no. 7, July, 1971) for this exhibition. Catalogue of the show (folio of loose pages) issued early 1972.

Art Disaster, John Baldessari, 1971. Art and Project Bulletin 41, July 3–15, 1971.

John Baldessari. NSCAD, Halifax, summer, 1971: "I will not make any more boring art. I will not make any more boring art. I will not make any more boring art." . . . etc., in which the students became the "whipping boys" for the artist, who was not present; anyone who wanted to wrote on the walls of the gallery, over and over again: "I will not make any more boring art"; videotape made. Baldessari also made a three-minute film in June, 1971, called "The Excesses of Austerity and Minimalism," a sheet of paper in a typewriter on which the title is being typed as fast as possible, over and over, in an attempt to do it with utmost speed and no mistakes.

Richardson, Brenda. "Howard Fried: The Paradox of Approach-Avoidance." *Arts,* summer, 1971.

Rosenberg, David. "Notes from a Conversation Tape with Vito Acconci, July 22, 1971." *A Space News* (Toronto), July, 1971. Excerpt:
Seems most of my pieces set up as kind of learning pieces, as ways to adapt to something, kinds of practice sessions for things which might happen. . . . Like lots of my stuff last year had to do with setting up regions . . . or people as regions . . . in ways that one region would intrude upon another region or combine with another region, like the piece where I'm standing near a person and intruding on his personal space, picking out a person looking at the exhibits and taking over his personal space by forcing him to move because I intrude on the space he set up for himself to look at the exhibit in . . . or like opening up a private region, or closed system, like I do in that piece with Kathy where she has her eyes closed shut & I try to force them open. . . . So seems lately I've been using mostly other people in my pieces, or animals. . . . Before it was mostly me turning on myself, involved with myself. . . . Now I'm thinking a lot more about interaction. . . .

Getting more and more difficult to separate the two, the art activity and the daily living, and that's what we're working toward, no separation. Tho ultimately *showing* it in an art context. . . . I find that kind of performance tends to clarify things for me, as a kind of a model experience . . . working toward the work. . . .

My sense now to be getting out as much work as I can, constantly, doing "public" things . . . so that what becomes public is not so much finished pieces but a *process* of working . . . Dislike my pieces considered in isolation . . . Like them more to appear as a kind of working notebook than finished pieces . . . Like to document them not just in photographs & description, but along with the notes in a notebook I keep while working on them . . . The way words, in the notes, can suggest the process of the pieces unlike photos & lead to sense & ideas outside it . . . Like one reason Nauman's work impresses me is that beautiful neatness and completeness to each piece, but it's almost the direct opposite of what I want myself . . . Like Oppenheim perhaps the most important influence on my whole sense of an artist today, but going back, I'd say for instance [William] Faulkner was the biggest influence of any kind I ever had, like his lack of desire to finish a sentence, his sense to keep on going beyond where you could possibly follow (did I say flow?), like sentences that go on for pages . . . with so many reconsiderations & hesitations & alternatives, his sentences seem to be consciously or unconsciously trying to subvert a fantastically conservative framework. . . . I think they win out . . . like in myself I sense as a kind of impulse to

Ulrich Rückriem. *Circles.* **Still from videotape. (The artist hammering a circle around himself.) Summer, 1971. Courtesy Videogalerie Gerry Schum, Düsseldorf.**

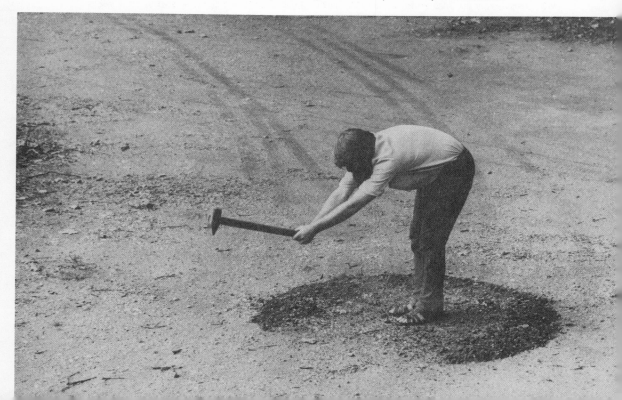

overcomplicate things, to mess things up, or thicken the plot, or my daily life, to where I almost can't handle it . . . & finding ways to put things back together . . . Just how far the risk goes: Still feel I've got incredible safety mechanisms built in, but the push toward opening things up . . . Learning something . . . about how it keeps together.

Jasper Johns' sketchbook notes the biggest that happened to me, in '64, '65, when I was feeling I'd reached my limits in writing poetry. . . .

A constant attempt to get to, to bring out, all that might be there . . . to get in, like I think the push is really toward content, *real* content, and because you're not concerned with perfection, like in Nauman's pieces, it can be very messy, you can use anything, any content, that helps you get there . . . Terry Fox & Howard Fried a couple of other artists I relate to as working in a similar way . . . concerned with the mental superstructure or process that is applied to everyday things & events . . . like Fried's moving into a new loft piece . . .

Andy Warhol? . . . The incredible examination of veneers, pushing of veneers or roles so far . . . But I'm concerned with acting as if the mask doesn't exist really, even though it does . . . Healthy would be the mask . . . that keeps you safe . . . so that acting as if that mask doesn't exist at least lets you get close to try to see what other possibilities are there and that's just what messes things up, because you get so accustomed to one mask—or one *home*—you keep trying as many masks as you can . . . probably the most natural thing would be a combination of many masks, this ability to combine in yourself . . . wherever you get too vulnerable, the art context, as you are true to it, keeps you safe. . . .

Sol LeWitt. Art and Project Bulletin 43, July 9–August 2, 1971. Two wall drawing projects for 10,000 straight lines; blank brochure folded into squares so it becomes a grid.

Alan Sonfist. ICA, London, July 29–August 31, 1971. Ten-page catalogue with statement by the artist mentioning a work exhibited in 1968: "Enclosures in which invisible micro-organisms from the air are picked up by a medium that fosters accelerated growth into visible patterns"; also worked with snails and schooling fish in 1969.

Attitudes Toward Photography. NSCAD, Halifax, August 5–18. Organized by Ian Murray.

Daniel Buren. Art and Project Bulletin 40, August, 1971:
. . . one of the characteristics of the proposition is to reveal the "container" in which it is sheltered . . . Acrylic on cloth visible recto verso cotton cloth (65′ 7¹/₂″ × 32′ 9 3/4″) with alternating white and blue stripes (each 3 7/8″) . . . Photographs from 11 different points of view of a piece installed before the opening of the VI Guggenheim International Exhibition and *censored* the same day by the museum at the request of some participating artists who felt that their work was compromised and endangered by the presence of this piece in the exhibition. (*Rep.*)

"Jan Dibbets in Conversation with Charlotte Townsend," *Artscanada,* August–September, 1971.

Jarden, Richards. *Hand Animation, Leg Animation* (August, 1971). Films shown at NSCAD, Halifax, September 12–19:
Hand Animation, 16-mm black and white:
A single-frame film loop in which I hold my hand as still as possible, and a series of still images is taken at the rate of 2–3 frames per second.

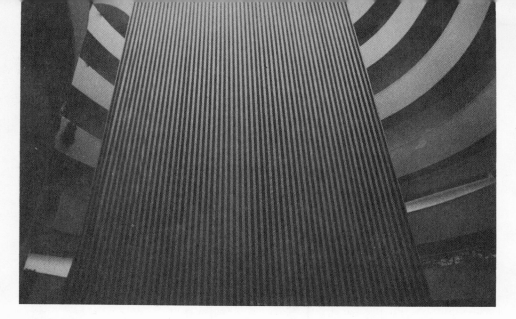

Daniel Buren. *Visible Recto Verso Painting.* 6 1/2' x 34 3/4'. 1971. Solomon R. Guggenheim Museum, New York, 1971 (removed from exhibition).

An attempt is made to eliminate activity within an extended actual period of time. The period of time taken as a whole normally establishes the character of the activity. When still images are projected at the same running speed at which they were recorded, the result is a naturalistic re-creation of actual motion. The interpretation of a film image is one of time and motion as continuous processes. The shaking of my hand over a period of time is not a continuous motion like that of waving, for example. Shaking is the result of scattered muscle spasms or twitches that take place at random, rather than in muscular order. When the film is projected at a speed faster than that used in recording an activity, the result is a distortion of time. Animation techniques applied to animated subject matter give the clearest example of this. So when the film is projected at normal speed it is in fact speeded up, but the effect of the time compression is minimized by applying it to a subject that shows very little change. The procedure is effectively counteracted by holding still.

Long, Richard. *From Along a Riverbank.* Art and Project, Amsterdam, summer, 1971. Twenty-page booklet of leaves.

***Yutaka Matsuzawa. Art and Project Bulletin 42,* August 7–21, 1971. "All human beings! let us vanish. let us go. ghatei ghatei. the anti-civilization committee."**

***Dennis Oppenheim.* CAYC, August 27–September 6, Buenos Aires. Folio catalogue of work and the artist's activities when in Buenos Aires.**

***Tony Shafrazi, Non-Projection.* NSCAD, Halifax, August 23–27.**

***Art-Language,* no. 3, September, 1971. Contributors: Burn, Cutforth and Ramsden, Howard, Bihari, Baldwin:**

The practical, theoretical and epistemic conditions of the area (domain) of discourse served by the journal have achieved de facto consolidation. Broadly, the editors had been concerned to preserve a specific art-theoretic basis. One of the upshots of this is that the contents of the journal demonstrate the vacuity (or inadequacy) of categorical restraints in a context which may well support fairly high epistemic generality.

Data, no. 1 (Milan), September, 1971. Gilberto Algranti and Tommaso Trini, eds. Contents include "Interview with Ian Wilson" by Tommaso Trini; "Book as Artwork 1960/1970" plus bibliography by Germano Celant; "Presenza Assenza" by Daniel Buren (on the Guggenheim affair, previously published in *Opus International,* May, 1971, as "Around and About"; in *Studio International,* June, 1971, and *Art Info,* July, 1971); "Buren, Haacke, chi altro?" by Michel Claura and René Denizotj; "Commento su Merz" and "Mario Merz: La Serie di Fibonacci" by Renato Barilli (excerpts follow). (Rep.) All texts in English and Italian.

What is the Fibonacci series?

It is the proliferation of numbers. Numbers reproduce themselves like men, bees or rabbits. If they did not reproduce they would cease to exist. The series is life. The numbers 1, 2, 3, 4, 5, 6, 7, 8 and 9 are the enumeration of dead elements. Instead the series is mathematics in expansion, that is to say living mathematics.

How do you apply this mathematical series to the visual activity of art?

I apply it by attaching numbers to certain "essential" elements in architecture. In the Guggenheim Museum I attached them to the balcony in spiral tension. The numbers increase the tension visually, or rather they make it felt. If numbers are visual art, then the Guggenheim balcony, Mies van der Rohe's house, the five windows of the Munich hall or the rampant spiral arch of Nuremberg Palace, other places where I have worked, are also art. It is through art, which is a method which has always been used to say something or to give birth to something.

What method did you use in your latest project in Munich?

The reason for my interest in the Fibonacci mathematical series is that numbers are an abstract invention by man, but become concrete when they are used to count objects. I am not interested in a direct physical sense, but rather in all that in an environment which is not physical although it can be counted. . . .

You used the Fibonacci mathematical series on other architectural structures, as for example at the Guggenheim Museum, at Krefeld and at Nuremberg.

Yes, at Krefeld I first had the idea of using this series, which I had already applied to the igloo and in other situations, to architecture as well, that is to say to the closed space which is expanded by the series. Here I used a spiral which began in the center of the museum and went toward the exterior. Its violence of expansion was directly related to the very fast "growth" of the Fibonacci numbers. . . .

If you should sum up what you have discovered about the Fibonacci series, putting it to use and reflecting on it, what would you say?

That there is an enormous volume of mental, and therefore physical, space at our disposal. This is the "political" value of the application of proliferating numbers to the areas which we make use of.

Has this research of yours anything to do with the question of the relationship between art and life?

Do you mean the problem of art going out into the streets, etc? This business of art and life can also be expressed in other terms. If we can apply this series to art, it means that in sociology (from art) we can include the terms of an idea which arises

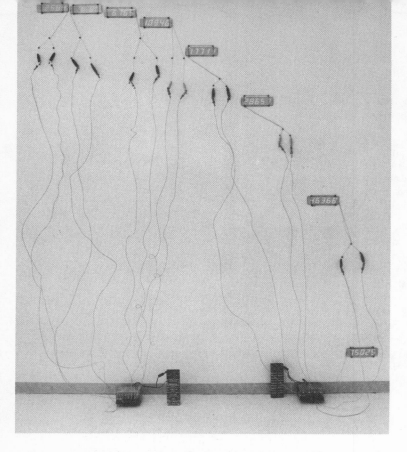

Mario Merz. *Relationships of Growth Within the Development of a Tree Outlined in an Unbroken Line According to the Fibonacci Series.* Neon, wire. 1970. Courtesy Sonnabend Gallery, New York.

from the study of plant and animal proliferation. The change from Roman numbers to Arabic numbers is the indefinable quality which has overturned a system.

Anonymous. "Evaporation Piece," "Strata Reverse Study," "Limestone Wash." University of British Columbia Fine Arts Gallery, Vancouver, September 13–October 2.

September 18, 1971: Card sent by anonymous "Orders & Co." to Sr. Jorge Pacheco Areco, then President of Uruguay, from New York, in Spanish:

Dear Dr. Pacheco Areco:

We have decided to put you under our orders. You will receive orders by mail at your duty time. The fulfillment of our orders will not occupy too much of your time or energy. We will dispose of certain zones of your time in the future because we consider that an individual with the accumulation of power that you have can only humanize himself by receiving orders.

In the case of a refusal, at the moment you receive each order, you must communicate it to the press. Copies of our orders will circulate among segments of the Uruguayan population, who, with us, will assume that you are fulfilling these orders unless you publicly express the contrary.

[The letter accompanying this first card explains that Orders & Co.] is a private organization with no economic interests in Uruguay. Its unique interest is to invert a little the relationship between orderers and those ordered, breaking the vicious circle of power. [Sample orders:] Oct. 5: Our next order is for the 15th of October. That day you will take special care to button your pants before going out into the street. Oct. 30: The 5th of November you will simulate normal walking but you will be conscious that for this day Orders & Co. have taken possession of every third step you take. It is not necessary for you to obsess yourself with this.

Scalar (Rep.). **Dorothea Rockburne, New York, September, 1971 (exhibited Bykert Gallery, January, 1972).**

Rockburne's work is based on the axioms of set theory, the surface sheets providing the "givens," the blots and stains the "variables." The arrangement follows an initially logical proposition. From the artist's journal:

Scalar and Sacshuamán

1) Aggregate those courses and tendencies which produce its observed character.
2) Study the circumstances in which both systems attain the freest action.

Dorothea Rockburne. *Scalar.* Paper, chipboard, crude oil, 8' x 12' (approx). 1971. Courtesy Bykert Gallery, New York.

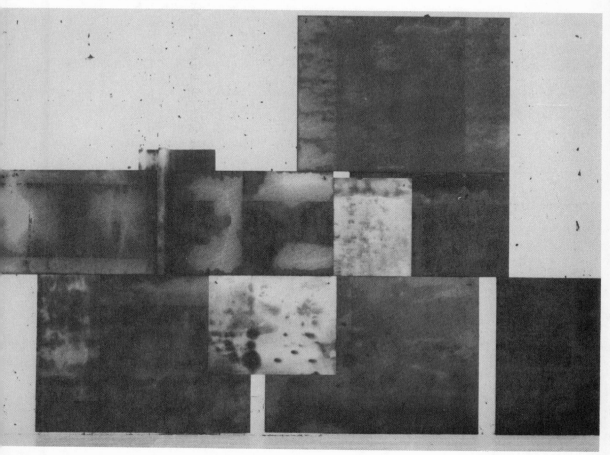

3) Determine to some extent the causes which are at work, though imperfectly or partially; the causes of their action.

4) The manifestation of order affords a presumption not measurable but nevertheless real.

Milieu Protektion (Denmark). September, 1971. Newspaper format; includes section on Barry Bryant's Street Works.

Robert Barry, fall, 1971: This work has been and continues to be refined since 1969:
It is whole, determined, sufficient, individual, known, complete, revealed, accessible, manifest, effected, effectual, directed, dependent, distinct, planned, controlled, unified, delineated, isolated, confined, confirmed, systematic, established, predictable, explainable, apprehendable, noticeable, evident, understandable, allowable, natural, harmonious, particular, varied, interpretable, discovered, persistent, diverse, composed, orderly, flexible, divisible, extendible, influential, public, reasoned, repeatable, comprehendable, impractical, findable, actual, interrelated, active, describable, situated, recognizable, analysable, limited, avoidable, sustained, changeable, defined, provable, consistent, durable, realized, organized, unique, complex, specific, established, rational, regulated, revealed, conditioned, uniform, solitary, given, improvable, involved, maintained, particular, coherent, arranged, restricted, and presented.

Taylor, Robert. "Chris Cook's Coming Years: Life as Process as Art." *Sunday Magazine of the Boston Globe,* September 26, 1971. Cover of the magazine used by Cook as a "Real Art Data" piece (a form to be filled out and sent to the artist).

This is Not Here: Yoko Ono. Everson Museum, Syracuse, New York, September–October, 1971. Organized by James Harithas and George Maciunas.

Smithson, Robert. "A Cinematic Atopia." *Artforum,* September, 1971.

Jappe, George. "A Joseph Beuys Primer." *Studio International,* September, 1971.

Hickey, Dave. "Earthscapes, Landmarks and Oz." *Art in America,* September–October, 1971.

Conversation between Douglas Huebler and Donald Burgy, Bradford, Mass., October, 1971 (excerpts from recording):
H: Do you recall a conversation we had on my sidewalk in the spring of '68 when I'd begun to dig into my lawn and do things out there?

B: I remember that conversation very well. One of the things I was asking you about at that point was boundaries. What did you consider in the realm of art and what was excluded, and how were you deciding that. I can remember looking down at the sidewalk and the grass tangent to the sidewalk and asking you questions about where the art began and where it ended.

H: At that time I began to make those little models, little earth models. I remember one in particular where I was making the kind of forms that I had been using to make minimal sculpture and started to encroach on the Charles River, making a diversion, just a simple channel that would be a simple right angle, straight line, parallel with the river and then back out again. Then doing that kind of thing was what really turned my head around because I realized that while I didn't have the line of concrete, I could just find a bend in the river and make a little canal across. And then I realized that all of these things could be very subtle.

B: That is very strange. I arrived at a similar but different position by constantly looking at the mirrored plexiglass works I was doing and seeing that the content of the art works was all of the surrounding environment that had supposedly been excluded from normal art works.

H: At that time I was trying to think of new ways of dealing with nature and imposing forms onto nature without being bounded; without having the frame, the content; . . . like the earth being flat. The earth being flat put a frame around it for man, and the earth being round created continuity. And space. Space itself. And a recognition of isolation as well. Continuity means space more than frames do . . . The little models I was making for the river piece blew the notion of frames. The issue of the frame, the context, preempted my interest in making the forms go in nature.

B: One of the important things lies in the fact that both of us were groping for a recognition that during the time we grew to be makers of art and conscious of art we had arrived at a historical state that had isolated art from other things. Artists were supposedly special or different people, who had different views of society. Now it becomes apparent that artists, like anyone else, just arrange the material of the earth, reprocess materials of the earth. We have realized that you cannot successfully isolate art from social or cultural or historical processes, that there is a constant feedback.

H: I wonder if there has been any time that art has been a manifestation of a culture that had no reason to believe it was not going on, and therefore could accomodate the forms of art as an adjunct, as something of cultural value alone. The tangible impermanence of a lot of things that are being made today may be an extension of a great pessimism about biological survival.

B: The kind of art we do can also be seen in the context of the evolution of the information-to-weight ratio of media, from the stone age hieroglyphs to the present high-information, lightweight media. We have been consistent with the recognition that you no longer have to have tons and tons of copper to convey importance. But still the sense of property, and of passing property on to your sons, and all that has always been involved when something is conceived of as a luxury item—all that still works in the art market. If art is isolated from culture and becomes a luxury item, it functions in very distorted ways. Size and weight become important factors.

H: Since our art has turned from making the luxury item and turned to the residue or information as the product, it is interesting to make a comparison with what had value up to now. Rather than be exhausted or polluted by objects of the world, we may become finally exhausted by information in the world.

B: But we don't participate in the information overload. There are two entirely different ethics going on. The work I do is highly distilled, highly processed information—highly abstracted ideas. I'm not recovering those ideas. I'm introducing them into the audience. There is a high degree of selection. We pride ourselves as artists that we select what we think is necessary for the situation we are in. On the other hand, the artists who work with redundancy, with accumulation, with the collage sensibility, are being wasteful. One important criterion to judge art is the artist's capacity to select the one factor that gives the most resonance.

H: That presumes somebody is paying attention.

B: If nobody pays attention, it isn't art. I believe that one cannot make art in isolation. The definition of art in part is that it is a relationship formed between an audience and an artist. . . . Television programs which are redundant and have an audience result in cultural paralysis.

H: One of the things that holds a culture together is redundancy of information. You say the same prayers over again, the same stories. You go to the same meetings and meet people saying the same things. . . . That kind of redundancy is precisely what forms the cultural base.

B: There are two entirely different approaches because the one point of view places the responsibility of filling in with the audience and the other places the task of filling in with the artist. One uses art as a vehicle of suggestion and the other as the vehicle of presentation.

H: In the work where you say "take that which is on the outside, bring it to the inside, and take the inside and put it on the outside"—that kind of thing is more ambiguous, more like my secrets, where the content is beyond that. . . .

B: That whole thing, the series of insides and outsides, is precisely concerned with the boundary conditions of identities, ego boundary conditions and cultural boundary conditions, and they function on several levels. In other words, we send an explorer out into the world. He comes back and what he reports to us tells us who we are. We extend our egos out into the world. We make art works that have to do with the world and they mirror who we are. On several levels it really has to do with placing the configuration, the question, in the audience's mind. It forces him to identify where his boundaries are.

H: But given that kind of reciprocity the boundaries constantly shift.

B: They do. They are dynamic boundaries, and that is why those inside-outside art works are so vague, to take account of the fact that boundary conditions are dynamic. . . .

H: Buren's article in *Studio International* this summer talks about Duchamp and how he still remained within the art context. And here's Buren, writing in the art context, still addressing himself to the art world, and he can never escape it. . . . The issue of context is always there. The issue of information is only phenomena, the posture from which you adjust or manipulate or direct the phenomena you choose to use. The stance from which the discretionary position is taken is more important than the subject matter. There's a misunderstanding that a lot of contemporary art is merely using information as a decorative, a picture-making device, another way of adjusting the apples, to paraphrase Buren. . . .

B: We were sold a bill of goods about dynamic avant-gardism, about the artist having the capacity to thrust cultural forms ahead of necessity; how the culture would suddenly wake up one morning and say we need that because of the problems we are in. What is incredible about the avant-garde posture is the belief that the cultural forms we have are no longer adequate to solve whatever problems we want to solve. What it means to be avant-garde is to constantly waste cultural forms; to throw them away; an obsolescence not of forms but of contexts as well. Now there are people who are throwing contexts away at the speed one would throw out a pair of tennis shoes.

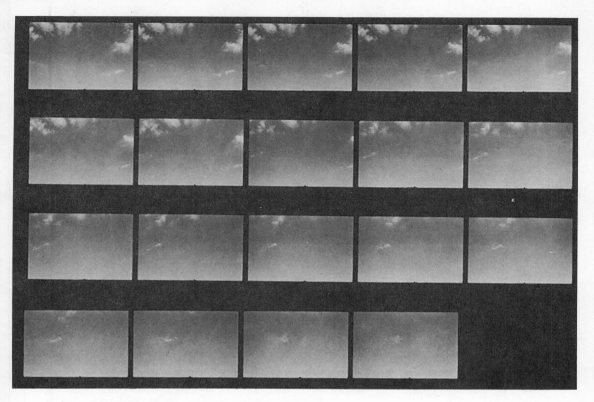

Alice Aycock. Segment of *Cloud Piece.* 1971.

Nemser, Cindy. "Subject-Object: Body Art." *Arts,* September–October, 1971.

Avalanche, no. 3, October, 1971. Contents: Interviews with David Tremlett, Ulrich Rückriem, Barry Le Va; writings, photo essays, and works by Bill Beckley, Joel Fisher, Gordon Matta-Clark.

Prospect 71. Kunsthalle, Düsseldorf, October 8–17. Organized by Konrad Fischer and Hans Strelow. Devoted entirely to projections: slides, films, video.

Arte concettuale. Daniel Templon, Milan, October, 1971. Art-Language, Burgin, Burn, Kosuth, Ramsden, Venet.

Alice Aycock, project for Mezzanine Gallery of NSCAD, Halifax, fall, 1971 (Rep.):
   The following project is based on the fact that small, fair weather cumulus clouds dissipate within 5 to 15 minutes after formation. It consists of a series of four photographic black and white contact sheets. There are 36 to 38 exposures per contact sheet. Each contact sheet shows a cloud or clouds photographed from a stationary camera position for a 10- to 15- minute time period and until the roll of film was completed. Each contact sheet can be read from frame to frame in order to detect transition/change: cloud movement, dissipation, formation.

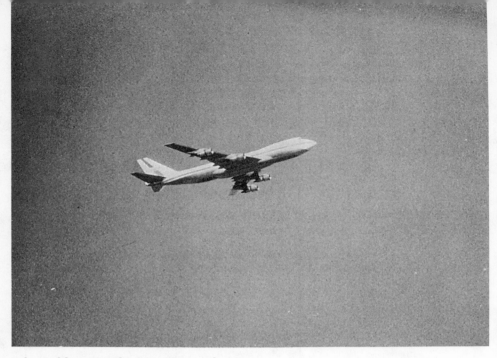

John Baldessari. *The Best Way to do Art.*

John Baldessari: Ingres and Other Parables. Konrad Fischer, Düsseldorf, October 8–22, 1971. **One parable follows (Rep.):**

The Best Way to do Art

A young artist in art school used to worship the paintings of Cézanne. He looked at and studied all the books he could find on Cézanne and copied all of the reproductions of Cézanne's work he found in the books.

He visited a museum and for the first time saw a real Cézanne painting. He hated it. It was nothing like the Cézannes he had studied in the books. From that time on, he made all of his paintings the sizes of paintings reproduced in books and he painted them in black and white. He also printed captions and explanations on the paintings as in books. Often he just used words.

And one day he realized that very few people went to art galleries and museums but many people looked at books and magazines as he did and they got them through the mail as he did.

Moral: It's difficult to put a painting in a mailbox.

Mel Bochner: 3 Ideas + 7 Procedures. Museum of Modern Art, New York, September 28–November 1, 1971.

Burn, Ian, and Ramsden, Mel. "A Question of Epistemic Adequacy." *Studio International,* October, 1971.

Roger Cutforth: Transpositions of Place, Situation, Direction, Relation, Circumstance. NSCAD, Halifax, October 22–30, 1971.

Hanne Darboven. Westfälischer Kunstverein, Münster, October 16-November 14. Text by Klaus Honnef and Johannes Cladders; thirty-eight-page typewritten piece and indexes by the artist, biography, bibliography. One page of the catalogue piece follows:

I

eins zwei

eins zwei drei vier fünf sechs sieben acht neun zehn elf zwölf dreizehn vierzehn fünfzehn sechzehn siebzehn achtzehn neun zehn zwanzig einundzwanzing zweiundzwanzig dreiundzwanzig vierundzwanzig fünfundzwanzig sechsundzwanzig sieben undzwanzig achtundzwanzig neunundzwanzig dreissig einund dreissig zweiunddreissig dreiunddreissig vierunddreissig fün funddreissig sechsunddreissig siebenunddreissig achtunddreis sig neununddreissig vierzig einundvierzig zweiundvierzig drei undvierzig

eins zwei drei

eins zwei drei vier fünf sechs sieben acht neun zehn elf zwölf dreizehn vierzehn fünfzehn sechzehn siebzehn achtzehn neu nzehn zwanzig einundzwanzig zweiundzwanzig dreiundzwanzig vierundzwansig fünfundzwanzig sechsundzwanzig sieben undzwanzig achtundzwanzig neunundzwanzig dreissig einund dreissig zweiunddreissig dreiunddreissig vierunddreissig fün funddreissig sechsunddreissig siebenunddreissig achtunddreis sig neununddreissig vierzig einundvierzig zweiundvierzig drei undvierzig vierundvierzig

eins zwei drei vier

eins zwei drei vier fünf sechs sieben acht neun zehn elf zwölf dreizehn vierzehn fünfzehn sechzehn siebzehn achtzehn neun zehn zwanzig einundzwanzig zweiundzwanzig dreiundzwanzig vierundzwanzig fünfundzwanzig sechsundzwanzig siebenun dzwanzig achtundzwanzig neunundzwanzig dreissig einund dreissig zweiunddreissig dreiunddreissig vierunddreissig fün funddreissig sechsunddreissig siebenunddreissig achtunddreis sig neununddreissig vierzig einundvierzig zweiundvierzig drei undvierzig vierundvierzig fünfundvierzig

eins zwei drei vier fünf

eins zwei drei vier fünf sechs sieben acht neun zehn elf zwölf dreizehn vierzehn fünfzehn sechzehn siebzehn achtzehn neunzehn zwanzig einundzwanzig zweiundzwanzig dreiun dzwanzig vierundzwanzig fünfundzwanzig sechsundzwanzig sie benundzwanzig achtundzwanzig neunundzwanzig dreissig ein unddreissig zweiunddreissig dreiunddreissig vierunddreissig fünfunddreissig sechsunddreissig siebenunddreissig achtund dreissig neununddreissig vierzig einundvierzig zweiundvierzig dreiundvierzig vierundvierzig fünfundvierzig sechsundvierzig

eins zwei drei vier fünf sechs

eins zwei drei vier fünf sechs sieben acht neun zehn elf zwölf dreizehn vierzehn fünfzehn sechzehn ziebzehn achtzehn neun zehn zwanzig einundzwanzig sweiundzwanzig dreiundzwanzig vierundzwanzig fünfundzwanzig sechsundzwanzig siebenundzw

255

Hanne Darboven. Untitled. Ink, on paper. 1971.

anzig achtundzwanzig neunundzwanzig dreissig einunddreissig
zweiunddreissig dreiunddreissig vierunddreissig fünfunddreissig
sechsunddreissig siebenunddreissig achtunddreissig neunund
dreissig vierzig einundvierzig zweiundvierzig dreiundvierzig vier
undvierzig fünfundvierzig sechsundvierzig siebenundvierzig

Preston McLanahan: Silence. **Apple, New York, October 2–10. "A writer, a theologian, an anthropologist, an industrial relations expert, an artist, and a publisher will convene in silence for fifteen minutes; after which they will discuss their experience." Conversation recorded and made available.**

Robert Morris, in conversation with L.R.L., October, 1971, New York:
   M: I never thought of myself as a conceptual artist. I always objected to being called one. I have done certain things that don't have a physical manifesttion, but it always seemed to me that what I was doing was initiating some process that had an existence other than just a mental one.

L: You and Iain Baxter seem to me to be the only two artists I've worked with who have no *style*. The process or the idea behind the work usually outweighs the particular look. Do you feel any lack of commitment to a style?

M: Well, I certainly have thought about it. I guess there are certain attitudes, certain themes that may be constant, but the visual manifestations are not. That really never bothers me much. From time to time, I've had misgivings about it, wished I could develop or run out all the permutations of something which gives one a style. But I never had the patience to do that. Often I go back and pick up something related to earlier work, but there is frequently so much distance intervening that it doesn't look like anything is continuous. I see themes that go through. That is the only continuity I have.

L: What would the themes be? Measurement, and process?

M: Yes, that kind of thing. I am concerned with how things are made.

L: Is the temporary aspect a theme or a variation?

M: That has been true of a lot of the work, that it was temporary, and on the other hand a lot of those things were temporary only by virtue of the situation. If the situation had been different they could have remained: for example, the plywood pieces were temporary but at any given time they can be reconstituted.

L: I wasn't thinking of those so much as the steam piece, the dirt pieces, the changing piece, the money piece, things where afterwards there was nothing left.

M: But they got documented like everything else.

L: Everybody's relationship to documentation is different. How do you see the documentation of a work and the work itself? Heizer's idea seems to be acceptance of the fact that nobody is going to be able to see his pieces except the few people who can afford a trip to Nevada.

M: I feel differently. I don't want to do things that are withdrawn to that extent. That gives them a connotation I don't like. It takes a religious pilgrimage to get to the art. That seems to me like putting it in a museum, only outside. Like this work I did in Velsen, Holland—I was pleased with the site because people could get to it, and insofar as I do something like that that is physical I want it to be experienced for what it is. It is important to me that it is *there,* and available. Other things, like the money piece, or very early pieces end up as photographs. But the removal of the work itself and a purposeful replacement of its existence with a photograph has never been a working method.

L: I'm not certain about the chronology of those earth pieces of yours.

M: The Circular Mound was made as a model in 1966. A work leading up to the outside proposals was *North-South Track,* which was a plywood piece with a compass in it; its orientation, if not its placement in the room, was specified by direction. The first thing I proposed for outside was *Track,* which would be a very long steel bar embedded in an earth embankment that supported the bar. That was proposed in 1965 to a person who had land in Florida. It was never carried out.

L: What is the relationship of the model? I've always hated sculptural models.

M: Well, it's very unsatisfactory. I haven't made any I liked. It seems like photographs of models are better than models. It's a problem of working. I don't want to make just the drawings. . . . The Dutch [Sonsbeek] work is the only thing I've ever done on the scale I wanted. It was 230 feet across and related to the 1966 *Ring.* Both involved the perceptual impossibility of taking in the work all at once, but the Dutch work also involves other elements dealing with time.

L: Why do photographs make something not real look more real?

M: Photographs function as a peculiar kind of sign. There is a strange relation between their reality and artificiality, the signifier-signified relation they set up is not at all clear or transparent. One of the things they do is to give too much information and not enough at the same time.

L: That *lack* of information hasn't been used in art. . . . I've never been able to figure what makes an abstract photograph uninteresting if I'm willing to be interested by, say, an abstract painting, or print.

M: I think partly it's the convention of how one sees photographs. They are consumable signs, yet something more. There's something inherently objectionable about seeing photographs on a wall. . . . In the beginning I used to take all the still photographs of my sculpture. I didn't like others' photographs. But when it comes to filming I don't like to operate the camera. I get a cameraman, preferably more than one. I try to give them a certain amount of instruction and if possible have several cameras and then take what I want from other people's looking at the situation. I can then deal with the footage as an immediate thing, as a photograph of something. . . . I want to see the artificiality of the scene and deal with that.

L: Once removed. You see a thing day after day for several days and you think you know it pretty well. Then you see the photograph and it's so completely different. Your memory fails you right at that point where the photograph replaces your memory. Five minutes before you have seen the photograph you remember a situation in such and such a way. The very second you are shown the photograph, *that* becomes the memory, and everything else, reality, bites the dust. People end up by living through their photographic memories instead of through reality.

Do you ever have thoughts of not being an artist? Is there a way for an artist not to be one?

M: I'm so involved in trying to get things done, working or trying to move things away from the clogged situation that exists now that I'm not really involved with that issue.

Fall, 1971. *Seven xeroxed leaflets* or essays by Ken Friedman, formerly head of Fluxus West, San Diego; among them, "Notes on Concept Art":

Concept art is not so much an art movement or vein as it is a position or world-view, a focus for activity:

One way to understand this world-view, these activities as focused, is to understand the doings of the first major group of concept artists, the Fluxus group. . . .

Henry Flynt, the man who named concept art, defined it as "first of all an art of which the material is 'concepts', as for example the material of music is sound." Through his exploratory work in the late '50's and early '60's in concept art, culture, politics, mathematics and linguistic philosophy, Flynt developed a philosophical basis for what he called concept art. The first known publication of the term is copyrighted in his 1961 essays on concept art [*in LaMonte Young and Jackson MacLow,* Anthology, *1963.*].

A short definition of concept art as it came to be practiced might be: A series of thoughts or concepts, either complete in themselves as work(s), or leading to documentation or to realization through external means. . . .

While there are indeed a great number of artists in the conceptual field today, there is a relatively small number of individuals who comprise the historical founding circle. These are, most outstandingly, Henry Flynt, George Maciumas, Yoko Ono, George Brecht, Robert Morris, Bob Watts, Simone Forti, Walter de Maria, Ben Vautier, Dick

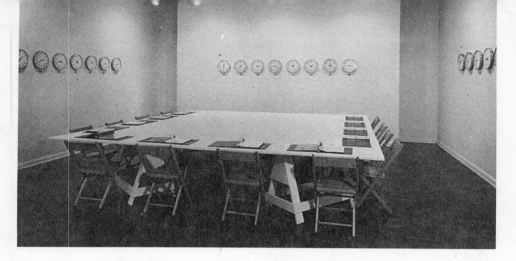

Joseph Kosuth. *The Eighth Investigation (AAIAI), Proposition Three.* Investigation supported by Dr. Giuseppe Panza. 1971.

Higgins, Alison Knowles, Nam June Paik, Ay-o, La Monte Young, Ray Johnson, Emmett Williams, Tomas Schmit, and Stanley Brouwn. Others, like myself, had been working, and came into the group slightly later following independent activity, such as Milan Knizak, Eric Andersen, Per Kirkeby, Joseph Beuys, Geoff Hendricks, Bici Forbes, Sigeko Kubota, Chieko Shiomi, Jock Reynolds and members of the ZAJ group. As well, a few quiet and indescribable individuals whose activity and variety, or whose quietude, places them beyond definition, among them Phil Corner, Toshi Ichiyanagi, Richard Maxfield, Bengt Af Klinberg, Wolf Vostell and Jackson MacLow.

Artitudes (Paris), no. 1, October, 1971. A monthly newspaper edited by François Pluchart; includes an article by him on "Body as Art," with statements by Acconci, Oppenheim, Gina Pane, Ben, Sarkis, Journiac.
    No. 2 (November) discusses Venet, Acconci, Gilbert & George.

APG Research Limited: The Individual and Organization. Prospectus and offer for sale of the Artists Placement Group. London. Twenty-three pages, fall, 1971.

Art-Language, no. 4, November, 1971. Contributors: Stuart Knight, Graham Howard, Terry Atkinson, and Michael Baldwin.

Millet, Catherine. "Notes on Art-Language." *Flash Art,* October–November, 1971. Also a double spread on Carl Andre.

November, Paris: Daniel Buren successfully contests the sale of a so-called Buren poster at auction.

Reise, Barbara. "Presenting Gilbert & George, the Living Sculptures." *Art News,* November, 1971.

John Goodyear: Earth Curve (A One-man, One-World-Ten-Fold Exhibition). Held in ten places, all over the world, beginning at MIT and the Quebec Museum in November, 1971. Deals in various ways with various aspects of the curvature of the earth. Among them, *Postal Card*

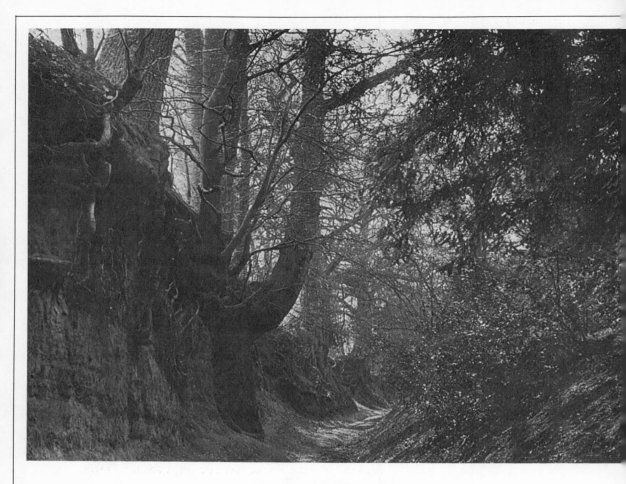

THE PILGRIM'S WAY
The main prehistoric thoroughfare in south-east England.

TEN DAYS IN APRIL
A 165 mile walk from Winchester cathedral to Canterbury cathedral.

We should be lowe and loveliche,
and leel, eche man to other,
and pacient as pilgrimes for
pilgrimes arn we alle.

Hamish Fulton. *The Pilgrim's Way.* April, 1971.

Piece: One Dollar—Tilt: **A postcard showing the angle of standing in your city in relation to another city participating in the exhibitions (executed in Boston and Quebec).**

Douglas Huebler. *Variable Piece # 70 (In Process) Global.* **November, 1971:**
Throughout the remainder of the artist's lifetime he will photographically document, to the extent of his capacity, the existence of everyone alive in order to produce the most authentic and inclusive representation of the human species that may be assembled in that manner.

Editions of this work will be periodically issued in a variety of topical modes: "100,000 people," "1,000,000 people," "10,000,000 people," "people personally known by the artist," "Look-alikes," "over-laps," etc.

"Dennis Oppenheim Interviewed by Willoughby Sharp" (documentation of a work shown in London under the auspices of Nigel Greenwood, October 1–November 6); also, "Notes on a Piece by Barry Le Va; Extended Vertex Meetings: blown; blocked; blown outward." *Studio International,* **November, 1971.**

Gina Pane. **M. et Mme. Fregnac, 32, rue des Thermopyles, Paris, November 24, 1971, 18 h. 30: "A minimum of 2% of your monthly salary must be deposited in a strong-box situated at the entrance to the place where I will perform." For an account by François Pluchart of this evening of "biological aggressions" (body works involving overeating, extreme discomfort, and pain), see** *Artitudes,* **no. 3, December, 1971.**

Smithson, Robert, and Müller, Grégoire, " . . . The Earth Subject to Cataclysms Is a Cruel Master." *Arts,* **November, 1971.**

The Five Years of Bernar Venet : A Catalogue Raisonné. **New York Cultural Center, New York, November 11–January 3, 1972. Texts by Venet and Donald Karshan. "The exhibition comprises the total output of the 30-year-old, internationally known conceptual artist who decided earlier this year to terminate a successful career as an artist." (Press release.)**

Group Activities: **"An open-ended situation of interaction between an unknown number of people." At Apple, New York, November 23–28 (Billy Apple).**

Changing Terms. **Museum School Gallery, Boston Museum of Fine Arts, December 3–January 14, 1972. Looseleaf catalogue; statements by artists, among them: Bochner, Castoro, LeWitt, Rockburne, Weiner.**

20–12–'71 **("Appunti per una tesi sul concetto di citazione e di sovrepposizione"). Studio d'arte contemporanea, Rome, December, 1971. Catalogue includes Ben, Rinke, Beuys, Prini, Dimitrijević, and others.**

Jacki Apple and Pamela Kraft. *Transfer.* **Apple, New York, December 21, 1971:**
There are four people in every relationship between two. Each as we see ourselves, and each as the other sees us.

In order to experience and reveal each other's view, Pamela and I shall relinquish our self-images and transfer onto each other what we each perceive the other to be.

Bartlett, Jennifer. *Cleopatra I–IV.* **Adventures in Poetry, (Larry Fagin) New York, December, 1971. Loose pages. First read, or "exhibited" publicly, November, 1970. Excerpts:**
Cleopatra's brother said to her, after returning from his first battle, men spill blood on continents women bleed on rags. He later drowned in the Nile.

Lamps. Off/On. Two states of existence. One thing or the other. Yes or no. A binary situation was one which faced Cleopatra being born, giving birth, having her brother killed, and dying.

Plugs and Sockets. Electric Cleopatra became a socket, a connecting point between currents and a vacuum cleaner sucking up Europe and Asia. She was a plug in her relation to Egypt and other women, a plug and socket for her brothers, a socket for Caesar. Plug is a noun describing an object used to fill a gap or act as a wedge, and any natural or morbid concretion acting thus. It is a kind of stopper for vessels or pipe. A socket is a natural or artificial hollow for something to fit into, or stand firm in, or revolve in, with an enlarged end to receive another. As ruler, as divine, as woman, as mother, was Cleopatra artificial or natural? Plug or socket? In what combination of artifice and nature can we name her as one? Was she a natural hollow for the Roman Empire in the persons of Antony and Caesar to stand firm and revolve in, or a plug stopping the rush of 3,500 years of history into the Mediterranean?

Gilbert & George: A Touch of Blossom (spring, 1971). *Art and Project Bulletin* 47, December 22, 1971–January 21, 1972.

Levine, Les. *Museum of Mott Art, Inc.* Protetch-Rivkin Public Art Hearings, Washington, D.C., December 4, 1971. Catalogue of the "museum's" services.

Rosenberg, Harold, "On the De-definition of Art"; also, Kim Levin, "A Different Drummer" (on Rafael Ferrer). *Art News,* December, 1971 ("The problem is not what to do. It is where to do it and how"—R.F.)

POSTFACE

Hopes that "conceptual art" would be able to avoid the general commercialization, the destructively "progressive" approach of modernism were for the most part unfounded. It seemed in 1969 (see Preface) that no one, not even a public greedy for novelty, would actually pay money, or much of it, for a xerox sheet referring to an event past or never directly perceived, a group of photographs documenting an ephemeral situation or condition, a project for work never to be completed, words spoken but not recorded; it seemed that these artists would therefore be forcibly freed from the tyranny of a commodity status and market-orientation. Three years later, the major conceptualists are selling work for substantial sums here and in Europe; they are represented by (and still more unexpected—showing in) the world's most prestigious galleries. Clearly, whatever minor revolutions in communication have been achieved by the process of dematerializing the object (easily mailed work, catalogues and magazine pieces, primarily art that can be shown inexpensively and unobtrusively in infinite locations at one time), art and artist in a capitalist society remain luxuries.

On the other hand, the esthetic contributions of an "idea art" have been considerable. An informational, documentary idiom has provided a vehicle for art ideas that were encumbered and obscured by formal considerations. It has become obvious that there is a place for an art which parallels (rather than replaces or is succeeded by) the decorative object, or, perhaps still more important, sets up new critical criteria by which to view and vitalize itself (the function of the Art-Language group and its growing number of adherents). Such a strategy, if it continues to develop, can only have a salutory effect on the way all art is examined and developed in the future.

Conceptual art has not, however, as yet broken down the real barriers between the art context and those external disciplines—social, scientific, and academic—from which it draws sustenance. While it has become feasible for artists to deal with technical concepts in their own imaginations, rather than having to struggle with constructive techniques beyond their capacities and their financial means, interactions between mathematics and art, philosophy and art, literature and art, politics and art, are still at a very primitive level. There are some exceptions, among them certain works by Haacke, Buren, Piper, the Rosario group, Huebler. But, for the most part, the artists have been confined to art quarters, usually by choice. As yet the "behavioral artists" have not held particularly rewarding dialogues with their psychologist counterparts, and we have had no feedback on the Art-Language group from the linguistic philosophers they emulate. "Art use" of elementary knowledge, already accepted and exhausted, oversimplification, and unsophistication in regard to work accomplished in other fields are obvious barriers to such interdisciplinary communication.

The general ignorance of the visual arts, especially their theoretical bases, deplorable even in the so-called intellectual world; the artist's well-founded despair of ever reaching the mythical "masses" with "advanced art"; the resulting ghetto mentality predominant in the narrow and incestuous art world itself, with its resentful reliance on a very small group of dealers, curators, critics, editors, and collectors who are all too frequently and often unknowingly bound by invisible apron strings to the "real world's" power structure—all of these factors may make it unlikely that conceptual art will be any better equipped to affect the world any differently than, or even as much as, its less ephemeral counterparts. Certainly, few of the artists are directly concerned with this aspect of their art, nor can they be, since art that begins with other than an internal, esthetic goal rarely produces anything more than illustration or polemic. The fact remains that the mere survival of something still called Art in a world so intolerant of the useless and uningratiating indicates that there is some hope for the kind of awareness of that world which is uniquely imposed by esthetic criteria, no matter how bizarre the "visual" manifestations may initially appear to those unacquainted with the art context.

INDEX

Note: Entries in *italics* are texts. Entries in **boldface** are works of art. Page numbers in roman indicate quotations. Page numbers in *italics* indicate citations. Page numbers in **boldface** indicate reproductions. Single quotation marks indicate exhibitions. (Inclusions in group shows have not been indexed.)

270